APPLE OF DISCORD

APPLE OF DISCORD

A SURVEY OF RECENT GREEK POLITICS IN THEIR INTERNATIONAL SETTING

by

C. M. WOODHOUSE

*Former Commander of the Allied Military Mission
to the Greek Guerillas.*

With a Foreword
by
THE RT. HON. LORD ALTRINCHAM,
P.C., K.C.M.G., K.C.V.O., D.S.O., M.C.

HUTCHINSON & CO. (Publishers) LTD
London   New York   Melbourne   Sydney   Cape Town

Printed in Great Britain by
William Brendon and Son, Ltd
The Mayflower Press (late of Plymouth)
at Bushey Mill Lane
Watford, Herts.

CONTENTS

iii

FOREWORD

COLONEL WOODHOUSE has, characteristically, said very little about himself in the pages of this book; and that is an omission which needs to be corrected if readers are to appreciate with what exceptional knowledge and authority he writes. I was not myself directly connected at any time with British action in Greece, because its local direction had passed from the Middle Eastern to the Central Mediterranean Command before I went as Minister Resident to the Middle East. But the branch of the organisation called SOE to which Colonel Woodhouse was attached was then still in Cairo, and I therefore heard a good deal of the exceptional service which he rendered, and of the courage and cool judgment with which he rendered it. Here, very briefly, is the outline of a most exacting experience which lasted over five years.

He was twenty-two years old when the war broke out. Having joined the Royal Artillery in October 1939, he won his majority in three years and was gazetted full colonel in 1944. Sent out to Greece in the first instance as an officer in our Military Mission, he served there throughout the operations until our evacuation of Crete in the spring of 1941. He returned to the island in December of that year in a fishing-boat; and after some preliminary experience in the organisation of resistance there, he was dropped in Greece itself on a mountain within ten miles of Delphi with Brigadier Myers, his immediate commander, on the night of 30th September 1942. He remained there for nearly two years in contact with all forms of resistance until just after Normandy D-Day in June 1944; re-entered as commander of our action in September of that year; and stayed till after the liberation and revolution, leaving again on New Year's Day 1945. Finally, he served as Second Secretary in our Embassy at Athens from June 1945, and completed his long and intimate experience of Greek affairs as Secretary-General of the Allied Mission which observed the elections in March 1946.

I should add that he speaks Greek like a native, and has a very deep personal affection for the Greek people, though this is little emphasised in the book. He has, moreover, no prejudices one way or the other so far as Greek parties are concerned, and in that country of violent political partisans was even a little suspect for the clear-eyed detachment with which he did his work. His knowledge of Greek politics is therefore impartial as well as exceptionally intimate, and official verification could be found at need for all his statements of fact. His book is indeed in a class by itself as a comprehensive survey of the complex, elusive, bewildering, kaleidoscopic play of forces in war-time Greece.

Where are these forces now carrying Greece in time of peace?

Colonel Woodhouse abstains from political argument; but few of his readers will, I fancy, close his book without reaching two broad conclusions on what has so far happened and on what has yet to pass. The first of these is that, but for Mr. Churchill's decisive intervention, Greece would by now have been completely submerged by the lava flowing from the red crater in the East. Prejudice against monarchy, and a most unwise failure to trust the Press with information, for a long time overlaid that essential truth both in America and here; but in neither is it now a matter of serious doubt. As regards the future, Colonel Woodhouse does not conceal his opinion that the odds have been weighted against our cause in Greece ever since Allied strategy determined that our concluding war effort should ignore the Balkans and concentrate on France. Greece and the Balkans are inseparable, and Greece's fate will be decided by the balance which is ultimately struck, on a much broader theatre, between the powers of East and West.

It is ridiculous that this great issue should be confused, as it has been, with the constitutional struggle between monarchy and republicanism in Greece itself; and nothing is wiser in Colonel Woodhouse's survey than his initial explanation of Metaxas' aims and his emphasis throughout the story upon the irrelevance of the constitutional issue to the real problems of Greece, though that issue has bedevilled Greek politics ever since the first Venizelos, whose memory I revere, was forced into it by his devotion to the Allied cause in the First World War. King Paul and Queen Frederika, who are now popular throughout Greece, will render a noble service to their country if they can lay it at last to rest. Greek problems, as Colonel Woodhouse insists, "are organic rather than political: the problems of starvation, homelessness, illiteracy, lack of communications, disease, destitution, lawlessness, superstition, vendetta." He writes, of course, first from the war standpoint of the United Nations and then from the peace standpoint of the disillusioned West. But he writes also with complete detachment from mere politics, because his heart is, first and foremost, with the simple, primitive and lovable people of Greece. He saw that people from every angle and in all parts of their country during the protracted loneliness and danger of the service which he undertook. He writes of them therefore with unrivalled understanding. Like most Englishmen, I am devoted to them as deeply as he; and I hope that on both sides of the Atlantic many readers will widen their knowledge of Greek affairs by reading this fascinating book.

Altrincham

Tormarton,
    1st *May*, 1948.

PREFACE

T H E purpose of this book can be summed up in a few paragraphs. It is an attempt to find an explanation for two perplexing facts about Greece, and to trace their consequences. One of them is a fact about the country's internal relations; the other is a fact about its external relations: but both are aspects of a single fact, which is that Greece's affairs, whichever way you look at them, are in an unhappy state. I will begin by isolating the two facts from each other and the complex, for the purposes of definition.

At the beginning of 1941, when Greece had been in the second World War a few months, the people seemed more united than ever, and the country was the apple of the Allies' eye. (The Allies, by a venial anachronism, include the USA and USSR, which shared the general esteem for Greece although they had not yet entered the war.) Soon afterwards Greece vanished in the darkness of enemy occupation. When its shores were reopened to the world in 1944 those two characteristics of 1941 had both been tragically altered. The people were no longer united; they were torn by antagonisms. The country was no longer the apple of the Allies' eye; it was their apple of discord. These changes had begun during the occupation, and have been consolidated since. Occupation was the root of both.

There were four things the plain Greek could do in the occupation: not the leaders, but just the plain Greek. He could sit and do nothing; he could escape from the country; he could collaborate with the enemy; he could fight the enemy. Those who chose the first two alternatives turned out, in the light of after-events, to have been wisest in their own interests; those who chose the third were not far behind; but most of those who chose the fourth seemingly committed at best a foolish mistake, at worst a crime. This, the source of the new antagonism that replaced the apparent unity, is the first of the two perplexing facts.

The political leaders, on the other hand, found new prospects coming into view from those years. The war intensified the interest of the Great Powers in Greece. The politicians found themselves wooed by ambassadors; each could incline to his choice. Now, a conflict of courtship between the Axis and the Allies was natural; but what added spice to the political game was that a similar conflict emerged between the Allies themselves, as the Axis rivalry began to be eliminated. For a time this was agreeable: everyone likes to be sought after. Then the war ended; and for the politicians the game was no longer, in the Greek idiom, "play and laugh." Greece became a theme of dispute that could be relied on to split Great

Britain from the USA, and both from the USSR, whenever it was raised. Greece was the apple of discord; the rivalry between politicians became suddenly a competition for the role of Paris. The internal politics of Greece reproduced in miniature the international rivalry of the USSR, USA and Great Britain. This contrast with the bliss of 1941 is the second perplexing fact.

Even as the two facts have been stated, it is impossible to segregate them absolutely. The first is primarily internal, the second primarily external; but both are aspects of the same Greek politics, and their mutual impact appears in the bare statement of them. They will not be kept separate henceforward, because any account of one entails an account of the other. I state them separately only to provide the reader with the guiding threads that will persist throughout the following chapters. They also help to fix the chronological limits: approximately from the year 1941, before the changes could be seen to have begun, to the year 1946, when they were sufficiently crystallised to be recognisable. But the narrative will range freely beyond those dates at both ends; for history, unlike history books, has no known beginning and no foreseeable end.

I do not suggest that this book approaches the dignity of history. Perhaps no man can write history about events in which he has himself played a part. The historian has advantages, too, which are denied to the writer on current affairs. His sources cannot rise up and call him a liar; political critics cannot juxtapose selected sentences to prove that he means the opposite of what he says. Lacking the scope of a historian, I must respect the former and resign myself to the latter. Nor do I expect, as an historian should, to meet with wide agreement. The widest agreement that seems possible on Greece is between two people, if one be away. It is not yet agreed, for instance, whether the events of December 1944 in Athens were the heroic self-expression of nascent democracy or the dastardly conspiracy of criminal megalomaniacs. But whatever else may be in dispute, the dual discord which I have defined is not. It is therefore a convenient thread on which to string the series of facts, which I hope may be useful to the historian when his time comes. Most of these facts have already been published in Greece; in England some of them are new. The opinions expressed on them are exclusively my own; and although they are partisan in the sense that they seek to justify British policy in Greece as the only possible policy, their more important function is to show why neither that nor any other policy could have completely succeeded.

CHAPTER I

THE BACKGROUND

*"When I am told that Mr. Popoulos, the Greek politician, is a little to the
left of Mr. Skopopoulos, I have no more notion what it means than the man in
the moon."*
A. P. HERBERT,
The Point of Parliament.

THE hardest part of my subject is to define its geographical and
chronological limits. To define the former as Greece and the latter as the
years 1941-6 exhausts my competence to speak with authority; but
the events of 1941-6 have roots in preceding years, and bear fruit in the
future. Where is the date-line to be drawn? Again, whatever happens in
Greece has repercussions in Greece's territorial neighbours; and whatever
happens in Albania, Yugoslavia, Bulgaria or Turkey has repercussions in
their territorial neighbours. Where is the boundary to be drawn? Even if
such limits could be fixed, no country lives in a vacuum insulated from
the influences of the Second World War and Great Power politics. Any
viewpoint that takes in less than the whole must be inadequate; yet
anyone less than a Toynbee must write within limits, or not write at all.
Whatever limits are chosen will be arbitrary, and leave ill-defined edges.
It is impossible to shed light on the Balkan darkness without leaving a
penumbra. This first chapter has such a penumbral character and the
inadequacies that go with it. There will be less precision, less fullness of
detail, more unsupported generalisation, than in later chapters. Its purpose
is to sketch the immediate penumbra which hazily surrounds the definition
of "Greece 1941-6." To do this, I shall outline a few of the events and
trends of political history in Greece and her Balkan neighbours during the
period framing the main subject.

1. Metaxas and the old Political World.

Ioannis Metaxas died on 29th January, 1941, three months after the
Italians attacked his country from Albania. No dictator was ever more
fortunate in the moment of his death. By his famous answer "No" to the
Italian ultimatum on 28th October, 1940; by his efficient conduct of the
Greek mobilisation; by the successes won against the Italians in every
phase of the war; by all these combined with the popularity of the Anglo-
Greek alliance, he had become endeared not only to the countries which
were to form the United Nations, but in an unprecedented degree to his
own countrymen. The war between Greece and Italy proved Metaxas a

military genius, backed by an able Chief of the General Staff (Lieut.-General Papagos) and a brave people. But the legacy of his dictatorship was hard. It might be endlessly debated what Metaxas would have done in the circumstances he bequeathed to his successor: but the very fact that the question cannot be answered, argues the difficulty of the problems he left unsolved and the fortune which saved his reputation from the stain of failure to solve them.

His was not a government designed to meet the problems of war and occupation. It was designed to rescue Greece from the chaos to which the abuse of democratic processes was reducing it. The character of "temporariness" was written upon it from the day Metaxas assumed dictatorial power on 4th August, 1936. But such a régime, established to bring about a certain end so that constitutional government may succeed it, is not the best (though it is the only effective) judge of the attainment of the end. Metaxas died without completing the task which he had set before himself; without providing for the future by creating a party or nominating a successor; and mercifully for himself, without being called upon to face the greatest of his country's calamities, the German invasion.

The task which he had set before himself and his ostensibly provisional Government was to *create* the Greek state: to give it the stability, the cohesion, the self-respect, which characterise an independent state and which, despite a hundred years of freedom, Greece had not yet secured. Hitherto there had been Greek statesmen, but there had been no Greek state. There had been Kharilaos Trikoupis in the nineteenth century, and Eleftherios Veniselos in the twentieth; but an examination of the lives of those statesmen reveals that behind and beneath them there was no *state*. So long as they were in power, there was progress in the welfare of the people and the condition of the country. But when the ordinary processes of democracy replaced them by their opponents, what they had achieved was undone. The achievements of Veniselos in particular raised the international status of Greece to one of wide respect; but the passage of time showed that although Veniselos himself was among the greatest European statesmen of his time, the state which he appeared to represent did not exist; the wide respect was being accorded personally to Veniselos and vicariously to Greek antiquity, but not to the Greek state. His intermittent displacement from office revealed behind the façade an administrative anarchy.

The fact which the Greek politicians would not face, and which Metaxas set himself to cure, was that Greece could not be a state as England or France was a state, in the twentieth-century European meaning of the term, until Greece had entered twentieth-century Europe. Metaxas recognised and proposed to remedy certain fundamental defects of the Greek community, which can unfortunately still be analysed in the present tense, because his radical cure was defeated by the war and his death. The analysis will confirm the principle on which Metaxas worked even if he did not formulate it: that the chief impediment to Greek political stability is the Greek politician.

The field over which the Greek politician has to exercise himself is wider (although on a miniature scale) than that of the western politician. However much English politicians may disagree with each other, there is a common ground that has been settled under their feet for ever by the accumulated progress of centuries. Because it will never be disturbed, they not only do not dispute it; they do not even mention that they agree. Such common ground is the inheritance of any state that has existed for several centuries: it is those centuries that Greece lacks. They are not easily made up, as Metaxas resolved that they should be, in a decade.

A week in the Greek mountains will confirm to any observer that the greater part of Greece is living in conditions several hundred years behind western Europe, but the fact is not easy to illustrate in words. The nearest equivalent to the picture that might be familiar is Boswell's description of life in the remoter parts of eighteenth-century Scotland, in his *Journal of a Tour to the Hebrides*. But in Greece (as no Athenian would fail to point out) there is an important exception: Athens. Athens, together with a few other small urban societies in Greece, belongs to twentieth-century Europe just as Paris and London do. The importance of the exception lies in this: that almost no native Athenian, and certainly no Athenian politician, knows any more about life in the wilds of Greece than the inhabitants of Paris or London. The Greek provinces are to them as much a foreign country as Tibet. Those who ever did know anything of them do their best to forget it. Their slogan, consciously or unconsciously (and often explicitly), is: "Athens is Greece."

Greek politics therefore present two unusual phenomena. They are composed of problems too primitive to be called political, and of politicians determined to obliterate them from their minds. There are certain qualifications to be made later, which do honour to individuals; but they do not modify the picture as a whole. This picture is composed of a large number of political parties, which may more easily be considered as a smaller number of political groups, since many of the splinter-parties are too small and ephemeral to be fruitfully analysed. The groups are indistinguishable in their attitude to the problems that really matter to Greece: which is, to ignore them. The question is, then, what does distinguish them?

It is often said that Greece has no true division into left and right, because most Greeks are small proprietors or *petits bourgeois* who can only be more or less conservative. The same argument is sometimes modified to prove that they are all more or less socialists because they are all poor. Whatever they are, this kind of argument runs, they are all the same. This fails to account for the fact that anything up to sixty different parties take the field at election-time. Worldly wise Greeks, who know how to explain their fellow-countrymen to the English, glibly say that the real distinction is not between left and right but between Communists and Greeks; others say that it is not between right and left but between Fascists and Greeks: each implying that their opponents are too monstrous to be accounted Greeks. These two kinds of glibness would themselves provide a criterion in the absence of any other: we could call the former the language of the right, and the latter the language of the left. But there are others. Many controversies divide the Greeks, and almost none of them cut across each other. The attitude a man takes towards one of them is expected to determine his attitude towards all of them; it is the sum of those attitudes that places him in politics on the left or the right or (if he is able to compromise) at the centre. On the left, he is assumed by antagonists to believe in a Greek republic, to sympathise with Bulgaria and Albania and with the autonomous aspirations of Macedonia, to favour the official adoption of the demotic language and the expropriation of industrialists, and so on. On the right, he is assumed by antagonists to believe in the Greek monarchy, in territorial expansion at the expense of Bulgaria and Albania, in the hellenisation of the Macedonians, in the sacrosanctity of the purist *katharevousa* language, in the inalienable right of industrialists to evade taxation, and so on. These are trivial, haphazard lists; it is characteristic that the first item is usually the most decisive. What all of them omit is everything fundamental to social life at its lowest. They omit these things not, as western Europeans might omit them from a political programme, because they are already solved or at least agreed, but because they do not want to think about them, nor to accept the status of personal inferiority entailed by an admission of national backwardness. They want, left and right alike, to play the same fascinating game of politics that is played in the rest of Europe and America; not a more primitive game indigenous to the Balkans.

The categories of western politics ought not to apply in Greece. Greek problems are organic rather than political: the problems of starvation, homelessness, illiteracy, lack of communications, disease, destitution, lawlessness, superstition, vendetta. The problem of life itself still needs to be put before that of the ideal life. But the categories of western politics *are* applied none the less. The Athenian politician can rarely say what his party's social programme is, for few of them have such a thing; domestic controversy is confined to the constitution. Because many of the senior administrative and executive posts, which in England are called "permanent," in Greece change hands with every change of government, the average politician is busier angling for "patronage" for himself and his family, than attending to the interests of his constituents and his country. Because too, Greece usually elects its Parliament (when it has one) by proportional representation,[1] there is a chance for any number of splinter-parties to obtain representation. Because there is little danger of these having to form a Government by themselves, they need not bother with a social programme; or with any sort of programme beyond the slogan, "Down with everyone else!" Even absolute power never corrupted so absolutely as absolute irresponsibility.

Disregard for the social needs of Greece does not prevent the Athenian politician from talking till kingdom-come about the problems that really interest him. Using the same counters as the Great Powers, he can be brilliantly fluent on global strategy, on the Slav menace, on atomic power, on the blunders of the Council of Foreign Secretaries, on nationalisation of industries which he has not got and rectification of frontiers which he has never seen. The difference is that he need not cash the counters; to him it is a game with words. A Greek Prime Minister can talk on equal terms with a British Prime Minister; but he cannot talk as the representative of Greece, as the Englishman can talk as the representative of England, because he has not the same reality behind him. There is no state for him to represent.

To understand this, we have to distinguish between Greece and Greeks. Greeks, as a nationality, belong to the same category as Englishmen or Frenchmen; Greece, as a state, does not belong to the same category as England or France. Greece is small and backward, but that is no reason why any individual Greek should be small or backward. A Greek politician can have as acute a brain as an English or French politician; often he has a more acute one, and an astonishing insight. He can talk as well as any western politician, if not better; and that is all he can do. He is the spectator who sees most of the game; until Greece has acquired the standing of a truly sovereign state, spectator is all he will be. He does not stand against the same social, administrative, historical background as the western politician; he can only take part in the international game as an intelligent individual, not as the representative of a state; that is to say that he can take no part in it. But he can understand, theoretically and academically, all the current political issues of the great world. He wishes to exercise his intellect upon them, and he does so; but he does nothing else, for there is still nothing else he can do. It is a scintillating exercise in a vacuum.

Metaxas lost patience with politics so conducted: he sought realities.

[1]The term "Proportional Representation" is here used to mean any system which aims to make every elector's vote count once and leave none wasted. The system by which the candidate who obtains more votes in a single constituency than any single rival is elected, even if more votes are cast against him than for him, will be referred to as "Majority Vote." Naturally small parties tend to prefer the former and large parties the latter. After trying many variants of both systems, Greece adopted P.R. in the general elections of 1936 and 1946.

Since 1917, when King Constantine and his Prime Minister, Eleftherios Veniselos, quarrelled over the entry of Greece into the first World War, the constitutional issue which they created had been almost the sole determining factor in internal affairs. Power had alternated between the supporters of the King, called the Popular Party or Populists, and the supporters of republicanism, called the Liberal Party or Veniselists. This is an imprecise dichotomy, because not all republicans were Liberals, nor all Populists royalists, but it serves the purpose of a broad picture. It is also verbally misleading, because neither party was popular or liberal in the English sense, and the only subject that separated them was the constitution. Their rule was punctuated by military dictatorship under Generals Plastiras, Pangalos and Kondylis; and apart from the majestic vision of Veniselos, and Pangalos' passing interest in the length of women's skirts, there were few issues that seriously agitated them, except the controversy between monarchy and republic. The election of January 1936 finally exposed the bankruptcy of democracy as conducted by these men, by leaving the balance of power in the House in the hands of fifteen Communist members. In April the House prorogued itself, and was replaced by a Committee which reproduced its proportions and defects; in the same month Metaxas became Prime Minister through a process of elimination by death. The deadlock precipitated his *coup d'état*, and left in the hearts of many Greeks the feeling that it was about time too.

It is a retrospective justification of Metaxas that Populists and Liberals alike emerged with almost no widening of their understanding or experience from the interlude of dictatorship and occupation from 1639 to 1944. The Liberals indeed suffered some schism, losing such offshoots as the Social Democrats under Papandhreou and the National Liberals under General Gonatas; the Populists lost a few individuals to the temptations of collaboration: but the hard core of both parties, as a brief anticipation will show, simply resumed the old quarrel in 1945 where they had left off in 1936. When a suggestion of coalition government was put to them in October 1945, the Populists refused principally on the ground that in 1922 a Government of revolutionary Liberals had shot six royalists, and the Liberals refused principally on the ground that in 1933 an attempt had been made to assassinate Eleftherios Veniselos under a Populist Government. When they were asked what divergences of social policy kept them apart, neither side could answer because neither could define its social programme. Though both were quick to take the hint and set about devising such a programme, no one supposed that elections would be fought on any serious issue other than the Monarchy. The Populists might well have remembered that the death-warrant for the six royalists in 1922 was signed by King George II; and the Liberals that Veniselos' dying wish in 1935 was that Greece should become reunited round the

King. But such weaknesses would have taken the spice out of the political game.

This is the point at which to soften the harsh outlines of the picture by indicating a few exceptions. First there are a few that are honourable: despite what has been said there are responsible Greek politicians who appreciate the twin facts that Greece's needs are administrative and social, and that they are not confined to Athens. They even believe that those problems can be solved by democratic methods. Some of their names will be put forward later: collectively they are defined as the Centre; but it is not easy to list them here, if this judgment is to hold good for the future as well as the past. The sequence of dictatorship and enemy occupation left a wide gulf in the political ranks between the very old and the very young. Among the former it is unprofitable in the long run to look for such exceptions; among the latter it is difficult because of their lack of political experience. But a few names at least will deserve to become prominent in this book; and the American intervention of 1947 gave them hope of a wider and more lasting prominence still.

A second exception has to be made which is larger and more controversial: the Communist Party of Greece, commonly known from its Greek initials as the KKE. This party does profess a social programme; it has a high degree of administrative insight and executive efficiency wherever it chooses to apply them; and it is not unaware of the existence and grievances of the semi-civilised world beyond Athens. In all these respects it is another exception to the generalisation made above.

The only characteristic which these two exceptions enjoyed in common was the disapproval of Metaxas, when he undertook the task of dragging Greece into the twentieth century. He disapproved of the former because they clung to the constitutional processes of democracy, which he considered bankrupt; he disapproved of the latter because they espoused a rival form of authoritarianism to his own. Democratic politicians and Communists were therefore equally his enemies, and both were indiscriminately suppressed. He proposed to achieve for his country in a few years what had taken Europe several centuries; he intended to have no patience with anyone who wasted his time with irrelevant nonsense like democracy, or obstructed his progress with rival dogmas like Communism.

The warmest defender of Metaxas must admit that he was ruthless, but his opponents should in fairness admit that he saw the problem. The disease of Greece was the imposition of a modern political system on a partially primitive society. Metaxas believed that the only hope of modernising the society lay in suspending the political system. His method drastically eliminated all the evils so far noticed. It eliminated the contrast between the backwardness of the people and the precocity of the political world, by eliminating the politicians. It eliminated the evils of the electoral system of representation by eliminating parliament. It eliminated the "spoils system" and "patronage" in the Civil and Armed Services by putting in nominees of the government, who could not be removed by a general election because there was not going to be one. In all this Metaxas might be compared to a doctor whose only cure for a headache was decapitation. It may seem a feeble justification to argue that at least he had correctly diagnosed the headache.

Nevertheless, to compare Metaxas' Government with the dictatorships of Italy and Germany is ridiculous. The term "Fascism" in connection with Metaxas is idle abuse, just as the term "Communism" was in connection with many of his opponents. He did not found a one-party state as the Fascists did; rather he founded a no-party state. He did not plan aggressive war. He did not preach racial nationalism or sanctify a *herrenvolk*. He did not attempt to create an ideologically hereditary succession, nor even nominate a deputy *führer* to take his place. He was personally unambitious, benevolent and even retiring. He did not appear in public in gaudy uniforms nor invent for himself grandiose titles; even the rank of General, which he earned more than any other Greek who had held it, was quietly dropped. He seems to have seen his dictatorship rather after the model of the dictatorship in the ancient Roman republic, as a *temporary* device to replace constitutional government in an emergency, intending ultimately to restore it when it could work. But however high-minded the motives for undertaking supreme power, it is a hard thing to resign. Whether Metaxas would ever have put himself in the tiny class of dictators who dared to retire when their mission was fulfilled, history denied the opportunity of knowing.

That is the crucial point about Metaxas' Government. It could only be judged when its work was completed, and it never was completed. It could only become permanent, for good or ill, when it was complete; being left incomplete at his death, it crumbled to nothing in a few weeks, leaving no mark on Greek life except in the memories of the people. It is not hard to make comparative lists of the good and evil that it did; but it is not relevant either. We can balance in one scale its success in making government departments work instead of plotting over the coffee-cup; in stabilising the currency; in establishing an export trade; in completing motor-roads instead of building a hundred yards and then thinking up another one; in organising an army which could meet the Italians at a few days' notice, and so on. We can balance in the other scale its injustice in suppressing freedom of the press; in imprisoning or exiling its opponents; in interfering with ecclesiastical elections; in replacing Trade Union leaders with its own nominees; in dragooning its children into an ideological youth movement; in setting up a secret police on the German model, and so on. But when we have struck a balance, we have not assessed its claim upon history. What matters is that it failed because it never completed its task. Although the laws of Metaxas' Government were not formally abolished until June 1945, his régime was extinct *de facto* from April 1941 and *de jure* from October of the same year. His five years were not enough.

Whether it ever could have completed its task is a difficult question, which implies another: How far did Metaxas intend to go in creating the Greek state? He could not hope in his lifetime to equip Greece to stand on equal terms in global war. He was engaged upon an internal revolution which could only be successful in an international vacuum. If Greece could have been insulated from Europe until Metaxas had worked his miracle, it might have come off; but Greece could not be insulated, as Metaxas found, for instance, when he was called upon by the League of Nations to support sanctions against Italy's Abyssinian adventure. To concentrate all his energy upon the internal revolution, however, he felt obliged to free his hands from all other problems. Three at least of these were charged with danger; and they were not removed, but swept under the edge of the carpet.

These three were the constitution; the Communists; and foreign affairs. The first two would eventually have caused the Metaxas Government serious, perhaps fatal embarrassment. They were shelved, not solved, when he decided that during his administration, Greece should be a monarchy, not a republic, and that the place for Communists was behind bars or in exile. The later history of these two problems, closely interwoven with each other, will form the fabric of later chapters. How they would have affected the Metaxist state is an academic question; for in fact it was the third of his unsolved problems that brought ruin.

2. *The Second World War in the Balkans.*

It was not Metaxas' fault that there was no solution in his last days for Greece's foreign problems. It was the operation of a law binding together the foreign policies of every Balkan government. They could not have independent foreign policies; and they could only have a collective policy as long as each sustained it. The Balkan Entente of 1934 had never been complete, because Albania and Bulgaria were not members. Even what was left of it collapsed when Italy occupied Albania unchallenged in April 1939, and Rumania adhered to the Axis in November 1940. After that no Balkan country had any principle left upon which to found a foreign policy, except the desire to postpone as long as possible its own entanglement in the Second World War. It was not merely because the Balkan countries hungered for each other's property; it was because the Great Powers needed their territories and resources for the conduct of the war. Certainly there were selfish groups and corrupt individuals ready to exploit their neighbours' difficulties; but there were also wise men who could have conducted their inter-related affairs with reasonable

B

harmony if they had been free to do so. It was the projection into the Balkans of the rivalry of the Great Powers that turned them into the playground of criminal bandits and set them back a hundred years.

Balkan politics in the first years of the Second World War revolved in two concentric orbits. In the inner were the countries of south-east Europe; in the outer the rival powers of Germany, Britain and the USSR. Of these three, the first two were at war, and both lived on terms of suspicion with the third. All had traditional and immediate interests in south-east Europe. Germany was concerned to occupy the Balkans as a preliminary to attack on the Middle East, and perhaps on Russia. Britain was concerned to save what she could of south-east Europe to protect the eastern end of the Mediterranean. The USSR was concerned to prevent Germany from occupying Constantinople and the Straits, which were then as always the crux of Russian foreign policy. Each was competing for the good-will of the Balkan countries. Of the three, Germany was the least popular; but Germany had what neither of the others had—a huge army on the spot. The effect of German diplomacy, by the exercise of this weapon, is the first subject to be discussed in approaching the position of Greece in the Second World War.

Having secured Hungary in the summer and Rumania in the autumn of 1940, the Germans intended to isolate and absorb successively Bulgaria, Yugoslavia, Greece and perhaps Turkey. The simplest wedge to insert between each pair of them in turn consisted in the importance of Salonika. This port had been a disputed prize of the Balkan Wars thirty years earlier; it had fallen to Greece, with the concession of a Free Zone to Yugoslavia; it was the natural capital of the still-disputed territory of Macedonia. Macedonia, a geographical term of indeterminable limits, was divided between Yugoslavia, Bulgaria and Greece; but each wished to extend its claim, and the object of irredentists in the first two was to prove that Salonika rightly belonged to their share. Although in thirty years Greece had almost hellenised it, Salonika remained a temptation to the unscrupulous governments of the Slav neighbours. It was never specifically offered by the Germans to the Bulgarian Government, as it was later to the Yugoslav; but Bulgaria was the first to be tempted by the prospect of territorial gains at the expense of Greece, which it was naturally understood would include Salonika. Two things held back the Bulgarian Government at the beginning of 1941. One was the attitude of the USSR, which had sent a special emissary to Sofia to keep Bulgaria out of the German camp: a task that was facilitated by the pro-Russian sentiment of the Bulgarian people. The other was the attitude of Turkey, which was bound by treaty and by the reiterated undertakings of its Ministers, to go to war if Bulgaria attacked Greece. The object of Bulgarian diplomacy was therefore twofold: to maintain an equipoise between German and Russian influences; and to gain territory from Greece without going to war. The object of Turkish diplomacy was to keep out of any war which, if it should involve the USSR, might lead to the permanent loss of Constantinople and the Straits. The object of the USSR was to prevent the Germans from turning Bulgaria as well as Rumania into an armed base on their frontier. From this triangle of forces a resultant must eventually emerge, perhaps determined by no policy, but itself determining Bulgaria's response to Hitler's offers.

Oblivious of inconsistency, Hitler offered the same bait of Salonika to Yugoslavia. He added to it the hint that Bulgaria itself would be part of Yugoslavia's reward for joining the Axis. The Yugoslav Government at the beginning of 1941 was unsteady, but there were sufficient ministers of character to harden it against bribery. On November 1st, 1940, the Yugoslav Government had declared its neutrality in the war between Greece and Italy; it did not intend to be dragged into any other war if it could avoid it. But if Bulgaria gave way to the Axis, it would become impossible for Yugoslavia to keep out of the war: for the route through Bulgaria to Greece lay along the Struma valley, parallel to Yugoslavia's eastern frontier at a few miles' distance. To protect that flank, the Germans had to be sure of the Yugoslav attitude; to supplement that exiguous route, the Germans would require the better routes into Greece: the Monastir and Vardar Gaps through Yugoslav territory. Sooner or later, the choice of Bulgaria would force a choice upon Yugoslavia. When those two choices were made, it was Greece's turn next.

Upon these events it was impossible for Metaxas to exercise a decisive influence. Like every Balkan leader, he could only play for a respite from day to day. It was a tragic dénouement to a policy that depended on peace and isolation. Greece's internal revolution could only have achieved entire success if everybody left the country alone; if Greece ceased to have foreign relations until the Greek state was established. Instead, in 1940 Greece was involved in a minor war that was bound to grow into a major one. Still Metaxas pursued to the last the habitual course of little men trying to keep out of big men's quarrels: because he could not avoid foreign relations altogether, he tried to be friendly with everyone. Thanks to the statesmanship of his predecessor Eleftherios Veniselos, he could retain the goodwill of the Turkish and Yugoslav Governments, with which Greece's relations had been good for several years. But perfect equilibrium could not be maintained. War with Italy had come, and war with Germany was coming, when Metaxas died. It was his personal fortune that he did not live to reap the harvest of a foreign policy which events beyond his control had forced upon him.

The successor who inherited the miserable legacy at his death was a banker called Alexandhros Koryzis. The unexpected choice which put him in office (it would be ridiculous to say in power) refutes the comparison between the Greek dictatorship and those of Germany and Italy:

Hitler and Mussolini would not have been succeeded by blameless public servants. Koryzis lacked even the personality necessary to conduct what was left of Greece's foreign policy, which passed into the hands of King George II himself. It did not escape the attention of the King's enemies that his mother had been a German. Yet although the time was almost past when anything Greece did could divert or even delay the pre-determined development of events, the shift of responsibility led to one immediate and brave decision. Metaxas, fearing to provoke Germany to an attack which could not be held, had refused to allow a British Expeditionary Force into the north of Greece until its size and especially its air support could be sufficient to ensure success. (He had shown similar caution in advising King Constantine to keep out of the First World War.) From the British point of view, the despatch of an expeditionary force to Greece might have one of two advantages: either to check the German advance in S.E. Europe, or at least to delay it and compel the enemy to occupy hostile rather than acquiescent territory. From the Greek point of view, the latter was hardly an advantage at all in comparison with the former; but the people's determination would nevertheless not have hesitated if discretion had not been imposed by Metaxas. Shortly before his death he agreed that in any circumstances British forces should be allowed to land in Greece, even if they were too small to save the country, as soon as German troops entered Bulgaria. It was likely that the margin of time would be too small; but even after this concession Metaxas would not allow British reconnaissance of northern Greece. The British authorities persisted, with an urgency which Gen. Papagos has logically attributed to the political importance of honouring, even by token, the guarantee given to Greece on 13th April, 1939.[1] Metaxas was stubborn and logical, but he was also dying. A month after his death, his successors waived his scruples, and the British Expeditionary Force began to arrive. It was chiefly composed of Australian and New Zealand troops drawn from General Wavell's already inadequate force in North Africa.

This decision did not by itself provoke the climax of German action in the Balkans: it simply came to meet it halfway. A temporary halt in the Germans' progress in Bulgaria had been brought about by combined pressure. The Bulgarian Government was restrained from surrender by a non-aggression pact with Turkey; by an explicit warning from the special representative of USSR; by another from the special representative of the USA, all the more forceful because Bulgaria and the USA had never been at war; and by a stern broadcast from Mr. Churchill. But there was an unbridgeable gulf between the wishes of the Bulgarian people, for whom the attitude of the USSR was decisive, and their rulers, for whom fear and greed were decisive. German infiltration

[1] *The German Attack on Greece*, (London, 1946), p. 12.

progressed throughout February; on 1st March the Bulgarian Prime Minister signed the Tripartite Pact.

The treatment applied to the Yugoslavs was almost the same, but the reaction was different. The offer of territorial gain at the expense of Greece was made; the consequences of refusal were hinted; the Tripartite Pact was duly signed (with a few reservations) on 25th March. But instead of acquiescing, as the Bulgars had, the Yugoslav peoples rebelled. A revolutionary government was formed, comprising every racial group and political opinion except the Communists; the Regency of Prince Paul for the boy-king Peter II was terminated; the quisling ministers were arrested and deported; Russians, British, and Americans were indiscriminately cheered throughout Belgrade. The Germans could not tolerate this insolence, although they were informed by the Yugoslav ambassador in Berlin that the Tripartite Pact was still accepted in principle. On 6th April they invaded Yugoslavia, as well as Greece; Belgrade suffered air-bombardment of a degree hitherto inflicted only on Warsaw and Rotterdam. The Yugoslav campaign was over in a week, and the revolutionary government escaped into exile. The Greek campaign was finished within the month. Before April was over, Koryzis was dead by his own hand, and the King and government had departed for Crete with the undestroyed remnant of the British and Imperial Expeditionary Force.

It is worth anticipating a little to point out the later development of this contrast between Yugoslavia and Bulgaria, because Greece was affected by it during the occupation. Two things might have been expected to emerge eventually from the contrast. Firstly, because Yugoslavia had carried out its own revolution before Germany attacked, it might have been expected that the new government would have enjoyed uninterrupted recognition by the Allies and re-established itself after the war with general acclaim. Secondly, it might have been expected that Bulgaria would eventually pay a heavy penalty. Neither of these expectations was fulfilled, and Greece was a principal sufferer from the fact that they were not.

The reason in the first case is that the new Yugoslav Government was no more "popular" (except in the sense of momentary enthusiasm) than its predecessor; it belonged at heart to the same *ancien régime*. The revolution was military; it started in the air force, and the new Prime Minister was a Serb general, Simovitch. (Another Serb general, Neditch, had been Minister of War a few months earlier and was to be the Germans' puppet Prime Minister a few months later; and another, Mihailovitch, was to lead the first resistance.) Simovitch did not denounce the Tripartite Pact, and thereby forfeited the right to invoke armed support from Turkey under the terms of the Balkan Entente. He patted himself on the back for refusing the offer of Salonika; but not long afterwards he laid public claim to Trieste in a broadcast from exile. These did not look like signs of a change of heart, even if Yugoslavia had, in Mr. Churchill's words, "found its soul." The Simovitch Government enjoyed for the moment the support of its peoples and of all the major Allies, including the USSR, which signed a treaty of non-aggression with it on the day Germany invaded Yugoslavia. But it was not an elected government; except in the face of disaster, it was not a cohesive government. When the Germans drove it into exile and dismembered Yugoslavia into its component parts, neither Simovitch nor any other Serb could re-unite the components into symbolical unity in exile. Yugoslavia still had its real revolution before it; Greece, which welcomed the *coup d'état* of Simovitch, had still to experience the discomfort of a Communist dictatorship on its northern frontier.

By a different process, the same result came about in Bulgaria, which derived uninterrupted benefit from the gulf between the people and its rulers. Throughout the war it had the advantages of its rulers' collaboration with the Germans; after the war it had the advantages of its people's sympathy for the Russians. That sympathy was evident from the first. Bulgaria's peasantry became a whispering gallery along which every voice from Moscow re-echoed, while Bulgaria's Government entered whole-heartedly into Berlin's plans for the dismemberment of Yugoslavia and Greece. Bulgaria's southern frontier reached the Aegean, and its western frontier marched with Fascist Greater Albania, while the Bulgarian population built up merit with the USSR. (It was even reported in 1941 that a visit from Himmler was necessary to put a stop to pro-Russian gossip in the coffee-shops.) Thus Bulgaria not only averted the dreaded war with Turkey, and acquired everything that its rulers had set their hearts on from its neighbours; but also at the end of the war effected an instantaneous transformation which, at the expense of some unwanted heads, a few months of war with the Germans, and twenty-four hours of formal hostilities with the USSR, substituted a virtuous dictatorship of the proletariat for the wicked dictatorship of the fascists, and left the country intact within its pre-war frontiers. It was the neatest trick of the war; but it was naturally unwelcome to the Greeks.

The two revolutionary developments which the German occupation precipitated on Greece's northern frontiers were supplemented by a miniature third in Albania. Metaxas had spoken in December 1940 of liberating Albania from the Italians. The Albanian puppets had grandiosely replied that "Fascist Albania, within extended frontiers, will form a valuable element of culture and progress in the new Roman Empire." They drew as dividend from Yugoslavia a slice of territory which included Kossovo, though nothing for the present from Greece. But as in Bulgaria, the people were in disharmony with their leaders. The occupation inspired them to a resistance movement, which in turn threw up the new government when the Axis was expelled. The point in common with Yugoslavia and Bulgaria is that from the Greek point of view the last state of all three was as bad as the first. In February 1941 they were dominated by powers hostile to Greece, namely Germany and Italy. In 1945 they were again under a domination hostile to Greece: thus whatever happened, Greece was the loser.

This gloomy future was not in the minds of the Greek Government or its British Allies in 1941, when they were occupied by dangers in a different direction. Crete, to which the Anglo-Greek authorities had retreated, was the immediate objective of the German High Command; for the moment the Balkans lay in the background. The Germans intended to cut the Middle East in half, in order to win the Arabian oilfields and to isolate Britain and the USSR from any possible alliance with each other, by seizing successively Crete, Syria, Cyprus, Iraq and Iran. Crete, and later Cyprus, were to be seized by air-borne forces; Syria was to be handed over by the Vichy Government of France; Iraq was to be wrested from British control by the revolt of Rashid Ali, its quisling Prime Minister; Iran was finally to be penetrated in the familiar way. The only flaw in the plan was the timing.

Greece had already held out unexpectedly long; the delay was increased by the defence of Crete. The King and his Government were there when the attack began, but their presence was a liability rather than an asset. When Koryzis committed suicide, the King, after presiding at the Council of Ministers for two days himself, had appointed a Cretan Prime Minister, Emmanuel Tsoudheros. But the gesture was viewed with indifference, for Tsoudheros was regarded as a royalist, and three Metaxist ministers, Maniadhakis, Dhimitratos and Nikoloudhis, remained in his Government; whereas Crete, the home of Eleftherios Veniselos, had a predominantly republican tradition. As the German attack began, the brave but super-fluous King made an adventurous escape, followed by his ministers, and left the islanders and the British and Dominion forces to fight it out. The defence lasted eleven days; captured operation orders proved that it was scheduled to last four. This discrepancy was perhaps one of the irregularities which threw Hitler's time-table out sufficiently to delay the start of the onslaught upon the USSR.[1]

The dislocation of the plan was soon evident. The revolt of Rashid Ali in Iraq began prematurely on 30th April. To sustain it, the Germans planned to send troops by air through Syria, thus anticipating the diplo-matic processes of annexation there. But although Crete was theirs by 1st June, Rashid Ali had already fled his country the day before; and the weakness of Vichy in allowing the Germans to use bases in Syria pre-cipitated a joint invasion from Palestine by Fighting French and British

[1] I have discussed this point (which is still controversial) more fully in *The Nineteenth Century and After*, January 1948. See also General de Guingand, *Operation Victory*, pp. 78-80.

troops on 8th June. Hitler nevertheless carried out his plans against the USSR by crossing their frontier on 22nd June, accompanied by Rumanian divisions at once, and by Hungarian, Slovak and Croat forces soon afterwards. This monumental lunacy had a magic effect upon the rest of the world. It produced the Anglo-Russian Alliance of 12th July; it produced the recognition by the USSR of the exiled governments of Poland, Czecho-Slovakia, Yugoslavia and Greece; it precipitated the occupation of Iran not by German but by Russian and British troops; it was followed within two months by the signature of the Atlantic Charter. Between April and August 1941 the course of the Second World War was settled so far as it affected the Middle East. There were still two great powers, Japan and the USA, to come into it, but there was no longer doubt about the opposing alignments. The pieces were in their places on the board: the Balkans occupied by Germany, the Middle East by the Allies, Turkey neutral at the centre. There were no more great changes to take place until the war passed its climax. There was at last a comparatively stable background against which the affairs of Greece could be seen.

The first visible result of the Eastern Mediterranean upheaval upon Greek affairs was the abolition of the régime that took its name from the Fourth of August, 1936. When King George II announced from his exile that the régime was defunct, he only recognised a *fait accompli*. In Greece it had already been replaced by an ineffectual puppet government under General Tsolakoglou, the man who had betrayed his people and disobeyed his orders by signing an armistice with the German and Italian commanders at Salonika on 23rd April. In exile it had been replaced by a provisional cabinet under Tsoudheros, pledged to restore constitutional government. The one subject on which the rival governments of Athens and London were unanimous was the denunciation of the Fourth of August. The years of occupation, therefore, began with a political *tabula rasa*. It has now to be seen where the next constructive marks upon the clean slate were to come from.

CHAPTER II

SCENES AND CHARACTERS

"It is unfortunate, though very natural, that the history of this period has so generally been written in hysterics."—CARLYLE, *The French Revolution.*

ALTHOUGH it wiped clean the political slate, the effect of the German occupation of Greece was not entirely one of simplification. Everything had to be begun all over again; but the characters who could make the fresh start, and the points from which it could be made, were not reduced but multiplied. The abolition of the Metaxas régime was an act of release rather than destruction. It not only restored but magnified the primeval chaos of Greek politics. From the summer of 1941, there were four stages instead of one on which the Greek drama could be recommenced; and the number of potential participants far exceeded the political world of Athens. These scenes and characters must be carefully introduced before the narrative goes further.

Greek politics, which had been conducted exclusively and somewhat parochially in Athens, became diffused by the occupation to three other centres as well. In Athens there remained the puppet Governments of the Germans, the *attentistes*[1] and the illegal organisations. In Egypt there were the *emigrés* and exiles; the headquarters of the armed services; and always at least part of the legitimate Government. In London there were intermittently the King and part of his Government. In the Greek mountains there were the armed rebels with their political directors. All these contributed independently to the development of Greek politics from 1941 to 1944. Each of them had a complicated system of internal and external relations. Each of them enjoyed direct or indirect, but in any case mutually independent, access to some representation of the allied authorities. In nine cases out of ten "Allied" in that context meant "British."

The last point is crucial. The German occupation entailed the direct entanglement of the allies in Greek politics, and circumstances dictated that the brunt of the entanglement should be borne by the British. Under Metaxas Greek politics had been a Greek affair; now they were everyone's, and chiefly ours. This will therefore appear to be a fundamentally Anglo-Greek story, in which the British will figure more than seems

[1]The word *"attentiste"* was coined by the French to describe those who decided neither to resist nor to collaborate, but to "wait and see."

25

right, and most of the other Allies less than they ought. Before embarking
on it, I shall introduce separately all the new participants which the
changed circumstances bring into it. The introduction will digress
freely into the past and future, but the picture which it is designed to
compose is primarily of the figures participating in the crucial period of
the occupation. The chronology needed to establish the individual
characters will be given, but it is not necessary to correlate the dates of
the various biographies in proper sequence, since that will be the function
of the next chapters. I shall here simply present them on each of the four
stages in turn, so that the reader can use this chapter for reference back
from the chronological survey which follows.

1. ATHENS.

From everything that follows, there is one initial exception: the
common people of Athens. Others abide our question; they are free.
They are not to be criticised, or even named except on bended knee.
They are exempt firstly because their role was politically passive; secondly
because such decisions as they made collectively came not from the head
but from the heart. One should never again think of Greece without
thinking first of the women who seized the brooms from the hands of
British prisoners scavenging the streets, to do their work for them; of
the street-urchins who flung the cigarettes with which they earned their
living into lorries loaded with British prisoners as they passed; of the
families that died in Khaidhari prison-camp for helping British prisoners
to escape. When the common people does such things, it too is influencing
the history of human relations; but not in the way that politicians do so,
nor for their reasons. The common people of Athens were not guided by
reason, but by emotion and instinct. What they did under the impulse
of those emotions has no place in a political survey; for under the impulse
of another emotion, they could easily do something entirely different.
It was, for instance, a girl belonging to the same heritage who returned
from a Communist demonstration in October 1944 exclaiming: "What
crowds! What enthusiasm! What a marvel! What popular democracy!
Just think what it will be like when the *King* comes back!" It is not
because these people's emotions are wrong or trivial or muddled that I
exclude them; it is simply because they are emotions, and therefore the
victims of alien impulses. Whoever mastered those impulses mastered the
common people: it is with those masters that I am directly concerned.
I leave the common people of Athens with homage, and turn to its
political scene.

The arrival of the Germans did not immediately revitalise political
life: vitality returned earlier elsewhere. In Athens one kind of political
death was substituted for another. Occupation did not release party
politics from the coma into which Metaxas had plunged them; nor did

it take over the Metaxist Government, as the enemies of Metaxas had predicted. Although the régime of the "Fourth of August" was defunct, most of the men who had held high office contrived to escape the country and evade the expected stigma of collaboration. The Germans found a political vacuum; but it would have been out of character to fill that vacuum by allowing a recrudescence of party politics. Even though Metaxas had not been their ally, and would never have collaborated with the Germans, nevertheless he had prepared the way for occupation by adapting the machinery of administration and accustoming the people to authoritarian government. The Germans therefore did not have to find a new kind of administration to fill the void; they only had to find a few men to fill empty chairs in the ministries.

(a) *Collaborators.* The first set of participants in the new drama on the Athens stage may therefore be called the "collaborators." It is wrong to use the more offensive term "Quislings," which applies only to those who conspired with the enemy in advance of the occupation: no Greek in high office committed the crime of Vidkun Quisling. The worst that can be said against the Greek collaborators, which is bad enough, is that they acquiesced in the occupation either for personal gain, or because they believed that the Germans had won the war, or because they saw no hope of survival for themselves and millions of others except by collaboration. Those three explanations, singly or in combination, account for the motives of all three collaborating Prime Ministers and most of their adherents.

The first of the three, General Tsolakoglou, accepted the post of Prime Minister under the Germans because his experience as a Corps Commander in Albania convinced him that the Axis had won the war and that Greece had to make the best of a bad job. His principal subordinate and rival was his Finance Minister, Gotzamanis. The second Prime Minister, Professor Logothetopoulos, not only shared that delusion but had personal ambitions; his German training in medicine, his German wife and his German sympathies gave him reason to expect a profitable career under German patronage as an agent of the New Order. The third, Ioannis Rallis, was a different case. He was the only professional politician among the three; he took office when it was already clear that the Allies would win the war. His motives must therefore have been different from those of his predecessors. He seems to have calculated that the Allies would be grateful to him for keeping the machinery of government in motion during the closing stages of the occupation, so that on their return they should find Greece in a state of passive orderliness, rather than disintegrated into a chaos from which only the Communists could profit. His chief act was the formation in the summer of 1943 of the Security Battalions, under the inspiration of the ex-dictator, General

Pangalos, and perhaps with the tacit acquiescence of the ex-revolutionary, General Gonatas. He was chiefly assisted by three men in his Government: Tavoularis (the nominee of Pangalos), Bourandas and Voulpiotis. The military commanders of the Security Battalions, Colonels Plitzanopoulos and Papadhongonas, were unimportant. Rallis regarded the force as a bridge across which Greece would pass from German occupation to Allied liberation without an interval of chaos; he intended to enjoy the best of both worlds, reaping the fruits of collaboration with both sides. His calculation was surprisingly shrewd.

(b) *Attentistes.* Rallis was not alone in making the calculation. A second group of prominent Athenians argued from the same premises without committing themselves to such downright conclusions. These included many of the old world of Greek politicians and its semi-political fringe; ex-deputies, businessmen, industrialists, civil servants, the pro-fessional classes, even the church, all reacted similarly, because in Greece, unlike England, there is no contrast of ethic between public service and private enterprise. But none of them needed to take sides in the open. The political world was free to conduct its policies over the coffee-cup; the industrialists and businessmen were free to re-insure themselves by discreetly financing every possible winner; the professional classes were exempted from judgment by the necessity of keeping life going under any political régime; the church could not openly exhort its flock either to the sin of collaboration or to the desperate alternative of starvation. Such men were obliged to sit on the fence. Of the professional politicians, it is hard to find anything interesting to say: they enjoyed the passive bliss of those who have no history. The right-wing quartet of Populists, Theotokis, Mavromikhalis, Tsaldharis and Stephanopoulos, were handi-capped in rehearsing their imperfect harmony against the day of libera-tion by the absence of the first in Corfu and the second in Turkey; the Liberals, Progressives and Agrarians (few of whom had any agricultural experience), ranged only from elder statesmen like Mylonas and Rendis to ancient monuments like Sophoulis and Kaphandaris; the new-statesmanlike Sophianopoulos spun his silent web as always in watchful isolation. Big business extracted as much profit as it could from the occupation and subscribed as much as it thought prudent to the resistance; the Church intervened in public affairs only on errands of mercy and dignity; the civil servant, the bank-manager, the policeman, the black-coated slave, hardly deviated from the customary routine of their lives.

Of the last, four examples will speak for all: Sbarounis, who served Tsolakoglou and Tsoudheros in turn as a financial expert; Dhimaratos and Evert, two of the heads of the City Police; and Spiliotopoulos, one of the heads of the Provincial Gendarmerie. All four held office during at least part of the occupation, and thereby served the Germans; all four did what they could (sometimes a great deal) to frustrate the intentions of the Germans and to aid the Allies; all four could plead that worse men in their positions would have brought worse tragedies to their people. Those who, being without sin, are inclined to throw stones, might profitably study the contrasting but unadvertised example of General Papagos. Having tried too late to rescind Tsolakoglou's surrender, he refused the opportunity of escape and submitted to house arrest. Although not rich, he refused the pension which Tsolakoglou offered him; he did his best two years later to join the armed resistance movement; and he endured more than a year in a German concentration camp with four colleagues. He behaved as a Greek general should have behaved in circumstances beyond his control. Those who criticise the class of Greeks to which he belongs ignore his example, and evade the inference that if every Greek had followed it, the Greek nation would have expired. It was right that the outstanding few should so behave: but it was in-evitable that the majority should carry on. There were exceptions who committed themselves whole-heartedly to the Germans, or gave up everything to support the resistance. But as classes their policy had to be that of *attentistes*. It did not look nice; it brought on many respectable men, even on Dhamaskinos, Archbishop of Athens, the hint of having collab-orated; but it was inevitable. These men too, therefore, played a part in the political development of the years of occupation: a neutral, hesitant, negative part, but not a negligible one. Indeed, their part might almost have been called decisive when, by a process of cancelling out extremes at the end of the war, the people who seemed to come out best were those who had done least one way or the other, having so calculated the balance of risks that they would not be much worse off whoever came out on top.

These two groups that have so far been introduced may be referred to henceforth as the Collaborators and the *Attentistes* of Athens, with the qualification that the line between them is imprecise and fluctuating. Two qualities can be detected on both sides of the dividing line: a tendency to live in the past, and a pathological terror of Communism. They lived in the past both socially and politically; perhaps in both cases because the narcotic administered by Metaxas to the life and thought of the Greeks, even when it began to wear off, still left them with the subconscious impression that they were back in 1936, if not earlier still. Most of them remained throughout the dictatorship of Metaxas, throughout the German occupation, and remain to this day oblivious of the social revolutions that have taken place in Western Europe. The retrogression of their political thought is still more marked: for the only lively political problem that divides them is still the constitutional question of Monarchy or Republic, which has been fruitlessly debated without intermission since it came into being in 1917. Apart from the coma into which Metaxas plunged their political consciousness, only one other thing has had the power to silence this controversy even momentarily: the even more paralysing fear of Communism.

With the confused foresight which characterises the Greek political world and its semi-political fringe, these two groups concurred in regarding not the Germans but the Communists as the principal danger. The alliance of the Western Democracies with Soviet Russia could to their minds only be a short-lived marriage of convenience, whoever might win the war. But they had no counter to the Communist menace except an instinctive reaction in the opposite direction. Instead of moving forwards in a parallel direction, their thought moved backwards into the world of constitutional controversy, which at least they understood because they had it always with them. Their purposeless debates on the respective merits of Republic and Monarchy as the best means of ensuring stability and averting Communism might be compared to a debate on the respective merits of steel-helmets and gas-masks as the best protection against atomic bombs.

(c) *Underground*. In all these respects the third group on the Athenian stage presents a strong contrast. It may be referred to as the Underground, though the connotation of that term is made difficult to define by the diversity of its constitution. As the occupation drew towards its close, the potential value of a claim to have belonged to an Underground movement rose visibly; efforts were made by the unlikeliest individuals to achieve imprisonment by the Germans, as the return of the Allies became daily more certain. Even at an earlier stage, some Athenians realised the value of re-insurance in this direction, provided they could avoid the attendant risks. In this way there came about an overlap between the *attentistes* and the Underground, just as between the Collaborators and the *attentistes*. An example was the formation in Athens at the end of 1942 of a Military Committee of six regular colonels (including Spiliotopoulos, who had been head of the Gendarmerie), for the putative purpose of organising and directing the guerilla forces in the mountains. Although the formation of the committee was a brave step to take before the battle of El Alamein, and as such it won the official recognition of the Greek and British Governments, no guerilla unit ever owed anything to it; its value was confined to the initial gesture and the collection of intelligence. Such activities lie outside my scope in speaking of the Underground.

The Underground of Athens as a political participant in this story consists essentially of two groups: the Communists and the younger politicians of the Left Centre. I except the many Athenians of all classes who contributed everything, even their lives, to helping the Allies during the occupation, not because their work was not valuable, but because it was not political. That enhances its merit in the eyes of those who regard politics as the curse of Greek life, but it makes it irrelevant to a political study. The definition of the political underground of Athens must be restricted to those who saw the conflict with the German occupation as primarily a political affair and as means to a political end.

The exception therefore covers not only those who had no consideration before them besides the war effort, but also those who saw the political implications of the occupation too late to exploit them as they would have wished if they had seen them earlier. An example of the former is the group of young men known as PEAN (the Patriotic Union of Fighting Youth), which in 1942 carried out one successful act of sabotage in blowing up the premises of the Greek Nazi Party, but was soon extinguished by the capture and execution of many of its directing committee. An example of the second is an organisation of which much has been heard since the occupation under the name "X" (pronounced "Khee" in Greek). This body, later known as the direct-action instrument of the Royalist right wing under the leadership of Colonel Grivas, has claimed to have been a resistance movement during the occupation. If that claim were true, it would be classifiable as the only resistance organisation of the right then active in Athens; but in fact its name was unknown until shortly before the Germans left; and even then the name signified nothing connected with resistance. Only in the years immediately after the war did it acquire significance: the sinister significance of a Ku Klux Klan. It too, therefore, has no place in this introduction.

The political underground on the Athenian stage will hereafter mean on the one hand the Communists, and on the other the energetic elements of the Left Centre: roughly the same pair that formed the exceptions to the general picture drawn in Chapter I.[1] The term Communist, though often loosely used as a term of abuse, is perfectly precise, and will only be used here in its strictest sense, to mean a member of the KKE. Such membership is not acquired at will, but by selection after rigorous probation, though it is often desired and even claimed by a miscellaneous fringe who have no right to it: in both respects its nearest equivalent in England is the Old School Tie. The term Left-Centre, on the other hand, is imprecise and subject to fluctuation. The latter will need some immediate clarification, whereas the former can be left to reveal its specific character in the mountains of Greece, where the different components are more clearly distinguishable.[2] There is, however, one aspect of the work of the KKE that must be dealt with here; that is the organisation of the workers who formed a separate department of the resistance movement confined to Athens and the few other big towns.

Before Metaxas, there had been two trends in the Greek trade unions,

[1] See page 15.
[2] See Section 4 of this chapter, pp. 59 seqq.

the Reformist and the Communist. The leaders of the former, whose inclinations resembled those of the Fabians in England, were Kalomoiris and Stratis: the leader of the latter, on behalf of the KKE, was Theos, and his chief assistant was Nepheloudhis. The two trends were roughly equal in the General Confederation of Labour, in which all workers were doubly represented, because the method of organisation was two-fold. They were organised hierarchically by occupations into unions, federations and confederations of particular trades, and by locality into workers' centres comprising all workers of particular districts. Both the Confederations and the Workers' Centres (of which there were fifty-six all over Greece) sent representatives to the periodical General Confederation of Labour, which elected a directorate and a general secretary to preside over it. Since the method of election before the war was by majority vote, not by proportional representation, the winning group captured every seat in the directorate, and a mixed directorate was impossible. Such was the system before Metaxas, and such more or less it became again in 1945, with the significant addition of a new political group. But from 1936 to 1944 the organisation existed only in name, because Metaxas and the Italians and Germans successively packed it with their own nominees. During the temporary uncertainty which followed the death of Metaxas, Kalomoiris was able to re-establish the General Confederation of 1936; but this lasted only three months, until the Germans and Italians took over. The workers therefore ceased to be democratically represented for more than eight years. But the Communist group under Theos took the initiative in forming an underground rival called "the Workers' National Liberation Front," and usually known by its Greek initials as EEAM.

This organisation contained all that was best of organised labour in Greece. Its importance was greatest in Athens, Piraeus, Salonika, Volos, and Patras; but wherever there was a working population, EEAM inspired it against the occupying authorities. Strikes and demonstrations were regularly organised to embarrass the enemy on every important occasion, whether it was the celebration of Independence Day or the attempt to conscript labour for Germany. The movement was successful because no political problem confronted the Greek worker at the time and no rivals competed for his allegiance. There was a clear-cut division between collaborating puppets on the one side and EEAM on the other; there were no fine shades, no indeterminate borderline occupied by ambiguous adventurers anxious to keep a foot in both camps. Outside EEAM there was no organised body at the time that could claim to represent the workers. After the liberation of Greece a new such body was formed by official action, and led successively by Hadjidhimitriou and Makris; but neither represented any serious section of opinion, and their group was not even in being before the early months of 1945. During the occupation, therefore, Greek labour was exhaustively represented by the coalition of Theos, Kalomoiris and Stratis. These three divided the Central Committee of EEAM between themselves in proportions which varied, but finally became stable at nine representatives of Kalomoiris, four of Theos (that is, of the Communists) and two of Stratis. That the Communists, who initiated the organisation, allowed themselves to be heavily outnumbered in this committee is significant. They could afford to do so because there was no division of purpose within the Labour movement, so long as the enemy remained in Greece to unite them. When the occupation ended, the internal relations of the workers changed: having agreed as a coalition to take over each of the fifty-six Workers' Centres in Greece when the Germans left, the Communist component of the Central Committee acted in anticipation of the agreement, and installed its own directorates as soon as the nominees of the Germans could be replaced. After that followed protests and evasions, quarrels and disruption: EEAM dissolved, and Theos unsuccessfully tried to re-create it as ERGAS (the Workers' Anti-Fascist League). But he stood alone, disowned by Kalomoiris and Stratis. This anti-climax earns no credit for the astuteness of Theos' democratic colleagues, but it does not detract from the Greek workers' achievement during the occupation. Although EEAM has been the least publicised component of the Greek resistance movement, it was perhaps the most successful. Its frustration of the Germans' plan to conscript Greek labour for Germany was one of the two or three greatest achievements of Greek resistance. The credit for organising this effort belongs largely to the Communists.

The one other source in Athens from which came an impulse to resist was intellectual rather than practical. The Centre in Athenian politics is a collective name for a cluster of individuals, rather than parties: especially during the occupation, when parties had not existed except in name for some years. Almost the only thing on which the extreme left and right in Greece have ever agreed is the non-existence of the centre. In this they are almost right, for as parties the centre barely survives; but as individuals, the centre includes much ability. The term evokes a picture not of organised masses of voters, but of a handful of outstanding men periodically oscillating to and fro in relation to each other and to Greece's political centre of gravity. Even among that handful selection must be made for the present definition. Sophoulis and Kaphandaris and their fellow elder-statesmen fall out as too old for revolutionary politics, though each was the titular head of a centre party. Papandhreou and Panayiotis Kanellopoulos and Sophoklis Veniselos must be excluded for two reasons: first, that although all three of them at various times flirted with the extreme left, they belong more consistently to a position rather to the right of the centre; second, that each of them played his most important part during the occupation abroad from Greece itself. They therefore belong to a later section of this introduction.

The men of the centre concerned in this definition are another breed; neither too old, like the first exceptions, not too undecided, like the second. They were unknown names in pre-war politics; they were mostly young as Greek politicians go. They often disagreed with each other, but more often, more decidedly, and more unanimously with the old political world: with the collaborators, the respectable *attentistes*, the unrelenting dotards of the pre-Metaxas world. Only one of them, Kartalis, had held a ministerial post before the war: the incongruous post of Minister of Labour in a right-wing government, whose policies he later abjured. One or two others had a slight fame for other reasons: such as Elias Tsirimokos, the son of a distinguished politician; or Svolos and Angelos Angelopoulos, the respected occupants of university chairs. The others constituted, before 1941, a list of unknown names: Petimezas, Pyromaglou, Peltekis, Kapsalopoulos, Katavolos, Pappas, Dhrakopoulos, Yiorgakis, and so on. At this stage of the narrative, these are still empty names; but they will acquire a significance, which is not likely to be permanently eclipsed merely because, like most active participants in the Greek resistance, they are temporarily consigned to oblivion. Their fortunes were the natural consequence of their principles. Each of them gravitated to a different political sector of the underground, without ceasing to preserve certain fundamental ideas in common. That gravitation separated them during the occupation; but what they had in common brought them together again in opposition to the post-war régime. In both phases they were trying to mitigate forces that were too strong for them; in both they personally failed, though their ideas were not without effect. There is no need to say more of them here by way of introduction, since they did not function as a group but as a leaven scattered throughout the resistance. Their individual contributions can be left to emerge from the impact of the organisations to which they gravitated; and although they belong essentially to the world of Athens, that impact occurred chiefly in the world of the mountains. Most of them will therefore reappear more distinctly in the fourth section of this chapter.

(*d*) *British Agents*. One of the above characters approaches the borderline which separates that group on the Athens stage from the next. Ioannis Peltekis, who later became known as a political figure in the left centre, was known during the occupation under a different character: as a British agent. In the current phraseology of Athens, he was a member of the "Intelligence Service," a title generally used by all Greeks in its English form, just as they would speak of the Gestapo or the Kremlin, and not even qualified by the epithet "British," because it is assumed to be unique. This title would be convenient to describe the last group in Athens; but as its implications are misleading, it is better to speak of agents of the British authorities. That term is itself invidious, partly because not all those agents were in fact *British*, and partly because it justly implies that none of them can be described as agents of the *Allied* authorities. In that last limitation is summed up much of the recent tragedy of Greece.

The *Greek* agents of the British authorities, of whom Peltekis was the most brilliant but not the earliest, must therefore be considered separately from the *British* agents in Athens. Their consideration must be detached from the more melodramatic associations of the word "agents." The function of these men in Athens was not political at all: it was to carry out espionage and sabotage; but this is not a history of either. Although it was no part of their work to become involved in Greek politics, it was equally unavoidable, whether they were Greek or British; for nothing takes place in the charged atmosphere of Athens that does not have its political aspect. The primary work on which these men were engaged must therefore be disregarded; only its indirect results matter here. The strictly political implications of their presence in Athens are themselves of sufficiently dramatic interest. They begin from the day our forces left Greece in 1941.

The first successful communication between the expelled British authorities and occupied Athens, apart from the casual intercourse maintained by refugees and couriers crossing the Aegean Sea in *caiques*, was achieved by means of a wireless transmitter that had been left in the hands of Colonel (later General) Bakirdzis.[1] Bakirdzis, who will figure often in this story, belonged in political sympathy to the Left Centre. He had acquired for himself in his unusual career a number of oddly assorted titles and associations. For his services in the First World War, he was made a member of our Distinguished Service Order. For his participation with other republican officers (notably Colonels Saraphis, Psaros and Tsigantes, whose names will recur hereafter) in the anti-royalist revolution of 1935, he earned a death sentence *in absentia* and the nickname of "the Red Colonel." At the beginning of the occupation he was an agent of the British authorities under the alternative names of "333" or "Prometheus"; before that occupation was over he had escaped to Egypt and returned to Greece as a senior member successively of two different and mutually hostile resistance organisations in succession. He was reinstated in the Army and promoted to General. He was a foundation member of a left-wing shadow government designed to frustrate the authority of the recognised government in exile; yet he largely helped to prevent a left-wing revolution in Salonika coinciding with the revolution of December

[1] A similar arrangement had been made in Salonika under the direction of a Veniselist Liberal of the old school, Aleko Zannas; a man highly respected throughout the country. But since his organisation gave up subversive work as early as 1941, and since Salonika requires separate consideration in conjunction with the rest of Macedonia, I will here confine myself to Athens.

1944 against the recognised Government in Athens. He deserved a better end than fate allowed him: in September 1946 the Greek Government sent him into exile, and in May 1947 he committed suicide on the Aegean island of Ikaria.

In 1941 his work as an agent in Athens did not by itself cause political repercussions (apart from a suspicion of British motives in employing him), because it did not last long enough. After a little more than one year, Bakirdzis was obliged by the pressure of German curiosity to escape from Athens. He left his wireless set in the hands of a young naval officer called Koutsoyiannopoulos, who became known as Prometheus II. The political sympathies of Prometheus II were similar to those of Bakirdzis; he too had been involved in the 1935 revolution. But his success in Athens was more limited: apart from arranging the infiltration of the first British parachutists into Greece in October 1942, he did not play an important role. When he was captured by the Germans in February 1943, the Prometheus succession died out. Another short-lived political contact was extinguished at almost the same time: that of Major Tsigantes (the younger of two brothers well known for their energy and their Anglophil sentiments) who had entered Greece by submarine in August 1942, and was killed in a gun-battle with Italian secret police in Athens in January 1943. The work of both their organisations against the occupation was continued by successors; but the loss of their personalities and influence on external opinion robbed it of political significance.

There were other Greek agents of the British authorities in Athens; there were many separate British authorities engaged in diverse activities there; there was consequently an almost incalculable number of Greeks in Athens who could claim to be British agents without fear of contradiction. This fact accounts for another considerable part of the tragedy of recent Greek history. But the pretenders and the small fry must be ignored in order to concentrate upon those that matter. Since it was considered necessary for every branch of the British clandestine war effort to have its exclusive representation in Greece—whether its object was to collect intelligence or prisoners of war, to organise guerillas or sabotage, to carry out relief or psychological warfare—it was inevitable that in the end half Athens and his wife, nephew, father-in-law and second cousin once removed should have been able, if they wished, to claim a place in the Intelligence Service; but the confusion so caused need not obtrude here. The only remaining Greek agent of the British authorities who must be considered in an exclusively political survey is the one whose name introduced this section: Ioannis Peltekis.

Apart from being the most spectacularly successful of our agents, Peltekis is remarkable for the alternate fame and notoriety which he has attracted. By jealous rivals in Athens, he was accused of collaborating with the Germans. By jealous officials in Egypt he was accused of collaborating with the Communists. In 1944 the latter charge was considered scarcely less abominable than the former; a court of inquiry had to be held before he was cleared on both counts. Later his fame spread in a more honourable manner. He was decorated with the D.S.O.; he enjoyed the confidence of British officials in Athens after the liberation of Greece; he became Minister of Mercantile Marine in the last unelected Greek Government under Sophoulis in 1945-6. If only by reason of his contacts with British authorities, quite apart from his outstanding abilities, he has been a permanent factor in the political development of the period under review. It is therefore important that, like so many others here considered, his political sympathies place him consistently left of the Centre, with a steady tendency towards the extreme.

Whatever the political intention of His Majesty's Government towards Greece during the occupation, a high proportion of Greek agents of the British authorities were nearer to the left than the right in political sympathy, and anti-monarchist in the constitutional controversy. The reason was fortuitous: the right wing and the monarchists were slower than their opponents in deciding to resist the occupation, and therefore little use to the Allies until it was too late. There were only two important exceptions, neither of them more than partial. One is Major Tsigantes, who certainly had little sympathy with the left. Although he had taken an anti-monarchist course by participating in the 1935 revolution, he had in 1942 sufficiently made his peace with the King of the Hellenes, or at least with his Government, to be sent on an official mission to occupied Athens with their approval. The other exception is General Spiliotopoulos, for a brief time the head of the Gendarmerie, who enters into this narrative at two points in the occupation without making a conspicuous mark at either. He was one of the military committee of the six colonels which plotted global strategy from Athens in 1942-3; and he was appointed Military Governor of Athens with Allied approval in 1944, before (but not much before) the end of the occupation. As the recipient at that time of British money and arms for the maintenance of order in Athens when the Germans left, he may just qualify for the title of a right-wing organ of British policy in Athens. But these two exceptions rather emphasise the general rule by contrast, than detract from it. It is a safe generalisation that the Greek agents of the British authorities belonged predominantly to the left.

The balance was partly, but not wholly, redressed by the presence of certain British agents in Athens. The British authorities reasonably desired to be represented in Athens by Englishmen; but the Germans made the desire difficult to fulfil. Before the occupation was a year old at least three Englishmen on special (but not political) missions had come to grief. The first was left behind at the time of the evacuation, and captured soon afterwards. A second was captured shortly after his disembarkation in the

Peloponnese. A third was captured in landing on the island of Antiparos, in conditions which brought disaster on several Greek agents in Athens. These unfortunate enterprises do not bear on the present subject. It is only with later arrivals that political implications are to be traced; it is only of them that a tendency to redress the balance of their Greek colleagues can be remarked.

Concerning the first arrival in Athens of an Englishman sent there by the British authorities on an official mission,[1] I will quote only the opinion of the *Ethniki Phloga* (a right-wing Royalist paper) in 1945 that he was personally responsible for the creation of the left-wing conspiracy against the liberties of the Greek people; coupled with the opinion of the *Eleftheri Elladha* (a Communist paper) in 1946 that he was personally responsible to Mr. Churchill for the intrigues by which a monarcho-fascist dictatorship was re-imposed upon the Greek people. The conflicting judgments are characteristic and illustrative. But the point is not important at this introductory stage, since the brunt of British representation in Athens was borne by others. Three characteristic examples will help to show the partial redress of the balance.

The first and most famous was Lieut.-Colonel Macaskie, who was taken prisoner by the Germans in the campaign of 1941. He escaped to the Middle East; returned to Athens on a special mission; was recaptured by the Italians; escaped and was recaptured several more times; was tried in Athens and condemned to death; was saved by the Italian armistice, and escaped into the protection of the Archbishop of Athens; returned to the Middle East again; returned to Greece by parachute in 1944; and very properly watched the German evacuation of Athens from the balcony of the Archbishop's house. These facts emphasise that the Athenian world to which his contacts belonged was that of which the Archbishop of Athens was the highest typification. Dhamaskinos had been elected Archbishop under Metaxas, who had invalidated the election for political reasons and replaced him by Khrysanthos; the German occupation had in turn replaced Khrysanthos by Dhamaskinos, who regarded himself as the rightful Archbishop throughout: but neither had played any part in the jerrymandering about their appointments, which did nothing to damage the reputation of either. Dhamaskinos was the centre of a world which contributed some of the noblest efforts to resistance in Athens. Its political affiliations were rather to the right of the centre; its constitutional sympathies were on the whole republican rather than monarchist. These were the natural associations of Lieut.-Col. Macaskie: whatever his personal sympathies, this was the milieu whose link with the outside world he became.

The second example was the late Lieut.-Col. Sheppard. After living

[1] Myself, in January 1943.

in the Greek mountains for over a year almost exclusively in the company of left-wing guerillas, he entered Athens in February 1944 with unmistakable sympathies for the left. Events did a good deal to shake those sympathies; but it was impossible, however much he might change his mind, that any Greek should regard him as anything but a left partisan. This adds to the tragic irony of his death in the revolution of December 1944; killed by a mine placed by the same guerillas for whom he had already sacrificed so much.

The third example is a contrast to both the preceding ones. Capt. Stott, a New Zealand officer, entered Athens in the autumn of 1943 to carry out sabotage. His courage and originality soon involved him in other, far more perilous, activities, in the process of which his political associations were largely of the extreme right. One of them was Gen. Papagos, Chief of the General Staff of the Greek Army under Metaxas in 1940-1; another, far less inoffensive, was the Mayor of Athens installed by the Germans. Through the latter he found himself entering into negotiations of a complicated character with the German occupation authorities. These communications were abruptly severed when they came to the notice of higher British authorities, who had not at first understood their gravity. But sufficient had already happened to convict British policy, in the eyes of malevolent critics, of collusion with the enemy.

The last example illustrates an important point about all British activities in Greece. A British officer in Greece does not, in the eyes of the Greeks, *represent* England; he *is* England. The lightest word that falls from the unguarded lips of the youngest second lieutenant in the British Army is assumed to be an inspired declaration of policy. If three British officers say three different things, that does not mean that any of them is wrong; it does not even mean that British policy is confused; it only means that it is more intricate and far-reaching than had hitherto been supposed. From this can be seen the importance to Greek calculations of the emergence in occupied Athens of a handful of Englishmen with different points of view. What such men said and did may have had no importance in the eyes of the British authorities in Egypt or London; they might be lightly dismissed as inconsequential by authoritative spokesmen with politely ironic smiles. But smiles of dismissal cut no ice in Athens; the authorities who had allowed these men to be sent to Athens were held responsible for their most trivial and whimsical actions: it might be wrong, but it was so. They were on the spot; they *were* England; whether they or anybody else liked it or not, they helped to create British policy and to affect Greek politics. With this forewarning, the presentation of the Athenian stage and its actors during the occupation is complete.

2. *EGYPT*.

The second of the four stages on which the Greek drama was rehearsed during the German occupation is Egypt. Apart from its strategic importance, Egypt has two other characteristics that matter here. It is very hot; and it is full of Greeks. Both set it apart from the third of the four stages, which is London: the former sets it apart also from the fourth, which is the Greek mountains. Examination of the kind of Greeks that Egypt was full of during the war will show that it also stands apart from the Athenian stage. Egypt is thus a distinctive scene. Being very hot and very full of Greeks (many of whom had lived all their lives there and never visited Greece), Egypt became a maelstrom of heated, often confused, often violent Greek politics. The general structure of the participants was in principle similar to that which has already been described in Athens; but the balance and the inter-relation of the components were different.

(*a*) *Greeks Abroad*. There were no collaborators in the strict sense of the word on this stage; there could not be in the nature of things. But both among the Greek colony that had always lived in Egypt, and among those who escaped from the mainland as the Germans advanced in 1941, there must have been some who doubted the possibility of an Allied victory, and some of the material from which in Athens collaborators and *attentistes* were made. There was certainly, too, a number of paid agents of the enemy in the miscellaneous flood of humanity which was swept out of Greece before the German advance; but there were probably none in high places. Outside Greece there was no incentive to collusion with the Germans, though there may have been grounds for doubts about the Allies. When, therefore, the charge of collaboration with the enemy is made (as it sometimes is) against Greeks of the exile, it must be interpreted as a figure of speech expressing strong dislike. The same is not true of the charge of communism; for although it is often used as a mere term of abuse, it is also the case that the KKE had positive representation in the outside world while Greece was occupied. The Greek Communist Party in Egypt (as distinct from the Egyptian Communist Party) was vigorous from the beginning of 1943, and was frequently reinforced by agents from occupied Greece. This constituted, as everywhere in the world where there was a Greek population, the strongest pressure group influencing external opinion.

These forces were working in Egypt upon a variety of the Greek mentality, whose nature it is important to define. The Greeks of Egypt are Greeks with a difference: very Greek, but very different. Many have never been to Greece; many who have been were just as much foreign tourists there as an American in England. The society of Alexandria and Cairo is both more Oriental and more westernised than that of Athens; the Oriental aspects of it have driven Egyptian Greeks, by a self-conscious reaction, to a greater degree of westernisation than those at home. A hint of an inferiority complex may be traced here, that is lacking in the resiliently self-confident atmosphere of Athens. The Egyptian Greeks are more prosperous, but perhaps less happy. Successful business men abound among them, and this fact in itself has political implications; for big business was the backbone of the Liberal Party under Eleftherios Veniselos. From such impulses springs a tendency to distrust everything in Greece that could be labelled reactionary or out of date. These are the seeds of sympathy for republicanism and of susceptibility to the more attractive features of the left.

During the occupation there was another impulse in the same direction. The devotion of Egyptian Greeks to their little country across the water has always been intense; it is exactly what the Englishman hopes and believes the Dominions will always feel. Yet it is even stronger: it is an insatiable nostalgia. When the Germans occupied Greece, the Greeks of the outer world suffered mental agonies as great as the physical agonies of their cousins at home: sympathy, in its literal sense, is the strongest of all the emotions that Greece has transmitted to the world. This sympathy in Egypt took the form of admiration towards every Greek who endured the torment of the occupation, coupled with a faint, ill-defined, but nevertheless real contempt for those who did not. It aggravated their inferiority complex; but it also did more. It predisposed them to believe that, wherever there might be a dispute, the Greek who had been through the occupation must be right, and the Greek who had left his country as the Germans entered it must be wrong. There was something glamorous about the suffering Athenian: there was nothing glamorous about the exiled King and his exiled Government. Such is the illogical but in-eradicable influence of emotion on political judgment: the heart has its reasons that reason knows nothing about.

The first effect was a propensity to attach overwhelming importance to anyone of the least significance who escaped from the mainland after the occupation had begun; but not too soon after, because merit naturally varied in proportion to length of endurance. Public opinion forced this same propensity upon the exiled authorities. Thus in 1942 Panayiotis Kanellopoulos was made Vice-Premier within a few weeks of his arrival in the Middle East; General Zygouris was made Commander-in-Chief soon afterwards in the same circumstances; Exindaris and Sbarounis were each in turn given government appointments soon after their escapes from Greece in the late summer of 1943; and in 1944 a general exodus from the mainland threw practically an entire cabinet under Papandhreou at the King's head, as well as a new Chief of General Staff, General Vendiris, and many staff officers and minor politicians trailing clouds of glory from the occupation. With few exceptions, these men had one characteristic in common: they had had to undertake the risks of crossing the Aegean Sea by *caiques* to escape worse risks at home. They were mostly men wanted by the Germans, either for what they had done or for what they might do. That means that they were on the whole men whose general tendency was to the left rather than to the right; to republicanism rather than to royalism. The Greeks whom the Germans left unmolested did not usually feel any motive to undertake the journey: having declined the risks of resistance, they were not inclined to take the risks of evacuation. The kind of Greeks who found it easiest to get on with the Germans were the kind of Greeks who found it easiest to get on with the old régime, the old way of life, the old social conventions; and therefore with the monarchy, as well as incidentally with the English. I am describing trends, not individuals: so countless exceptions can be found. To name but two, Zygouris and Vendiris both left Greece at the instigation of Spiliotopoulos and the Committee of Six Colonels; if they left in fear of anyone, it was not of the Germans (whom they had done nothing to annoy) but of the Communists. In general terms, however, the influences which at first filtered and ultimately streamed out of occupied Greece were predominantly left and republican. The Greeks of Egypt assumed that the influences predominating inside occupied Greece must be the same. The Greek Communist Party in Egypt displayed (or rather, concealed) its customary skill in exploiting this luck.

(b) *Exiled Government*. All this was distasteful to the King of the Hellenes; but he himself preferred (or was made to prefer) England to Egypt for the greater part of his exile. There was little, therefore, that he could do about it; so little that his introduction belongs to the next section rather than to this. On the other hand, his government always retained at least a representative échelon in Egypt, even when it was established in London, so that the attitude of its members is relevant here. At first only the service ministers stayed in Egypt, to look after the Greek forces serving under the British Commanders-in-Chief; but in 1942 they were reinforced by a Vice-Premier, Panayiotis Kanellopoulos. Since he had lately escaped from the occupation, his presence justifies the inclusion of the exiled government in this section, not only because of his status, but because he was the only minister who could speak with authority about Greece under the Germans. His entry into the government also marks a turning-point in the trend of its composition.

That trend may be represented as a progress, co-terminous with the duration of its exile, away from the right and the monarchy towards the left and republicanism. It became tacitly understood, as a consequence of the King's increasingly liberal pronouncements in public, that to join his Government did not commit a man to any particular views on the post-war constitution. Many republicans entered the Government on this understanding. Kanellopoulos and Papandhreou were perhaps the best known; but not the least remarkable was Sophoklis Veniselos, whose

father had been the arch-enemy of the King's father. The hereditary
republicanism which was expected of him had cause to be modified by
his father's dying wish, that the old quarrel should be forgotten and the
Greek people re-unite around their King. It must also be remembered of
all these three that, although they would have opposed the unconditional
restoration of the King in 1944, they acquiesced in it in 1946. On the
other hand, the exiled Prime Minister, Tsoudheros, who was once
described as the only royalist in his own cabinet, subsequently declared
himself converted to republicanism in 1945. These were the perplexing
symptoms of a precise reversal: the steady trend away from the royalist
right in the years of the occupation turned into a regression from the
republican left in the years immediately after liberation; so that in the
quality of the individuals composing it, the last state of King George
II's Government was not greatly different from the first. The causes of
this reversal will emerge later: what matters here is the first of these two
trends, because it alone characterised the Egyptian period of the exiled
Government. To a Greek royalist with no means of foreseeing the
future, this presented itself as an alarming and undeviating progress in
the wrong direction. The progress can be seen by comparing the beginning and the end of the occupation. The first exiled Government was the
recognisable heir of the Fourth of August, and therefore unquestionably
loyal to the monarchy: it included three Metaxist ministers when it
left Greece, and one even when it was reconstituted in England. But the
last exiled Government was predominantly republican: it included two
Communists and no relics of the Fourth of August. Whatever qualifications may be needed in detail, the general propensity was unmistakable.
The transplantation of Greek politics to Egypt had brought the republicans
to the top.

Though the Greek Court had reason to be alarmed by what had
happened to Greek opinion in Egypt, it was trivial in comparison with
the apparent effect of the same atmosphere on the British authorities.
Ominous signs were patent from the first day. King George II had himself
suggested, when he left his country, that it was desirable to concentrate
whatever activities the British authorities proposed to engineer in occupied
Greece under a single direction. This wise suggestion was ignored. To
the Greek Court it must have seemed that the diverse individuals and
organisations involved in such activities had only two things in common:
a pronounced susceptibility to the atmosphere described, and a consequent
antipathy to the King. The hostility became mutual, and extended to
embrace the whole resistance movement recognised by the British
authorities. The causes of this situation come next for discussion.

(c) *British Authorities.* It is hard to extricate a consecutive thread of
policy or personality from the complex tangle which must be collected
under this general name: the authorities in Egypt responsible for British

relations with Greece and Greek affairs during the occupation. The cumbersome length of their title itself suggests confusion; but they have to be taken together, if only because they were all British and all had a finger in the Greek pie. As individuals, there was little else they had in common, for they held between them every possible opinion on Greek affairs. As officials their inter-relations were intimate and complex. It would be convenient to represent their structure in the form of a chart like a genealogical tree; but it would be quite impossible. A family tree connects people by a single straight line, either vertical or horizontal; but this chart would show a mass of inter-connections at all angles, by means of lines which in many cases would not be straight at all, but highly tortuous, and would sometimes run with imperfect concealment underneath the paper. All that can be attempted here is to convey a part of the complex by means of simple enumeration.

Those who had a right to be consulted on Greek affairs in Egypt included in the first place the Resident Minister of State in Cairo, who was responsible directly to the War Cabinet; the Commanders-in-Chief of the three services, each of whom had Greeks under his command; the commander and staff (both military and civilian) of the subordinate head-quarters responsible for the execution of operations in Greece during the occupation. All these were permanently involved, but none of them was represented by the same individual from 1941 to 1944. In the second place, each of these was multiplied by two when a separate Central Mediterranean Command was established in Italy in 1943, having the Middle East Command subordinated to it. In the third place, the throng was joined by the British Embassy to the Egyptian Government in Cairo during the period of disorganisation after the collapse of Greece, and by the British Embassy to the Greek Government in Cairo when that was established in 1943. In the fourth place, the approaching liberation of Greece in 1944 added to the list the headquarters of the liberating forces under Lieut.-General Scobie, and that of the organisation known as "Military Liaison" under Major-General Hughes. Most of the above were susceptible at all times to the awareness of an equivalent official of the USA discreetly observing him in the background: sometimes offering advice, sometimes criticism, sometimes help.

But to show that these men and their multitudinous staffs far from exhaust the complexity of the scene, one specimen may be isolated for examination: the headquarters responsible for the execution of operations in Greece during the occupation. The clearest permanent title for this organisation is Special Operations Executive (Cairo); it will therefore be referred to hereafter as SOE Cairo for short. It was one of many similar, but less ambitious, organisations maintaining connections of different sorts for different purposes with occupied Greece. It was responsible partly to the Ministry of Economic Warfare through its headquarters in London, partly to the Foreign Office through the diplomatic representatives of the latter, partly to the Commanders-in-Chief for its operational activities. This triple responsibility was not defined as such on paper; but it was a reality and a source of confusion. More perplexing still was the internal confusion which can be shown by personal statistics. During four years of active existence, it was known under seven different names (besides that of SOE Cairo, which I have adopted as a portmanteau). Each change of name corresponded to a change of structure and nature; often slight, but always real and significant. During the same period there were eight different heads of the same organisation, sometimes concurrently; three of them were civilians who did not entirely trust soldiers, and five were senior officers who did not entirely trust politicians or diplomats. The successive replacements of these men and their staffs did not always, though it did sometimes, coincide with those other rearrangements which periodically changed the name of the whole organisation. Able and conscientious individuals were therefore not always in a position to do their best as an organised whole.

Because SOE Cairo was unique, it was liable to the disadvantages which come from lack of continuity. It could not, like a permanent department of a Ministry, persist through change and survive re-organisation. Its functions were not quickly learned, nor did any prior experience contribute towards making them easier. The gap between it and those serving under it in the field was wider than is normally the case in military formations. So wide was it that, for example, four months after the first party of British parachutists had been dropped in Greece, SOE Cairo could not even trace any record of their names.[1] But being out of touch is a two-way relation, the blame for which could often as easily be laid at the other end, and always more fairly on distance and difficulties of inter-communication. The result was that sometimes an unhappy atmosphere prevailed between its staff in Cairo and its subordinates in Greece, for which neither side was to blame, since neither was in a position to understand the problems of the other. The gulf was caused not by the individuals but by the system: the same thing would have occurred in reverse if the individuals had changed places. Endless criticisms and explanations could be maintained on both sides without ever reaching a balanced judgment. This is not the place to examine them; but it is fair to add as one of the psychological influences on the Egyptian scene, the multiplicity, the perpetual flux, the deficiency of internal cohesion, which characterised the organisation. These will account for the unconscious vagaries of policy to be recorded in the next chapter.

[1]For this barely credible incident, see *We Fell Among Greeks* (by Denys Hamson), p. 149.

There are two more items to be added: the relations which these representatives of the British authorities collectively maintained with the international press and with the exiled Greek Government. Both were unsatisfactory for various reasons, of which the principal one is in each case the same: an exaggerated notion of secrecy. Security was carried far beyond the necessities of military operations, to the point at which it only bred suspicion. The ironic fact is that precisely opposite suspicions were bred in the minds of the press and the Greeks. The press became convinced that there was a plot to sell Greek liberties as the price of restoring the King; the exiled Greek Government became convinced that there was a plot to sell the King's rights for the sake of a deal with the extreme left. The British authorities insisted that they had no evil intentions of either kind. This was true; but in the absence of any corroborative evidence, all of which was diligently suppressed, it was greeted with hollow laughter from both sides.

None of those concerned was blameless. Because newspapers are the source from which the public usually learns whether anyone is good or bad at his job, there is a popular fallacy that all newspaper-men are good; for dog does not eat dog, and no one else has a chance to. Newspaper-men are their own advertisers; the advertisements speak well of them; but they are not necessarily right. In 1944 the press in Cairo was on the whole a poor lot. Since it was in Cairo that the trouble started with the press, this fact is important. The Middle East had ceased to be a theatre of war before the end of 1943. The principal newspapers of the world did not maintain the pick of their war correspondents in Cairo. Of those that happened to be there as the liberation of Greece approached, a few were kept in the Middle East by a special interest in Greece; a few by interests so special as to have nothing whatever to do with war correspondence, or even with the press at all; a few by accidents of sickness or travel; and not a few because their employers had no use for them anywhere else. Their limitations made it specially dangerous to antagonise them by withholding information and spoiling their stories. It was arguable that some of them would not recognise a fact if they saw one; but they might reasonably have been allowed the benefit of the doubt. The decision not to trust them was taken even before they had proved themselves untrustworthy. Consequently when the British authorities fell into trouble at the end of 1944, the press of almost the entire world rejoiced. The principal exceptions, Mr. Capell of the *Daily Telegraph*, Mr. Sedgwick of the *New York Times*, and Mr. Salusbury of the *Daily Herald*, were in such a tiny minority as to be suspect of heresy. The press deserved the strictures which Mr. Churchill passed upon it; but Mr. Churchill's subordinates were themselves partly responsible for the tragedy.

They were equally responsible, with an opposite result, in their dealings with the representatives in the Middle East of the Greek authorities. The first subversive activities to be organised by agents of the British authorities in Greece were divided into those which were co-ordinated with the Greek authorities and those which were concealed from them; the latter were the more numerous and important. The first infiltration of British and Greek agents into occupied Greece was usually done without any prior consultation of the Greek authorities.[1] The reasons for this secrecy may have been solely for the sake of security; but the Greek authorities, when they found out, suspected that the reasons were political. In theory this state of affairs was terminated by the formation in 1942 of the Anglo-Greek Committee in Cairo, consisting of representatives of SOE Cairo, the Resident Minister of State, and the Greek Government, which was to be kept informed of British activities in Greece. This neither ended secrecy nor allayed suspicion; but it ceased in any case to function in 1943, when the Greek Government itself moved from London to Cairo. Thenceforward the link between SOE Cairo and the Greek Government was the British Ambassador, Sir Reginald (then Mr.) Leeper. But this was at best an imperfect liaison since HM Ambassador was himself kept in the dark about the activities which SOE Cairo was directing. It is difficult to pick out any two individuals who saw exactly eye to eye from beginning to end; a misfortune which can be ascribed not so much to the personalities involved as to the facts of arithmetic and to the place where they worked. When a dozen brains fail to arrive at a single policy, it is not because they are antagonistic or incompetent, but because they are a dozen; perhaps nowhere in the world do their discrepancies become more aggravated than in the unwholesome atmosphere of Egypt.

The conclusion which emerges is that there was no such thing as a collective will in the make-up of the British authorities in Egypt; there was simply a conflict of individual wills. This was not because any of them failed to understand the problems: they could not have disagreed without understanding; and Greek affairs are a subject on which disagreement is admissible even between experts. The fault lay not in the individuals but in the circumstances. No group of men, for instance, could have had a more sympathetic understanding of the Greek problem than the Commander-in-Chief of the Middle East Command and his immediate staff in 1944. But as soon as they began to bring it under control, the tide of war swept it out of their hands into those of the Central Mediterranean Command: no less competent hands, no less sympathetic men, just as capable of understanding the problem, given six months' experience.

[1]To give only two examples within my own experience: my first entry into Crete during the occupation with two members of the Greek armed forces was carried out without informing the Greek authorities at all; my first entry into the mainland of Greece was only notified to the Greek Vice-Premier (Panayiotis Kanellopoulos) on the day that it was due to take place.

But that could not be given; the system gave the individuals no chance. Scanning the emergent result, the Greek Royal Court read into it an antipathy to themselves. But they were wrong: some were for it, some were against it; but neither were decisive, and neither were a majority, for the majority was simply indifferent. What tipped the balance, to create the appearance of antipathy, was the skill of the Greek Communists in exploiting the divergences.

3. *LONDON*.

From London, unlike Egypt, Greek affairs were apt to look small and remote. Both during and after the war, London was the centre of so many eddies of such vast circumference, that what concerned Greece alone was easily swallowed and forgotten. In Egypt, a Greek atmosphere permeated not only the war effort but the social life of the country; in London a Greek was a vaguely interesting phenomenon, faintly recalling complicated associations, half-forgotten names and never-understood initials. In Egypt the Greek drama was lived as intensely as in Greece itself; in London it was recorded as an earthquake on a seismograph, occasionally exaggerated by pressure groups. Yet the analogy is not wholly valid; for in London there was also a handful of men who exercised, even from their dispassionate aloofness, a decisive control over the affairs of Greece. They occupy the farthest and highest point to be reached by this survey: the farthest in remoteness from Greece, and the highest in authority. The Greek Government in exile having been dealt with already, there remain only His Majesty's Government (hereinafter called HMG) and the late King of the Hellenes to be introduced in this section; for although the latter, like his Government, led a divided existence between London and Cairo, it is fair to suggest that Claridge's rather than Zamalek was his spiritual home for the duration of his exile.

(a) *His Majesty's Government.* In the judgment of some critics, these are the villains of the whole story. To the relationship of HMG and King George II alone they attribute the tragedy of Greece since 1941. That this is a superficial conclusion will emerge plainly enough later on; but the complicated nature of their relationship can be partially shown in introducing the individual characters. The relationship was complicated because, unlike the Greek monarchy, HMG did not consist of one man. It contained not only various political opinions, but various practical opinions on the course of the war. The latter, which were so much the more important that they cut across and frequently obliterated the former, divided themselves on the relative importance of strategic and diplomatic considerations. It was this division, rather than political ideology, which determined the attitude of the highest levels in London towards the King of the Hellenes. There seemed to some of them to be an incompatibility between the immediate requirements of military operations and the long-term requirements of British foreign policy in the Eastern Mediterranean. Those who put the war effort first tended to have an adverse opinion of the King, because practically all resistance to the Germans in Greece was carried on by republicans; those who put long-term considerations first looked with favour upon the King as the most likely guarantee that Greece would not pursue an anti-British policy after the war. This division of opinion lay not between politicians of opposite parties, nor even entirely between political leaders on the one side and military leaders on the other; it was rather a periodical fluctuation of emphasis between the two considerations, so that each alternately predominated in the individual minds of the participants and the collective wisdom of HMG.

These fluctuations were never determined either by the war alone, by Greece alone, or by King George II alone. They emerged rather from the wider interaction of British foreign policy as a whole and the state of world affairs as a whole. Greek affairs were simply one small component of the vast complex, here detached from their context for isolated study. There was no such thing as HMG's policy towards Greece, in the sense of a fixed set of objectives laid down in advance. British foreign policy has never been something that is laid down in advance, to be achieved regardless of what may happen between its formulation and its execution; it is rather an emergent character which can gradually be detected amongst the welter of *ad hoc* decisions. It has principles by which the problems are to be solved, but it does not boast a programme which announces what the problems are to be. It cannot be precisely defined in advance; it can only be recognised in retrospect.

This general warning leaves little that can be usefully said about the individuals responsible for determining HMG's policy towards Greece; except that there was an unexpectedly large number of them. The War Cabinet alone had the power to issue binding directives; but it was open to the advice of the Chiefs of Staff, representing all three services, and to that of the Foreign Office and the Ministry of Economic Warfare. The minister in charge of the last department was responsible for the execution of British policy in Greece during the occupation, through the head-quarters that has already been introduced in Cairo. His military advice came from the Chiefs of Staff; his political guidance from the Foreign Office; his orders from the War Cabinet. But this simple arrangement was subject to the same lack of definition in practice as the conduct of affairs in Egypt. In London the latent conflicts were brought into relief by the daily impact upon each other of the men ultimately responsible for them. The Ministry of Economic Warfare was subject to all the stresses that operated independently on lower levels of the hierarchy. It contained an unresolved contradiction within its own

D

nature, besides having to attempt a reconciliation between contradictions external to itself. The internal contradiction was that, having been founded to enforce the blockade upon occupied Europe, it found itself also charged with part of the responsibility for breaking that blockade to save Greece from starvation. The external contradiction lay between the diplomatic and strategic considerations of British policy, to both of which the Ministry had to give full weight. The Foreign Office could consign certain of its difficulties to the service departments, and they could do the same to it; but the Ministry of Economic Warfare had to accept both kinds of problem, to solve both, and to make both solutions work as one. This was difficult. Consequently part of British policy towards Greece during the war appeared, both to the Greeks and to those who had to execute it, to be incoherent and undigested.

The incoherence and indigestion were not due to political causes. There was almost no political consideration before HMG at the time which could be solved by a party member with a purely party solution. Too little was known about Greek politics at the time to enable an English politician to decide that such-and-such a Greek party thought on lines parallel to his own, and was therefore right. Even when more became known, it only showed that any attempt to draw parallels was vicious in circumstances so radically different; consequently the Labour Government of 1945 found itself committed, willy-nilly, to a conduct of Greek affairs that was politically just as indeterminate as that of the Coalition Government of 1944. There was, however, one permanent factor in the policy of the Coalition which was absent from the policy of the Labour Government, and to which a political character can rightly be attributed. This was the personal devotion of Mr. Churchill to King George II. It was political because it was a matter on which opinion was sharply divided between the two major political parties of Britain; it was personal because it was not universally shared by Mr. Churchill's colleagues of his own party. The motives for it were disinterested. They sprang hardly at all from the consideration that the restoration of the King would ensure the friendship of Greece towards England, because as a matter of plain fact almost any Greek Government that was not Communist would be friendly to England; they sprang almost entirely from gratitude and loyalty to the man who had stood with us when everything seemed lost. The practical question is, was it worth while?

(b) *King George II of the Hellenes.* Those who have tried to do justice to the late King George II have found it dangerously easy to be unjust to the Greek people; the converse is equally true. In this contrast is summed up the psychological crux of the whole question: the King was not a Greek. He thought and talked and acted like an educated Western European; so did the small circle of sophisticated Greeks who formed his court. His position *vis-à-vis* the Greeks was not unlike that of King George III of England: he belonged to the third reigning generation of a foreign dynasty, still incompletely assimilated to its adopted country. Neither he nor any possible heir to the Greek throne had any Greek blood in his veins; the one member of the Greek royal family who had was *ipso facto* debarred from the throne.[1] Perhaps the late King owed to this his objectivity, his consistency, his balance and his coolness; for these are not characteristically Greek qualities. But to this also he owed his lack of intimacy with the Greek people and his acceptance of the insulation which his entourage threw round him. Even when he was in Greece, his life was one of permanent quarantine.

Three things combined to keep up that quarantine which separated the King from his people. For two of them he was not to be blamed: the heritage of his dynasty, and the enforced sojourn in exile (mostly in England) from 1941 to 1946. Of the third, for which he was responsible, history has still to judge: the dictatorship of Metaxas. A few words on his part in each of them will help to establish his position in this survey.

George II was the eldest son of King Constantine, who had, like other Balkan monarchs, two distinct reigns separated by an exile. Constantine was unique even in the Balkans in that on his second accession to the throne he succeeded his own younger son, and on his second deposition he was succeeded by his eldest. King George II then won another record for the family by having three distinct reigns separated by two exiles, each terminated by an overwhelmingly favourable plebiscite. All this, though it makes confusing reading, shows the width of the gulf which divided the unstable people of Greece from their persevering monarch. The crucial point which emerges first is that George II was associated in his own mind and public opinion with the causes of his father's first exile.

The conflict of King Constantine and his Prime Minister, Eleftherios Veniselos, about Greece's entry into the first World War reached such a degree of bitterness in 1917 that one of them had to go. The western Allies decided that it should be Constantine, who had tried to keep Greece out of the war on the advice of Gen. Metaxas. He was accused of being pro-German; an argument that public opinion based almost entirely on the fact that he had a German wife and a German field-marshal's baton. By accompanying his father and leaving the throne to his younger brother, whether voluntarily or under compulsion, the Crown Prince George shared his father's reputation. Alexander, the younger son, died after a brief and popular reign. Constantine, the father, was restored against the wishes of the western Allies, and was again deposed in 1922 after Greece's disaster in Asia Minor. George II then came into his invidious inheritance, accepting with dignity the responsibilities, the dangers, and

[1]Alexandra, the daughter of King George II's brother, the late King Alexander, by a morganatic marriage; she became the exiled Queen of King Peter of Yugoslavia.

the odium attached to it. Although he was deposed in 1923 and not restored until 1935, his name was never free, in the gossip of enemies, from the stigma of German sympathies which his father had conferred upon his family. For this it was unfair to blame him: it was simply an inescapable legend. But within a year of his first restoration, a graver association became attached to the King's name; and after his second absence, a graver still.

On 4th August, 1936, Metaxas persuaded the King to sign two decrees; one suspending those articles of the constitution which affected the liberty of the subject, and one dissolving Parliament. Metaxas took this action to avert the threat of a general strike on the following day; perhaps to avert a civil war such as was raging in Spain. He considered himself justified by the fear of Communism, and by the proved incompetence of Parliament to face a crisis. The King's acquiescence involved a breach of the oath which he swore at his accession. There was nothing unprecedented about most of the actions to which he allowed Metaxas to commit him; they had been taken before, and some of them were taken again in 1945. Nor was there anything final about them, for it was assumed that what had been suspended was to be restored. The appearance of temporariness which characterised the régime of Metaxas has already been noticed. But however good the intentions of the King and his Prime Minister, the facts were that constitutional government had not been restored when Metaxas died four and a half years later; that they were restored only in name when the King and his Government went into exile in 1941; and that the death of Metaxas left the King to bear the responsibility before the Greek people. It was a large target for the King's enemies, and a heavy burden for his new reign. It was aggravated during his exile by another.

The King's second departure, in 1941, released the energies of the republican liberals whom Metaxas had treated hardly less severely than the Communists themselves. The Communists were naturally the King's enemies; so were the Germans, against whom he had led his country to war. Many of his adherents accompanied him into exile. There was thus left behind in Greece a comprehensive alliance of incompatibles dedicated to calumniation of the King: the republican liberals, the Communists and the Germans. Since the first two made up the resistance movement, and the last were the backbone of the occupation, there was no active element in the life of Greece for three and a half years that was not hostile to the King. All this he owed to his loyalty to the allies. His decision to accompany the British out of Greece was a hard one: if he stayed, he would be called a collaborator, on account of his German blood; if he left, he would be called a deserter, out of touch with his people. He could not avoid being represented as a puppet either of the Germans or of the British. Still worse, the division of his country's life between Greece and the world outside was certain, whichever choice he made, to reopen the unhealed division between monarchists and republicans. Where he was, the monarchists would flock; where he could not be, the republicans would flourish. Either way, King George was doomed to end up as the leader of a political group. This is an impossible situation for a constitutional monarch: but constitutional monarchy had ceased to be a practical possibility. He could not mediate impartially between the political parties when his own person was the wedge that divided two groups of them from each other. The political world of Greece was not divided, like Britain's, between His Majesty's Government and His Majesty's Opposition. It was divided first between those who acknowledged the King and those who did not; and only within the first division was it subdivided between His Majesty's Government and His Majesty's Opposition. But the second division contained much of the educated Greek world; and because it was energetic it had to be suppressed. During the King's second absence it reached a strength which appeared to give it undisputed control over the future of the country; all the more severely did it later have to be controlled. Good government might be possible, but constitutional monarchy was not.

King George was therefore saddled on his second restoration with a triple burden: the heritage of his father's quarrels; the responsibility for an unconstitutional dictatorship; the leadership of a political group. His successor, King Paul, was in the less unhappy position of inheriting only the first of the three, intensified though it had been by his elder brother. It argued courage that King George persisted in his task; and this was one of the kingly qualities that still left open the possibility, if he had lived, that he might in some unforeseeable way have succeeded.

Two other such qualities deserve to be mentioned: his loyalty and his consistency. His loyalty to his allies was proved not only by his leadership of Greece against the Axis, but also by his acquiescence, often against his better judgment, in the wishes of HMG at every crisis during his exile. His consistency was proved by the fact that he was almost the only figure in this story who took up exactly the same stand from beginning to end. The pendulum of war, the pendulum of politics, the pendulum of diplomacy, time and again swung past him from one extreme to another; but they always passed him at the same point. The external relation which he maintained with the world outside Greece was to his credit; but his internal relation with his own country was not the less unhappy for it. He was perhaps the only foreigner with the courage to take on his job, and the only one also whom circumstances had conspired to disqualify from it. His own qualities had nothing to do with this fact, either for good or ill: what mattered was that his name was a symbol of controversy.

The loyalty of Mr. Churchill, and to a lesser degree of his Government, towards the late King was thus morally justified by his conduct towards his Allies rather than by his conduct towards his people. Its practical justification is less certain, for it was one of two things that combined to keep Greece divided. The other, which might never have flourished if the first had ceased to exist, was the power of the Communist Party of Greece. The supporters of the late King naturally argue the opposite: that if the KKE had not been allowed to grow powerful, the position of the King would never have been jeopardised. Because they suggest further that it was the folly of British policy during the occupation which allowed the KKE to grow powerful, it is worth anticipating to point out that the growth of the KKE during the occupation was neither caused nor sustained by British support, since it had already established itself impregnably before the first British contact was made with the Greek armed resistance. It was, on the contrary, solely due to British succour that any political rivals of the KKE survived in the resistance movement, which would have become a Communist monopoly if there had been no British intervention. The constitutional question, and with it the King's position as part of the constitution, became reopened not by British support of the wrong kind of Greeks, but by the admission (made by King George himself through his Government in exile) that the Metaxist régime of the Fourth of August was based upon a constitutional illegality. The proof of these two propositions will come later; but these are only points of detail. The real weakness of the late King's position, which is itself revealed by the arguments of his supporters, is that he should need supporters at all. The King of England has no supporters in this sense, because he has no enemies. The practical argument against the policy which Mr. Churchill imposed upon his cabinet is therefore this: that however right the King might be, he was debarred by circumstances beyond his control from being able to unite the Greek people. The policy pursued in London of supporting King George could only perpetuate the schism of the Hellenes. His death in April 1947 removed many of the causes of the schism, but not the schism itself. His youngest brother, King Paul, was an easier and less controversial figure for the western allies to support: but it was certain that all Greek Communists, and most Greek Republicans, would vicariously carry on against him the campaign which they began against his predecessor.

The relationship between HMG and the Monarchy was the most important element in the Greek drama as it was rehearsed on the London scene. Since London, like the other stages, presented a microcosm of the entirety of Greek life during the war, it was not the only element in the drama: but the others had been exhausted on the way before they reached the rarefied detachment of London. It was only in London, and only because of his presence there, that the King's matter dominated the Greek problem, leaving the rest to be agitated in the restless atmosphere of Egypt or the remote obscurity of occupied Greece. It is one of the peculiarities of the four stages that although each of them faced the same set of problems, a different aspect of them preoccupied the participants on each; even when communication was comparatively so easy between them as it was between London and Egypt. This will appear even more forcibly in examination of the last of the four stages, where the King's matter was actually believed during the occupation to be defunct.

4. THE GREEK MOUNTAINS.

The physical, geographical and psychological differences of this fourth stage from all those that have been discussed are too great to be depicted in detail. It must only be emphasised and remembered, whenever the political developments of the Greek mountains are in question, that they constitute a world apart, belonging to another century and another continent; in which there are none of the utilities and amenities of western civilisation, and in which the personal background was composed of quick-witted but largely uneducated peasants. Upon this world the politically conscious organisation of the impulse to resist the occupation was imposed from without. In describing how it was imposed, I shall introduce for the first time the various organisations which have become known under different sets of initials; and the discussion will range back to overlap the field already covered in Athens, where the mountain organisations had their roots.[1]

That the resistance movement was imposed upon the mountains from without and not generated spontaneously from within, is of such importance that it may properly serve as the starting-point for introducing those to whom it applies. It is another facet of the contrast between Athens and provincial Greece. For it was not the easy-going peasants who started the resistance to the Germans in the mountains. That was the last thing they wanted: they had hardly seen a German, or noticed the slightest difference in their way of life, until the talkers from the towns arrived with exhortations to take arms against the invader. For them the resistance movement meant the loss of their livelihood, the burning of their homes, the looting of their property; all of which they endured as long as they believed the cause to be a good one; but none of which they would have inflicted upon themselves without prompting. The participants in this section, therefore, can be divided into those who belonged there and those who did not: and the division coincides with the still more important division into those who did not know where they were going and those who did. There are exceptions on both sides of these divisions; but generally speaking the rank and file of the guerilla organisations in the

---

[1] I am concerned exclusively with the *political* significance of the resistance movement. Its intrinsic importance as a *military* contribution to the war effort must be taken for granted, and fortunately rests on higher authority than mine: for instance, F.-M. Wilson's dispatches as Commander-in-Chief, Middle East Command.

mountains were composed of the indigenous peasantry; the leadership and guidance were provided from elsewhere, as a rule directly or indirectly from Athens.

(a) *The Plain Greek*. The point which this illuminates is that discussion of the resistance organisations in the mountains must not start by segregating them into categories under their various sets of initials, and tying the same label on to every individual who comes under the same alphabetic heading. It must not start with a *vertical* division, but with a *horizontal* division. The horizontal division is between those who knew where they were going and those who did not know; the leaders and the led; the active and the passive; the aware and the unaware; in the idiom of the British soldier, those who had a clue and those who had not. This dividing line ran uninterrupted throughout the whole of Greek life during the occupation; not only through the world of resistance, but through the worlds of those who actively and passively opposed the resistance; through the collaborators and the *attentistes* as well. It is a permanent feature of Greek politics, but it is most easily seen in the resistance organisations. The importance of it is that *below* this line, which divides the politically conscious from the politically unconscious, there are no vertical lines of division. Below the line there is only the undifferentiable mass of Greek humanity; above the line alone do the customary divisions into vertical categories correspond to differences of nature.

Although it is right to draw the vertical distinctions between the various political branches of the resistance movement, as well as between those collectively and the various other categories of collaborators and *attentistes*, this must not obscure the fact that below the line no distinctions apply. Those who, not as leaders but as followers, joined the ranks of whatever resistance movement came upon them; those who, with the same qualification, joined the Security Battalions which were formed by the Collaborating Government to fight the Communists; those who, acquiescing in the example of wiser men, sat at home waiting to see what would happen; all alike below the horizontal line were just plain Greeks. (I omit the few who were just plain criminals: these occur in every country above the line as well as below.) However well a man knew the ordinary Greeks before the occupation, there was almost nothing to tell him which would be their individual decision when the crisis was upon them. There was indeed nothing to decide them, except the first glib tongue that reached their ears from above the line; when the decision was made, there was still no mark to distinguish them from their friends in the next village, or the next house, who had made the opposite decision for the same reasons.

This implies the heterodox opinion that the Greek peasant does not really understand politics. It is indeed his national sport, but still he does not understand it as played by professionals. The Greek word πολιτικὰ is not as simple as it seems: although it is the source of the English word "politics," it is not a precise equivalent to it. From the day when Aristotle first called man a "πολιτικὸν ζῷον," the Greek word has always meant something wider than what we call politics. Aristotle meant that man is an animal who cannot live except in society, not a man who cannot live without (what we call) politics. In the same way, a Greek soldier to-day who exchanges his uniform for his "πολιτικὰ ροῦχα" is not intending by that token to plunge into (what we call) politics; he is simply putting on his civilian clothes. In fact, "πολιτικὰ" includes more than politics: it includes most of the senses in which we use the words "social" and "civilian" as well. Everything that appertains to the citizen (πολίτης) is included in the Greek word which we crudely translate "politics." Those who wearily implore the Greeks to give up their mania for politics are asking them (in their own language) to give up their interest in social life.

In the wide sense, then, Greek politics belong to everybody: the right to express an opinion is universal. In the narrow sense, Greek politics belong to the professional politicians, whose place is above the horizontal line. But the wide sense is so wide, so diffuse, so diluted, that acquaintance with politics in this sense is no help in the intricacies of the professional game. A Greek peasant, thinking in terms of his own family and his own patch of stony soil, will vote Communist because he has been told that Russian planes will then come and sow his fields from the air so that he need never work again. He will also vote for the King because he has been told that the British will then divert the stream from the mayor's water mill to irrigate his corn. He will pair off with his brother to vote opposite ways in order to have the best of both worlds. His only objection to Metaxas was based on a law restricting goats in the interests of re-afforestation. His wit is quick, but his judgment is weak. These are not imaginary instances: they are records of fact, which may help to explain why ideological conflict so quickly becomes confused in personal vendetta.

This huge majority, having in common only a terrible ignorance of its direction, its dangers, its personal stakes, was divided up and blindly led by the minorities who did know where they were going. Because all the latter were determined to tolerate no rivals, the ordinary Greek—the man in the street, in the field, on the hillside—was not even free to stay still; for even the decision to stay at home and do nothing was a positive decision involving concrete consequences. He was obliged to choose between the alternative leaderships offered to him: to become either a collaborator or a Communist or a republican or whatever it might be, unaware that these alternatives were not exhaustive; often only dimly aware that they were mutually exclusive. Lifelong friends, who had been driven or cajoled into opposite choices, were sometimes not easy to convince that they had thereby become lifelong enemies: such is the simplicity of the common man. Every choice was a lucky dip; more often an unlucky one. Apart from the eloquence of the recruiters, no guidance was available except the necessity of coming out on the winning side. But if there was one thing certain in Greek politics, it was that, whoever won, the loser would be "the poor bloody man in the street"; or, as the Greeks call him, "ὁ φουκαρᾶς ὁ λαός."

A classic example will show in one paragraph how the whole principle worked. The protagonist is Nikolaos Beis, who had been a shepherd, a butcher, and an emigrant to the USA. He was living in his mountain village in 1942 when he heard that British parachutists had landed in the neighbourhood. He said to himself (I quote his own words): "God has sent us Englishmen from heaven; it is my duty to go and help them." He not only helped them; he saved their lives. When they no longer needed his help, he joined the left wing resistance movement, because it was the first in his neighbourhood. (They were on top then, so he was right.) He was awarded a British medal; he received the ribbon before the end of the occupation, and was wearing it prominently when he accompanied his comrades in the march on Athens to fight the British in December 1944. (He did not know who was on top then, or whether he was right or wrong.) When he reached Athens, he surrendered his weapon to the first British officer he met, drawing attention to his ribbon as he did so. (The other side were on top, but this might still leave him all right.) A year later he was received at the British Embassy in Athens, and the medal itself was pinned on his breast by His Majesty's Ambassador. As he left the embassy, a Greek police officer recognised him as a man wanted for—who knows what? The next day he was in gaol. (Someone else was on top, so he was wrong.) Thanks to British intervention, he was released soon afterwards. But that will not have been the end of his story; and it is the archetypal story of the impact of Greek politics upon "the poor bloody man in the street." That is why, in every Greek election, the poor bloody man in the street takes care to vote for the side which he knows is going to win.

Nikolaos Beis is above the average of those below the horizontal line, but he will do as an example. It happened that he joined the movement which was dominated by the Communists, though he was no Communist: he might as easily have happened in other circumstances to join the Security Battalions formed to fight the Communists, though he would still not have been pro-German. He would not have been a recognisably different individual if things had happened otherwise; but recognisably different things would have befallen him. His fate did not rest in his own hands, but in the chances which brought him into contact with men from above the horizontal line; chances that were largely geographical. If he lived in one part of the mountains, he was more likely to be in contact with the Communist influence first; if in another, with the non-Communist resistance; if in the plains, with the Security Battalions and the collaborating authorities; and so on. But in any case his destiny was decided for him by chance and the forces above the horizontal line.

Passing up across that line I come to the alphabetic designations which long constituted the whole of the English-speaking public's knowledge of the Greek resistance movement. I have withheld them up to this point, in order to label the ingredients one by one before describing the mixtures they made. Having so far tried to avoid the confusion which these initials inspire, I must now plunge head first into it; taking them roughly in their order of chronological seniority, which happens also, not unnaturally, to be their order of size and importance. This section will cover every significant element in the mountains, not excepting the liaison officers whom the Allied Governments sent to participate in the resistance, and the collaborating forces whom the Germans armed to fight them. I pause only to stress for the last time that although the following designations formally penetrate below the horizontal line, it is only above it that they correspond to real differences.

(b) *EAM/ELAS and its Satellites.* The resistance movement of the extreme left consisted primarily of two organisations known as the National Liberation Front and the National Popular Liberation Army. These will henceforth be known by their Greek initials, EAM and ELAS; the latter being identical in pronunciation, and almost identical in spelling, with the Greek name for Greece, which made it conveniently confusing for embodiment in slogans. Where there is no necessity to distinguish their particular functions, but only to speak of their over-lapping membership as a whole, I shall speak of EAM/ELAS; for except in function, and not always there, no real distinction separates them. EAM was theoretically a political coalition, ELAS the army of the people: but both represented the same point of view and spoke with the same voice. Only to distinguish between a purely political question and a purely military one, is it important to separate them; and such purity is rare. In referring to them without qualification, I shall normally mean the leaders rather than the rank and file; those above the line rather than those below. Confusion over this point has vitiated most controversy about EAM/ELAS. Those who assert the evil character of the movement usually mean the leaders when they speak of EAM/ELAS; those who hymn its virtues usually mean the rank and file; and although the dis-putants believe themselves to be contradicting each other, they seldom talk about the same subject. I hope to avert this error by the above warning.

The spiritual identity of EAM and ELAS is not a matter of doubt.[1] I shall only briefly illustrate it, to make clear the nature of what they had in common, since the common character which united them is the all-important fact about both. It is that both were created and controlled by the KKE: not dominated or influenced or penetrated, but entirely created and exclusively controlled by the KKE. When the Communists had manufactured the "National Liberation Front" in name, they threw it open to any other parties that wished to join. They presented it as composed of independent parties, all of which were masks of the KKE. Only two independent parties were taken in (in both senses of the phrase): the Popular Democratic Union (ELD) of Tsirimokos, which remained EAM's show-piece throughout the German occupation; and the Socialist Party of Greece (SKE), whose names included a few major stars such as Stratis, and many minor satellites such as Dhrakopoulos. Neither of these accessions was more than a nominal adherence of individual leaders. Two years passed before the followers of ELD learned what Tsirimokos had committed them to; and the Socialists, who learned earlier, split among themselves, so that Greece had two Socialist parties, one inside EAM and one outside. Tsirimokos and the acquiescent Socialists persisted as fellow-travellers without having any doubt whom they were following. From the first, then, the KKE was the brain and backbone of EAM. This is not said in disparagement of EAM/ELAS or the KKE: the important thing is not to pass moral judgments but to reach the truth about them; this is simply one of the facts.

It has often been argued[2] in criticism of British policy in Greece that our mistake lay in not persuading patriotic democrats to enter the EAM coalition, and so exercise a favourable influence upon it, before it fell under the control of the KKE. The argument must be disposed of once for all, by pointing out that the first part of it describes exactly what British policy *did* try to do, and the second part contains the fallacy which prevented it from succeeding. There was no such time as a period before EAM/ELAS fell under the control of the KKE, because it was created by the KKE. This point may be clarified by describing EAM and ELAS as they were found by the first representatives of the British authorities who came into contact with it.

EAM was founded, by its own account, which there is no reason to doubt, on 27th September, 1941. Its initial composition is uncertain, but it is not in dispute that the KKE took the initiative in forming it. Its first year was devoted to organising its activities on the Communist cell-system throughout Greece, as well as to clandestine publications and some

---

[1] All doubt should be dispelled by a study of Appendix F, where the terms EAM, ELAS and EAM/ELAS are used indifferently in a document drafted by themselves.

[2] E.g., by Capt. F. Noel-Baker, *Greece: the Whole Story*, p. 43; and similarly in a letter in *The Times*, 28th February, 1946.

subversive activities in Athens through its satellite EEAM. The most notable fruits were a series of successful strikes. It did not put armed forces into the field outside Athens until the following year; but the network of *cadres* was so efficiently woven and deployed that when, in the summer of 1942, the first guerilla bands under the name of ELAS appeared in the mountains, they multiplied quickly. When they could they swept out of their way or absorbed all rival bands that they came across. This fact gives a clue to the purpose of the ELAS units, whose leaders did not regard the war as being fought between national groups but between rival ideologies, which cut across national groups and were called Progress and Reaction. This justified progressive Greeks, such as ELAS, in attacking reactionary Greeks, such as everybody else. It was formally proclaimed by EAM/ELAS that anyone who did not belong to them was *ipso facto* a traitor.[1] Fighting the Germans was a secondary, though not a negligible, consideration for their leaders. To many of their followers and junior commanders this qualification only applies in the sense that they were not as free as they wished to fight the Germans, though many of them did so wish and chose their areas of operation accordingly. Their principal areas were the mountain ranges running north-westwards from Athens to the northern frontier, and were known by the provincial names of Roumeli, Thessaly and Macedonia. Only the north-west corner of Greece (Southern Epirus) and the southern peninsula (the Peloponnese) were for the present dead ground to them. All this is written from retrospective knowledge; for up to the point so far reached, the late summer of 1942, no Englishman except an occasional escaped prisoner-of-war had seen the Greek guerillas. Such was the situation of EAM/ELAS when the first official British Mission encountered them in October 1942.

Perhaps many Englishmen who first met EAM/ELAS in those far-off days, and even more recently in the occupation, could hardly remember how or when they first realised that EAM and ELAS were under the control of the KKE. They were first struck by trivial things: by Russian methods of saluting and presenting arms; by the system of command in ELAS under a committee of three, one of whom was always a political adviser; by the habit practised in the *élite* unit of ELAS of wearing black fur caps in imitation of the Russian Cossacks; by the preponderance in the EAM clandestine press of Communist propaganda; by the clichés on every tongue about the imperialistic character of the war until the USSR entered it. Certain universal marks of Communist methods were unmistakable: the belief in violence, not only as a justifiable means to an end, but as welcome for its own sake; the claim of a small clique to represent the real will of the people, whatever the people might think to the contrary; the "iron discipline imposed by a central committee

[1] In the clandestine press and by leaflets, March 1943.

with wide powers," which Trotsky laid down as indispensable; even the technique of the "popular front" itself. But these things, even cumulatively, only amounted to an alert perplexity, in face of the assertions of the EAM/ELAS leaders that their ranks were open to everyone, including Royalists. Doubt was not always set at rest by the presentation of a specimen Royalist for examination.

The conviction ultimately came that the KKE was the directing power behind EAM/ELAS; with the conviction came a doubt about the motives of those who took such pains to conceal the fact. The revelations which brought that certainty to the minds of the first British observers in Greece reinforce the argument made above, that there was no time before the KKE were in control of EAM/ELAS, and therefore no time at which British policy could have forestalled the Communists' control. Obviously the British authorities could not have done so before they were in contact with it; but even if they had been in contact with it on the day of its foundation, it would still have been too late.

The point is not that EAM/ELAS were composed entirely of Communists; it is that their leadership was *controlled* entirely by Communists. The difference is wide. For instance, the first Englishmen in Roumeli met many ELAS guerillas who were delighted to meet them; but they met only three men who exercised the command over ELAS. These three were called Aris Veloukhiotis, Pelopidhas and Tassos Eleftherias; all three names were pseudonyms, and all three men were members of the KKE. The first Englishmen in Thessaly encountered the same contrast. The leaders were called Karayioryis, Yioryios Kissavos, and Kozakas; all three names were pseudonyms, and all three men were members of the KKE. The first Englishmen in Macedonia had the same experience. The leaders were called Kikitsas, Markos Vaphiadhis and Lazanis; all three of whom have this extra qualification, that in 1947 their names were among the leaders of the new rebellion in Macedonia against the Government of Athens. (Of them all, Kikitsas is the only one who was perhaps not then a Communist.) The first Englishman sent from the mountains to Athens[1] met six representatives of the Central Committee of EAM at two conferences in January and February 1943; and at the two conferences only two men altogether spoke. Their names were Andhreas Tzimas and Yioryios Siantos; and both were members of the KKE.

The same experiences were reproduced in the case of every British officer who came to Greece during the occupation. Another common character of these experiences is that almost all the Communists so encountered denied being Communists until the fact was found out by other means. The only ones whose membership of the KKE was declared from the start were Aris Veloukhiotis and Siantos. Complete and invariable secrecy would be justified as a measure of security; but partial and

[1]Myself, in January 1943.

discriminating secrecy implies deception. The suspicions thereby aroused were multiplied by the repeated discovery of new disguises under which the KKE masqueraded. The party's preference for anonymity made it largely independent of personal idiosyncrasies, and therefore not easily identified by the simple process of pointing to individuals. Individuals count in the KKE, but only behind the scenes. For instance, after the liberation of Greece a doctrinal dispute broke out in 1945 between two rivals who had both been Secretary-General of the Party; but this dispute did not reach the public. In public there is only one KKE doctrine, only one orthodoxy, only one party line: at least, only one at a time. But although this anonymity makes it hard to identify the shapes of the Communist Proteus merely by identifying individuals, it also proclaims itself in uniformity of manner, conduct, speech and thought which experience renders unmistakable. By means of this guidance the following disguises of the KKE can be penetrated.

The most important subsidiary was EEAM, which has already been introduced in Athens. This organisation of the trade unions was entitled to nominate a member to the Central Committee of EAM, and the privilege was continued when the purely Communist component of EEAM reorganised itself as ERGAS after the liberation. The nominee has usually been Theos, whose deputy is Nepheloudhis.

The second subsidiary is EA, whose Greek name can perhaps best be translated as the "National Co-operative." It was a mutual benefit organisation designed to help victims of the war, especially villagers whose homes had been destroyed by German reprisals. Some of its work was good, although it had a tendency to discriminate in favour of members of EAM, which made it an uneasy partner for the British authorities delegated to the same task. Thus, a British representative would provide financial help to victims in proportion to their needs; EA would collect the money back and redistribute it in proportion to party loyalty. Those who did not get enough were advised to complain to the British; and especially, when in due course it became possible, to the Americans.

The third subsidiary was OPLA (Units for the Protection of the People's Struggle), which combined for the KKE the functions of Gestapo and SS. It had the advantage, for use as a popular slogan, of being identical with the Greek word for weapons. Its counterpart at the visible level was EP, the National Civil Guard, founded towards the end of the German occupation to sustain the KKE's conception of public order. Proposals for the dissolution of this body in December 1944 were among the immediate occasions of the outbreak of revolution in Athens.

The fifth subsidiary was EPON, the National Panhellenic Organisation of Youth, an unhappy echo of the least pleasant invention of Metaxas, which had been known as EON. It is not surprising that the head of EPON, Professor Yiorgalas, had also been prominent in EON.

The last subsidiary, a minor appendage of ELAS, was ELAN, the National Popular Liberation Navy, which ran a small but efficient service of armed *caiques*, chiefly in the Gulf of Corinth.

Two other names have to be considered here, both rather different cases. Those mentioned in the preceding paragraphs were formally organisations of a lower order, subsumed under and controlled by EAM/ELAS. But of the next two to be considered, one was formally an organisation of a higher order, subsuming under itself EAM and all its tributaries; the other was an organisation which EAM/ELAS, having helped to create it, proved unable to control. The former was called PEEA, the Political Committee of National Liberation: it was founded in March 1944 as the shadow government of EAM/ELAS in rivalry to the other existing governments. The latter was called SNOF, the equivalent of EAM among the Macedonian Slavs of Greek nationality. The first hint of its formation was made privately at a meeting on Greek soil of representatives from all the Balkan Partisans in the summer of 1943: but the name SNOF was not heard till many months afterwards. This organisation was theoretically subordinated to EAM/ELAS in Macedonia, but proved unamenable to Greek discipline and repeatedly declared its preference for service under Tito's Macedonian leader, Tempo. As early as November 1943 Tito's "Radio Free Yugoslavia" broadcast a message of adherence from a South Macedonian leader; the unit of SNOF commanded by a Macedonian known variously as Gotsi and Gotchev revolted from ELAS on at least three occasions. To these slavophones, it was more natural to be a nationalist than a loyal communist in Greek Macedonia.

Most of these organisations will recur hereafter. It would be confusing to say more here than that they are all in varying degrees manifestations of the KKE's activity. The variation in degree does not mean that the strength of Communist control varied; it only means that the proportion of Communist composition varied. The Communists controlled every body they entered; if they could not control it, they disrupted it. But it was not always necessary for them to dominate *numerically* even a controlling committee, still less the obedient rank and file. In EAM/ELAS their numerical proportion was minute; in controlling positions it varied from two out of three (for instance, in most ELAS HQs down to platoons) to 100 per cent. To revert to the notion of the horizontal line transecting the whole of Greek life, the structure of EAM/ELAS could be described as follows: within the vertical division known as EAM/ELAS, the KKE component below the horizontal line was small; above the horizontal line it was high, if not an absolute majority over all other components. But in other cases where they could find fellow-travellers to do their work for them as well as to make it look respectable, their numerical proportions fell still lower. In EEAM their proportion was four-fifteenths:[1] in PEEA it was perhaps as low as one-fifth. This numerical proportion had nothing to do with executive power. It may seem at first sight incredible that a majority can be so dominated by a minority; but it is the object of this work to make that hard saying less hard. It may be illustrated by a simile: the non-communists in EAM/ELAS enormously outnumbered the Communists, just as the sticks that make up a fire enormously outnumber the match-stick that lights them.

If all this was achieved by a tiny numerical minority, then that minority must have been made up of outstandingly able personalities. This is not an easy fact to illustrate. Although a few names have already been mentioned among the Communist minority which controlled EAM/ELAS, most of them were pseudonyms. It does not greatly matter if these men are not known by their real names, since their common quality is what mattered to the KKE; but it does make it difficult to give them individual credit. The following, however, can be singled out, if only by pseudonyms, as the pre-eminent personalities of Greek communism.

Yioryios Siantos was Secretary-General of the KKE during the German occupation, deputising for Nikos Zakhariadhis, who was in a German concentration camp; and although both were able men, their alternation in office caused some mismanagement after the restoration of Zakhariadhis in June 1945, at least until the death of Siantos in May 1947. Aris Veloukhiotis (whose real name was Athanasios Klaras) was the fighting genius of ELAS; but although he took part in the attack on the Gorgo-potamos viaduct on 25th/26th November, 1942, most of his other fighting was against Greeks, and it was in civil combat that he met his end on 16th June, 1945. Of the other Communist leaders in the field, none was outstanding against the Germans, but two of them in Macedonia, Markos Vaphiadhis and Lazanis, and one Thessalian, Yioryios Kissavos, have won a retrospective glamour by their leadership of the revived guerillas of 1946-8. Of the political leaders, the best known during the German occupation were Andhreas Tzimas (a Macedonian by birth) and his wife, Petros Roussos, Zevgos, the lawyer Porphyroyennis, the agriculturalist Gavrielidhis, the journalist Karvounis, and Dhespotopoulos; but after 1944 these lost ground (and Zevgos lost his life by assassination in March 1947), while others moved forward: notably Ioannidhis, Partsalidhis, Khrysa Hadjivasiliou (the wife of Petros Roussos) and Theos. They all have in common certain unmistakable characteristics, of which the chief are ruthlessness, lust for power, and a sense of conspiratorial security; most of them have also a devoted loyalty to Moscow.

Certain conclusions are now possible about the activities of EAM/ELAS and its satellites during the occupation. It can be seen why the KKE, having been for many years an illegal and unpopular party, found it

[1]See page 33.

E

wise to camouflage itself under different forms. It can be seen why the German occupation gave a natural start, in the organisation of underground resistance, to a party which had already become accustomed to living underground during a hostile dictatorship. It can be seen how easy it was for the KKE to attract to its ostensibly patriotic organisations, EAM and ELAS and the rest, a large proportion of the patriotic population, most of whom were sufficiently humiliated by the national tragedy to seize the first opportunity to contribute to the national resurgence. What cannot be seen so easily is why, if EAM/ELAS was in fact only a cover for the KKE, the non-Communists who joined it for patriotic reasons remained in it when its true character gradually became revealed.

This question is not difficult to answer in the case of those below the horizontal line. Several different and independently satisfactory arguments can be put forward. In the first place, the true nature of EAM/ELAS never was revealed to many of them; they simply continued to believe the propaganda to which they had become conditioned; they rejected the suggestion that it was false, because that was the easiest reaction. In the second place, many of them were bound by fears of two kinds. One fear was that of the oath, for which every Greek has a natural respect; and the oath by which recruits were bound to EAM/ELAS was of a strong and uncompromising kind, calculated both to appeal to their initial enthusiasm and to discourage subsequent apostasy. The other fear was of the ruthless and mysterious ways of Communists in disciplinary matters; Aris Veloukhiotis, to name no other, was known to have shot one of his men for stealing a chicken, to say nothing of the more formidable crime of betraying the movement. In the third place, membership of EAM/ELAS gave the ordinary Greek the opportunity to do things that he had vainly longed to do, to be someone that he had never been before. Some of its opportunities were meretricious: to domineer over the stay-at-homes, strutting about in the picturesque get-up of the guerilla; to fleece his personal enemies in the levy of supplies, or discriminate against them in the imposition of communal duties; to be assertive and powerful and arrogant instead of a nobody. Others were noble, especially that of fighting the occupying powers; for this, although secondary, was never a negligible consideration to EAM/ELAS. In the fourth place, whatever might be said by the rich, the respectable, and even by the church, Communism has a natural appeal of its own to the needy, to those who have a grievance against society, as many Greeks in this category had. If the Communists had not lost their heads at the end of 1944, they might have won and kept a majority of the people on their side by this last consideration alone.

Although these reasons explain why EAM/ELAS could keep its hold over the rank and file against the power of any disillusionment, they do not account for the acquiescence of the more sophisticated. That the membership of EAM/ELAS above the horizontal line included many intelligent and patriotic democrats is not in dispute; nor that practically all of them sooner or later discovered the true relation of EAM/ELAS with the KKE. What calls for explanation is not only that most (though not all) of them continued to remain in EAM/ELAS despite that discovery; but also that from 1943-6 the democratic component of EAM/ELAS above the horizontal line actually grew. This can be illustrated by a list of names. In the first half of 1943 the only leaders of EAM/ELAS known to myself both in person and by name were the following nine: Siantos, Tzimas, Karvounis, Roussos, Dhespotopoulos, Klaras (Aris Veloukhiotis), Yiphtodhimopoulos (Karayioryis), Vlakhopoulos and Tsirimokos. All except the last were Communists; and the last never in my presence uttered an independent opinion. At that time no important military figure joined ELAS in the field. During the following twelve months (from the middle of 1943 to the middle of 1944) there was a respectable accession of civilian and military personalities to the support (but not invariably to the *membership*) of EAM/ELAS. The principal politicians were Svolos, Askoutsis, Angelopoulos and Hadzimbeis, all of whom became members of the shadow Government set up in the Greek mountains in March 1944 under the name of PEEA. Still more impressive was an influx of unmistakably anti-revolutionary civil servants and professional men: doctors like Kokkalis; teachers like Professor Yiorgalas; intellectuals like Roghas, the translator of Shakespeare; even priests like the Bishops of Kozani and Elis. Open adherence or private sympathy was won from four of the ablest generals of the regular army, Saraphis, Bakirdzis, Mandakas and Othonaios; as well as countless regular officers of lower ranks, who had no inclination to gamble with their careers. The accession of Saraphis enabled ELAS in July 1943 to set up a speciously respectable GHQ, whose only abnormality was that it had three commanders instead of one: Saraphis being the military member, Aris Veloukhiotis the popular leader (called Capetanios), and a variable third (always a Communist) being the political adviser. The respectability conferred on this GHQ by Saraphis' position in it attracted other regular officers to ELAS; and their accession in turn helped to confer political respectability on EAM/ELAS as a whole. The process was cumulative and self-propelling. It was also impressive, for these men could not all be laughed off as inconsiderable; they contained some of the best of Greek democracy.

But they are not the last; there is a still more remarkable development to be recorded. After the liberation of Greece, after the exposure of the KKE, and after the failure of the revolution in December 1944, the cause of EAM/ELAS (though again not necessarily its membership) continued to draw adherents from the educated democratic world. Most of the men who were named earlier as participants in the resistance movement in

Athens[1] drifted nearer to EAM/ELAS after 1944, although before that date they represented other organisations which were in open or clandestine hostility to the KKE: these men include Kartalis, Petimezas, Pyromaglou, Peltekis, Yiorgakis, Pappas. They were still minor stars in the political firmament, but they might grow in magnitude. More notable figures inclined in the same direction; even General Plastiras, head of the Government that saw out the revolution in January 1945, later lent his presence to public meetings convened by the KKE; even Sophianopoulos, Foreign Secretary in that same Government, consistently intrigued with them. It almost looks as if the policy of encouraging democrats to join EAM/ELAS, which HMG was bitterly criticised for not pursuing, was all the time bearing unnoticed fruit. But this is delusive, because the approach of these men did not modify the nature of EAM/ELAS: on the contrary, EAM/ELAS modified them. Even the cataclysmic events of 1947-8, which tended to renew disgust with the KKE and to diminish antipathy against the legitimate authorities, only partially restored the balance.

The fact that the KKE has no fear of the influences which such accessions may bring with them into EAM/ELAS, can be observed from the indifference with which they have accepted, when it was convenient, the adherence of their proclaimed enemies. Examples will be pointed out later among officers occupying senior positions in the rival guerilla organisations with which ELAS was in a more or less permanent state of civil war. That EAM/ELAS were equally willing to accept reformed collaborators was shown when they were joined by Gen. Sariyiannis, who was connected with a firm accused of industrial collaboration with the Germans, and by Colonel Dhimaratos, whose name has already been mentioned in connection with the Athens police. There is nothing discreditable about Dhimaratos' adherence to EAM/ELAS, since he held his appointment under the collaborating Government only for about two months in 1941; but his case makes an interesting contrast with that of Spiliotopoulos, who held a parallel appointment in the gendarmerie during exactly the same period. Spiliotopoulos also resigned in 1941, but did not join EAM/ELAS; he has therefore been one of their principal targets of abuse ever since. The principle which these cases illustrate is that the KKE did not care tuppence for the opinions or past conduct of the miscellaneous membership which it roped into EAM/ELAS, since it only required the use of their names and was confident of its own control over their future conduct. This principle has continued to operate throughout the post-war years.

It is a feature common to all Communist parties that although they take pains to attract visitors, they only issue one-way tickets. Many well-meaning patriots of liberal sentiments have conceived the idea of

[1]See page 34.

gaining the confidence of the Communists by moving towards them, in order subsequently to use their influence in drawing the Communists closer to themselves, and in bridging the gap which separates them from the constitutional life of the country. In place of the sound maxim that the way to *defeat* the Communists is to move to the left yourself, they substitute the perilous maxim that the way to *mollify* the Communists is to move to the left yourself. But Communists do not come half-way to meet them. Such idealists can therefore be divided into two classes: those who have drawn back before they got near enough to make themselves felt, and those who have been swallowed alive. The 1945-6 contingent of fellow-travellers still belonged to the first category when 1947 began: the 1943-4 contingent already belonged to the latter. They had not become Communists; indeed, some of them insisted that they had left the EAM/ELAS coalition. But their contemporaries knew that they were wrong; as independent forces they no longer existed, because no one would believe in their independent existence. The belief, by its own force, created the fact.

The ground is now cleared for an answer to the question: Why in that case did these people persist in gravitating to EAM/ELAS and voluntarily staying in it? The answers given in the case of the rank and file apply only with negligible force, and others must be found.

The first is not a creditable one, though it is valid. It must be prefaced by a point which has already been made, that the KKE alone existed in an organised form at the beginning of the occupation, since the Communists alone had resisted the disintegration of political life by Metaxas. Indeed, persecution had sharpened their skill. No other left-wing politicians had a party worthy of the name left in 1941. Being by nature neither demagogues nor conspirators, many were content to accept the existing machinery and leadership of the KKE, rather than put themselves to the difficult and dangerous task of building up their own following in competition with it. With an exact appreciation of their dilemma, the Communists took pains to offer them flattery, privilege, obsequious attention, everything that goes with responsibility except power. Since at every level of the hierarchy of EAM/ELAS the executive power was held by Communists, it was easy for the KKE leaders at the top to acquiesce from time to time in the proposals of their non-Communist associates; with the certainty that if such proposals did not conflict with the KKE policy, they could do no harm and would create good will; and if they did conflict, they could be quietly suppressed or amended in execution at a lower level. Both the spider and the fly were for the time being perfectly happy.

But this could not last. Only a coward or a fool could put up with it for ever. Some of these men were both cowards and fools; but few or none of the important ones who have so far been named were either. It is true that the adherence to ELAS of Saraphis and some other officers was obtained at the point of a pistol; that some civilian members of PEEA were persuaded to toe the line in the mountains by hints about the dangers to which their families were exposed in Athens; that some of the figure-heads of EAM/ELAS were past their prime of youthful vigour and political alertness; but these were exceptions. It is with the men whose judgment and conduct really mattered that we are concerned, and we must look farther for the explanation in their case.

The second and third possible answers are complementary, because one of them comes to an end where the other begins. During the German occupation, the advice of the British authorities, which no Greek could afford (and few wished) to neglect, *seemed* to favour the participation of democratically minded Greeks in EAM/ELAS. This argument, which operated powerfully during the occupation, came to an end with the liberation, and especially with the revolution of December 1944. The complementary motive then began to operate. The reaction against the conduct of the KKE threw power increasingly into the hands of the more conservative politicians, and ultimately into the hands of the Royalists: this process also *seemed* to enjoy the approval of British policy. But Greece was now free, and republicans had less respect for British policy than during the occupation. The abuse of power by those to whom it passed in the years 1945-6, coupled with the probability that King George II (whom they feared hardly less than the KKE) would return to his country, turned the sympathies of democratic republicans back in the direction of EAM/ELAS. In both those evolutions can be traced the influence of what was believed, usually mistakenly, to be the policy of HMG. Positively or negatively, this influence was never far from the foreground of Greek politics.

The fourth and last possible answer contains the most powerful argument of all. It was the growth of the conviction that EAM/ELAS was bound in the long run to win the game in Greece; a conviction which carried with it in every Greek mind the corollary that British influence would succumb to Russian, and the iron curtain would clang down over the last remnant of the Balkan peninsula. If they argued thus, it may nevertheless have crossed their minds fleetingly, especially in 1947, that British influence might succumb not to the USSR but to the still more powerful USA; but it would do so only to vanish in despair, because in the judgment of Athens the political ineptitude of the Americans is even more abysmal than that of the British. In any case, the more immediately important part of the argument is that which concerns EAM/ELAS alone. EAM/ELAS, as it rightly claims for itself, is not a political party; it is not even a coalition; it is rather the symbol of a way of life. If the remark can be taken as involving neither blasphemy nor a judgment of approval, it could be said that EAM/ELAS differs from the rest of the Greek political world rather as early Christianity differed from the rest of the ancient religious world. There is one parallel, and no more, between Communism and Christianity: that both came to alter not this or that detail, but the entire structure of life. Communist thought, however good or evil it might be, had made a clean break with the past in which the rest of the political world continued to dream and stagnate. Because the rest was plainly moribund, and EAM/ELAS represented something that was at least alive, however frightening it might be, it must certainly have a future; indeed, it looked as if it were the only thing in Greek life that did have a future.

With few exceptions, even the most high-minded Greek politician is an opportunist; if he is not he is a suicide. His patron saint is the Vicar of Bray, whose circumstances were similar. Once he became convinced that EAM/ELAS was not as others are—not simply a political party that would be now in power, now out—but the forerunner of an inevitably approaching way of life, whether he liked it or not he had to make his peace with it. I have already emphasised the importance to a Greek of being on the winning side, of voting for the party that is about to win the elections, of cheering for either the King or the Republic whenever the appropriate change is imminent. The alternative is extinction; and the art of survival is naturally ingrained in a people which has spent most of its recent centuries under enemy occupation. There is therefore nothing surprising in the conduct of these far-sighted men. This explanation accounts for the decision to adhere to EAM/ELAS in a high proportion, if not all, of educated Greek democrats. The implications of their decision will emerge later in this chapter; whether they were right or not it is the purpose of this book ultimately to unravel.

The introduction of EAM/ELAS can now be concluded without giving a potted diary of their progress such as will be necessary in introducing the smaller and more ephemeral organisations; for the biography of EAM/ELAS is co-extensive and inter-penetrated with the political history of Greece as a whole during the years under consideration. The two are even in a sense identical, because the history of the period is also the history of the successive attempts of EAM/ELAS to seize absolute power. But although this makes a diary of their development unnecessary here, it is worth summarising the general trend of that development. It can be done by comparing the schools of thought which prevail on EAM/ELAS, which resolve themselves into two extremes with almost no middle opinion between them. One maintains that EAM/ELAS was the tool of a ruthless conspiracy of Slavophil Communists; the other maintains that EAM/ELAS embodied every progressive force in Greece. The important thing about these two statements is that both are perfectly true: what they are not, despite the ferocious antagonism with which they are supported, is incompatible. Between them, however, the supporters of these two doctrines have done Greece a cruel disservice which neither

of them, nor anyone else, could have done alone: they have accustomed
world opinion to the identifications (which are wholly fallacious) of all
Greek resistance with EAM/ELAS, and of all EAM/ELAS with the KKE.

(c) *EDES*. Like EAM/ELAS, the military organisation of General
Zervas had political roots in Athens. Its armed forces took the field in
north-west Greece in the summer of 1942; its political foundation in
Athens was somewhat earlier. But the political and military components
were not discriminated by separate names: both were known as EDES,
the Greek initials standing for the "National Republican Greek League."
This unity of political and military structure paradoxically caused a lack
of co-ordination between political and military policy; because instead
of being directed by two authorities harnessed in parallel, like EAM and
ELAS, it was directed by one authority who could not be in two places at
once. Politics were mainly conducted in Athens; military policy mainly
in the mountains. The titular head of EDES, General Plastiras, was not to
be found in either place, but in the south of France: in Athens his place
was filled by a committee, and in the mountains by General Zervas, who
remained there from the middle of 1942 till the latter half of 1944. His
energies were almost wholly devoted to organising his army, which was
built up by his personality rather than by the corporative skill in administration which characterised ELAS; it consequently remained smaller
and needed more work from its commander. He had only an indirect
familiarity with the political development of EDES in Athens, some of
which was very queer indeed, as well as very divergent from its development in the mountains. Whereas the first task, in considering the EAM of
Athens and the ELAS of the mountains, was to show that in spite of
having different names they were substantially indistinguishable, the first
task in considering the EDES of Athens and the EDES of the mountains
is to show that in spite of having the same name they were really different.
This difference was eventually crystallised by Zervas in the adoption of
of a separate name for his military force, EOEA (National Bands of
Greek Guerillas). But although the name was suggested by the British
authorities, it did not stick and was not consistently used even by them.
The confusion of the political EDES in Athens and the military EDES in
the mountains therefore persisted.

The principal link between them has already been introduced: his
name is Petimezas. Since his post-liberation associations veered towards
the left,[1] it is striking that those of General Zervas veered even farther
towards the right. This divergence is characteristic of EDES, and began to
become visible even before the end of the occupation. The crucial point
which it illuminates is that there was no *positive* character holding the
organisation together. It was a miscellany of negatives; the principal one

[1]See page 68.

of which was anti-communism. If we compare its name with the quality of the men who composed it, its atomic nature becomes plainer. The crucial word in its title is "Republican"; a qualification without which General Plastiras could never have been claimed even as its titular head from his exile in France. The Greek word for "Republican" is "δημοκρατικὸς" from which we derive our word "democratic." That word sometimes also means "democratic" in Greek; but in relation to domestic politics its proper meaning is "Republican"; that is what it means in the title of EDES. To confirm this, it would be enough to read a few paragraphs of the EDES charter as it stood in 1943; for one of its first provisions was that the organisation should oppose the return of King George II until the Greek people had declared in his favour by a plebiscite. The greater part of Zervas' adventurous past tended to identify him with the Republican cause. He had joined the armed force formed in 1917 by Eleftherios Veniselos to fight in the first World War on the side of the Allies and in opposition to King Constantine; he had formed the "Republican Guard," which in 1926 maintained the republican dictator General Pangalos, and then broke him in favour of his republican rival General Kondylis (who subsequently smashed Zervas' force and abjured his own republicanism); and he had been imprisoned under the Royalist dictatorship of Metaxas. All these details of Zervas' biography are unimportant now, since in 1946 he himself repented and became a supporter of the King, at least for the time being; but they were important in 1942, since the character of the organisation and its leader determined what kind of men joined it.

In 1942, then, the composition of EDES *above* the horizontal line tended to be republican in sympathy; those *below* the line were the same as any other Greeks below the line. In Greece republicanism is not strong to the right of the political centre: consequently the influences on EDES policy at this time were of the same kind, though not in the same degree, as the left-centre influence in EAM/ELAS. Thus, the political sentiments of Petimezas, of EDES in Athens, and Pyromaglou, the second-in-command of EDES in the mountains, coincided not only very closely with each other, but reasonably closely with those of (say) Tsirimokos or Dhrakopoulos in EAM. This means no more than that they were all republican, all progressive, all left of the centre. After the occupation, however, men of these opinions drew still closer together for the time being in reaction against the domination of the right. The range of oscillation of this nucleus of EDES thus lay entirely to the left of the centre; but although such men represented the true nature of EDES at its foundation, they became quite early a dissident minority.

The crisis which opened the gap took place in March 1943. The British War Cabinet made it clear that in supporting the military operations of the various groups of guerillas, HMG would veer in favour of groups willing to support the King of the Hellenes and his Government. This decision was made subject to operational necessity; it did not mean that republicans would be cut off. But British support was expected to be an increasingly valuable factor in the resistance movement, in which at that time there was no effective unit in the field affiliated to any but republican organisations. It was useless to expect a change of heart on the part of EAM/ELAS, and it was not long before the decision was in their case tacitly forgotten: they continued to preach aggressive republicanism and to draw British supplies, for reasons which the events to be recorded in the next chapter rendered inevitable. Zervas, however, had often shown himself amenable to British persuasion; a fact to which he owed a good deal of his later misfortunes. He was therefore approached[1] with the suggestion that he might send a telegram of non-committal greetings to King George II, on the timely occasion of Independence Day, 25th March, 1943. The intention was that he and the exiled authorities should at least return to speaking terms; but Zervas went a great deal farther than was expected. He sent two telegrams, one to the King and one to HMG. The first was far from non-committal, but it did serve the purpose of restoring some form of intercourse. It deplored equally the misrepresentation to which the resistance movement had been subject, and the militant activities of the KKE; but it was at least what was wanted to the limited extent of being addressed to the King. The second telegram was more important. It informed HMG that Zervas would not only be the first to welcome the King back if the Greek people expressed their free opinion in his favour, but even that if HMG wished the King to be restored "for wider reasons and even without the people's wishes," he would not oppose it. For that declaration there are two names: one is unscrupulous opportunism; the other is unquestioning loyalty.

　　King George sent a polite reply and HMG sent none. That Zervas' gesture was not received with enthusiasm was due to the prevailing atmosphere in London and Egypt, where he was regarded by the Greek authorities as hardly less disreputable than EAM/ELAS. One telegram gave them no reason by itself to modify their disapproval; and this stubborn fact wrecks the parallel which has been drawn between Zervas (who was treated with uniform distaste by the Greek exiled Government) and Mihailovitch (who held a ministerial post in the Yugoslav exiled Government). The *status quo ante* was, in fact, left unaltered by the interchange in March, at least in the world outside Greece. Neither HMG nor the King of the Hellenes committed themselves to anything which they had not already publicly avowed. The War Cabinet's directive only reasserted HMG's support for the King and his exiled Government, which had already been publicly declared in the House of Commons. The King in his reply to Zervas only reasserted his intention to base himself on the will of the people after his return to Greece, which was his

[1] By myself. In retrospect I am inclined to regard this as a mistake.

declared policy throughout his exile. But although nothing was changed in the outside world, Zervas had precipitated a violent reaction in occupied Greece.

His enemies denounced his conduct as that of a quisling; for in the judgment of EAM/ELAS, to collaborate with the King was as bad as collaborating with the Germans. But royalists throughout Greece began to take him seriously for the first time. By reason of these two reactions combined, EDES came to be regarded as the asylum for everyone, especially royalists, who hated and feared the KKE. Zervas' armed force expanded to rival ELAS in the Peloponnese, Roumeli, Thessaly and Macedonia. Even some adherents of EAM/ELAS did their best to transfer their allegiance to EDES, until it became more than their lives were worth to attempt it. But the important point is that Zervas had decided on his own initiative to transform the nature of EDES. Only after the decision was taken did he consult his political committee in Athens. Owing to the length and difficulty of communications between Athens and N.-W. Greece, such consultation was impracticably slow and seldom undertaken. It was hardly surprising that the subsequent development of EDES took different directions in Athens, which Zervas never revisited until the occupation was over, and in the mountains, where he was able to shape it to his will. The first effect of Zervas' *volte face* was that it became respectable to join EDES; the second was that it was joined (among many others) by a number of people who deserved no respect whatever.

The form which this effect took in Athens was worse than in the mountains. EDES had always had a disreputable fringe in Athens, derived principally from Zervas' adventurous past. This fringe began to accumulate a following derived from the antagonism that was widely felt towards EAM/ELAS. The negative nature of the bond enabled it to embrace a variety of men, who came before long to constitute the controlling element of EDES in Athens. They ranged from ambiguous opportunists like General Gonatas, a natural revolutionary and former Veniselist, to downright collaborators like Tavoularis and Voulpiotis. The disgust and alarm which this development evoked in the republican element of EDES led to a more or less openly acknowledged split. It is said that at one secret meeting of the underground in Athens, two distinct groups attended each claiming to represent the Central Committee of EDES. But there was not for long any doubt which had the upper hand. It might not be charitable to inquire why several of the section that succumbed, including Petimezas himself, spent the last years of the occupation in a German prison, and emerged to find themselves irrevocably superseded.

What Zervas thought about this from his mountain stronghold in N.-W. Greece is a question admitting two answers: at first he disapproved; at last he acquiesced. It is doubtful at what point he made the transition. Because the matter was a political one, and British support was given to

Zervas on the understanding that he would never again take part in politics, it was not brought up between Zervas and the British authorities, except when it was forced upon them both by his rivals in EAM/ELAS. Early in 1944 the leaders of EAM/ELAS convicted Zervas of having admitted collaborators into his organisation, by persuading him to abjure them publicly by name; three of those named were Gonatas, Tavoularis and Voulpiotis. But two qualifications must be made of this apparently damning self-indictment. The first is that those so denounced belonged only to the political EDES of Athens; the second is that no officer serving under Zervas' direct command was ever guilty of such a crime. The admission therefore reflects adversely on Zervas' political judgment and ability to control his political following; it does not convict either himself personally or his military force of collaboration with the Germans. Such a charge would be refuted by his record of military operations against the Germans and of implicit obedience to British orders, however much he disliked them. Nevertheless, since the charge of collaboration has been maintained against him, not only by his Greek enemies but also by some responsible British authorities, a little more must be said.

The difference between the Greek and the British authors of this charge is that the former had a long and direct acquaintance with the political and military EDES, whereas the latter had none with either. The former were thus in a favourable position to manipulate the facts in order to impress the latter. One of the characteristics of the KKE was that in their single-minded determination to monopolise the resistance move- ment they were willing not only to accuse their rivals of collaboration, but even to drive them into a position where they had either to collab- orate, or to submit to EAM/ELAS, or to be liquidated. The method was to attack them with a campaign of vilification, followed by an armed assault until they made their choice. When the only hope of survival lay in joining EAM/ELAS, or throwing themselves upon the mercies of the Germans, they duly made their choice and that was that. It will be shown how almost all the remaining guerilla organisations were presented with the three choices, and all chose. But Zervas was a tougher nut to crack; he fought back. At one time, in November 1943, he was reduced near to the fatal choice; some of his officers in parts of Greece remote from his immediate control were confronted with it and made it. It is they whose conduct forms the principal basis of the charge as presented by EAM/ELAS.

There is no certainty that any senior officer under Zervas' command made the choice of going over to the Germans; but it is probable that some did. Their choice does not indicate any sympathy with the Germans: it simply indicates a belief that the Germans were a lesser evil than death or EAM. It is also probable, but not certain, that some fought literally to the death. There is, however, one certain case of a prominent officer of

EDES who made the third choice and unwillingly agreed to go over to EAM/ELAS: his name is Lt.-Col. Ghikopoulos. The circumstances of his conversion are only interesting because they were almost identical with the steps by which General Saraphis had preceded him into ELAS, and by which other senior officers were to follow him. He was first accused of collaborating with the Germans; then he was caught and held under arrest with the daily threat of death over his head; evidence was alleged in confirmation of the charges against him; finally he emerged after a secret purgatory of variable duration into membership of EAM/ELAS. The conclusion must be in every case either that the evidence was forged, or that EAM/ELAS had no objection to a collaborator provided that he belonged to their side. It is a short step from this to the conclusion that the accusations made by EAM/ELAS against Zervas need not by themselves be taken seriously; especially as it is known that they made several attempts to persuade him to become their own Commander-in-Chief in place of Saraphis.

The British supporters of the charge go further, however. They allege that Zervas was personally in touch with the German authorities, both directly and indirectly. The indirect contacts are indisputable, for Zervas had a wide and indiscriminate acquaintance of every kind. Like everyone who could afford it, he dealt on the German-sponsored black market. He was in communication with General Mihailovitch,[1] whose collaboration with the Germans is generally assumed. He was in communication with the Bishop of Ioannina, who was himself in personal contact with the German headquarters in that town. He was in communication with one of the leaders of a force armed by the Germans in Macedonia to fight ELAS; with them I shall deal later.[2] He was in communication with the Greek and International Red Cross, which acted as avowed go-betweens. These were the normal intercourse of war. All except one of the cases quoted were specifically authorised by SOE Cairo, the British authorities responsible for allied operations in Greece.

Only three examples have come to my knowledge, purporting to prove collusion between Zervas and the Germans, that are based on his actual conduct of operations. The first is an armistice which he was alleged to have signed with the German commander in N.-W. Greece in October 1943. The second is the inactivity of his forces against the Germans in the summer of 1944. The third is the lack of interference by the Germans in the disembarkation of allied supplies for Zervas on the west coast of his area in the same summer. The principal sources of these three charges were, in order: of the first, the GHQ of ELAS, especially

---

[1]In November 1942, Zervas showed me a letter (in French) from Mihailovitch, containing greetings and a vague suggestion of co-operation. In June 1944 two officers sent by Mihailovitch reached Zervas' GHQ, but were rebuffed on British instructions.

[2]See page 95.

Aris Veloukhiotis; of the second, several senior British officers of SOE Cairo; of the third, a British Socialist MP who took part in the operations in question. I mention these notable authorities so that I shall not be thought to damage Zervas' reputation merely by protesting too much.

On the first charge, the evidence which Aris produced to prove that Zervas had signed an armistice with the Germans in October 1943 was a telegram from an officer commanding an ELAS division in Zervas' neighbourhood. But Aris had misunderstood the message. The ELAS commander reported that, having been told by Red Cross representatives that they had just persuaded Zervas to sign an armistice of fourteen days with the Germans, he had agreed to do the same.[1] That Zervas had not done so was proved by two facts: first, that an English officer with an exceptional knowledge of Greek had been present throughout his meeting with the Red Cross representatives; second, that the meeting was followed within a few days by one of the longest and most ferocious battles that ever took place between Zervas and the Germans. Neither of these facts, however, prevented the GHQ of ELAS from publishing their version; nor did they prevent Aris Veloukhiotis from launching upon Zervas a flank attack at the height of his battle with the Germans. The evidence in this case therefore reflects discredit on EAM/ELAS, but none on Zervas.

The second charge is only interesting for an odd and secondary reason. The allegation that Zervas refrained from harassing the Germans during the summer of 1944 has been sustained by senior British officers of SOE Cairo. It is true. But during the summer of 1944 Zervas was under orders to refrain temporarily from operations against the Germans, in order to avert reprisals and to conserve his force for the final operation of harassing the Germans' withdrawal; those orders were transmitted to him by the staff of SOE Cairo. When he eventually received the order to attack in September, the results which his force then achieved against the Germans could be described[2] as coming up to expectations, which were high. Zervas thus obeyed his orders throughout. That the orders and the criticism both emanated from the same quarter is an inexplicable misunderstanding.

The third charge has the added importance of having been made by

[1] The operative words in Greek were: ἐδώσαμεν παρομοίαν ὑπόσχεσιν. This document was presented only to myself, on 12th October 1943 at Pertouli (Thessaly). No one outside EAM/ELAS ever saw it again, so that in any dispute about its contents, their word stands against mine. It is the only incriminating document ever produced by any Greek party that I know for certain to have been genuine. Greeks interested in discrediting political opponents are ready to provide, or at least to accept, forged evidence; but that cannot be true of the present case, since the party incriminated by the document accidentally showed it to me themselves. For a discussion of the general nature of such evidence, see Appendix A.

[2] In my report on the final phase of the Occupation, dated January, 1945.

a member of the House of Commons.[1] It is the most serious of the three, and the purport of it is convincing. In 1944 British naval units were employed to deliver supplies to the west coasts of Yugoslavia, Albania and Greece for the use of their respective guerillas against the Germans. The guerillas in the first two countries belonged to the left-wing movements of Tito and Enver Hoxha; in the third case they were those of General Zervas. In the first two cases the difficult operation of disembarking supplies by night was regularly harassed by the Germans; in the third case it never was. Yet it is known that the Germans were aware of the operations in the third case as well as the other two, for a German intelligence summary[2] was afterwards captured which contained this information. The suggestion, in its mildest form, is that the Germans allowed the operations to be carried out unhindered in Greece, and opposed them in Yugoslavia and Albania, because they knew that weapons delivered to Zervas would not be used against them, as weapons delivered to Tito and Enver Hoxha would. Obviously, a much less mild inference could alternatively be drawn.

Three answers can perhaps be made to the argument: or rather, one answer (that it is mistaken) can be made in three ways. The first is that the contrast between the Germans' interference on the Yugoslav and Albanian coasts, and the absence of it on the Greek coast, could *prima facie* be attributed to greater efficiency and better security on the part of the latter. It might mean that the Germans did not interfere with the Greek operations simply because they did not know about them in time; the captured German intelligence summary, for what its evidence on this point is worth, only reported the operations after they had taken place. This argument is possible but improbable, and will not appeal to those who already have a predisposition against Zervas and in favour of Tito and Enver Hoxha.

The second answer is that if the evidence proves an indifference on the part of the Germans (to put it no more strongly) whether Zervas received weapons or not, it also proves by the same token an indifference on their part whether ELAS or anyone else in Greece received weapons or not. A proportion of the supplies delivered to the west coast of Greece was not destined for Zervas, but for the territory of ELAS many days' journey inland to the east, to which they were transported (with Zervas' help) over a mountain barrier by trains of mules. This fact also became known to the Germans, when in April 1944 they intercepted a mule-train *en route*, and captured many of the stores, as well as Greek and British personnel. It might at first sight be deduced from this that the

[1] This is an example of a general and common argument: but since it was made in private conversation, in September 1945, it would be improper to name the source.

[2] German XXII Mountain Army Corps' Intelligence Summary, dated in Ioannina 7th August 1944.

Germans *were* concerned to prevent such supplies from reaching ELAS, and therefore intercepted them only at the stage *after* Zervas had taken his share. The deduction is invalid, because in the first place it was so enormously more difficult to intercept them at this stage, than at a known point on the coast, that no calculation could be based on the possibility of doing so; in the second place the interception of the mule-train in April 1944 was plainly an accident, which was never repeated. It follows that this argument can only be used against Zervas by turning it against ELAS as well. This is legitimate, but improbable, and useless to Zervas' enemies.

The third answer is decisive. Collaboration with the enemy is not a matter of words but of deeds. It is conceivable that the Germans believed that weapons delivered to Zervas would never be used against them; but if they did so, there was a shock in store for them. They could not be expected to know that Zervas' inactivity against them during the summer of 1944 was the result of express orders from the British authorities; it has already been seen that some of the British authorities responsible for issuing those orders did not know it either. In referring to Zervas' "lawful attitude toward the German troops," the intelligence summary already mentioned is attesting not his disloyalty towards his allies, but his obedience to their orders; not the success of the German authorities, but their wishful thinking. When Zervas received orders to attack the Germans during their withdrawal in September 1944 he did so. If, therefore, the Germans had in fact allowed supplies to be delivered unhindered to Zervas throughout the summer, that proves not that he was a collaborator but that they were fools. The charge under examination is not that there was an explicit agreement between Zervas and the Germans (which would imply a double-cross on his part), but that the Germans tacitly turned a blind eye to operations on the west coast. Of explicit agreement there has been no evidence, nor has it been suggested. Of tacit acquiescence it can only be concluded that it is possible, that it must await further evidence from German archives, that it does not incriminate Zervas, and that it convicts the Germans of an expensive mistake.

The only residue of the argument is regret that the charge should exist to be answered. Throughout the occupation Zervas' conduct was unexceptionable. As a soldier, he punctiliously obeyed his orders, not (as his critics argue) because he knew which side his bread was buttered: he did so even before butter had been offered at all. For a major operation in the summer of 1943 he issued orders consisting simply of the sentence: "Between the dates 20th June and 14th July all units will do exactly what they are told by the British liaison officers attached to them." As a politician, he had no opportunity to be a collaborator himself, being established in the isolation of the mountains; but he was too tolerant in providing an asylum to every opponent of the KKE indiscriminately, and therefore to a number of quasi-reformed collaborators. These men he publicly abjured in the end, whatever his private sympathy for their position. But as the occupation drew to a close, and he began to foresee post-liberation probabilities, it was rather towards men of this type than towards his old republican colleagues that he found his sympathies leaning. Whether or not they had been collaborators (and most of them had been nothing worse than *attentistes*) seemed to matter less when the fighting was over; less still when December 1944 had committed the Communists to crimes quite as terrible. It was from such henchmen that in 1945 Zervas formed a new party, with the new name of the National Party of Greece, in association with an abortive coalition, modelled on EAM, under the title EME (the National Front of Greece). The old associates went their own way, drifting steadily nearer to EAM. When General Plastiras returned to Greece from his French exile at the end of 1944, it was already ridiculous to regard him as the leader of EDES. EDES was dead; split, as is the fate of its kind, between two extremes.

Zervas' military force was extinguished soon afterwards by violence. It was one of the victims of ELAS in the December revolution; and although the events of the end of 1944 will be dealt with in detail later, it is worth anticipating a little on account of the discredit which the annihilation of Zervas' force by ELAS brought upon the British authorities, for having supported him, as well as on himself, for succumbing so easily. There are two reasons why the discredit is unjustified. The first is that Zervas' defeat by ELAS in December 1944 was irrelevant to the reputation of his force and his own abilities. It did not prove, as his enemies contended, that his army was never any good and that the British had been fools or hypocrites in backing him. It only proved that his army was inferior to ELAS at fighting other Greeks: a creditable fact which needed no proving. But there is no logical connection between their capabilities in fighting Germans, which was their function, and in fighting Greeks, which was not. This is simply an illustration of the difference between Zervas' forces and those of ELAS: that the former were formed to fight the Germans and the latter to fight anyone, whatever their nationality, who obstructed the ideological aims of EAM.

Even if Zervas' forces had fought ELAS with undivided enthusiasm, there was a second reason why they would still have been beaten. Towards the end of the occupation Zervas had been assigned, by the British authorities,[1] a zone which suited his purposes as a guerilla fighting the Germans, but exposed him on three sides out of four to superior positions held by ELAS as soon as the Germans had gone. The orders of the British authorities were justified on the assumption that when the Germans had gone, all fighting was over: they therefore even went farther. They required Zervas to prepare his force for demobilisation, which he was doing a few days before ELAS attacked him; and they required him to

[1]As part of the "Caserta Agreement"; see Appendix H.

F

surrender his reserve of small arms ammunition as soon as the Germans had left his area. It seemed to Zervas unreasonable that the recipients to whom he was obliged to surrender his ammunition were ELAS, after the Germans had also left all their areas.[1] Yet these orders were scrupulously executed. The collapse of his forces is thus directly attributable to his men's reluctance to fight other Greeks and to his own obedience to orders. Neither of these causes deserves ridicule; nor do they reflect discredit upon the British policy of supporting him during the occupation. But the fact that these things were not made public at the time illustrates another important fact about the British military authorities in Egypt: that the extinction of Zervas' force and the discrediting of his leadership were not universally unwelcome. The BBC even announced his force's disintegration in advance. British opinion was in fact sharply divided about Zervas, as it still is. In December 1944 the ascendant had passed from his supporters to his enemies.[2]

Despite these internal divisions, it is perfectly correct to say, as many critics of British policy do, that without British support Zervas' army would never have existed: what is wrong is to make it a criticism. It is not true that he was induced to take the field as a counterweight to ELAS; neither ELAS nor any other guerilla organisation had ever been heard of at the time when British agents first tried to induce Zervas to take the field. It is not true that he was given preferential support: the final balance was in proportion roughly even; for ELAS did better in 1943, Zervas in 1944. What is true, however, is that Zervas' forces would have been annihilated sooner than they were if they had not been backed by British support. Critics argue that it would have been better to give up that support as we gave up our support to Mihailovitch. The argument is based on a superficial identification, which is itself of recent date: indeed, Zervas had not even been heard of when the agitation against Mihailovitch in December 1942 took its first form, an arbitrary association between the "reactionary" policy of supporting him and the "reactionary" policy of supporting Darlan in North Africa. Zervas' conduct too was different from that of Mihailovitch, especially in military obedience. But the criticism is really political in content; it is on political grounds that it has to be met.

If Zervas had not been supported, the whole of Greece would have been controlled by EAM/ELAS when the Germans left it. This is not conjecture; it is ascertained fact, observable from what happened in every

[1] This ammunition was partly shot back at those who supplied it in December 1944 and partly hidden for later use; in 1947 a bill for the costs of transporting it from Zervas to ELAS was submitted to HMG at the instigation of the KKE.

[2] In the interests of establishing bias, I should add that I was one of the supporters. The evidence on which the foregoing paragraph is based unfortunately cannot be given in detail, because the report on EDES' last campaign, in which I set it out, is still a secret document.

other part of Greece. Nor is the fact in dispute: the point of the critics is not that this would not have happened, but that it would have been better if it had. The last chapter of this book will suggest that controversy on this point is irrelevant to the real problem; but the critics should know what they are defending. Two propositions which I hope to leave beyond dispute are that EAM/ELAS was and is the instrument of the KKE, and that the KKE was and is the instrument of the Soviet Government. The chain of causation which would have led from the abandonment of Zervas to the domination of Greece by the USSR is certain. Whether that would be a good or a bad thing is irrelevant. Those who criticise British policy on this matter must commit themselves to desiring the ultimate absorption of Greece into a Soviet Federation of the Balkans. They may be right and wise to do so; but they are not often open about it.

This is no lamentation for the death of EDES. The political organisation of that name had become detestable, and the military force had served its purpose. It was proper that both should expire after the liberation of Greece; just as it would have been proper for EAM and ELAS to expire on the same day, had they been what they pretended. The difference in their fates lay potentially in their natures, for EDES lacked both the political cohesion and the revolutionary ardour of its rival. But EDES had one thing which not even dissolution could take away: the dynamic personality of its leader. Far the most important part of EDES at all times was Zervas; so much so that there was a propensity to think of the organisation entirely in terms of his name, in contrast with the anonymity of EAM/ELAS. Of Zervas himself, to draw together the threads, this summary may be made. As a soldier, none of the charges made against him could be sustained; as a politician, the charges were easier to sustain after the end of the occupation than before. His appointment as Minister of Public Order in 1947 may have seemed to his henchmen the crown of his career; to his true friends, however, it must seem a melancholy anti-climax. His political conduct in 1945-7 appeared to give retrospective validity to charges made in 1942-4. Nevertheless, they were not true in 1942-4; years in which he rose to heights of personal greatness which his previous career had not foreshadowed and his later career did not maintain. If he had died, like EDES, on the day of liberation, he would have died a national hero; and rightly so. If he had even respected his often repeated pledge to abstain from politics when the Germans were expelled, almost all attacks would have failed. But for all his faults he stands out alongside his rival, Aris Veloukhiotis, as one of the only two great personalities that the Greek resistance movement produced.

The big battalions of the resistance movement, both political and military, have been covered. What remains is a number of smaller resistance organisations having certain features in common. The first is that they were all late into the field. The second is that none of them survived the occupation. The third, which was the cause of the second, is that EAM/ELAS hated them all. The fourth, which was the cause of the third, is that they were characterised by the same general respectability of composition. Their constitution was not identical: if it had been, they would have been one organisation instead of several; but it was drawn from the same classes, which can best be described as bourgeois, in the sense most offensive to doctrinaire Communists. Their military leadership was derived from the regular army; their political leadership, such as they had, was derived from sober democrats; their following was derived from the same material that has already been distinguished below the horizontal line transecting Greek life. Between themselves they had minor differences, not major gulfs such as separated them all from EAM/ELAS. They lacked the revolutionary spark and the toughness of moral fibre that were needed for the guerilla movement. They lacked that ability which set the KKE apart, to see in another Greek as bitter an enemy as the Germans. Their warfare was not ideological but patriotic: it could not, as that of EAM/ELAS so easily could, be translated at a moment's notice into civil warfare. In much of this they did not stand apart from EDES; the difference of EDES was that it was older, bigger and tougher. Here as elsewhere the essence of the rivalry which split Greek life can be represented as a conflict of EAM/ELAS versus the rest. But the following paragraphs will show that there was still enough to divide the rest if there had not been two things to keep them friendly: the existence of EAM/ELAS to drown all disputes in a common fear; and the geographical separation of the minor organisations from each other in the field.

(d) EKKA. The earliest of this group was called "National and Social Liberation," and usually known by its Greek initials as EKKA. Its military leader was Colonel Psaros, who was accompanied in the field for a time by his friend Bakirdzis. The ambiguity of their relationship was resolved when Bakirdzis deserted EKKA in March 1944 to become the first president of the EAM/ELAS shadow government, PEEA. EKKA's principal political leader was Kartalis, whose name has already been introduced: a former right-wing politician to whom EKKA was an intermediate stage in his progress towards the left. His brilliant intelligence and western education distinguished him among the political figures in the mountains, but did not enable him to save EKKA. The political support of the organisation in Athens included Kapsalopoulos, Katavolos and Pappas, of whom the last two (as well as Kartalis) subsequently held office in unelected governments of the centre, in 1945-6. The quality of these names vouches for the democratic integrity of EKKA. But more was needed for survival in the ungentlemanly hurly-burly of the mountains.

EKKA hesitated fatally long before putting an armed force into the field in March 1943. Psaros chose to revive the 5/42 Regiment, which he had once commanded, in his native district of southern Roumeli. He was popular in that area and attracted a large following, and won British support. But these advantages carried with them the enmity of EAM/ELAS. In the summer of 1943 he was twice attacked and his force twice annihilated by ELAS. Twice he reformed it. In the autumn he was invited to join EAM/ELAS in a civil war against Zervas, but his officers bought them off, in his absence, with a benevolent neutrality. To punish his lukewarmness, EAM/ELAS accused him of collaborating with the Germans. In April 1944 came the final attack. The 5/42 Regiment was destroyed for the last time, and the fate of its senior officers exactly illustrates all of the three choices which the enmity of the KKE invariably presented. Part of the force escaped under two senior officers to take refuge with the Germans and the Security Battalions in Patras; part under other officers allowed itself to be incorporated in ELAS; and Psaros paid for his obstinacy with his life. It can be seen in retrospect that there could have been no other fate for the only guerilla commander who was what the British Army calls an officer and a gentleman.

The political membership of EKKA survived, but not in the mountains. It continued after the occupation to provide the Centre with such backbone as it still has, including its only significant newspaper, the *Eleftheria*. From that paper the residuary legatees of EKKA took their subsequent name, the "*Eleftheria* group," which remained a power in Greek politics; but it failed to provide the Centre with any positive principle to hold it together. This lack can be seen in the differences of principle that separate the Centre from the two extremes. What separates it from the left is opposition to Communism, which to a patriotic Greek means the diminution of his country's independence in the interests of Slav imperialism. What separates it from the right is opposition to the monarchy, which in the memory of a republican Greek is still associated with the dictatorship of Metaxas. At every crisis, the reactions of the centre are determined by the relative intensity of these two enmities. If hatred of the monarchy is uppermost, the centre moves to the left; if hatred of Communism is uppermost, it moves to the right. When the intensities are approximately equal, nuclear fission takes place and the disintegrated atoms gravitate to opposite poles. In the crucial months before the elections of March 1946, for instance, the gravitation of the Centre was towards the left. It is to the credit of the "*Eleftheria* group" that they moved that way in a body, instead of suffering the same disintegration as EDES. But in 1947 the rival fields of force again wavered in relative intensity, and by 1948 the Centre was back in a state of fatal fluctuation. It still includes many of the ablest individuals in public life, and the association between it and the former components of EKKA is lively and encouraging. But the prospects for a group which believes in democracy are not bright in a political world governed by extremes, which find the forms of democracy valuable and its substance ridiculous.

The three organisations which have so far been considered, EAM/ ELAS, EDES and EKKA, constitute a class apart in their relations to the British authorities. They were the acknowledged resistance in the field, because in the summer of 1943 they, almost alone, existed to be acknowledged. The distinction was crystallised in the signature of an agreement by each of them and the representatives of the British authorities in July 1943, by which they were recognised as armed forces under the command of GHQ Middle East under the common title, "National Bands of Greek Guerillas." They, with one British representative, formed the Joint General Headquarters (JGHQ) which was set up at the same time to co-ordinate operations.[1] Although the JGHQ was short-lived, and the "National Bands" Agreement was soon a dead letter, the status of these three forces as members of the Middle East Command was never repudiated. In this respect they differed from all other resistance organisations on the mainland.

They were not, as their opponents have argued, first in the field because they were given preferential treatment by the British authorities: on the contrary, they were given preferential treatment because they were first in the field. They were first because of that quasi-revolutionary nature which has been held against them, and which they proclaimed in their very names. ELAS was the *popular* army; EDES was the *republican* league; EKKA stood for *social* liberation. Men who wanted the state of things in Greece to be different after the war naturally took the initiative before those who were content that it should be the same. This desire, and not the unalloyed sense of a duty to expel the enemy, was what brought their first leaders (but not their first followers) into the field. The remaining organisations were all more conservative, not necessarily supporting the King because he was George II, but supporting the established government because it was established. They had not, therefore, the same motive for asserting themselves in a hurry. They regarded all Greek questions as having been put into cold storage for the duration of the occupation; and no more to them than to their rivals above did it occur until later that a patriotic duty was involved.

(e) *Minor Resistance Organisations.* Two early examples of the formation of resistance movements in the interests of the *status quo ante* occurred in the Peloponnese, which has a traditional reputation for what its enemies call reaction. Because the men who organised EAM/ELAS there were particularly alien to Peloponnesian temperament, and the men who followed them were of a particularly poor type, there was a welcome for

[1]See Appendix C for the terms of the "National Bands" Agreement.

the rival organisations which called themselves the "National Organisation of Officers" (EOA) and, rather pretentiously, the "Greek Army" (ES). Theoretically the relation between these two was similar to that between EAM and ELAS, but the practice was less clear cut. Guerilla bands calling themselves by both names took the field with little co-ordination in the early summer of 1943. The leadership was drawn from regular officers, of whom the chief were Colonels Papadhongonas, Karakhalios and Yiannakopoulos. The familiar contrast between EAM/ELAS and the rest was emphasised in the Peloponnese by the adherence to EOA and ES of representatives of EDES (Colonel Yioryiou, who claimed the supreme command by virtue of his relationship to General Zervas) and EKKA (Lieut. Kokonis). It was further emphasised when civil war broke out between these well-meaning unfortunates and ELAS, with the familiar consequences. The attack by ELAS began early in August 1943 and succeeded by the end of October. Of the principal leaders of ES, Papadhongonas escaped to join the Security Battalions, Karakhalios was killed, and Yiannakopoulos went into hiding, where Yioryiou had long already been. Of the subordinate commanders, Kokonis joined the Security Battalions, and two of his colleagues joined ELAS. The remainder, unable to decide what to do or to obtain advice from their sponsors in Athens, dispersed disconsolately to wait for something to turn up. The accustomed pattern was once more completed.

For the sake of completeness, a small number of insignificant bodies purporting to be resistance organisations may as well be briefly recorded and dismissed at this point. They had enough in common to make periodical attempts to merge themselves into coalitions on the model of EAM; but even the two most strenuous attempts, under the designations of LAE and EDEM, were stillborn. In their effect upon the movement in the mountains, they do not noticeably surpass the nonentities of Athens; but they qualify for admission here by virtue of the fact that, unlike "X" or the six colonels, they did at least send representatives into the mountains on their own initiative. Some of these joined other forces already in the field; others looked round and went home; but time spent in reconnaissance, we are told, is never wasted.

The first of these organisations was called AAA (a conventional symbol). It has two points of interest: that one of its founders was George Papandhreou, later Prime Minister, and that it was the first organisation to back General Saraphis in the field, before he underwent transfiguration into Commander-in-Chief of ELAS. He had once before enjoyed a brief initiation into EAM/ELAS, from which he repented when he discovered that it was controlled by the KKE. AAA won him on this first rebound, and he took the field in Thessaly as a rival to ELAS towards the end of 1942. His lieutenants in the field were Majors Kostopoulos and Vlakhos, both strange bedfellows for Saraphis; the latter at least was a declared royalist. His military sponsors in Athens were Major Tsigantes and General Pangalos, who have already been encountered separately. Their communication with him was conducted through Sarandis, the Nomarch (County President) of Trikkala, who contrived to ingratiate himself successively with the collaborating Government, with the Italians, with Saraphis, with EAM/ELAS, with Zervas, and with the restored Government of 1945, but apparently never (to his credit) with the Germans. His connection with the Italians was the occasion of a belief that Saraphis was supported by the occupation authorities. This was the excuse for armed attack by ELAS upon Saraphis' embryonic force in March 1943. He was taken prisoner and threatened with death for his crimes; but once he was safely back in the bosom of EAM/ELAS, with all the moral fervour of a reformed renegade, it was discovered that the charge rested on misunderstanding, and that he had not been collaborating after all. AAA, however, passed out of the picture for good.

There are three more minor names in this category which it is difficult to distinguish with precision. They may each have had a diverse composition in Athens, but from the Greek mountains they appeared to amount to the same thing: and that, *quoad* resistance to the enemy, was nothing at all. One was called the National Committee, one the Sacred Brigade, and one the Union of Enslaved Victors. The first of these sent as their representative to the mountains in December 1942 a provincial magistrate called Tsimbos, who soon returned to Athens after much amiable but ineffectual conversation. When he came back to the mountains six months later he appeared to represent the second of the three, whose name referred collectively to the senior generals of the regular army. Before he could be stopped, he produced one of them in the mountains, and was barely prevented from producing another: the former was Gen. Tsipouras, a retired officer of great courage who had unfortunately held an appointment under the occupation; the latter was no less a figure than Papagos, CGS of the Greek Army in the Albanian campaign of 1940-1. This distinguished officer would have been as out of place among the guerillas as Aris Veloukhiotis at the Royal Court: it was not his kind of war. But the organisations concerned had decided that the time had come to remove the command of the guerillas from the uncouth ruffians who had created them, and give it to the senior generals who had done nothing for them at all. They were wrong: the time had not come; it had long gone by. The fallacy underlying their plans was illustrated by the sole contribution of the Union of Enslaved Victors, who sent to the British authorities a beautifully typed letter offering, in almost perfect English, to do whatever might be useful in the way of vaguely getting things going. It was not to be expected that men who had only got as far as that after more than two years of enemy occupation would make a noticeable mark in the resistance movement. Nor did they.

The kind of officers who made up the military component of such organisations found their level when the occupation was drawing to a close, in organisations such as X, SAN, and RAN. The first is a conventional symbol; the second stands for "League of Young Officers"; the third took its initials from the areas in the north which irredentists wished to add to Greek territory. All were largely composed of regular officers pledged to fight Communism. The first grew up among unemployed officers in Athens, under Colonel Grivas; the second grew up among serving officers in the Mediterranean Command; the third was formed in both places in turn by Gen. Vendiris, who had been associated with the republican revolution of 1935 but later made his peace with the King for fear of Communism. When the occupation ended, the line between them was less clear cut, and in hostile propaganda they were treated as identical. There was some excuse for this in the persistency of certain names in association with them: the same kind of names that had been associated with the minor organisations trying to stake their little claims in the resistance movement. The reason is that the corps of Greek officers as a whole was at a loss what to do, both during the occupation and during the two years of uncertainty which followed it until the King was restored. They were men devoted to the established order who could find no established order to warrant their devotion. They would have rallied to any reputable leader, whatever his political associations: even to the Republican ex-dictator General Plastiras, the titular head of EDES, whose return to Greece as Commander-in-Chief was seriously mooted in 1942 and later. The only leadership they would not accept was that of the KKE; but it seemed that in most parts of Greece no other was available. In small and fluctuating groups, therefore, they drifted to and fro across the wilderness, hesitating between greater and lesser evils, vainly searching for an oasis. They were willing to try anything, subject to infinite precautions and reservations, and many of them did in fact try everything. That is why the minor organisations were so many, so difficult to distinguish, so kaleidoscopic, so small and ineffectual.

A more honourable addition to this class is the National Organisation of Cretans (EOK), whose name speaks for itself. Two dominant features of Cretan politics are its separatist tradition, since like other islands it resents centralised control from the mainland, and its devotion to the name of Veniselos, the Cretan who founded the Liberal Party and inspired the Greek Republic. The instinct of the Cretans is therefore to distrust most mainlanders, but republican liberals less than the rest; on the other hand, the internal freemasonry of Cretan blood is so strong that even a rare sport such as a Cretan royalist can be trusted and forgiven because he is a Cretan. EOK therefore had a catholic range of membership, which excluded only the outlandish creed of Communism imported from the mainland by EAM. Even with EAM, so long as its local composition was mainly Cretan, EOK contrived to have no quarrel; there was even some reciprocity of leadership between the two. Among outstanding Cretans who might have been expected to assume respectively the political and military leadership of EOK were the former Veniselist Askoutsis and the former revolutionary General Mandakas; but Askoutsis was deported to the mainland by the Germans in 1942 and Mandakas crossed voluntarily in 1944, both to end up in privileged membership of EAM's shadow-government, PEEA. EOK neither resented nor regretted their loss: its own leadership rested in happier hands. The chief of its leaders in the field were at first Emmanuel Bandouvas and later Petrakoyioryis, both wealthy landowners who were born leaders of the *Capetanios* type; the best of its political leaders was Emmanuel Papadhoyiannis, a royalist whose integrity was universally respected. It was characteristic of the genuine patriotism which inspired EOK that these and other far more diverse Cretans remained united until the Germans surrendered in May 1945, and only disbanded when their task was completed. It was also character-istic of Cretan good sense that EOK never became involved in civil war with EAM/ELAS. EOK was therefore unique among nationalist organ-isations in being the only successful one indigenous to a particular locality.

What usually happened to these attempts can be seen in the example of two eccentric individualists, one in Central Greece and the other in the far north-east. The first was called Athos Roumeliotis, a pseudonym derived from Roumeli, the area which he purported to govern. Having originally commanded a unit of ELAS and quarrelled with his immediate subordinate, the more notorious Aris Veloukhiotis, he retired to the most inaccessible part of the Pindus range of mountains and set up an indepen-dent state, while Aris set up the more dynamic power of ELAS GHQ. Athos emerged periodically to take a flamboyant part in whatever negotiations happened to be going on within the resistance movement; but generally he confined himself to levying taxes, conducting weddings, and performing the other functions of a medieval chieftain. For a time the British authorities were tempted to treat him seriously; perhaps as a living embodiment of the spirit of "The Napoleon of Notting Hill" he deserves a sympathetic tear. But few were shed when his force was disbanded by ELAS in August 1943; one of their few actions that enjoyed the approval of practically everyone in the Greek mountains.

The second individualist was known by the Turkish nickname of Andon Tsaous; for his native area in north-east Greece is one where Turkish is still an important language. He was nevertheless an intensely patriotic Greek. His purpose was to ensure that Eastern Macedonia and Greek Thrace remained Greek; and since both were occupied not by the Germans, who were a temporary calamity, but by the Bulgars, who might be a permanent one, he had no temptation to collaborate with the enemy. In that area the only Greeks who could seriously be accused of collaboration were EAM/ELAS, for in the complicated circumstances which prevailed there, little substantial difference of purpose separated the Bulgarian Army, the Bulgarian Partisans, and the KKE; a tripartite inter-relationship in which the connecting liasion was provided by a man known variously as Radev and Rhodhopoulos, a Greek by birth, a Bulgar by naturalisation, and an international Communist by persuasion. This was what Andon Tsaous set himself to combat. Because he began his task only towards the end of 1943, neither ELAS nor the Bulgars had time to eliminate him before the end of the occupation. He and his "Cape-tanioi," as they were called, successfully held off all enemies, and came in the end to enjoy exclusive British support, by reason equally of military merit and political orthodoxy. They are the one relieving feature of the gloomy waste presented by the development of resistance in the extreme north of Greece. Andon Tsaous also acts as a bridge to bring into the field of this study the most complicated and controversial area of Greek affairs. It was in the extreme north that the most violent and various opposition to EAM/ELAS was generated during the occupation.

The next victim of EAM/ELAS that has to be considered had chosen for its area of operations this dangerous ground of Macedonia. The term Macedonia here means that part of the wider Macedonian heritage which fell within the frontiers of Greece and the occupation of the Germans. It does not include the extension of Macedonia into the territory of Yugo-slavia and Bulgaria; nor the eastern extremity of Greek Macedonia (referred to in the preceding paragraph), which from 1941 to 1944 was not *occupied* by the Germans but *incorporated* into Bulgaria. The River Strymon is the eastern boundary of the area now in question. This German-occupied part of Greek Macedonia had been almost exclusively the preserve of EAM/ELAS from the day that resistance began. A few independent popular leaders had taken the field alone; a few semi-reformed bandits had insensibly transfigured themselves into popular leaders; but both had either allowed themselves to be absorbed by ELAS, or resisted absorption and been annihilated. There remained considerable feeling against EAM/ELAS in Macedonia, since the population associated them with Communism, Communism with Panslavism, and Panslavism with Russian imperialism. To them, therefore, the domination of EAM/ELAS foreshadowed the loss of part of their country, including Salonika, to the Slavs across their northern border; as well as other personally distasteful consequences, such as being forced to regard the Bulgars as their brothers. The only brotherly sentiment which Greek Macedonians felt towards the Bulgars was a disposition to raise Cain. In the north of Greece, therefore, men were politically divided not by ideology but by nationalism. The right were more terrified of Panslavism than even of Communism; they not only feared a Slav incursion across their frontiers, but were fanatically expansionist in their own outlook northwards. The left sought an accommodation with Slavs who shared their own internationalist theories; but even this accommodation was precarious. Both sentiments were deeply rooted. They account for the prolonged resistance to EAM/ELAS from Greeks in Macedonia, of which the protagonist was the organisation known at first as "Protectors of Northern Greece" (YVE), and later, when they wished to extend their protection to the whole country, as the "Panhellenic Liberation Organisation" (PAO).

One of the reasons for this change of name was that EAM/ELAS had convicted YVE of collusion with collaborators. The Greeks of Macedonia found it hard to determine which was the greater evil: the Germans or the KKE. On the ground that the Germans were probably temporary, and the KKE permanent, many patriotic Greeks became colour-blind and were seduced into collaboration with the Germans. The line dividing collaboration from more respectable activities was fine in Macedonia; the KKE wished to delete it altogether. Having discredited YVE, they spared no pains to discredit its successor PAO as well. But the new leaders of PAO had learned their lesson. What brought about their final downfall was not a crime but an error of judgment.

The Central Committee of PAO was established in Salonika, the second most important town in Greece and far the most important in Macedonia on account of its port. It had not hitherto played a considerable part in resistance to the enemy. EAM had a committee there; so had EDES in a small way; in 1941 a subversive group of Veniselist Liberals had worked there under Aleko Zannas. But Zannas' group had given up subversive activities before the end of 1941, leaving only the growing EAM and the discredited YVE in organised being. Reformed out of YVE, the Central Committee of PAO set about filling the gap in the last months of 1942, renewing especially the broken links with the British authorities in Egypt. PAO was in fact the first group in Salonika to provide SOE Cairo with a competent system of intelligence.

In 1943 it wished to put armed guerilla bands in the field to fight the Germans; but its leaders knew that this would be interpreted by EAM/ELAS as a gesture hostile to themselves. British representatives sent written advice to the PAO leaders in Salonika to send a senior officer first into the mountains, to co-ordinate the activities of PAO with those of its rivals in advance, and not to put any forces in the field until the acquiescence of ELAS was assured. This advice recognised (but did not sanction) the intention of EAM/ELAS to monopolise the resistance by force if they could. The purpose of the letter was to avert bloodshed between Greeks. It failed because it arrived too late; the delay in delivery was almost certainly due to the intervention of EAM/ELAS. The result was that the forces of PAO took the field unheralded in July 1943; its two successive representatives, Lieut.-Cols. Mousterakis and Aryiropoulos, did not make the proposed contacts until August; in September ELAS launched against it charges of collaboration with the Germans, and armed onslaught designed to make those charges come true. By the end of October, the forces of PAO were annihilated, and its officers faced the usual choice. Some were killed; some escaped to the Germans; Aryiropoulos escaped with British help to Egypt; Mousterakis became, by the usual process, successively a traitor, a collaborator, a prisoner, and a divisional commander in ELAS.

Greek rivalry towards EAM/ELAS was not ended in Macedonia by the annihilation of PAO. It hardly could be so long as there existed EAM's slavophone cousin SNOF. The function of SNOF was to justify the existence of an autonomous Macedonia in a southern Slav federation. Although the relations between its nationalist rank and file and the patriotic rank and file of ELAS were uneasy, the identity of policy between the Communist leaders of both was regarded as damning by the generality of nationalist opinion among the Greeks of Macedonia. In their eyes SNOF was a devilish invention of Tito, and EAM was in partnership with the devil. Their judgment was supported by rumours of agreement between EAM/ELAS and the Bulgarian authorities, to connive at the independence of Macedonia when the occupation came to an end.[1] The rumours were so circumstantial that in 1944 the leaders of EAM had to devote strenuous efforts to rebutting them. Whether true or not, the fact that they were widely believed was enough to account for the identification of EAM with the enemy, which prevailed among Macedonian Greeks.

(f) *Minor Armed Collaborators*. Without passing out of the confines of northern Greece, this survey can now cross the line, which it has already closely approached, into the sphere of armed collaboration in the field with the enemy occupation. Macedonia contained the seeds of all forms of collaboration with the Germans, especially those which were only manifestations of hostility towards the Communists. Most of the organisations armed by the Italians and Germans to fight against EAM/ELAS are to be found in Macedonia; from them, though they are not the best known, this section can conveniently start. They fall into two categories: those which made use of the occupation to achieve private ends, and those which came to regard the Germans as a lesser evil than the Communists.

The former category contains three members, all sprung from discontented racial minorities in the Greek population. It does not include the two contented minorities: the Turks of Western Thrace, who chose to remain when Greece and Turkey exchanged populations in 1923; and the Jews of Salonika, whom the Germans naturally made no attempt to employ but only to exterminate. The Greeks had never persecuted the

[1]See Appendix A, para. (g).

Jews, since between two races of equal genius there could be no balance
to be redressed by force; but by 1944 the Jews were almost extinct.
Unlike Yugoslavia, therefore, Greece is left with almost no religious
division, and with only three racial minorities, whose spark of nationalism
is normally feeble. The last are the Slavophone Macedonians (commonly
called Bulgarians), the Vlachs (commonly believed to be akin to the
Rumanians), and the Chams (a Moslem people commonly called
Turko-Albanians). These were poor material for the occupation authorities to exploit against Greek unity; but they did their best. From the
slavophone Macedonians were formed counter-guerilla bands in
Macedonia called "Comitadjis": a word used throughout the Balkans to
mean guerillas. These caused ELAS some irritation in Macedonia, but
would never by themselves have been formidable antagonists. From the
second group, the Vlachs in south-western Macedonia, the Italians
formed in 1941 a semi-autonomous state and an armed force known as
the "Legionaries"; thus stressing their racial kinship with the Rumanians,
who were currently oppressed by the "Legionary State" of General
Antonescu. This attempt to divide the Greek nation was a pitiful failure,
for the discontent of the Vlachs was inconsiderable. The whole fabrication
crumbled in 1942 almost before ELAS had time to suppress it. The third
group, the Chams, do not strictly belong to Macedonia but to Epirus;
but this is the most convenient place to consider them, especially as the
frontier question between Greece and Albania has similarities in principle
to that between Greece and her other northern neighbours. The Chams
were not Albanian by blood, but Greeks of mixed blood who had become
Mohammedanised during the Turkish occupation, when southern
Epirus lay in the Albanian Pashalik and was administered by an Albanian
Governor. Since both Hitler and Mussolini had adopted the Moslem
world into their protection, it was natural that the occupation should try
to make trouble between the Chams and the Orthodox Greeks. But they
were not successful, partly because the Chams were a wealthy community
disinclined to risk a fight with anyone; partly because General Zervas
found them a nuisance in his area, and in 1944 ejected most of them in a
short and bloody campaign. They took refuge across the border in
Albania, whose post-war government became their champion in virtue
not of any blood relationship, but of their value in the international game
of Tom Tiddler's Ground on Greece's northern frontier. Such were the
three pathetic attempts made by the Axis to scrape together armed support
from racial discontent.

The second category contains the Greek forces of Colonels Poulos
and Khrysokhöou, and the armed villagers of Mikhalagas in west
Macedonia. What they all had in common, apart from their hatred of
Communism, was a conviction that they were on the same side as the
western Allies. They considered that by accepting arms from the Germans

to fight EAM/ELAS, they were doing the Allies a service. Englishmen attached to ELAS units paid for that delusion with their lives; but the fact that ELAS once killed a New Zealander by an act of criminal negligence has obscured from the public view that other Greeks, fighting against ELAS in the field, shed even more British blood. This fact in no way derogated from their conviction of virtue on the day of liberation; for they simply did not believe that there could be British officers with ELAS and attributed the misconception to Communist propaganda. There could be no clearer illustration of the mental confusion that prevailed in Macedonia during the occupation.

Poulos and Khrysokhöou were senior officers of some reputation. It was suspected by EAM/ELAS that they were in touch with the leaders of PAO, some of whom were men of the same background; for there is a subtle freemasonry among senior officers of any regular army. Mikhalagas was a man of different type. He was a peasant from an area in which some villages are still predominantly Turkish. He was himself as fluent in Turkish as in Greek; but his movement was not a symptom of racial discontent. It sprang from the ordinary peasant's distaste for the KKE, and enjoyed the support of the villagers around him. There is another difference between Mikhalagas and the two colonels. The force of armed villagers which he commanded never took the initiative in attacking ELAS; their purpose in taking arms from the Germans was to keep ELAS out of their villages, thus protecting themselves from the depradations of the one side and the reprisals of the other. It was characteristic of Mikhalagas that his followers first shot at British officers with ELAS, because he did not believe that they were British, and afterwards saved from a German search-party two RAF pilots, because he was certain what they were. It was also characteristic that he was on personally friendly terms with the regular officer commanding the ELAS division against which he fought; for this officer, Colonel Kalambalikis, was sufficiently out of sympathy with the KKE commissars who controlled him to see a good deal of Mikhalagas' point of view.

Like Poulos and Khrysokhöou, Mikhalagas hoped, as the tide of the war turned steadily against his German patrons, to enlist the sympathy of Zervas, who was willing to give asylum to almost any victim of EAM/ELAS. A representative of these unhappy collaborators was flown across Greece in a German aeroplane to facilitate their approaches to Zervas; for the Germans were naturally ready to further any enterprise which might add to the bitterness between EAM/ELAS and its rivals. But although Zervas was disposed to sympathise, he was obliged by British advice to harden his heart. This was the first indication of the intended attitude of the Allied authorities towards such people: they were to be given a fair trial when Greece was liberated, but they could not be forgiven. That was the Allied intention; but two things went wrong with it. The first was that ELAS "liberated" Macedonia before a sufficient Allied force could be sent there. The second was that the merciless treatment which EAM/ELAS accorded to such collaborators as they caught disposed everyone afterwards to be merciful to those who still survived.

(g) *Security Battalions.* The classic example of this rule was the Security Battalions, who were almost confined to the southern part of Greece, especially the Peloponnese. They were formed in the latter half of 1943 by Ioannis Rallis, who was then Prime Minister, and after whom they were sometimes called. The influences behind them were Generals Gonatas and Pangalos, but their commanders were lesser men. They were represented as a *corps d'élite,* and they included a unit of Evzones, the kilted pride of the Greek Army. They were popular with the population of the provinces outside the resistance movement; the resistance organisations, on the other hand, unanimously denounced them with Allied approval in February 1944.[1] They owed their success to the unpopularity of the resistance movement at the time of their formation, which coincided with the civil war between ELAS and EDES. The fact that they prospered most where ELAS was dominant speaks for itself. Although EAM/ELAS and its defenders interpret that fact to prove that they alone were fighting the Germans, it does not prove anything of the sort; for the Security Battalions were not pro-German but anti-Communist. As such the villagers of southern Greece welcomed them. It is worth a chronological anticipation to study the result, so important were its consequences.

The familiar distinction must be made between those above and those below the line of political awareness, in order to estimate the criminality of this organisation. The position in 1944 was doubtful according to the letter of the law. The Rallis Government had no constitutional standing; its leader had been formally deprived of his Greek citizenship by the legitimate government in Egypt; the members of the Security Battalions had been publicly warned by the Greek and Allied authorities to lay down their arms by a specified date, under threat of being treated as war criminals; even after that date the warnings had been repeated on several occasions by two successive Prime Ministers of Greece, broadcasting from Egypt, as well as by Allied commanders. There could be no doubt of the proclaimed intentions of the Allies; the commanders of the Security Battalions knew what to expect. Below the line there may have been misunderstanding; for those above it there was no excuse. They sinned against the light, and they persisted in their sin because Rallis let it be known that the Allied proclamations were a bluff; that he was in touch with the British authorities, and everything would be all right. This rumour appalled EAM/ELAS. Their leaders repeatedly asked for British

[1]See Appendix E.

assurances that it was unfounded; they repeatedly disbelieved those that they received. When liberation came, events did little to dispel their disbelief: the trouble was that there was no law that the formation of the Security Battalions had infringed.

At first the treatment of the Security Battalions after the liberation coincided with the announced intentions of the Allies. They were disarmed and confined to await trial. But when the revolution of December 1944 broke out the situation altered in two ways. First, a great many of them escaped; second, the behaviour of EAM/ELAS (and especially OPLA) convinced people with short memories that there was a lot to be said for the Security Battalions after all. When order was restored in 1945, and the treatment of collaborators became a matter for the Greek Government, there was an inclination not only to forgive them but to reward them. Decorations and promotion, denied to Greek officers who had served in the resistance organisations, were conferred on those who had served in the Security Battalions. When the services of the commander of the Peloponnesian Security Battalions, Colonel Papadhongonas, were cited in the Gazette in connection with his posthumous promotion by two ranks, the matter became such a public scandal that the order had to be reversed; but more discreet examples passed unhindered. The effect upon thoughtful Greeks was not only a profound shock, but an inclination to blame the British.

The inclination was natural, but British culpability went no farther than a failure to give sufficient consideration to the gravity of the question. There was no calculated policy of protecting collaborators, because in detail there was no calculated policy at all. Two arguments against British intervention are unassailable. In the first place, it was purely a Greek affair; in the second place, there was no article of Greek law under which those who served in the Security Battalions could have been indicted. No lawyer could wish for a better defence of British abstention from interference: but there are two points which it does not touch. The first is that if the threat to treat the Security Battalions as criminals could not legally be executed, it should not have been made; the second is that the British authorities approved its publication, and associated themselves with it. The Greek Prime Minister in 1944 could not address his people over the wireless without the express consent of the British authorities. Even if they were not responsible for what he said, they knew that all Greece would assume their agreement. Such agreement was asserted in general terms during 1944 by General Eisenhower and General Wilson, speaking on behalf of the two inter-Allied commands in Europe. But the British authorities were even more deeply committed. In February 1944 a document denouncing the Security Battalions was signed not only by representatives of all the resistance movements, but also by the authorised representative of the Greek High Command in Egypt and the

British authorities, and by an American officer on behalf of the US authorities.[1] The phrase "instruments of the enemy" was also applied to the Security Battalions over British signatures by the Caserta Agreement in September 1944.[2] These commitments were never repudiated: they were quietly forgotten; but not by the Greek resistance.

The logic is inescapable. It may have been right to threaten the Security Battalions with punishment; it may have been right to let them off: but it cannot have been both. The British authorities were at least morally, if not juridically, at fault in ignoring the generosity of the Greek authorities in 1945 towards those who had served in the Security Battalions. This must be said with no vindictiveness against the members of the Security Battalions, but in justice to the Greek people: not so much because they are to blame for having joined the Security Battalions under provocation in the first place, as because they *persisted* in committing what they were warned was a crime. The rank and file ought not to be victimised for what they did, any more than the rank and file of ELAS for what they did; but the leaders could and should have been punished, and the British authorities could and should have exercised the pressure required of them by their own responsibility. There is something incongruous about the persistence with which HMG addressed protests to other Balkan countries about their domestic conduct, in comparison with the official silence in which it accepted the disregard by each successive Greek Government of their obligations to punish men whom they had already formally stigmatised as traitors. This is one of the worst sores to be presented for inspection, and one whose accumulated poison has not grown less deadly.

(*h*) *Military Missions.* Perhaps not every British officer who served in Greece during the occupation would agree with the foregoing judgments. There were often differences of opinion among them, if only because one unique characteristic set them apart from all similar missions to the Balkan guerillas: they were accredited, as a single unit under a single command in the field, not to this or that one of the rival guerilla groups, but to all of them collectively. But although they are the last of the participants to be introduced upon this last of the four stages, not much will be said about them here or hereafter. This is not because they had no influence on events; their conduct and example had a great influence. It is for two other reasons. The first is that I am prejudiced in their case, having been their second-in-command (under Brigadier E. C. Myers) for nearly a year, and their commander for more than another year. The second is that it is incongruous to mention them without devoting several chapters

---

[1]The last two were myself and Major G. K. Wines respectively: the document will be found in Appendix E.

[2]See Appendix H, para. (1) (*e*).

to the things they were really sent to Greece to do, which had nothing to do with politics and much with winning the war. From this I am debarred by the unanimous assurances of those who know, that no one wants to read about such things any more. There are therefore only one or two points of strict relevance to this work to be made.

Most of them entered Greece for the first time with no previous knowledge of the country, the people or the language. They came by their task accidentally, when the first twelve of them were dropped by parachute to attack the Gorgopotamos viaduct, and afterwards, the operation having proved successful and evacuation difficult, were left in Greece without warning to carry on a different mission.[1] Few of them had political opinions, but their unconscious sympathies were rather to the left than the right. What formed their prejudices was not how they thought but whom they liked. In most cases, that meant whatever guerillas they were with. If the unit was bad, they left it; if they were bad, they were relieved; if the two were incompatible, an interchange was arranged. That was the only way the guerilla war could work. One other characteristic was also essential. They had, in common with other irregular units operating in the Eastern Mediterranean, a levity of outlook upon their grim life, which at its best enchanted the common Greek population with a sense of sympathy, but at its worst inspired serious-minded Greeks with angry despair. The latter were sometimes right in detecting a tacit assumption that Mediterranean countries were designed as playgrounds for adventure-seeking *herrenvolk*. This spirit still permeates most books written at second hand on the subject, and even some written at first hand; but most Englishmen engaged in such operations grew out of it, leaving a minor handful of journalists and MPs to grow into it.

The last important point is that only one of them was ever sent into the country on a specifically political mission; and by a tragic irony he was one of the few killed in action. With the exception of two or three at the top, none of them received any political brief or was authorised to make any political pronouncement. From the day the first of them arrived in Greece on 1st October, 1942 their task was to fight the occupation: later, under pressure of political complications, it was enlarged to military liaison; but it was never specifically political. Their name, therefore, was British Liaison Officers, or BLOS; their unit was the British Military Mission to the Greek guerillas, or BMM. Only their name, and not their politically neuter nature, was altered when they were transformed, by the arrival of American officers in 1943, into Allied Liaison Officers, and their unit into the AMM. But they could not even open their mouths

---

[1] I was myself the single exception, being the only British officer in the party destined from the start to remain in Greece. By 1944 the force numbered nearly four hundred officers and other ranks of various nationalities.

without finding their remarks interpreted as having political significance and official sanction. It has therefore not been possible, as they would have wished, to leave them out of this survey altogether.

Now that the introduction of the participants who were actually on the stage in the four scenes of action is complete, one common fact stands out. Most of them had a double relation: a lateral relation with those present on the same stage as themselves, and a vertical relation with those belonging to the same category as themselves on the other three stages. This can be seen most clearly in the case of the last participant introduced, the Allied Liaison Officer, or ALO. He had a lateral relation with the guerillas among whom he lived, and a vertical relation with his HQ in Egypt and the Government to which he was ultimately responsible in London or Washington. Not all the systems of relations were complete, but they were all intricate; and they had two effects which can again be illustrated in the case of the ALO. The first was caution in committing himself to anything for which he was responsible vertically, so that decisions were often delayed and enterprises of great pith and moment were apt to lose the name of action. The second was that it was sometimes not clear, even to himself, what he meant by the word "we": since it could refer equally, and sometimes did so indiscriminately, to the guerillas and himself collectively, or to his own authorities and himself collectively. This dual relation produced some confusion not only in the words but in the thoughts of everyone who has so far been introduced.

5. VOICES OFF.

But the process of introduction is even now not complete: there remain the voices off. Although this survey, like the circumstances it describes, has so far made Greek politics look like an exclusively Anglo-Greek affair, they are in fact an international affair. All the United Nations have a stake in the Greek question, because it is one that becomes periodically liable to break up the structure of their organisation. This fact was first emphatically illustrated to the public when the Greek question was debated by the Security Council in January 1946, and again when a commission representing eleven United Nations was sent in January 1947 to investigate the state of Greece's northern frontiers. This was the culmination of an awakening which began in 1945. The British Dominions were among the most active newcomers to the Greek problem: Australia and New Zealand had memories of comradeship-in-arms from 1941; Canada opened an Embassy in Athens in 1945, and South Africa a Legation in 1946; South Africans joined the British contingent in supervising the Greek elections of March 1946. France too created a new interest for herself by participating in the supervision of the elections with Great Britain and the USA; in addition to a close association through the international relations of trade unions, and the long-standing interest of French merchants in the export of Greek wine. During the war, however, the number of voices off that affected Greek affairs was limited to two on each side: Germany and Italy as the occupying powers; the USA and the USSR as the largest of the Allies.

(a) *The Axis*. The conduct of the first two speaks for itself. Their object was to exploit Greece for their war effort, and to crush resistance by dividing the Greek people against itself. The Italians, however, complicated the matter for themselves and everyone else by capitulating in September 1943. The effect in Greece, as well as elsewhere, was that the Germans then had the additional task of dividing the Italians against themselves. One Italian division (the Pinerolo, under General Infante) with a handful of hangers-on, instantly changed sides, while the rest of the Italians in Greece surrendered to the Germans. General Infante, who had served as Italian Military Attaché in London and Washington, knew well enough to which side he belonged at heart, and had the satisfaction of knowing that his initiative was sanctioned by his own High Command. But he only signed an agreement with the Greek guerillas because it was sponsored by the British Military Mission at their side; between himself and ELAS, which he had fought bitterly in the past, there could be no real confidence. Twelve thousand well-equipped Italians were more than the guerillas could stomach in their midst, well though some of them proceeded to fight against the Germans. Within a month of the signature of the agreement, EAM/ELAS had contrived to carve up General Infante's men into isolated units which could easily be disarmed. Infante's protests were received with sympathy and evasion; until on 14th October, ELAS GHQ agreed in the morning to give the Italians a separate sector, and disarmed them in the afternoon. The effect of this first of all essays in co-belligerence was that ELAS had an addition to its armoury of twelve thousand modern weapons, and the starving Greeks had an addition to their population of twelve thousand helpless Italians. As usual the Germans were the principal gainers.

Every complication that the mind of man could devise was by then inherent in the politics of occupied Greece, so that all the Germans had to do to create confusion was to pluck an occasional string. When the guerillas were at war with each other, the Germans would insinuate into the minds of each that their own sympathies were with the other, in order to exacerbate the struggle. When civil war stopped, the Germans used the Security Battalions to start it again. Their tactics persisted up to the day of withdrawal, when the emergent political situation was clear enough to give them the opportunity for a last master-stroke. Knowing that EDES would support the legitimate Government and the British authorities, and hoping that ELAS would fight them, the Germans left behind stores of weapons and ammunition within the reach of ELAS as they withdrew, but none within the reach of EDES. So well did they calculate their plan that one ammunition dump was left within a few hundred yards of the boundary between the two, with the certainty that ELAS would reach it first. These stocks played a part in bringing the revolution of December 1944 near to success. But there was no criminal compact between the Germans and the KKE: the matter was at once simpler and subtler than that. The Germans did not need such a compact; they only needed to convince the other party that there was one. The seeds of discord were already there without any action on their part. All that they needed was cultivation. The influence of the Germans upon Greek politics was thus wholly disruptive.

A cynical observer might say the same of the last two voices off, but it would be entirely unjust of the one and perhaps also of the other. The USA and the USSR both had in Greece the interests of Allies concerned to win the war, and both had historical connections with the country. If their periodical interventions in Greek affairs during the occupation seem from the British point of view to have been consistently unhelpful, two things must be remembered. One is that the British authorities did not help them to be helpful by taking them fully into their confidence. The other is that the British authorities had a monopoly of the persons of the exiled Greek authorities. To the least suspicious of men that might have looked like a monopoly of their opinions as well. Neither Americans nor Russians are, in regard to England, the least suspicious of men. When they spoke, therefore, although the tone of their voices was different, what they said was oddly similar. The fact that it was invariably echoed, and sometimes anticipated, in the English press, added to its plausibility.

(b) USA. The American authorities must be paid the compliment, which they never paid the British authorities, of acknowledging that in regard to Greece they were actuated by honourable motives. It must be assumed, as they never assumed about ourselves, that in Greece they were interested in only two things: the success of the war against the Germans, and the welfare of the Greek people after the war. If both those objects could be attained by the same means, the American people and the American Government would have been sincerely glad. American public opinion came to the conclusion that both could be attained by the same means; the means was EAM/ELAS. A part of American official opinion hesitantly concurred. In the case of public opinion, it can partly be attributed to pure ignorance, as it can in England; but in the case of official opinion that cannot be the whole explanation.

The cynical observer would incline to stress three characteristics of the process by which American opinion was formed; none of them was reproduced in England, though there were others just as harmful. The first was a Greek minority in the USA, who might be expected to know their fellow Greeks, and whose collective vote was important. This minority was inclined sympathetically towards EAM/ELAS, partly because that organisation alone paid attention to propaganda abroad; partly because it was simplest to think of Greece's gallant struggle in terms of one protagonist, and the natural one was the only organisation that extended over the whole country. The second thing was the lurking remnant of the ancient grudge against England, which encouraged propagandists of EAM to argue that they were only doing what the Americans themselves had done in 1776; the more recent parallels of Palestine and Eire gave conviction to the argument. The current form of the ancient grudge was to assume that all British diplomats were twice as slick as the plain American, and that everything the English did in any country outside their own was another manifestation of their notorious imperialism. The third thing was the American belief that kings, however ornamental at cocktail parties, were out of place on thrones. The three converged to one conclusion. EAM/ELAS had won the American-Greek minority; EAM/ELAS was regarded with disfavour by the British authorities; EAM/ELAS was opposed to the Greek monarchy. It followed that there was much to be said for EAM/ELAS. This perhaps summed up the reasoning of American public opinion, and exercised a subconscious influence on part of American official opinion.

That is the worst side of the picture. The cynical observer has been allowed his say first in order to have done with him. The whole picture is more complicated. Despite the simplification of Anglo-American disagreements over Greece into a conflict between British support of King George II and American support of republicanism, from time to time those roles were precisely reversed. When, for instance, towards the end of 1943, British persuasion had almost induced the King to let his return to Greece be subject to the Greek people's decision after the liberation, it was American influence that changed his mind at the last moment and determined him to stand firm on his constitutional rights. But this is still far from the whole picture. The reason why the whole is so confused is that the years under consideration coincided with a transition of American foreign policy. For a hundred years American foreign policy in Europe had been, as it were, a second-hand policy. It did not exist until it was known what British policy was: then it might be either the same or the opposite, but in neither case had it a positive existence. The second World War ended those happy days for the State Department; they will presumably never return. Indeed, some people fear that the reverse may happen: that twisting the lion's tail is giving way to taking the lion's share of the international burden. At any rate, the justifiable distaste of the American people for the entanglements of European diplomacy has had to be overcome.

The world first became aware that the USA had rejoined it when President Roosevelt signed the Lease-Lend Act in March 1941. The date was supremely significant to the Balkan peoples, since it coincided with the moment when the last of them was about to succumb to the Axis. President Roosevelt stressed the significance of the new outlook, so far as it affected the Eastern Mediterranean, by sending within the same year his personal representative, Colonel Donovan, to the Balkans; his son to Egypt and even Crete; and in the next year his rival, Mr. Willkie, to all that remained accessible of the Middle East. Greece recognised the significance of President Roosevelt's decisive conduct by making him a citizen of Athens and renaming one of its principal streets after him. By signing the Atlantic Charter in August of the same year, the President committed himself to a renewal of the task in which Wilson had failed. History can already confidently say that President Roosevelt succeeded: not, of course, in creating a Utopia of this world, but in making certain that whatever its fate the USA would share the task and the responsibility. That commitment of the American people is now, happily for everyone, an accomplished fact; but at the time when Greece was occupied it was only beginning.

Its progress could almost be traced in miniature by following the sequence of American representation in Greece from then until now. There too, on a small scale, the same advances and recessions and oscillations took place. Because the American authorities had no right to share Greek responsibilities with the British when the occupation began, and no inclination to do so when it ended, it is easily forgotten that between those two dates there was a fruitful period of nearly a year when they did entirely share it by representation in the Greek mountains. The first American officer to enter Greece during the occupation arrived in September 1943. Although his declared interests were confined to cavalry warfare, the KKE convinced him that crusading for EAM/ELAS against the British was practically the same thing. Before he could commit himself too deeply he was relieved in December 1943 by a more senior officer, Major Wines, whose arrival marks a turning-point. With the happy balance of an American born in the north and established in the south, he devoted himself to the inseparable tasks of understanding Greece and helping its people. He was one of the few Americans in official positions who understood at that time that these tasks were not only not incompatible with working alongside the British, but were actually what the British were also trying to do. The time had not come for a general realisation of this fact by the American authorities; nor did the British authorities help them realise it. Major Wines was replaced by a still more senior officer, whose instructions implied that the best thing the representative of the USA could do was to keep out of the political quagmire and concentrate upon killing Germans. His success in doing the latter left the American view of the former unchanged when the day of liberation came. The fact that he was accompanied in the field by American troops of Greek descent was an additional complication. Some of them, while enjoying the prestige of American citizenship and American uniform, could not avoid becoming recognised and involved as Greeks: one of them, for instance, was the exiled Prime Minister's son. It was a weakness of many Greek agents that they liked to please a foreigner by telling him what he wanted to hear, whether it was true or not. They had treated the British to the same courtesy; but when the British first came to Greece in 1942, it was not yet certain what they would like to hear, so their diet of propaganda contained variety. When the first Americans came in 1943, it was already believed that American sympathies lay with EAM/ELAS; the American-Greeks sent by the USA to Greece thus became an innocent channel for KKE propaganda. American official opinion was therefore in a muddle on the day of Greece's liberation; but it was a muddle for which they were inclined to blame the British rather than EAM/ELAS.

When Greece was liberated, the USA enjoyed two advantages over all other comers. One was that their Ambassador, Mr. Lincoln MacVeagh, had a longer acquaintance with Greek affairs than any other foreign diplomat in Athens. The other was that the bulk of the relief supplies, without which Greece could not survive, came from America. These advantages were partially offset by two British advantages: the enormous majority of troops in the country were British; and the Greek Government would not take a step without British advice. The tragedy was that these should be called "advantages." If they had been divided equally between the USA and Britain, there would have been no sense of rivalry, and no chance for opportunists to drive a wedge between them. There would have been a common policy and a common responsibility; and part of the Greek tragedy could have been averted. Some of the rivalry has since been eliminated; some of the balance of advantages has been evened. American opinion changed when its Greek minority became able in 1945 to communicate again with their relations in Greece, and to find out the truth about EAM/ELAS. By 1946 it was recognised as nonsensical on the British side to regard the American authorities as ill-informed and irresponsible; and on the American side to regard the British authorities as unscrupulous imperialists. It was recognised that the Government of the USA would have to take over most of the responsibility which HMG had hitherto borne in Greece. All this had been clear to those in Greece since the beginning of 1944, when Major Wines was the representative of the USA; American responsibility was involved in many decisions jointly taken there before the end of the occupation. But official opinion changes more slowly than that of individuals, and the process of mutual education took a long time. The result was that when the USA entered at last upon their responsibility, instead of taking half they had to take the whole.

From the point of view both of Greece and Anglo-American relations, this was a tragedy. Most Greeks, including most Greek politicians, were anxious to do what they were advised, provided the advice came with one voice from London and Washington. Intricate ingenuity was devoted to interpreting the wishes of the two Governments; but not even with the inspired help of the returned emigrants known as *Brooklidhes* could any certainty be reached about those wishes, except that they must be different from whatever the two Governments said. Later criticisms will gain point if they are read not as criticisms of British or American policy as the case may be, but as criticisms of Anglo-American policy; the chief defect of which was that it did not exist. Not until 1946 did the two Governments set about contriving an Anglo-American Balkan policy into which an Anglo-American Greek policy could be integrated. The next year the whole burden passed to the USA; 1947 was too late for integration between Britain and the USA as equal partners.

(*c*) *USSR*. Why it was too late can be partially explained in the introduction of the last participant in the Greek drama, the USSR. The Union of Soviet Socialist Republics is an intentionally elastic term, whose content can expand without changing its form. For that reason it is convenient (though not yet formally correct) to include in this section all Greece's northern neighbours. The principal effect of Germany's policy of atomisation in the Balkans was, by destroying the old links that the Balkan peoples had in common, to make it easier for the USSR to fashion new and brighter links to reunite them more closely. German policy had inevitably dismembered the Balkan States, because it was committed differently to each of them. Rumania and Hungary had become irreconcilable with each other, even within the Axis, since the Vienna Award of 1940 had given Transylvania to the latter; Bulgaria was neutral to the USSR; Yugoslavia had to be carved up to provide the Balkan satellites with territorial spoils; Albania (like Greece) was recognised as part of Italy's *lebensraum*. It was impossible for Hitler to impose on them all a uniform policy. The USSR, on the contrary, could use the common impulse of resistance against the Germans to generate a new, homogeneous spirit. The lesson which gave rise to the Communist resistance, and later to the Communist Governments of the Balkans, was learned by the Russians during the occupation of their own territory by the Germans: uniformity of policy emerged from uniform experience. These uniformities, which extend to the whole of Balkan life outside

Greece, in fact if not in name, are the excuse for including Greece's northern neighbours in a section devoted to the USSR. The questions which require answers can therefore be put as follows: firstly, to what extent were the activities of the extreme left in Greece directed from Moscow; secondly, what was the relation of the KKE and its satellites with their comrades in other Balkan countries?

The position of Greece in relation to the first of the questions is different from that of any other Balkan country, because except for Turkey, which is in every sense a case apart, Greece is the only one among them that has not emerged from the war with a government dominated by Communists and aligned in policy with the USSR. It is therefore not enough to rely on the *a priori* argument that because all other Balkan Communist parties are directed from Moscow, therefore the Greek Communist party is also. In the case of Greece it must be particularly remembered that for every visible policy of the USSR there is a corresponding invisible policy. The two vary independently, though they may approximate towards each other, as they do in countries where the supporters of Russian policy are already in power. This is another way of explaining the difference that sets Greece apart from the rest in their relations to the USSR. In Yugoslavia, Bulgaria and the rest visible and invisible policy can be allowed more or less to coincide, because the local Communist parties are in more or less complete control. In Greece they cannot, because declared opponents of Communism are in power. The USSR is obliged by diplomatic formality to recognise a Greek Government which it would prefer to see removed, and to conduct its real policy under cover. At the beginning of the German occupation of the Balkans, this was the position of the USSR *vis-à-vis* all the Balkan Governments; but in all except Greece it is no longer the case. This is the formal reason why the KKE was not *ab initio* included in Cominform, when it was set up in October 1947; for Cominform was a creation of visible policy, which had no necessary connection with the invisible policy concurrently pursued by the Soviet Government.

In pointing the contrast between the visible and invisible policies of the USSR, there is some danger of Anglo-Saxon hypocrisy. Every country has private policies which it keeps to itself. But the difference between the practices of the USSR and (say) the USA and Great Britain is one of kind rather than degree. The American and British Governments both have secrets which they do not want to air in public: but they do not (except to deceive their enemies in time of war) cover these secrets with a camouflage of falsification, designed to represent them as something different. If they do not want to talk about them, they keep off the subject altogether: they do not go out of their way to insist that black is white. Nor would they succeed in disguising their invisible policy as a different visible policy if they tried; at least so long as they are subject to a free press. In the USSR the organs of publicity can be used as a part of the conspiracy of silence or distortion: in the west that is impossible. The technique of diplomatic secrecy is therefore different between the USSR and the western democracies; it is in this sense that I distinguish the visible from the invisible policy of the USSR in the Balkans.

The foregoing paragraphs to some extent beg the main question, in order to reinforce one important point: that no *overt* evidence can have much relevance to the question of Russian relations with Communist parties in non-Communist countries. Everyone assumes them to exist; everyone would be surprised if they did not; but they can never be proved from the kind of evidence that makes up the daily material of newspapers. The USSR can always point in reply to its visible policy, and deny the existence of its invisible policy; no evidence derived exclusively from the visible sphere of international politics can have any relevance one way or the other. To take a concrete example, when the Secretary-General of the KKE announced at the Seventh Party Congress in Athens in October 1945 that his party did not take its instructions from Moscow, no statement could have shed less light on the question; for the probability that he would have made it if it were true, and the probability that he would have made it if it were not true, are precisely equal. The statement was an act of visible policy; the truth is a fact of invisible policy. There is no connection, either of validation or of invalidation, between them.

But there are two clues, of which the second is an extension of the first. The first is the uniformity of Communist tactics which emerges from uniform circumstances. If we except Greece in order not to beg the question again, the conduct of the Communist parties in the Balkans has been nearly identical since the entry of the USSR into the second World War. What was sauce for the goose was sauce for the gander: what went in Bulgaria or Yugoslavia went in Rumania or Albania. In this sense the USSR alone can be said to have a Balkan policy, instead of simply having, as Britain has had, a Yugoslav policy, a Bulgarian policy, an Albanian policy and so on. Mr. Churchill revealed the difference of principle in the House of Commons on 25th May, 1944, when he remarked of our attitude towards Greece and Yugoslavia: "In one place we support a king, in another a Communist . . . There is no attempt by us to enforce particular ideologies." Those words described a democratic policy; but the actions of the USSR, although not democratic in our sense, made a more consistent and tidy policy. To the atomising policy of the Germans, they opposed a synthesising policy of their own: HMG only had a policy of rival atomisation. It is therefore possible in the case of Soviet policy to make deductions which are impossible in the case of British policy. By way of an inductive generalisation from the remainder of the Balkans, a plausible conclusion can be reached about Soviet policy towards Greece.

The second clue is an application of the first to the relation between the visible and the invisible policies of the USSR. The general rule is that invisible policy only becomes visible when it has practically succeeded. While it secretly pursues its objective, it is covered by a different visible policy of words and gestures; when the objective is reached, the invisible policy replaces the visible and is itself—who knows?—perhaps replaced by another invisible. Since this may be what is to happen to Greece, it is worth examining how it has happened to Greece's neighbours. This is not an accusation of clandestine imperialism; it is a description of conduct, and very prudent conduct at that. Whether the USSR behave as they do from fear or aggressiveness is an academic question, which the second World War has exposed as being almost meaningless. Their conduct in 1939-40 towards Finland, for example, can be attributed with equal plausibility to either motive; so can their conduct in 1941-45 towards the Balkans. What matters is what they do and what they are likely to do. The task of predicting the course of Soviet policy in Greece is made easier by the fact that in the rest of the Balkans invisible policy has already graduated into visibility. Visible policy towards Greece still coincides with the visible policy maintained towards Yugoslavia and Bulgaria during the war; but in Yugoslavia and Bulgaria the invisible policy which was then covered has now become visible. By comparing what happened there with what is happening in Greece, a probable conclusion can be drawn for the whole of the Balkans.

The visible policy of the USSR when they first entered the war was not encouraging to an orthodox Balkan Communist. It looked as if the fear of defeat had driven the Soviet Government to compound with reaction both at home and abroad. At home, an early consequence of the war was the restoration of religious freedom and of the State's relations with both Orthodox and Moslem faith. In the army political commissars were abolished; badges of rank, regimental insignia, decorations and orders were restored; regulations prohibited entering cinemas or other public places with badly pressed uniforms or badly polished buttons. In foreign affairs the Soviet Government showed an unorthodox amenability towards the policy of its capitalist Allies. Instead of ignoring the imperialist war in 1941, the USSR openly condemned Bulgaria for adhering to the Axis, and informed the Hungarian Government that their share in the attack on Yugoslavia had created a particularly bad impression. The revolutionary Government of General Simovitch in Yugoslavia, which in the eyes of a Communist was hardly less reactionary than its predecessor, was offered a military alliance while Germany was preparing to attack Yugoslavia. It was explicitly recognised in exile; its diplomats were enabled to escape from Axis territory by the neutral Government of the USSR. In announcing their respect for the independence of the Yugoslavs, Poles, Czechs and Greeks, the Soviet Government expressed its interest in their restoration "on a national basis without interference in their internal regime." Before the end of 1942 the USSR supported the British and American Governments in a declaration of similar intentions towards Albania. Still more troublesome to the orthodox conscience of Balkan Communism were the agreement signed with the British Government on 12th July, 1941 and the Anglo-Russian treaty of 11th June, 1942. These concessions to heresy were rubbed in by the joint invasion of Iran in August 1941; by the elevation of the representatives of the USA and the USSR at each other's capitals from the rank of Minister to that of Ambassador; and by the exceptionally cordial treatment of Allied diplomats, even down to the Ambassador of Russia's least friendly neighbour and Britain's most important neutral, Turkey. The culminating blow to the orthodox supporter of Communism in the Balkans was the dissolution of the Third International, which had been his headquarters in Moscow, on 15th May, 1943.[1]

But all this was on the surface. Below the surface, the Soviet Government always had been in more intimate contact with Communist parties abroad; there has been no reason to suppose that the dissolution of the Third International affected that contact. It was taken for granted by the Germans that the principal resistance would come from Communists under Soviet guidance. Every round-up of suspects by the Germans in Sofia or Belgrade was described as an operation against the Communists; even the guerillas of General Mihailovitch fell into the same category. But it was only after large areas of Russian territory had been occupied by the enemy that the potentialities of these contacts with Balkan Communists came to be fully realised. Having learned, from personal experience in Byelorussia and the Ukraine, the value of guerillas behind the enemy lines, both to attack communications and to preserve the spiritual unity of occupied peoples with the USSR, the Soviet Government applied the same lesson in the occupied Balkans. A Pan-Slav Committee was set up in Moscow to issue co-ordinated encouragement and exhortation to the various countries. Resistance had already begun in all of them; but its value as an instrument of Soviet policy was not exploited until experience on Russian soil had shown the way. The campaign to capture the political leadership of the Balkans through the resistance movements was planned in 1942 and executed in 1943; it reached fruition in 1944. By then Yugoslavia was dominated by Tito, and Albania by Enver Hoxha. Even in Bulgaria a strong movement had been created, associated with two almost forgotten names that were soon to renew their significance: Georgiev, who had led the revolution of 1934, and Dimitrov, the hero of the Reichstag fire trial. These were

[1] It was not announced until 22nd May.

the men who conducted the invisible policy of the USSR in the Balkans, while the visible policy of words and gestures remained unaltered on the surface until the time was ripe. Diplomatic relations were maintained by the USSR with the established Governments of Yugoslavia in exile and Bulgaria under the Axis. But when the Allies sought the help of Moscow in bringing together the rival guerillas of Yugoslavia in May 1943, the first ominous evasions were met, on the grounds that it was unwarrantable for the Allied Governments to interfere with the internal affairs of other countries. This was the first symptom in Yugoslav affairs of the coming emergence of invisible policy to the visible level. A few other examples are worth recording for the parallel with Greece.

In November 1943 Tito set up in Yugoslavia an Executive Committee of National Liberation, invested with the status of a temporary Government and responsible to a Partisan Assembly having the functions of a parliament. This step was applauded in the USSR. Less than three weeks later, Moscow Radio announced the dispatch of a military mission to Tito's headquarters. Tito assured the head of the British Military Mission already with him that he had no intention of making Yugoslavia an appendage of the USSR, and hinted at future economic concessions to Britain in return for post-war relief. In April 1944, again with Soviet approval, the Committee of National Liberation sought to establish its status by requesting representation in UNRRA, and asking that the credits of the Yugoslav National Bank in London should be blocked. In June the deadlock between this shadow Government and the powerless Government in exile appeared to be broken when Tito (by permission of the Soviet Government) and Shubasitch (by permission of King Peter) met to negotiate in Italy. A new coalition was formed on paper and the dispute appeared to end. Nevertheless, Tito had the whip-hand and King Peter had nothing but the name: before the end of the year, the USSR had recognised Tito's Government, and within two years the Karageorgevitch dynasty had been abolished.

The parallel of Greco-Soviet relations with the account given in the last paragraph is precise up to the last sentence. The difference is that the invisible policy of the USSR towards Greece has not broken the surface of visibility because it has not achieved success. It has several times come near the surface; it has even come near success; and in spite of failure it is still persisting in the same object. A brief survey of the interest displayed by the USSR in Greece during the last few years will confirm the identity of the visible policy with that outlined above; and a few clues will be shown to point also to the identity of the invisible policy, which never became visible because it did not succeed.

Almost the first public reference to guerilla activity in Greece was a Russian report in August 1942, which estimated the number of guerillas at 30,000. This was almost exactly the date at which organised guerillas first took the field. Two months later British officers became the first to make direct contact with the Greek guerillas; a long silence followed on the part of the Russians. The next significant event took place in the summer of 1943, when congresses of EAM and ELAS in the Greek mountains were attended by representatives of Yugoslav, Bulgarian and Albanian partisans. Still there were no Russian representatives; the Soviet Government courteously went through the pretence of seeking all its information about the Greek resistance movement from HMG. When civil war broke out in the Greek mountains between the rival guerillas at the end of 1943, Moscow Radio supported HMG's appeals for unity in its broadcast on New Year's Day 1944. After that the invisible policy began to protrude its head in a way that was unmistakably similar to what had happened in Yugoslavia.

When EAM/ELAS set up its Shadow Government in the mountains under the title of PEEA (Political Committee of National Liberation) in March 1944, the Soviet press acclaimed it and began to denounce the "reactionary" Government of Tsoudheros in Cairo. The same had happened when Tito took the same step: in both cases the "reactionary" Government soon fell. When HMG sought, on 5th May, 1944, to discuss the danger of a divergence of policy towards Greece, the Soviet Government argued that it would be improper to join in making public pronouncements on political matters in Greece. The same reply had been made to similar suggestions of co-operation in reuniting the Yugoslavs. In July 1944 a Soviet Military Mission (detached from Tito's headquarters) arrived at ELAS GHQ. Its arrival was soon followed by an event parallel to the Tito-Shubasitch agreement of the same date. For some weeks the leaders of EAM/ELAS had been ostentatiously hesitating to join a Coalition Government, which Papandhreou had formed in succession to Tsoudheros. Within a month of the arrival of the Soviet Mission they decided to accept office under Papandhreou. Up to this point the parallel with Yugoslavia had been exact: but it then broke down. When revolution broke out in Athens in December 1944 the USSR took no steps to recognise or help the Greek Communists, as the example of Tito's success had led everyone to expect. Representatives of the KKE appealed in Sofia and Belgrade for the assistance of the Red Army or Tito's Partisans; but they were refused. The invisible policy of the USSR was not ready after all to break the surface in Greece.

The reasons were simple. One was that the Yalta conference was about to take place; the other was that British troops were already in occupation of Greece. To have supported the KKE at that moment would have entailed a dislocation of the course of Allied relations; a public outbreak, in fact, of contradiction between visible and invisible policy. The war with Germany still did not allow the risk of a rupture with the western Allies over a matter on which for the first time the British authorities seemed to have made up their minds. HMG had allowed the rest of the Balkans to fall into the USSR's lap; but Greece it was obviously determined to save. From the view-point of Soviet foreign policy this determination was illogical, but since it was the case December 1944 was no time to oppose it. The KKE had chosen their time badly, almost certainly without consulting the USSR, and the penalty of their folly had to be paid. True children of nature, the USSR abhor a vacuum, and hasten to fill it wherever they find one; but they were not prepared for the risky process of dislodging a solid body already in occupation. The invisible policy of the Soviet Government retired beneath the surface. It has not broken its invisibility again; but it has continued to exist, to grow, and to learn from experience. The last months of 1947 caused suspicions that it might be probing just below the surface in Greek Macedonia, preparing for the next opportunity.

Visible policy over the same period began as one of studied indifference, conveying the impression, almost too forcibly to be convincing, that nothing could be of less interest to the USSR than the antics of the Greeks. For more than a year after the liberation of Greece no Soviet ambassador arrived in Athens. Relations were maintained at first by the head of the same military mission that had unexpectedly arrived in the Greek mountains in July 1944. When it became obvious that he had no military function to perform, he was withdrawn. The USSR was then represented in Athens for the greater part of 1945 by the Tass News Agency, by an agency for distributing Russian films, by a Greco-Soviet league for the promotion of cultural relations, and vicariously by the Yugoslav chargé d'affaires. When this anomaly was repaired by the dispatch of an ambassador, he turned out to be an admiral surviving from the Tsarist regime. The impression created by this conduct, that the USSR was not really interested in Greek affairs (except perhaps the Dodecanese), but disliked what they knew about them, was reinforced by several incidents during 1945. When the Tass representative received a collection of propaganda documents for dissemination in Greece none of them was in Greek; all had to be translated. When the Greek Regent and Prime Minister telegraphed their congratulations to Stalin on VE-day no reply was received; a similar telegram on the same occasion from the Central Committee of EAM was politely acknowledged. The Soviet press, echoed by the press of Albania, Yugoslavia and Bulgaria, published scurrilous attacks on leading Greeks and poured scorn on Greece's territorial claims. The Soviet Government refused to join France, Britain and the USA in supervising the elections in Greece, on the ground that this constituted an interference in Greek internal affairs. But by the end of 1945 the pose of indifference gradually gave way to frank hostility. At the beginning of 1946 this manifested itself in the Security Council of the United Nations, in accusations that the Greek Government was kept in

H

office by British intervention, to the danger of the peace of the world.

This course of visible policy showed that the USSR had no hope of winning to themselves the mass of the Greek people by open means. This was the essential difference between the Greeks and those Balkan peoples which the USSR had so far successfully penetrated. Bulgars and Yugoslavs felt a racial kinship with the USSR that was independent of ideological sympathy. A Bulgar or a Yugoslav could be a Communist and a Nationalist at the same time; a Greek could not. The simplest test-case is the Macedonian question. If the Balkan Communists had their way, Macedonia would become reunited as an autonomous unit in a Balkan federation. It would be a new and enlarged Slav unit alongside a majority of other Slav units. Greece would be reduced by the loss of territory and population, and still more by the loss of Salonika. Since this is Communist policy, it is easy for a Slav nationalist to be a Communist, but impossible for a Greek nationalist. There is therefore some truth in the contention of Greek nationalists that the KKE is a fifth column in their midst. What is remarkable is that there should be such things as Greek Communists at all, since the ideology entails the resignation of patriotism. The dialectical acrobatics to which Greek Communists have been driven by questions on which all other Greeks are instinctively united, prove how hard it is to be a Greek Communist and keep a balance. Greek Communists (other than semi-Slavs such as Tzimas) need to be more sincerely devoted than Slav Communists to the pure ideology. This accounts for the personal ill-feeling prevalent between the leading Yugoslav Communist, Tito, and the leading Greek Communist, Zakhariadhis. It would consequently be impossible for the KKE to be subordinated in the Balkan hierarchy to the Yugoslav Communist Party. The belief that it is so subordinated is freely held by Greek anti-Communists, whose only interest is to denigrate the KKE; but *a priori* probability and evidence are both against this conclusion.

It is plain, however, that the Communist Parties of the Balkans work in co-ordination. It has been plausibly suggested that the Balkan branch of the Third International simply transferred its seat to Sofia when it was formally dissolved in Moscow. Pan-Balkan congresses of the Communist Parties have been held since 1943 both openly and secretly. Regular interchange of ideas and communications between Communist Parties of Greece, Yugoslavia, Albania and Bulgaria, even if it were not independently ascertainable, could be inferred from the consistency of their behaviour. When communications were difficult, the Communist Parties of the last three countries, as well as even those of Turkey and Egypt, were used as channels of communication from Moscow to the KKE. But the crucial point is that channels of communication do not constitute a chain of command. There is no evidence that instructions to the KKE were ever initiated in any other Balkan centre. Whatever form of association links the Balkan Communists, it is an association of equals. Although Cominform, when it was first set up in October 1947, was not exclusively Balkan, did not include the KKE, and had ostensibly no executive functions, it may also be cited as appearing to apply the same principle to its members. They are harnessed, if at all, in parallel and not in series.

The question whether they are harnessed at all is not one on which any reasonable man to-day has the least doubt. The fact that every Communist Party in every country in the world always marches in step (even if it has to stand on its head to do so) establishes a probability that some common impulse inspires them. In the Balkans the similarity far exceeds the possibility of chance. The common impulse may be that they are all so indoctrinated that they know what to do in any circumstances, or that they take specific orders on each occasion from some common authority. There is little difference between the two cases, since there can be no other source for either indoctrination or orders than the headquarters of international Communism. Probably both alternatives occur; in Greece at least there is some evidence for both. The whole of the KKE's political bureau, and most of its Central Committee, are known to have been trained in Moscow. Its Secretary-General, Zakhariadhis, was nominated by Moscow, and for that reason was unquestioningly restored on his release from captivity in 1945, although his deputy Siantos had conducted the affairs of the party throughout the crucial years of the war. Although some opposition to the Moscow line was developing inside the KKE, the background of these men makes it presumable that on all but the most critical occasions they could interpret the party line correctly without specific instruction. On the other hand, specially important occasions might be expected to call for direct orders; but such orders would only be communicated, probably orally, to one or two men at the top. It looked as if this was what happened in 1944, when the KKE abruptly changed its mind about joining the Government of Papandhreou three weeks after the Soviet Military Mission reached ELAS GHQ. Almost as certainly, the KKE was not specifically authorised by Moscow to launch the revolution of December 1944; so that it is not surprising that a wholesale purge of the party took place after that blunder. These are only probabilities, but their degree of probability is high.

The answers to the two questions with which this section began can therefore be given in the following working hypotheses: that whatever the vagaries of visible policy may be, the Soviet Government maintains a more persistent invisible policy through the KKE; that the invisible policy is co-ordinated with Soviet policy in other Balkan countries partly by means of ideological indoctrination and partly by means of direct orders; and that the relation between the KKE and other Balkan Communist Parties is one of brotherly equality, not of subordination. The objective of Soviet policy is a Balkan federation of autonomous units. Visible policy is a cover for this plan, with which it only begins to coincide when the plan approaches fruition. Such an approach towards fruition could be recognised in 1944, when British action checked it, and again in 1947, when American action checked it. From the Soviet view-point both those checks were regarded as temporary. They were tiresome, but the USSR was infinitely patient. One conviction may be supposed to sustain the Soviet Government: that the long-term effectiveness of those interventions would last exactly as long as the interventions themselves, and no more. On the day they ended, Greece would again become a vacuum unless they were instantly replaced, as German influence instantly replaced Italian in 1943, British instantly replaced German in 1944, and American instantly replaced British in 1947. From the view-point of Soviet policy, each of these replacements was nothing but a postponement of the day when the abhorred vacuum would recur for them to fill. That is why it will become plain that every attempt by the KKE to win power in Greece was an anticipation of the recurrence of such a vacuum. Although they failed three times, they appeared to see no reason why they should not succeed in the end. Unless the American intervention of 1947 worked a miracle, which it might do, it seemed that nothing short of a major war or the disintegration of international Communism could prevent them from being right.

With many anticipations and digressions the setting of the stages upon which the drama of Greek politics was rehearsed during the German occupation has now been completed. I say "rehearsed" because the crucial performance did not take place until Greece was liberated. Everything that happened prior to the day of liberation was a preparation, sometimes tentative, sometimes decisive, for the great day on which all the participants came together, and all the stages were reduced again to the one stage of Athens. So far only the participants have been introduced; there remains to be considered the chronological sequence of events by which they came to play their eventual roles in the tragedy. But it is already possible to summarise, in the dramatic metaphors which Greek affairs persistently invite, a few of the causes of trouble which emerge from this chapter. In one sentence, they are these: the cast of characters is too numerous; the four stages had been rehearsing four different plays; and there was no producer.

CHAPTER III

THE FIRST ACT

"Our concern, however, is neither to approve nor to disapprove, but to understand." TOYNBEE,
A Study of History.

1. *APRIL* 1941—*JANUARY* 1942.

A chronological survey must be able to keep in view at the same time all the separate scenes introduced in the last chapter. It would not be difficult to follow their trends separately, for more or less persistent labels can already be attached to the characters on them. The prevalent character of each can be defined roughly in permutations of the familiar antitheses: conservatism and revolution, royalism and republicanism, collaboration and resistance. Firstly, the dominant trend of London could be called conservative and royalist. Secondly, in Egypt it could be called republican with a conservative bias. Thirdly, in the Greek mountains a trend of republican resistance predominated with a revolutionary bias. Fourthly, in Athens an unstable equilibrium emerged from the conflict between conservative collaboration and revolutionary resistance. Of the voices off, the USA sympathised with the second; the USSR with the third. But these trends did not develop in isolation from each other, nor are their definitions rigid. Their interaction varied from practically nothing to intimate contact. The way they affected each other was often due not to what was happening in each of them, but to what was erroneously believed to be happening. Even London and Egypt were divided by this gulf; still more so were Athens and the mountains: but between either of the former and either of the latter it was immense, and only guesswork could bridge it.

The divergence is easy to see by reason of an initial coincidence. The first step taken by all the participants, wherever they were, was identical; from it they proceeded in separate directions. That first step, the repudiation of the régime of the Fourth of August, is therefore a convenient starting-point for a comparative survey. It is the one point on which every Greek, in London or Egypt, in Athens or the mountains, independently agreed. But the significance of the repudiation was different for each of them. In London and Egypt, that is to HMG and the exiled Greek authorities, its significance was primarily constitutional. Their problem, having agreed upon the extinction of the Metaxist system, was to determine what constitutional settlement should take its place, and how it should be brought about. In Athens, that is to the occupying authorities, the collaborating Government, and the people in general, its significance was primarily administrative. Their problem, when the existing machinery had been swept away, was how to run the country without it. Constitutional procedure was of even less immediate importance to them than the administration of Greece was to Greeks who had been expelled from it. In the mountains, however, that is to the resistance organisations, the significance of the repudiation had something of both these characteristics, as well as a primarily social content. Their object was to replace the old system with a new kind of administration, operated under a new constitution, to create a new way of life. But since no activities of political significance took place in the mountains until the second year of occupation, they can be temporarily left on one side. What mattered first was the constitutional significance outside Greece, and the administrative significance in Athens, of the independent decisions to abolish the régime of the Fourth of August.

(a) *Among the Greek Exiles.* Debating the constitutional question was almost the only political activity open to the Greeks in exile. Greece itself was a closed book to them, and its administration was in other hands. They themselves were guests on foreign soil; their armed forces were maintained and commanded by foreign headquarters. But where the King and his Government were, there alone could this question be legitimately discussed. Not only was it the only political matter that they were free to discuss: it was one that their own actions obliged them to settle. The constitutional question was not forced upon the late King George II and his Government by dissident minorities. It was brought upon them by the King's own actions in 1936 and 1941; it could not have been ignored by them even if no one else had ever raised it; it was already agitated among them before the republican clamour arose from their occupied country. Because this problem was embedded in every political crisis of the next few years, and implicit in every political speech, it is important to understand what it was really about. The technical aspects of it were often obscured by the irrelevant passions which it aroused.

The basis is the Constitution of 1864, the year in which King George I (grandfather of King George II and King Paul) was called to the throne. This was revised and reframed into a new Constitution in 1911, which has intermittently persisted ever since. In 1927 it was abolished and replaced by a Republican Constitution, which lasted only eight years, until the restoration of the monarchy in 1935. The Constitution of 1911 was then restored, subject to revision by a Constituent Assembly; but the disturbed state of Greek politics during the following year made it impossible for the work of revision to be carried out. On 4th August, 1936, when Metaxas determined to arrest his country's progress towards anarchy, no finality had been reached. When he presented to the King his two decrees dissolving parliament and suspending articles of the constitution, he raised a problem that should have been as disturbing to a constitutional lawyer as to a passionate democrat. The first of the two decrees was certainly legal, but only if fresh elections succeeded the dissolution: these Metaxas never held. The second of the two was the source of all subsequent complications. It suspended eight articles of the restored 1911 constitution. It was based, however, not upon the 1911 constitution itself (which provided for no such suspension), but upon a Constitutional Act passed in May 1935, which provided for such suspensions in the Republican Constitution of 1927 alone. Since this Constitutional Act could have no reference to the 1911 Constitution, the second decree of 4th August, 1936 was technically invalid.

This fact was eventually admitted by the King and his Government in exile. The first year of the occupation was spent in a gradual approach to the admission, and the next year in an attempt to work out what could be done next without losing face. These were the principal preoccupations of the exiles during 1941 and 1942. They were so, and they were bound to be so, independently of republican sniping. Even if the entire Greek world had been solidly behind the King of the Hellenes, there would still have remained for settlement the constitutional problem which he had created, by signing in 1936, and not repudiating till 1941, an illegal decree. Moreover, the monarchy was an integral part of the constitution: so that by acting unconstitutionally, he had reopened not only a question affecting the constitution, but also a question which could be made to affect his own personal position. This was the fatal embarrassment of the first year of exile, and the reason why every step towards a disentanglement of the constitutional problem was taken by the King and his ministers with circumspect hesitation. They feared that as soon as they took the decisive step of repudiating the Metaxist decree, they would thereby open the door to the Republicans. Their fear was justified; but it must be remembered that the initial irregularity was committed by the King, not manufactured by his enemies.

Even the extinction of the Fourth of August did not ease the King's problem; for its ending de facto had been no more constitutional de jure than its beginning. Having been begun by an illegal decree, it was ended in 1941 not by a formal return to the Constitution, but by the death of its founder and the anarchy of defeat in war. A complete break in constitutional continuity had to be mended. The King's dilemma was this: if he ignored the anomaly, then he was presiding over a constitutional vacuum; if he tried to rectify it, he had first to admit the irregularity of his own position and so expose himself to republican attack. While the

Greek political world watched with mingled anxiety and avidity, the King and his Prime Minister strove to bridge the dilemma with carefully chosen words. So sensitive was the political register that there was a direct connection between the development of their phraseology and the composition of their cabinet. The franker their formulae became, the farther their ministers moved away from the Metaxist tradition. When their vocabulary was exhausted, their Government collapsed. Emmanuel Tsoudheros, appointed Prime Minister in the week of the evacuation of Athens, was three years later the last, lingering, hesitant royalist in the King's Government.

The process was punctuated by moments when the King and his Prime Minister looked like winning: for instance, when the King became the hero of an adventurous escape from Crete, and won the DSO. But Crete had been bequeathed a strong republican tradition by Eleftherios Veniselos, and the scent of discord was already in the air before the King left the island in May 1941. During the occupation perhaps the last month in which the chances were decidedly favourable to the King was January 1942—a turning-point in his fortunes after which the odds declined steeply. These two dates bound the first phase of the King's problem in exile.

The first exiled Government was the recognisable heir of the Fourth of August, although it was headed by Tsoudheros, a native of the island which was the first stage of exile. There were two vice-premiers, General Mazarakis and Admiral Sakellariou, and three Generals as ministers of the three services; there were five civilians, including Maniadhakis, Nikoloudhis, and Dhimitratos, who had served prominently under Metaxas. No member of this cabinet failed to satisfy the taste of the most exacting royalist. But even before Crete was abandoned, an agitation swelled through the island for the inclusion of Veniselist liberals in the Government. The first month in Egypt revealed a rift between monarchists and republicans in exile, such as had not made itself felt (although it had existed) for the last five years in Greece. Before June 1941 was out a new Government had been formed under the same Prime Minister, who also held the portfolios of Finance and Foreign Affairs. Admiral Sakellariou was again vice-premier, and took over the Ministry of Marine as well: Dhimitratos was still Minister of Labour. The archangels of the Fourth of August, Maniadhakis and Nikoloudhis, retired from the Government, from sight, and even from Egypt; but the continued presence of Sakellariou and Dhimitratos guaranteed the persistence of the old régime. It was not until August 1941 that the first great step forward was taken: Varvaressos, a distinguished banker, was appointed Minister of Finance. He did not hold the post long, though he returned to it in still gloomier circumstances four years later; but both his appointment and his acceptance of office were signs of the rift with the past.

For several weeks the political life of the exiles was in merciful suspense, while they travelled from Egypt, by way of South Africa, to England. The service ministers, including the Minister of Merchant Marine, stayed behind because the centre of gravity of their work lay in the Middle East. The party which reached England in September consisted of King George II, the Crown Prince Paul, the Prime Minister, and the Ministers of Finance and Labour. The Greek Minister in London was invited to join them as Under-Secretary for Foreign Affairs, and the cabinet was for the time being stabilised. At this point the Prime Minister, later aided by the King, set about the task of finding appropriate words for a public attempt to bridge the constitutional dilemma.

In his first broadcast from London to occupied Greece on 7th October, Tsoudheros took the opportunity to repudiate what he called the "authoritarian exercise of power" which had (he explained) been accepted for a brief period "as a reaction against political anarchy." This distant allusion to Metaxas was heard by a small proportion of the population in Greece and passed on to the rest. They were starving for news as well as food; so far as it went, this was good news. But although it stated facts which everyone wished to believe, it did not confer constitutional finality upon them. A hint from Mr. Churchill persuaded the Greek Government that it still had to face the problem squarely. Shortly after the broadcast, Mr. Churchill addressed a letter to the Greek Prime Minister, in which he expressed his gratification that Greece had now been declared to be a democratic country under the beloved constitutional monarchy; and he added that as such it enjoyed the confidence and support of Britain. This was a gratifying letter for an exiled Prime Minister to receive, but it made one thing clear: there was to be no evasion of the implications. The constitutional problem had to be truly settled before the beloved constitutional monarchy rested on its laurels.

Tsoudheros set about sorting out the tangle. On 20th October his cabinet passed a Constitutional Act which formally restored and supplemented the Constitution of 1911; making it plain at the same time that this was a provisional measure, enforced by enemy occupation, until the Greek Parliament should be free to legislate again. The effect of this act was to confirm the invalidity both of the Republican Constitution of 1927 and of the illegal decree of 1936. It only remained to trim the last loose ends by public pronouncements from the King and his Prime Minister. The King had his opportunity on 1st January, 1942 when his New Year broadcast to Greece ended with an expression of his belief "in the return of liberty and prosperity to a free, constitutional country." To his people the words "free" and "constitutional" were the cream of his speech. The Prime Minister's opportunity came soon afterwards, when he addressed a letter to Mr. Eden on the new Constitutional Act. He explained that the continuation of government without a Parliament was now solely a temporary measure enforced by the occupation, and not a legacy of the Metaxist tradition. He added that on the return of peace two things were to take place in Greece; the establishment of a free and democratic constitution; and the replacement of his own Government. This letter, sent with the express concurrence of the King, set the tone of all future references to the last two matters. They were only clarified, never amended, by every public statement of the two men concerned.

A satisfactory step seemed to have been taken without endangering the position of the King. This agreeable result was pointed by two other events of January 1942. The first was the dismissal from the Government of the Minister of Labour, Dhimitratos, the last relic of the Metaxist heritage. The second was the signature in the presence of Mr. Eden of an agreement between the exiled Governments of Greece and Yugoslavia, by virtue of which, if all had gone well, the first step would have been taken towards a liberal federation of the Balkans. The agreement set up three "organs" of co-ordination between the two governments: a Political Organ (for foreign policy); an Economic and Financial Organ (for the development of a customs and monetary union); a Military Organ (for the planning of common defence). This document expressly envisaged the future adherence of other Balkan countries. A speech by King Peter of Yugoslavia linked it with a plan of Central European Union, which was to emerge from a similar agreement signed by the exiled Prime Ministers of Poland and Czecho-Slovakia. The prospect for the Balkans that the beginning of 1942 opened up in London foreshadowed three benefits for Greece: a stable constitution; a democratic Government; a free and amicable union with her Balkan neighbours. The frustration of that happy prospect can be traced concurrently in the occupied Balkans, where the situation was already such that the decisions made in exile bore only an academic relation to reality.

(b) *Under the Occupation.* In occupied Greece, the Metaxist régime had been abolished as decisively as in exile, but the result was different. In Athens the constitutional problem was trivial compared with the administrative breakdown. There was no effective government at all. The Germans were interested in Greece only as an area containing their lines of communication. As their thrust turned from a southward direction to an eastward direction, the importance of Greece to them as a country became smaller still. It had not, for instance, the value of Bulgaria, which provided two ports on the Black Sea for the campaign against Russia, nor the value of Rumania, which provided grain and oil. The material resources of Greece were small; even Greek man-power was not at first considered worth the trouble of draining. The German policy towards Greece was therefore simple: as long as their own narrow line of communication through the country was secure, the people could shift for themselves. At every point the Germans took the easiest way out. They let the Italians take the lion's share of occupation; they acquiesced in the monstrosities of Vlach Legionaries and Macedonian Comitadjis; they let the Bulgars help themselves to Eastern Macedonia and Western Thrace. They installed in Athens the first convenient puppet who came to hand as Prime Minister: the soldier who had let them in by signing an unauthorised armistice. General Tsolakoglou accepted the privilege of government, which he had earned by placing his signature beside those of General Jodl and General Ferrero in Salonika on 23rd April, 1941. But there was still in effect no government at all; for what the Germans would not do, Tsolakoglou could not.

Tsolakoglou tried to enlist the services of capable men, and received some help from Dhamaskinos, the new Archbishop of Athens who replaced Metaxas' nominee Khrysanthos. But few would serve him long. He sounded Panayiotis Kanellopoulos without success; he could not retain Spiliotopoulos and Dhimaratos in the Gendarmerie and Police beyond a few months; nor did Sbarounis last long as Financial Adviser to his Government. In his first declaration of policy Tsolakoglou laid almost exclusive stress on living conditions and supplies. The black market was already beyond control; this remained the fixed point of his tenure of position without power. The only powers in Athens were the German and Italian authorities, who had no policy between them beyond a competitive interest in consolidating their *lebensraum* at each other's expense. With this object, the Italians used Tsolakoglou's Minister of Finance, Gotz-amanis, as their own rival puppet, thus multiplying his impotence by two. By the autumn Greece was beyond his control. The Bulgars were exterminating the Greek population of the north-east provinces; Vlach autonomy was spreading chaos in south-west Macedonia; sabotage began both on the mainland, and especially in Crete. The Black Market became so formidable that on 21st September Tsolakoglou appointed a new Minister of the Interior to suppress it, with the aid of special courts and a special police force composed of "incorruptible ex-service men." Starvation and disregard for the law, endemic diseases of the occupation, had already established their grip.

Both evils in the end became so bad that the Germans could no longer afford to ignore them. The death-roll from starvation reached a length which could not be concealed. Greece, which had never been self-supporting, had imported 475,000 tons of wheat in 1938 and 273,000 in 1940; but in the first half of 1941 the imports amounted only to 50,000 tons, and in the second half, thanks to the occupation, they were still lower. The Swiss, Swedish and International Red Cross struggled with the problem; the Germans only attributed it to the Allied blockade. By the autumn of 1941 the pressure of neutral opinion, stimulated by the exiled Government, compelled the Germans to allow relief ships to import supplies of food, chiefly of American and Canadian origin; a measure which was demanded by humanity, but naturally delayed by the triple obstacle that the Germans were indifferent, the Turks relentlessly neutral, and the British determined to maintain their blockade. The difficulties were overcome largely by the initiative of the Greek War Relief Association of the USA; but even after ships had begun to sail in October, the starvation of Greece continued to be so appalling that a plan for the evacuation of children from the country was discussed in December. The ordinary Greek under the occupation was glad to hear that he was going to be liberated and given a democratic constitution in due course; but he was still more interested in his daily bread.

There was even more cause for gloom in the state of the world around him during the winter of 1941-2. Since the signature of the Atlantic Charter in August, news had been uniformly bad. The Russians had steadily retreated: Odessa had been captured by the Germans in October, and Moscow was declared in a state of siege a few days later. The British offensive in North Africa was petering out again. Turkey, seeing her Black Sea ports menaced from the Bulgarian coast and her Aegean ports from the Greek Islands, succumbed to the Commercial Treaty which the Germans had long and ardently pressed upon her. An important part of Greece had been incorporated in Bulgaria. A single week in December included the catastrophic opening of the war in the Far East and the declaration of war between all Greece's enemies and friends, with the singular exceptions that neutrality persisted between Bulgaria and the USSR and between Finland and the USA. Finally Yugoslavia, Greece's favourite neighbour in the Balkans, had been totally dismembered.

(c) *In the Balkan World*. It was this last fact which made the exiles' enlightened vision of a Balkan Union, based on the Greco-Yugoslav agreement, as unreal to occupied Greece as the constitutional palaver. Greece indeed still existed, even if its legitimate Government had lost touch with it; but Yugoslavia did not even exist. After Hungary, Bulgaria and Albania had taken their pickings (and Rumania had tried without success to do the same) the Germans carved the remainder into its component parts. It is a melancholy criticism of the Serb rule of Yugoslavia that the dissection presented no difficulty. The Croats welcomed it; their puppet Pavelitch worked loyally with the Germans during the greater part of the occupation. The Serbs, who did not welcome the disruption because the ruling caste of Yugoslavia had belonged almost exclusively to them, nevertheless also threw up a puppet Prime Minister who was as loyal to the Germans as Pavelitch, and more respectable. General Neditch was one of three men between whom the Serbs divided an indiscriminate fervour during the occupation, the other two being General Drazha Mihailovitch and King Peter; or rather, their fervour was undivided, for they regarded all three as equally symbols of the same ideal: Greater Serbia under the Karageorgevitch dynasty. During the occupation, as always before, Serbia stood apart from the rest of Yugoslavia in a privileged solidarity. The exiled Government was thus able to speak for Serbia, since men after its own heart ruled both the occupied capital and the free mountains; but it had no right to speak for Yugoslavia.

Several things combined to keep the exiled Government of Yugoslavia predominantly Serb. One was the fact that all the allies succumbed to the glamour of the revolutionary cabinet of General Simovitch. The British Government gave it asylum; the Government of the USA expressed open indignation to the Yugoslav Ambassador in Washington at Germany's behaviour; even the Soviet Government promised Yugoslavia the restoration of its national independence, "without interference in its internal régime." A second factor was that in the race to escape from the occupation, fewer Serb ministers than others had fallen by the wayside. The Government that arrived in England was therefore in form the same that fought the Axis, but its substance was different. A third factor was that Serb royalists had a foot in every camp: General Simovitch was in London, General Neditch in Belgrade, General Mihailovitch in the Serbian mountains. When Mihailovitch became *in absentia* War Minister in Simovitch's cabinet in December 1941, and Neditch gave up broadcasting attacks against him as a Communist bandit, the homogeneity of the Serbs attained a completeness unparalleled by any other occupied country. But it was not the unity of the Yugoslavs.

Below the surface two forms of dissidence had already begun, both initiated by the Croats. The first was purely disruptive, and depended on structural defects of Yugoslavia from which Greece was free. Under the Germans' puppet Pavelitch, the Croats already considered the hated union of Yugoslavia under the Serbs at an end. The racial schism was widened by a religious schism, in which one of the antagonistic creeds (Roman Catholicism) was shared by more than a third of the population with one of the occupying powers. This disruptive influence reached the exiles in the form of political mutinies in the armed services, which soon ceased to contribute to the Allied war effort. The second form of dissidence was still more ominous for the exiled Serbs, because it aimed not at the disruption of Yugoslavia but at its reconstruction into a new federation of all the southern Slavs, including both Bulgars and Macedonians. The movement was led by the Communist Tito (Josip Broz), who was not named until 1943, but had begun his work on the entry of the USSR into the war. This influence also reached the exiles, again first in the form of service mutinies, which left King Peter with hardly a formation to call his own. But both influences were more important on a higher level, bringing down one Government after another by disagreement on the questions which they agitated. Simovitch was succeeded by

Yovanovitch, Trifunovitch, Puritch; and finally in 1944 by the Ban of Croatia, Shubasitch, as sole Minister to negotiate with Tito.

The successive appointments were admitted stages in the weakening of Serbia's monopoly over the King's Government. Meanwhile the Germans' puppet Neditch embarrassed King Peter's Government by behaviour that was, for a collaborator, unorthodox. Instead of denouncing Mihailovitch and King Peter, he began to supply German arms to the former to fight the Communists, and commiserate over the air with the latter as a prisoner of the British. The King's own broadcasts to his people added to his difficulties. It was foolish, for instance, in his broadcast of 6th September, 1942 to denounce the Croat "collaborator" Pavelitch without also denouncing the Serb "collaborator" Neditch. It was still more foolish in a broadcast in March 1943 to provoke the wrath of the USSR by calling upon all Yugoslav guerillas to unite round Mihailovitch and "conserve their strength," at a time when Russian propaganda was clamouring for a second front in Europe. These things combined to weaken and discredit the exiled Government of King Peter. The first step towards its downfall had already been taken in January 1942, when Yovanovitch replaced Simovitch. The signature in that month of the agreement between Greece and Yugoslavia was therefore already too late: both Governments had lost effective contact with the realities which they were trying to control.

There is another, wider reason why January 1942 was already too late for the policy which that Greco-Yugoslav agreement implied. To succeed, the policy had to be a Balkan policy: but Britain had no Balkan policy; still less had the USA. HMG had a Greek policy and a Yugoslav policy; it was preparing a Bulgarian policy, a Rumanian policy, an Albanian policy, and so on. But in the circumstances it was neither democratic nor constitutional, in our sense of those words, to have a Balkan policy as a homogeneous whole. It was made impossible by two principles which characterise the traditional diplomacy of Britain towards the Governments of foreign countries: that they should manifestly represent the wishes of their people; and that they should be constitution-ally established. His Majesty's Governments, whatever their politics, have never liked to create or recognise Governments born of unconstitutional processes. British policy was therefore left during the occupation of the Balkans with its hands tied. The legitimate Governments of Greece and Yugoslavia were installed on British territory, and however unsatis-factory they might be, neither hospitality nor diplomatic orthodoxy left any alternative but to accept them. In the rest of the Balkans legitimate Governments did not exist, and in the view of HMG could not come into being until the various countries were liberated. The USSR accepted none of these limitations. Only two conditions, both unattainable, could have enabled HMG to devise a seamless policy for the Balkans as a whole. One was to determine, at least in its own mind, what specific régime it intended to support in each Balkan country when the German occupation was over; the other was to ensure that the Balkans were liberated by Anglo-American forces and not by the Red Army. In fact, HMG needed to decide more firmly and rapidly than the USSR. But on both conditions the decision of the Soviet Government was already taken; by January 1942 it was impossible for HMG, even had it wished, to assert any contrary decision of its own. Even if the Greco-Yugoslav agreement signed in that month had not been stillborn between the two Governments which HMG was able to bring to the conference table, it would still have died an early death as soon as its range was extended to the rest of the Balkans, where British influence was already vanishing.

2. JANUARY 1942—AUGUST 1943.

The bright prospects for Greece's political future in the new Balkans were therefore delusive. Neither Greek nor Balkan affairs were any longer in the condition which those prospects presupposed, and both changed steadily for the worse. Of this process in Yugoslav affairs it need only be said that it was parallel to that in Greek affairs, and more rapid. This section will trace the development of Greek affairs from the false dawn of January 1942 to the storm which broke out in March 1943, and was barely weathered by August of the same year. The width of the gulf between exiled Greeks and occupied Greece will again be apparent, and the separate courses pursued on either side of it will have to be separately mapped. But in this second phase there are points at which the two courses converged to a narrow gap that could almost be bridged. The tragedy is that the bridges were not built, and the paths again diverged more abruptly than before.

(a) *Among the Greek Exiles.* After the happy events of January 1942, the Greek Government in exile hoped that the constitutional question was shelved. The next Anglo-Greek interchange of commitments, an agreement regarding the Greek forces of the Middle East in March 1942, bore no reference to any delicate subject beyond the "complete liberation of Greece and the re-establishment of freedom and independence." At the end of March the same armed forces were reported to have received their King and Prime Minister with an ovation on Independence Day. But a shock came in April when the first important political refugee, Panayiotis Kanellopoulos, arrived in the Middle East from occupied Greece, followed soon afterwards by his colleague, Tzellos. They confirmed, what had been uneasily suspected, that a wave of republican feeling had spread over Greece with starvation and disorder; that the King and his Government needed to commit themselves more strongly to the restoration of constitutional liberties; and that a referendum on the constitution was likely to be the minimum demand of popular opinion when the occupation ended: a demand which had already been embodied in a document signed in Athens, sometimes referred to as "the protocol of 31st March." They might casually have mentioned two organisations called EAM/ELAS and EDES, which were liable to cause trouble later unless steps were taken in the right direction. It was not hard to read between the lines that the first step in the right direction would be to make Kanellopoulos a cabinet minister and his fellow-refugee Tzellos an under-secretary.

After prolonged wrangling, this was done; but not exactly on Kanellopoulos' terms. He wished to become Minister of Defence in charge of the armed forces in the Middle East. He was appointed instead Vice-Premier without portfolio, and established in Cairo to represent the cabinet of London. By taking office under the King he sacrificed the admiration of Greek exiles for a refugee from the occupation, as well as the confidence of the colleagues whom he left behind in Athens. He had, in fact, simply become one of the exiles; a new victim of the judgment that five minutes after leaving occupied Greece a man no longer enjoyed the right to speak for it. Feeling the obligation to justify himself, he made two broadcasts in May and June 1942: the first re-emphasising the extinc-tion of the Metaxist régime; the second, specifically addressed to occupied Greece, explaining his decision to take office.

Tsoudheros again reorganised his cabinet to meet the new situation. He assumed himself the Ministries of Foreign Affairs, Defence, the Interior and Labour; he substituted Admiral Kavadhias for Admiral Sakellariou as Minister of Marine; he offered an appointment to Sophoklis Veniselos, who was at the time in the USA. The last offer was not taken up till long afterwards; but like the replacement of Sakellariou, it was a decisive step away from the royalists and towards the liberals. It was perhaps part of the same policy that in June 1942 the King set out for a visit to the USA accompanied by Tsoudheros, and followed shortly afterwards by the King of Yugoslavia and his Foreign Secretary.

For several months the rot appeared to have been halted without further concessions. In September 1942 Colonel (later General) Bakirdzis turned up in the Middle East, bringing from Athens a tale not dissimilar from that of Kanellopoulos, and reinforced by his prestige with the British authorities. But one Red Colonel did not make a crisis; Bakirdzis seemed to be content with a back seat. Almost simultaneously the first British parachutists were dispatched to Greece by SOE Cairo; but that was no cause for worry yet. In October Kanellopoulos visited England, and created the impression of being able, loyal and far from revolutionary. On New Year's Day 1943 he issued an order of the day to the Greek forces in the Middle East, which could not have been excelled even by the most old-fashioned reactionary in its references to Greece's "inveterate bad neighbours," the Bulgars.

The behaviour of Greece's Balkan enemies was enough to hold any Greek Government together. The Bulgars, as the result of a visit to Berlin by their War Minister, had exchanged the disagreeable alternative of sending troops to the Eastern front for the agreeable alternative of taking over a larger area of Greece. They were consolidating Bulgarisation of Eastern Macedonia and Western Thrace by confiscating the land of those Greeks who fled, and conscripting or deporting as hostages those who stayed. The Albanians, having conceded everything to the Axis, from fine words about their place in Italy's *lebensraum* to an agreement for the construction of a military road through their territory to connect the Adriatic with Sofia and Rustchuk, had nevertheless been soothed by British assurances that their country would be "restored to independence" after the war. Greek opinion was offered the consolation that Albania's southern frontier would only be determined at the Peace Conference. But the Greeks regarded any friendly reference to Albania as an affront, although Metaxas had stated the same policy in December 1940. Incidents such as these could hold together the most dissident of Greek Ministers, and Kanellopoulos was far from that. He extended his public denunciation of Bulgaria on New Year's Day, into a private hint of disapproval to HMG about their policy towards Albania, when he revisited England in the same month. Conservative Greek opinion found no unorthodoxy to deplore in the new Vice-Premier.

Kanellopoulos' second visit to England in January 1943 was the occasion for a new attempt to clarify certain matters which his entry into the Government had again obscured. He was an avowed republican: yet a year earlier the constitutional question appeared to have been settled in favour of the King. In London Kanellopoulos specified five aims to which he considered the exiled Government to be pledged. The first was to raise the Greek armed forces in the Middle East to the highest pitch of efficiency. The second was to deal with the food shortage in Greece. The third was to solve the problem of Greek refugees from the mainland in the Middle East. The fourth was to collaborate with the United Nations in preparing the transition of Europe from war to peace. The fifth was to prepare the ground for the unhampered working "of a free constitution in the new Greece." This was a great expansion of the limited functions open to a Greek Government eighteen months before. At that earlier date none of the five aims except the last would have fallen within the effectual competence of Tsoudheros' Government. But greatly as the Government had extended its competence, the last was still the only one of the five aims which depended exclusively upon Greeks for its decision; and it had not in fact been decided at all.

Although the efforts of 1941-2 had legally reversed the blunder of

I

1936, they could not abolish the five years of history which lay between them. In 1943 memory revived among the victims, and reports of opinion in Greece were again disquieting. At this stage SOE Cairo was able to enter the debate as an informed participant, though the diversity of its sources and the differences of verdict among its members left excuses for the Greek authorities to ignore it. But on one thing every source, whether Greek or British, seemed to agree: the uninterrupted growth of republicanism. It was even suggested that the King's best policy would be to stay away from Greece when the country was liberated, on the ground that, since the first Government would be bound to fall within six months of taking office, this discredit might best be left to his enemies[1]. Whether wise or not, the advice implied a serious situation at the beginning of 1943. The intervening year had tacitly undone the ostensible achievement of January 1942; but the Greek authorities were not yet ready to admit it.

Kanellopoulos' reference to the constitution at that point was a momentary lapse. It was covered up during the following months by a systematic attempt to divert Greek curiosity from the position of the King to the position of his Government. Kanellopoulos added to his statement an explanation that his visit to London had given him the opportunity to consult with the King and the Prime Minister on their return from the USA. Their conclusion was that as soon as Greece was liberated, the present Government would relinquish its mandate to a new Government, representing "every political and social current and all parties and groups which during the occupation have shown themselves able to interpret the Greek people's will to liberation." This revised definition of the provisional character of the exiled Government was made more precise by a speech of Tsoudheros on 30th April, in which he promised to resign as soon as his Government had "brought the Greek flag back to Athens." It was left to be understood that the King would accompany the flag, for this was the accepted policy of the period. A triangular interchange of telegrams between HMG, the Greek resistance movement (through the BMM), and King George II, helped to clarify the point to those concerned.[2] The communications were not published at the time they were sent, in March 1943, because they contained nothing new: HMG only reaffirmed its support of King George II and his exiled Government, and the King reaffirmed his intention "after his return to Greece, to base himself on the will of the people." The meaning of these generalities could not be given greater precision at the time.

But vagueness was not enough for the republican elements among the exiles. The crisis was upon Tsoudheros even before the tactful

---

[1] In putting forward this suggestion myself in May 1943, I specifically referred it to EAM. In a sense the policy might be said to have been accidentally carried out in 1944-5.

[2] This was the occasion of Gen. Zervas' modification of his republican policy, referred to on p. 74.

platitudes were framed. In March 1943 mutiny took place in two Greek brigades in the Middle East, and committees of junior officers and NCOs took charge. The mutiny was not violent, nor was it designed to hinder the Allied war. The rebels demanded a new Government to prosecute the war more vigorously, and the removal and court-martial of Metaxist and defeatist officers. Their grievance was justified by the activities of a small clique of officers, once devoted to Metaxas, who had intrigued to sabotage the war effort. The rebels hoped that the British authorities would intervene to remove such men. It is therefore worth noting three new appointments, of great importance to Greek affairs, that had taken place among the British authorities just before this disturbance broke out. In February General (later Field-Marshal) Wilson, who had commanded the Imperial Forces in Greece in 1941, was appointed Commander-in-Chief, Middle East Forces. He was soon joined by his Chief of Staff, Lieut.-General Scobie, whose fame was yet to come. In March Mr. (later Sir) Reginald Leeper was appointed His Majesty's Ambassador to the Greek Government in exile. These three newcomers played a large part in the events which followed the mutinies.

The first reactions were swift and drastic, but not altogether satisfactory to the Greek authorities. British brigadiers were put in command of the two brigades; Kanellopoulos and Tzellos resigned; the King and Tsoudheros hastened to the Middle East from London; the decision was taken to redivide the Greek Government between London and Cairo, with a heavy emphasis on the latter. In April a new Government was formed, in which George Roussos replaced Kanellopoulos as Vice-Premier and Karapanayiotis became Minister of War. Although several ministries remained temporarily vacant, the Government was obviously to become predominantly republican. The objects of the mutiny were thus attained, and the mutinous troops were not severely punished. The two British brigadiers were joined by two new Greek colonels, with the ultimate object of taking over command when the trouble had been settled. 122 officers and 116 other ranks, who refused to return to duty, were interned in the Sudan; but 113 of the total number, all below the rank of captain, later repented and asked to be allowed to return. In June Greeks of the 1943 class in Egypt were called up to restore the army's numbers. In the same month a minor mutiny broke out in a destroyer, perhaps encouraged by the leniency shown towards the soldiers. The continued instability in the armed forces hampered Tsoudheros' task in completing his new cabinet.

Controversy revolved round the names of two candidates for ministerial posts. Since both were known as liberal republicans, the decision of the controversy was bound to affect the future course of Greek affairs. One was Sophoklis Veniselos, who was still in the USA; the other was Admiral Voulgaris, who subsequently became Prime Minister in

1945. In both cases the historical interest of the controversy is that it was largely fought out not between the political leaders, but between the various sects of Greek public opinion in Egypt, London and the USA. The Egyptian Greeks, being predominantly republican, pressed for the inclusion of Admiral Voulgaris; the London Greeks opposed it, fearing a one-party Government of the liberals. The Greeks of America disputed whether Sophoklis Veniselos should accept Tsoudheros' invitation to join his Government; but both sides were united in respecting Veniselos, and only divided on his best interests. In the end, the supporters of the inclusion of both won: Voulgaris became Minister of Air; Veniselos became Minister of Marine. The only major cause for anxiety was the fruitlessness of Tsoudheros' attempts to persuade the official Liberals, Populists and Progressives in Athens (led by Sophoulis, by Theotokis and Tsaldharis, and by Kaphandaris respectively) to send out representatives to the Middle East. The attempts had begun in April, but two months later no one had yet arrived, and it was impossible to wait longer. On 10th June the new Government was formally established on Egyptian soil. In the same month Varvaressos, formerly Minister of Finance, became Ambassador at large, charged with problems of post-war reconstruction. For the time being political stability again appeared to be restored.

The fall of the Yugoslav Government under Yovanovitch, in the same month in which Tsoudheros completed his new Government, reminded the Greeks that the appearance of stability was unreliable. They could read the ill omens for Yugoslavia in the refusal of the Soviet Government in May 1943 to join HMG in exercising pressure on Mihailovitch and Tito to co-operate, as well as in HMG's warnings to Mihailovitch that he would only receive further support from the Allies if he turned his activities against the Axis. But their own omens were at least better than the Yugoslavs'. At the beginning of July word came from occupied Greece that the dubious organisations of the resistance movement had united themselves under the title of "National Bands." They were reported to be sending a delegation to Egypt in the following month. Two days after the "National Bands" Agreement became known in Cairo, the King of the Hellenes took advantage of the temporary settlement of Greek affairs to make, on 4th July, his most important broadcast up to date, which was endorsed by Mr. Eden in the House of Commons three days later. The King repeated many points which had already been made by his ministers, and some he made more specific. He confirmed Tsoudheros' promises of impartiality; he confirmed that Tsoudheros' Government would resign on its arrival in Greece; he promised free elections for a Constituent Assembly within six months of that date; he repeated that the Constitution of 1911 would remain in force, until the people should have expressed its sovereign will; he added that he would himself be the first to respect the decisions of the Constituent Assembly. These words committed him more explicitly than any before. But it was the end of his speech that had the most immediate significance. "Meanwhile operations are impending," he said, "and I am confident that the Greek people will co-operate with those who land on its coasts to drive out the invader."

While he spoke, a British raiding-party was already operating on Crete, and others followed on other islands of the Aegean. Although retrospective warnings were published to the Greek people not to assume that they were about to be liberated, they could hardly have drawn any other conclusion from what their King said and what their Allies did. What in fact was in progress was a gigantic bluff to divert German attention from the impending invasion of Sicily. The Germans were successfully deceived, but almost everyone in Greece was deceived as well, with incalculably important results which will be described later. The King, however, was free after his significant broadcast to set out with an easy conscience upon a tour of inspection of his army and navy for ten days. It was only in August that he and the Anglo-Greek authorities began to reap the consequences of the two crucial events of July: the successful pretence that Greece was about to be liberated, and the decision to evacuate from the mountains a delegation representing the resistance movement.

(b) *Under the Occupation*. The roots of the crisis which followed in the Middle East are to be found in the events in occupied Greece during the period that has just been covered. The preceding crisis of March 1943 had no roots in occupied Greece, except in so far as certain minds naturally moved in sympathy; nor had it any that are verifiable in Communist agitation. But the crisis of August 1943 had roots in both. There is no connection between this derivation and the escape to the Middle East of Kanellopoulos, except as two symptoms of the same process in occupied Greece. The process may be described as a transition of Tsolakoglou's incompetence from one sphere to another. Starvation was gradually being overcome, thanks to help from abroad; but it was being succeeded in 1942 by the breakdown of law and order, and the outbreak of political resistance, both of which Tsolakoglou's Government proved as incapable of controlling as it had been of arresting starvation. The escape of Kanellopoulos and Tzellos, when they were wanted for illegal political activities, was one example of the administration's incompetence. Worse examples occurred in the following twelve months, and it was to these that the next crisis in the Middle East owed its ultimate origin.

The puppet Government had degenerated steeply throughout 1942. In March of that year Tsolakoglou reorganised it, taking charge of public security and concentrating responsibility between himself and Gotzamanis. The rivalry of these two continued to reflect the rivalry between the Germans and the Italians, and to make efficient administration impossible. Tsolakoglou was still regarded as the Germans' favourite; he therefore took conspicuous care to conciliate the Italians by the warmth of his welcome to Mussolini, who passed through Athens on his way back from Libya to Italy in August. This gesture was offset by the invitation of Gotzamanis to Berlin in September to discuss, alongside the representatives of Rumania, Croatia and Bulgaria, how best the Balkans could improve their contribution to the New Order. Nothing was achieved in Greece by these antics: the breakdown of the Government's control which attended them can be read in a brief list of events. In May 1942 the University of Athens was closed on account of the indiscipline of the students; in June outbursts of sabotage were reported all over Greece, especially on the aerodromes of Crete; in August the first attempt to recruit labour for Germany yielded less than 8,000 men; in September a bomb destroyed the premises of the Greek Nazi Party in Athens; in the same month the civil servants of Athens went on strike; in October the price of an English sovereign rose above 4,000 drachmas; in November the destruction of the Gorgopotamos viaduct temporarily stopped the use of the only railway line through Greece, thus interrupting the supply of Rommel in Africa and the transport to Germany of Greek labour. In the same month Tsolakoglou resigned. The conclusion drawn by the Germans was that it had been a mistake to allow the Italians the lion's share of control over Greece; it was soon confirmed by a similar breakdown in Italian-occupied Albania, which endured four changes of puppet government during the first five months of 1943.

The Germans sent to Athens a special commissioner, by name Neubacher, to straighten out the tangle and to replace Tsolakoglou. The Italians hastened to save face by sending a special commissioner of their own, by name Agostini; his special commission was an entirely futile attempt to restrain Neubacher. The results, apart from increasing inter-Axis friction, were meagre. Trifling successes, but no more, were won against the saboteurs whom the British sponsored in the principal towns. Bakirdzis had been compelled to withdraw from Athens; Zannas had been caught in Salonika and deported to Italy; Tsigantes was killed in a gun-battle; Koutsoyiannopoulos was captured, but rescued by the ingenuity of Ioannis Peltekis, who accompanied him to the Middle East a few months later. The Germans appointed the Austrian General Löhr to be Commander-in-Chief of south-east Europe, in order perhaps to use the traditional Balkan experience of Austrian administration, and sent a new Governor-General to Crete. The German Command of southern Greece extended its control and began to make preparations to confront an Allied invasion of the Balkans. Logothetopoulos was made Prime Minister; defences were built along the Greek coasts; the experiment in Vlach autonomy was abandoned; the surrender

of private wireless-sets in the German zone was ordered; civilian mobilisation of Greeks between the ages of 16 and 65 was decreed, and the classes
called up were sent to Germany as slave-labour. German propaganda in
the Balkans adopted the theme that Britain had sold out their interests to
the USSR. The Italian contribution to this outburst of energy was to
proclaim martial law in the Italian zone, and to declare a partial amnesty
of Greek prisoners in order to facilitate the conscription of slave-labour.
But thanks to the initiative of the KKE and EEAM the attempt at civilian
conscription was a failure. In Salonika the Germans were obliged to close
the recruiting offices, after arresting a number of students in April for
demonstrating against the decree. In Athens an outbreak of strikes under
the direction of EEAM rendered the work of conscription impossible. A
few contingents of workers were dispatched to Germany by press-gang
methods up to November 1943; but it was already obvious four months
earlier that orderly conscription had failed.

In no department of the administration was the rot checked. By
April 1943, while Hitler and Mussolini met to discuss the Balkans, and
the Germans took over control from the Italians, disaster was already
appallingly near. The Greek provinces were threatened, and the mountain-
ous parts of them entirely controlled, by the guerilla organisations of
EAM/ELAS, EDES and EKKA. Aided by British officers and supplies,
they had outgrown the phase that could be represented as unorganised
brigandage. The Germans' one relief was that much of their energy was
spent in fighting each other; but the fear that they might present a
common front against the occupation was at least intermittently realised.
The next measures which Neubacher took verged on panic. Defences
against possible invasion were hastened in Macedonia and the Peloponnese.
Logothetopoulos, who had proved a broken reed, was replaced in April
1943 by Ioannis Rallis, who took office in the conviction that his task
was to prepare the country for the early return of the Allies. The Germans
made use of his delusion to secure a partial restoration of order by the
formation of Security Battalions. He was helped in good faith by Generals
Gonatas and Pangalos, and the first reports of their results came in
July.

The vanity of these efforts was demonstrated by two other events of
the summer of 1943. In April the Germans offered an amnesty to all
Greeks who would surrender illicit weapons by 20th May; but no
weapons were surrendered. In June the Asopos railway viaduct was
destroyed, with the same effect upon German communications as the
destruction of its neighbour across the Gorgopotamos seven months
earlier. To the German High Command these two events confirmed that
control over two-thirds of the country had passed into the hands of the
Greek resistance movement. The ironic fact is that the most damaging
blow of all, the attack on the Asopos viaduct, was not carried out by the

Greek guerillas at all. This paradox will serve as a characteristic introduction to the situation which had arisen in the Greek mountains, followed by the consequences which it entailed upon Greek affairs in exile.

(c) *In the Greek Mountains.* The general character of the resistance movement in the Greek mountains has already been described. This section may be confined to its comparative maturity in the early months of 1943, when the guerillas of ELAS and EDES were already established, and those of EKKA were about to take the field. By that date three crucial events in the history of the guerillas were past: British officers had been sent by SOE Cairo to join them in October 1942; the Gorgopotamos viaduct had been destroyed in the only successful co-operation of the rivals, EDES and ELAS, in November; and in January 1943 direct contact had been made between the British and their various political leaders, especially those of the KKE, in Athens. The last two events combined to transform a handful of British officers attached to a handful of guerillas into a British Military Mission attached to a multiplicity of political armies. The pattern of their development was already well laid. The chief organisations, though not fully deployed over Greece, were firmly rooted. They were also sharply segregated, despite an attempt in December 1942 by ELAS to persuade Zervas to become its Commanderin-Chief. ELAS covered nearly four-fifths of the country with a network of guerillas: a network of wide meshes which could quickly be drawn tight. The other organisations can be pictured rather as isolated rashes of varying density: EDES in southern Epirus and western Roumeli; EKKA in southern Roumeli; Saraphis in western Thessaly. A few others were also in the field, but it was already obvious that the individualist could not survive against the big battalions; so that the many who could not bring themselves to join any of the known organisations sat at home kicking their heels. They did not draw confidence from the presence of British officers with the guerillas, for the BLO was still an unknown quantity. There were barely a score of them composing the BMM in the first months of 1943. Although the senior of them was a brigadier, they were not yet all under his command. The separation of command appeared to reflect a division of policy on at least two points among the British authorities. One was the relative value of ELAS and its rivals; the other was the function to be expected of the guerillas. These two divisions amounted compositely to a single division between those who preferred ELAS because it behaved as an army, and those who preferred its rivals because they behaved as guerillas. To such doubts the cautious stay-at-home added the consideration that British supplies also were scarce. Five or six aeroplanes a month at most could be expected to drop supplies; only a very meagre quantity of British gold was forthcoming to supplement them. There were solid grounds for hesitation about the potentialities of Greek resistance at the beginning of 1943, which adds to the credit of those who did not hesitate. But the division even among them, of those who knew where they were going from those who did not, was already marked; the horizontal line was already drawn.

The period of approximately eight months, here to be covered as a single phase of the resistance movement, was especially important from the military point of view. If this were a history of operations, it should properly be defined as extending from the destruction of the Gorgopotamos viaduct in November 1942 to the guerilla operations covering the Allied landings in Sicily in June and July 1943. These contributions by the guerillas to the strategy of the Mediterranean theatre compose the background to this account, since they were the justification for the guerillas' existence. But in a survey of political history, their importance must be taken for granted. Considered from the political point of view, the limits are slightly different. The relevant period extends from January to August 1943: from the month in which the political implications of the Greek resistance movement were first forced by events upon the attention of the Anglo-Greek authorities, to the month in which they caused the Greek political crisis in Egypt. This period may be called the first phase in the campaign of the KKE for absolute power. It is also the first period in which the British authorities came to close quarters with Greek Communism.

Two questions permeate all discussion of the relations between the British authorities and the Greek guerillas. The story of this first phase can be put in the form of answers to them. The first question, raised by supporters of the left both inside and outside Greece, is: Why did not the British authorities give more support to EAM/ELAS instead of their rivals? The second, raised by opponents of the left, is: Why did not the British authorities give more support to their rivals instead of EAM/ELAS? What is common to both questions is the conviction that it was a mistake to divide British support between irreconcilable rivals. The first part of the answer is that they could not be proved irreconcilable except by trying: it may have been true that conflict between them was eventually inevitable, but it would have been absurd to precipitate it by saying so. The more important part of the answer is that British policy had no alternative. I shall briefly show how this came about, in order to answer the two questions definitively.

In the first half of 1943, the rivals of ELAS that mattered were three: Zervas, Saraphis and Psaros. There were minor rivals in all parts of the country, such as ES and EOA in the Peloponnese, Athos Roumeliotis in Roumeli, YVE in Macedonia: but none of these presented any danger if the big three could be eliminated. Zervas, Saraphis and Psaros had characteristics in common which set them apart as dangers to the hegemony of EAM/ELAS. They were all regular officers of republican antecedents: therefore their survival presented the Greek people with an alternative to EAM if, as almost everyone then supposed, Greece should become a republic. They each commanded a rapidly growing, independent force, which was apt to attract recruits away from ELAS. Where their forces existed, they each enjoyed the confidence of the British authorities, as represented by the BMM, to a greater degree than EAM/ELAS. Zervas enjoyed these advantages from 1942, Saraphis from January 1943, and Psaros from March 1943. Where their forces did not exist, and only those of EAM/ELAS did, that is in more than half the country, ELAS enjoyed the undivided support of the British authorities and in the main justified it by their conduct. But that was not enough for the KKE, which wished to monopolise not only the areas where ELAS alone existed, but also the areas in which other forces existed. Their determination to do so was strengthened by suspicions based on two grounds: that the first BLOS were at one time all concentrated at Zervas' HQ, and that the first aeroplanes scheduled to drop supplies failed to reach ELAS more often than EDES. That both were accidents, although true,[1] was too much for EAM/ELAS to believe.

They set about eliminating their rivals with characteristic vigour. Saraphis' force was dissolved and he himself was captured with most of his staff in March 1943. Psaros' force, variously known by its military designation as the 5/42 Regiment and by its political designation as EKKA, suffered the same fate in May 1943, barely two months after its formation. Zervas' force, being the oldest and largest of the three, was treated more cautiously. Successful attempts were made to break up outlying formations of EDES; but its hard core was more than EAM/ELAS dared to attempt during this phase. One reason why Zervas' main force survived was that it was backed by the British authorities, who supplied it (as well as ELAS) with arms and small but increasing sums of money in gold. The same reason saved Saraphis and Psaros from death: Saraphis to change his mind, and accept the post of Commander-in-Chief of ELAS; Psaros to re-form his own independent force. Although Psaros was again attacked and again rescued by British support in June, the final outcome of this phase was that peace was restored between the rivals by the signature in July 1943 of the "National Bands" Agreement, by which the forces of ELAS and Zervas and Psaros were recognised by the British authorities as independent formations under the command of GHQ, Middle East. A Joint General Headquarters was set up in the mountains, comprising representatives of all three together with the commander of the BMM; and all three organisations combined to send a joint political delegation to meet the Greek exiled Government in Egypt a month later. The upshot of the six months' struggle was that EAM/ELAS had absorbed one of its rivals and failed to eliminate the

[1]This can be verified from *We Fell Among Greeks*, by Denys Hamson.

other two. These are the bare bones of the story. It is clear that the comparative failure of EAM/ELAS was attributable to British intervention. The first question is, why?

The political reasons which retrospectively justified this decision have been sketched in Chapter II[1]. What they amount to is that if EAM/ELAS had been allowed to monopolise the Greek resistance movement, Greece would have been dominated by the KKE and absorbed into the Balkan annexe of the USSR. But decisions are not always taken for the reasons by which they are justified: in this case the decision was taken for military reasons by the BMM under Brigadier Myers in the field and only endorsed for political reasons long afterwards. The Greek guerillas were supposed to be organised to fight the enemy occupation; the fog of political controversy has obscured the fact that they actually did so. The distrust felt by the BMM towards ELAS units in areas where they coexisted with their rivals was based not upon the conviction that they were Communists (which most of them were not) or that they were politically unreliable (a judgment which meant nothing to nine BLOS out of ten), but upon the fact that they could not be relied upon to fight the enemy in the way that the strategy of the Middle East Command required. This does not apply fully to the areas where only ELAS existed; nor does it mean that ELAS units would not fight the enemy at all. It means only that in the areas where both ELAS and their rivals existed, the latter proved more dependable as military units.

The BMM attributed this difference to a contrast in structure. The forces of Saraphis (while they existed) and Zervas and Psaros were commanded by trained officers. At that time the forces of ELAS were commanded by committees of three, two of whom were always Communists and the third usually a nonentity. EAM/ELAS themselves admitted the military superiority of Zervas by their repeated attempts to induce him to become C-in-C of ELAS; but these attempts always broke down, on EAM/ELAS' side because they objected to Zervas' allegiance to Plastiras and his practice of paying his men, and on Zervas' side because he objected to tripartite command. Nevertheless, his ability justified their anxiety to absorb his force, for he was the first to grasp the essence of guerilla operations. While the amateur strategists of ELAS set about building up army corps and divisions, which were useless for guerilla fighting but excellent for imposing martial law on the mountains, Zervas deployed his forces in small guerilla bands commanded by comparatively independent junior officers. The full contrast between the two is subtle and complex: words such as "centralised" and "decentralised" do not adequately explain it. ELAS, for example, could be either centralised or decentralised, in whatever degree suited it. Since each HQ at each level contained a representative of the KKE, all equally indoctrinated with the

[1]See page 82.

party discipline, it was possible when necessary to take crucial decisions at comparatively low levels; but since the chain of command was also a military hierarchy, the simplest decisions could reasonably be referred to higher authority when it was not convenient to take them. In a different way the same contrast applied to Zervas' force. There the uniformity at each level was provided by the military background of the trained officer; although Zervas kept all the reins in his own hands, it was known throughout his force that no decision at any level could be wrong if it were sanctioned by a BLO. EAM/ELAS was organically decentralised and operationally centralised; EDES was on the contrary organically centralised and operationally decentralised. Zervas' force thus possessed the advantage both of military experience and guerilla technique, but the disadvantage of not expanding easily. ELAS had the converse disadvantage as well as the converse advantage; and the respective advantages exercised a conflicting attraction upon various elements of the British authorities, both in the BMM, which tended to prefer that of Zervas, and in SOE Cairo, which tended to prefer that of ELAS. Success at the Gorgopotamos viaduct gave an impulse to the formation of a large, centralised army, from which ELAS was the natural beneficiary; and by encouraging this development SOE Cairo incidentally stultified its own control over the resistance movement. There was, in fact, a conscious alliance of principle between Zervas and the BMM, and an unconscious one between ELAS and SOE Cairo; the former working more slowly than the latter, and finally succumbing to it altogether. This competition eventually forced Zervas to change his organisation; but during the first half of 1943 it was nearly ideally adapted to its purpose of harassing the occupation within a small area. It was hoped by the BMM that Psaros and Saraphis would serve the same purpose, because in other ways they closely resembled Zervas; but at the time of their first submission to ELAS the hope had not yet been justified, and it was later entirely disappointed.

EAM/ELAS wisely allowed the same principle to operate in some units outside the areas where they coexisted with their rivals. Having a larger force at their disposal, they could detach units to please the BMM by operating in the way the British recommended, while the bulk of ELAS remained available for their own purpose of consolidating their control of the country. It was possible for them to win the approval of observers confined to a partial view, while at the same time fighting Zervas and imposing their will upon the countryside with the main body of their army. Smaller forces could only defend themselves against ELAS by devoting every man and gun to the task; so that when a civil war was in progress, the admirers of EAM/ELAS could point to the fact that they were at least doing something against the Germans at the same time, while Zervas (or whoever it might be) was doing nothing but fight ELAS.

This re-emphasises what has been said already: that for the leaders of EAM/ELAS (though not for many of their followers, whose enthusiasm was so easy to exploit), fighting the Germans was a secondary consideration, to be undertaken only for purposes subservient to the primary objective of winning political power.

An illustration of the principle is provided by comparison of the two most important operations undertaken during the first year of guerilla activity. The first was the destruction of the Gorgopotamos viaduct in November 1942; the second was the destruction of the Asopos viaduct in June 1943.[1] These two operations achieved the same result on the same railway line; but the former was carried out jointly by a British force and guerillas of both EDES and ELAS; the second was carried out by a British force without any guerillas at all. The explanation is that it had not been the intention of EAM/ELAS to take part in either operation: but in the former their hand was forced, and in the latter it was not. When the first party of British parachutists landed in Greece in October 1942, they landed fairly near both to the Gorgopotamos viaduct and to the ELAS unit commanded by Aris Veloukhiotis; Zervas was a hundred miles away to the west. More than a month passed during which the British party was unable to make contact with Aris. At the beginning of November a second party of British parachutists fell by chance into Aris' hands; he sent them to rejoin their comrades, again without offering to assist in their plan. Soon afterwards the first British party made contact with Zervas a hundred miles away, and brought him across Greece by forced marches to attack the Gorgopotamos bridge. That changed everything. When Aris understood that the attack would be made even without his force he could not take the risk of allowing Zervas to win all the credit: he at once offered his services. The result was a combined operation, which would probably never have taken place but for Zervas, nor succeeded but for Aris Veloukhiotis. But when, seven months later, the same operation was required against the Asopos viaduct, there was no possibility of enlisting any guerillas to help except ELAS; for Zervas was again a hundred miles away, and ELAS had entered upon its phase of internecine belligerence which made it impossible to think of inviting him back. The forces of Saraphis and Psaros had been annihilated: that of Zervas was threatened. Since there was no danger this time of any rival stealing the credit, EAM/ELAS refused to undertake the operation. (It was undertaken by a British party of six, and was also successful.) Other

---

[1]The KKE has published another version of these episodes in "Agents of Churchill," by Th. Vokos. In that version the arch-villain is myself. Future historians may easily find it as plausible as my own. But mine at least accounts for the fact, which is peculiar on any other hypothesis, that the Gorgopotamos operation has been incorporated by EAM/ELAS into their legend of the resistance, in which the no less brilliant success of the Asopos operation is entirely ignored.

examples such as these could be quoted to show why the BMM felt unable to rely upon ELAS to carry out the requirements of Allied strategy: these were the reasons which at the time justified the decision to continue supporting Zervas and Psaros.

There is therefore the second, precisely opposite, question to be answered: Why did the British authorities give EAM/ELAS any support whatever? Their political opponents maintain that if British hostility had been publicly asserted against EAM and ELAS, both would have broken up. The argument is fallacious, and was proved so whenever any such attempt was made; the effect was rather to consolidate EAM/ELAS, and to convince even waverers that it was better to cling to an organisation that was at least Greek, rather than submit to foreign dictation. But although the political argument is false, the preceding paragraphs suggest that it was, at least from the military point of view, a waste of money to support ELAS. A further examination of the second case quoted in the last paragraph will partly help to answer this argument.

Although no forces of ELAS co-operated in the attack on the Asopos viaduct, it could not have taken place if ELAS forces had not existed in the neighbourhood. Greece was already divided into "occupied" and "liberated" areas: roughly, the plains and the mountains. All military targets naturally lay in the former, though some (including the Asopos viaduct) lay on the borderline between the two. The most important targets lay in the vicinity of ELAS, and not of Zervas. It was impossible to approach such targets without guerillas to sustain the "liberated" character of the area through which the approach was to take place. ELAS provided in such areas what may be called an operational background: they hardly helped towards the operations, but they could have prevented the operations taking place, either by withdrawing, and thus letting "liberated" territory become "occupied" again, or by deliberately betraying them. But that is not all; British policy did not consist simply of an expensive subsidy to ensure Communist neutrality. The essence of the argument is not that ELAS would not fight the Germans, but that they preferred to fight the Germans in their own way. The operation against the Asopos bridge is an important instance of an occasion when their way was not our way. But a few weeks later they were fighting the Germans in large-scale operations conducted in almost precisely the way that the BMM required. Since the purpose of British policy towards ELAS was to turn instances of the former situation into instances of the latter, it is worth seeing how it was done. Again the argument will be confined to the reasons why the decision was made at the time; retrospective political justification will play no part.

The essential datum is that when the first BLOS reached Greece, EAM and ELAS were firmly established, capably organised, and increasingly well armed. During the following year they grew by leaps and bounds, whether the British supported them or not, undeterred by German opposition and propaganda, undeterred even by Stalin's dissolution of the Third International in May 1943. The alternatives open to the embryonic BMM were to use the services of EAM/ELAS against the occupation on their own terms; to undertake a futile struggle against them; or to do nothing. Having arrived by parachute, it was not even possible for the BLOS to leave Greece. For the first three months of their stay, they were hardly ever in communication with their headquarters, SOE Cairo. They therefore decided at the beginning of 1943 to adopt the first choice. So far as any detailed policy towards Greece could be devised by the British authorities in Egypt at that time, the decision adopted by the BMM was approved, though SOE Cairo placed itself in an uncomfortable position by its reaction to the triumph of the Gorgopotamos viaduct. It had hoped for a large-scale development of guerillas in Greece under the centralised control of the Six Colonels in Athens, on behalf of the exiled Government; but control from Athens was impracticable, and centralisation suited only EAM/ELAS. Thus to plan a large movement was to play into the hands of EAM/ELAS, which alone had an organisation of the requisite structure and magnitude; to plan a controllable movement was to sacrifice size and effectiveness. From this dilemma the course charted by the BMM under Brigadier Myers seemed to offer a way out. It entailed an attitude towards EAM/ELAS of hopeful and calculated friendliness instead of total capitulation or fruitless hostility. With periodical deviations, that relationship was accepted by EAM/ELAS: by the Communist leaders half-heartedly, because they regarded the British as only temporarily less dangerous enemies than the Germans: by their non-Communist rank and file as whole-heartedly as the Communist leaders would allow.

The first half of 1943 provides examples illustrating the whole process. When Saraphis and Psaros were attacked, relations between EAM/ELAS and the BMM underwent a strain, one of the consequences of which was the refusal of ELAS to co-operate in the attack on the Asopos viaduct. British disapproval was manifested in a document which all guerilla leaders were required to sign, guaranteeing their respect for each other's independence, and their willingness to obey the orders of GHQ, Middle East. This was the first draft of the "National Bands" Agreement.[1] Ironically, the new name for the guerillas had been chosen by Saraphis during his independence; but after his subjugation by ELAS, although everyone else was ready to sign the Agreement at once, he was obliged to support his new masters in presenting endless objections. The point at issue was apparently a small one, but in principle it was crucial, for it raised the question of the sovereignty of EAM/ELAS. The draft Agreement sought to place all guerillas under GHQ, Middle East,

[1] Texts of the first and final drafts will be found in Appendices B and C.

represented in Greece by Brigadier Myers, the Commander of the BMM. Brigadier Myers at last had all BLOS placed under his command; it was his intention that through himself and them all the orders of his superiors should be transmitted to the guerillas. EAM/ELAS considered that it derogated from their dignity to receive orders from British officers. They demanded that the channel of communication should be through their own GHQ, which had been formed in June of Aris Veloukhiotis, Saraphis and Tzimas; respectively the *Capetanios*, the Military Commander and the Political Adviser. Their GHQ, according to this plan, would receive general directives from GHQ, Middle East, and interpret them into detailed orders to their formations. It was not only a question of pride; it demanded the recognition of ELAS as an independent army, with political consequences which they can hardly have expected to remain unforeseen. The proposal was rejected by SOE Cairo; the early summer was consequently spent in violent outrages by ELAS against all its rivals, and in violent recriminations with the BMM.

When it became obvious that British supplies might become forfeit, EAM/ELAS began to show a more conciliatory manner. They apologised for their treatment of Psaros and his fellow-victims; they offered to rehabilitate their forces; they explained that the series of attacks had been unauthorised outbursts of irresponsibility under provocation; they offered a more reasonable revision of the draft "National Bands" Agreement.[1] Their version provided for the formation of a Joint General Headquarters representing all the guerillas "in proportion to their strength," together with the Commander of the BMM; this committee was to be the channel through which orders should pass to the guerillas. Although BLOS were still entirely omitted, the new draft was a more acceptable document than their previous conduct had led the BMM to expect; but it was rejected again by SOE Cairo on the ground that the proportions of the JGHQ would grossly favour EAM/ELAS. Tzimas argued that EAM/ELAS should have three members of the JGHQ, and each other representation (EDES, EKKA and the BMM) should consist of one member: a total of six. The proposal was defended alternatively, either on the ground that three was the number of their own GHQ and the number natural to their tripartite system of command, or on the ground that it fairly represented their numerical superiority. Neither of these arguments exercised the BMM in favour of concessions. But at the critical moment information came from SOE Cairo that the imminent invasion of Sicily from North Africa imperatively required large-scale operations by the Greek guerillas, to distract the Germans' attention towards the Balkans. Such operations could only be carried out with the help of ELAS; the help of ELAS could only be won by continuing to supply it with arms, ammunition and money; those supplies had been

---

[1] Texts of the first and final drafts will be found in Appendices B and C.

made conditional upon the "National Bands" Agreement; without that Agreement the freedom of the guerilla movement was certain to succumb to the domination of the KKE. The dilemma of strategic and political motives was complete.

Tacit blackmail and counter-blackmail persisted throughout the summer. For weeks neither side would give way, while time ran out and the invasion of Sicily drew nearer. EAM/ELAS did not know the nature of the operations, but it was clear to them that something important was impending. They realised how much importance HMG attached to events in Greece when a representative of the Foreign Office, Major Wallace, arrived in July to join Brigadier Myers' staff. They fought for their hegemony over the resistance movement with the same intensity which the BMM devoted to the twin aims of justice to minorities and effective action against the Germans. Because EAM/ELAS had one aim, and the BMM two, it was inevitable that the final concession came from the latter. The deadlock was broken by instructions from the British authorities in Egypt that the Commander of the BMM might at his discretion come to terms with EAM/ELAS if there were no alternative. With a few further amendments to reintroduce the BLO, at least in name, into the Agreement, it was at last signed in July; triumphantly by EAM/ELAS, reluctantly by Zervas, hopefully by EKKA, anxiously by the BMM.

There was certainly no alternative if the co-operation of ELAS were to be secured; but two other considerations tipped the balance. One was the conviction, deliberately implanted in everyone in Greece, that the country would be liberated at the latest within a few months, so that the effect of concessions to EAM/ELAS would not be far-reaching. The other was the belief that ELAS would at least be largely dependent for its material supplies upon British aeroplanes, and would be restrained from further misbehaviour by the knowledge that these supplies were about to be substantially increased. Both these beliefs turned out to be delusive. Nevertheless, the immediate result was that friendly relations were resumed; the supplies continued; the operations took place with success; the "National Bands" came into being under their Joint General Head-quarters.

The fabric of goodwill was strengthened by the undertaking of the BMM to secure increased supplies of heavier equipment and of gold. Heavy equipment was essential to full effectiveness against the Germans, whose artillery and mortars were practically unopposed. Gold was a more controversial matter.[1] It was argued by the guerilla leaders, and accepted by the BMM, that to meet their responsibilities towards their

[1]Since EAM/ELAS tried to create for themselves, in contrast to Zervas, a reputation for indifference to gold, it is worth recording that the BMM's first payment of sovereigns to both took place within a day or two of each other, in November 1942. This leaves out of account what EAM/ELAS received from British (and probably other) sources in Athens.

men and the civil population, a sum equivalent to two sovereigns monthly *per caput* of their forces under arms was needed. It was uncertain what their real strength amounted to, but the agreement gave them an incentive to falsify nominal rolls. It was also uncertain whether such a prodigious figure was necessary; for no one eats gold. Sovereigns were simply a substitute for efficient administration in bringing supplies out of the hands of the occupation and the black market; the administration was encouraged to remain corrupt by the supply of sovereigns to remedy its deficiencies. A popular resistance movement on a small scale, or an efficient one on a large scale, might not have needed sovereigns to do its work. The supply of them was well accommodated to the German practice of printing unlimited bank-notes as they needed them; but since sovereigns brought no new goods into Greece, they increased inflation, and set in motion a snowball which swallowed up more of them as it grew. Once the first sovereign had been let slip, the process became cumulative; the supply increased the demand. It is therefore perhaps true that when the principle of supplying gold was accepted, the quantity could not have been kept within lower limits. What is doubtful is whether the principle need have been accepted; whether it was worth the confusion which it generated both during and after the German occupation. These doubts were not expressed by the guerilla leaders; for they stood to gain in the short run, and it was only the plain Greek who stood to lose in the long run. The immediate effect of the British undertaking was therefore to increase confidence and encourage the growth of the resistance movement.

Mountain Greece was already a different world from that depicted at the beginning of the year. Guerillas had spread to every village in the mountains, and to many in the plains. Links had been forged with other Balkan resistance movements: by Zervas distantly with Mihailovitch; by EAM/ELAS more intimately with Albanian, Yugoslav and Bulgarian partisans. All organisations were now theoretically free to expand wherever they wished, though the predominance of ELAS in the JGHQ guaranteed that they would not expand too fast or far. Most of the minor organisations, and some reformed collaborators, felt encouraged to spread their wings about July 1943, tempted by the prospects (which few survived to enjoy) of British weapons and gold. But the future still lay with those who had taken an earlier initiative, and shown that they could stand on their own feet with or without foreign help.

The initiative of EAM/ELAS justified their predominance, though not their tyranny. Having acquired control of almost the whole country, except the principal communications used by the Germans, they had given it things that it had never known before. Communications in the mountains, by wireless, courier, and telephone, have never been so good before or since; even motor roads were mended and used by EAM/ELAS. Their communications, including wireless, extended as far as Crete and

Samos, where guerillas were already in the field. The benefits of civilisation and culture trickled into the mountains for the first time. Schools,
local government, law-courts and public utilities, which the war had
ended, worked again. Theatres, factories, parliamentary assemblies began
for the first time. Communal life was organised in place of the traditional
individualism of the Greek peasant. His child was dragooned into EPON,
his nest-egg levied into EA, his *caique* commandeered to equip ELAN.
Much of the early work of the JGHQ itself was of an administrative
nature, on the border-line between military and civil affairs; some of it
was dangerously near to legislation. Followed at a distance by the minor
organisations, EAM/ELAS set the pace in the creation of something that
Governments of Greece had neglected: an organised state in the Greek
mountains. All the virtues and vices of such an experiment could be
seen; for when the people whom no one has ever helped started helping
themselves, their methods are vigorous and not always nice. The words
"liberation" and "popular democracy" filled the air with their peculiar
connotations. Uneasy stirrings were breaking the surface everywhere, but
only the KKE knew how to give them direction. Some Greeks feared the
stirrings, and some welcomed them but feared the direction. With the
exception of the KKE, all alike, whether in EAM/ELAS or outside it,
felt that the presence of the BMM (which was expanding well into three
figures) was a guarantee that things would turn out all right. Symptom-
atically, for the first time regular officers flocked to the guerilla organisations. Their accession grew from the changed atmosphere in the
movement, and in turn encouraged the change. It had been more or less
respectable from the first to join EKKA, and almost respectable to join
EDES after Zervas' interchange of telegrams with the King in March
1943: now it became respectable even to join ELAS. ELAS modified its
language and verbally disowned its monopolistic tendencies; EDES
diluted its outspoken republicanism to a vague neutrality on political
matters; EKKA maintained its agreeable moderation in all things. There
were alarmists still to preach the danger of social revolution, but July
1943 was a month of hope and excitement as well as wonder and fear
in the mountains of Greece. This development had been latent in the
nature of EAM/ELAS from its foundation. Its rivals followed suit
because they had no alternative but to acquiesce or succumb. Whatever
they or the BMM did, the free mountain state was coming. All that the
presence of BLOS could ensure was that it was not a Communist
monopoly.

The relation between the BMM and the rival guerillas can now be
summed up. In some parts of Greece only EAM/ELAS existed; there
they behaved reasonably and fought adequately against the Germans.
In other parts both ELAS and their rivals existed; there the latter were
less ambitious and more reliable as an operational instrument against the

Germans. In both cases political consolidation was the primary object of EAM/ELAS. This was a situation which the BMM found and did not create. Their first alternative was to encourage ELAS to eliminate its rivals, from which on the above premises would have followed a diminution of the effectiveness of operations against the Germans. Their second alternative was to try to eliminate ELAS, which was too far beyond human possibility to be considered. Their third was to do nothing, or to get out of the country, which were only variants of the first; for in the absence of the BMM, only EAM/ELAS would have survived the resistance movement. Their fourth was to support ELAS in the areas where it alone existed, and to support its rivals in the rest. This was equivalent to giving the whole of ELAS a proportionally diminished support, since their centralised command freely transferred its assets from one area to another. The last alternative was to try to harness the guerilla units into a homogeneous military organisation, in which everyone would be entitled to his own political opinions, and everyone would take operational orders from a single command. This was the alternative which was adopted in the "National Bands" Agreement. If it broke down (as it did in due course), the only possibility would be the fourth alternative (and so it became); but this too was a variant of the principle of dividing support between the rivals, which was fundamentally inescapable.

The immediate reasons why the decision was taken by the BMM on the spot, have been distinguished from the long-term reasons why higher policy of the British authorities eventually approved it. The retrospective justification must be stated in terms of wider political and military considerations which were not accessible at the time to those who made the decision. The purpose of this chapter is to give a chronological account of what happened at the time: so the crucial point is not that the policy embodied in the "National Bands" Agreement was endorsed by higher policy and justified by events, but that its initiation in March 1943 and its consummation in July rested in the discretion of the Commander of the BMM. He was guided by the immediate military situation; his discretion was influenced only by the considerations which have been outlined. Since the "National Bands" Agreement, and the JGHQ which it embodied, were an outcome of the initiative expressly delegated to him by the British authorities, there is no reason at this point to account for the policy in the wider terms of wisdom after the event.

Nevertheless, the long-term implications of the decision soon began to show their nature, when the end of the extensive operations in July left a respite for stock-taking. When the six members of the JGHQ met for the first time at Pertouli, in West Thessaly, on 19th July, the atmosphere of their protracted debates barely concealed the instability of their equilibrium. They were in no ordinary sense a military headquarters, for they represented forces which retained their individual autonomy, and only carried out the collective orders of the JGHQ when it suited them. Since the political objectives of the constituent members, EAM/ELAS, EDES and EKKA, were inseparable from their military functions, it is important to see what brought them together and what was likely to drive them apart; for therein lay the seeds of the trouble which followed in the Middle East. Briefly, what drew them together politically was their fear of Greeks outside their circle, especially of Greeks in exile; what promised to split them apart was fear of each other. Extensively they were united; intensively they were divided. Each of these fears was aggravated by a suspicion that the British were consciously or unconsciously supporting the other side.

Since all the participants were subject to these conflicting motives, their conduct was not always consistent. For instance, when they assembled at the seat of the JGHQ, it was discovered that EDES and EKKA had no intention of appointing representatives of the same calibre as EAM/ELAS. This was not surprising, since the seat of the JGHQ had been chosen to coincide with ELAS GHQ. Although everyone professed himself satisfied with the agreement by which the JGHQ was established, neither Zervas nor Psaros was ever seen there more than once; the representation of each declined first to their senior political adherents, Pyromaglou and Kartalis, and then to a handful of staff officers. In this way, the JGHQ became nothing more than the GHQ of ELAS with a few appendages. When each party had thus indicated its estimate of the JGHQ, its disintegration was only a matter of time. But while the internal fear drove them apart, the external fear drove them together; while they cautiously eyed each other at Pertouli, at the same time all the guerilla leaders joined in presenting a united front to the outside world.

The occasion for them to do so was furnished by the construction in the Greek mountains of a landing strip large enough to receive aircraft. This made it possible for the principal Greeks inside and outside Greece to meet for the first time during the occupation. The opportunity was not universally welcomed by the exiled Greeks, some of whom blinded themselves to the fact that a reunion which must in any case take place eventually had better take place sooner rather than later. The entourage of King George II had been so alarmed by rumours of republicanism in Greece, which had come out through both Greek and British sources, that they preferred to blame the sources rather than face the facts. They could have gained little by postponing the evil day; but even that choice did not lie with them. On 9th August, 1943, the Greek and British principals of the resistance movement set out by air for Cairo, leaving behind their understudies to implement the "National Bands" Agreement. The task of those left behind was temporarily light, since military operations had come to an end with the invasion of Sicily, and the political centre of gravity was transferred to the Middle East. A detached and unreal harmony enveloped the JGHQ, as it enlarged its debates in equal remoteness from the operations which it purported to control and the scarcely veiled civil wars which brewed under its aegis. In Egypt, however, there was not even a pretence of such harmony. For the first time it was revealed how small was the possibility of extending agreement *among* those inside Greece into agreement *between* those inside Greece and those outside. Divergences on the different stages had gone too far; the first re-union served only to widen the rifts.

3. *AUGUST* 1943—*NOVEMBER* 1943.

The delegation from the mountains to Egypt was ill-fated from the first. Although the Greek and British authorities in Cairo expected it, they did not all realise its size and importance. In particular, HM Ambassador had been led to expect a small group of two or three individuals coming for a friendly chat and a pat on the back. Instead there arrived six men representing three organisations which were coming to regard themselves as the future rulers of Greece.[1] Their names were Tzimas, Petros Roussos, Dhespotopoulos and Tsirimokos, representing EAM/ELAS; Pyromaglou, representing EDES; and Kartalis, representing EKKA. The first three were all Communists. The last three were all more or less of the left centre; and although they represented three rival organisations at the time, their trends of thought were among those which gradually converged after the liberation of Greece. What divided the party has already been seen. What united all six men was a common language in discussing the future of Greece, which did not coincide with the language current in Egypt or London. The difference which separated the world of the mountains from the world of Egypt or London is best expressed by this metaphor: the six delegates spoke the same language, even when they used it to disagree among themselves; the Greeks of the exile spoke a different language, even though they might on some matters use it to agree with some of the six. A similar difference separated the British authorities from the principal British officers accompanying the delegation. Most of the British authorities had no familiarity with Greek thought,[2] except in the sophisticated language of the Court and Cairo. Brigadier Myers, the Commander of the BMM, had already spent nearly a year in the mountains learning a different type of Greek thought. The Foreign Office representative, Major Wallace, who accompanied him, occupied an intermediate position, having spent a little over a month in the mountains. Where all these diverse voices disagreed, many of the disagreements could be attributed to differences of language; but

[1] The technical hitches which caused this misunderstanding can be briefly summarised as two: a telegram was misinterpreted (perhaps deliberately) by the KKE, and several others were fatally delayed in the process of deciphering.

[2] The head of the Balkan section of SOE Cairo was an expert on the Baltic.

because this was not immediately recognised, and little could have been done about it, the disagreements grew to formidable proportions.

(a) *In Egypt and London.* The situation was unprecedented and needed to be delicately handled. What was especially confusing was the collision of a political atmosphere permeated by the Communist question with one permeated by the King's matter. In occupied Greece the latter had none of the urgency of the former; in Egypt the import of the former had scarcely begun to be realised. The conversations which took place in Egypt were therefore carried on at cross-purposes. The alignments which formed themselves within the group of characters reassembled on the Egyptian stage were complicated. From occupied Greece had come six Greeks united on the King's matter, and potentially divided on the Communist question, to meet Greek authorities divided upon the former but potentially united on the latter as soon as they became aware of its menace. Other things being equal, there was little to separate the moderates of the six delegates from the bulk of the exiled cabinet: that is, Pyromaglou of EDES, Kartalis of EKKA, and even Tsirimokos of ELD, from newly sworn ministers such as Sophoklis Veniselos and Karapanayiotis. All of them were republicans and none were extremists. But other things were not equal. The republican ministers were subject to a pull towards the right from the royalists with whom they shared power; the moderate delegates were subject to a pull towards the left from the extremists who accompanied them. Tsirimokos, representing almost the only independent party within EAM, was already a committed fellow-traveller of the KKE. Pyromaglou and Kartalis were handicapped by the lack, indeed by the impossibility, of a plan of approach to the discussions which could reconcile their various loyalties.

The misfortune was that on 10th August none of those concerned had a plan, except the KKE delegation. The King and his adherents had a principle, which was to accept no change in the constitutional position during their exile from Greece, but no plan to combat an unconstitutional attack. The exiled Government did not even know when the delegation was coming until after it had arrived. The delegation as a whole had concerted a plan of approach with each other and with the Commander of the BMM, which might have saved many tears if it had been followed: but it was not. The plan envisaged an approach across the gap between the resistance and the exiles in three stages. The first stage was to secure recognition of the guerillas by the exiled Government as a part of the Greek armed forces. Recognition was to have included interchange of liaison officers between the regular and irregular forces of the Greek army. The second stage concerned the more delicate subject of civil relations. Administrative and even legislative functions had become involved in the activities of the resistance, and especially of the JGHQ. The exiled

Government was certain to regret this, as did everyone else except the KKE; but no rigid line can be drawn between military and civil functions when an army is living in the midst of a population. To regret the duality of the resistance organisations was simply to regret their existence; many Greeks of the exile, who did regret their existence, behaved as if it would cease if it were ignored. The second part of the plan was therefore to overcome this attitude. The third, which flowed from the second, was to indicate, and if possible remove, the dangers which arose from the unrepresentative nature of the exiled Government. Apart from some officials of SOE Cairo, the Greek and British authorities tended to underestimate its dangers. If that Government, and especially its sovereign, were to return to Greece when the country was liberated without any further modification, the result would have been a revolution: the new wine would have burst the old bottles. It was futile on the part of the King's adherents to blame this fact upon the British authorities for supporting republican organisations in Greece: there had been no other organisations in Greece visible without a microscope. The effect of the British intervention had not been to encourage republicanism, but to limit Communism: yet whatever it had been, the King's adherents could not abolish the problem by blaming it on someone else. The presence in Egypt of ex-agents of the British authorities, notably Bakirdzis and Peltekis, made this refuge the more tempting but none the more helpful. The King's circle still had to learn, what they had already been told numberless times by reliable but suspect informants in Greece, as well as by SOE Cairo, that the character of their Government in exile did not yet meet the changed sentiments of its subjects under the occupation. The change might be artificial and temporary, but it was real. This enlightment was to be the third phase of the plan devised between the Commander of the BMM and his six Greek companions.

The plan was not executed because the KKE delegates never intended that it should be. Their moderate companions were left speechless by the headlong violence with which Tzimas, the strongest personality in the party, plunged his adherents straight into an extreme form of what was to have been the third phase of the plan. Sweeping aside the initial stages, over which disagreement within the delegation was most likely to become apparent, the four delegates of EAM forced an ultimatum upon the King within four days of their arrival. By a characteristically precipitate approach, which left no pause for consideration of internal controversies, they confined the issue to the King's matter, on which all the delegates from the Greek mountains were formally agreed. Not only was it impossible for the delegation to become divided on this issue: the six were even joined by the only two Greek politicians of note who had escaped from Greece to Egypt during the occupation: Kanellopoulos, who had fallen from office as a consequence of the mutinies in March,

and needed a gesture to rehabilitate himself; and Exindaris, who had
arrived in Egypt shortly before the resistance delegation, on an express
mission from Athenian republicans (the solitary result of Tsoudheros'
invitation in April)[1] to state their case to the Greeks of the exile.
Happy timing thus enabled the KKE delegates to secure eight signatures to the document which presented their views to the King and
his Government.

The opinion expressed over the names of Tzimas, Petros Roussos,
Dhespotopoulos, Tsirimokos, Pyromaglou, Kartalis, Kanellopoulos and
Exindaris was that King George II should not return to Greece before a
plebiscite had been held. At the same time it was suggested that three
portfolios of the exiled Government should be held inside Greece. The
King indignantly reasserted his intention to return to Greece when it
should be liberated, at the head of his armed forces, and ignored the
suggestion regarding his Government. The British authorities, after
anxious debate and some division of opinion, supported the King's
position, on the constitutional ground that no hasty decision could be
justified while Greece was under enemy occupation. Nothing could be
more unconstitutional and undemocratic than to concede the King's
legitimate position to the clamour of an acknowledged minority: a
vocal, organised, even armed minority, but still with no recognisable
means of proving its claim to speak for anyone but itself. The argument
for rejecting the ultimatum was logical, even though the principal
beneficiary from it had himself done most to undermine the constitution.
British policy in 1943, like American policy in 1947, might have been
easier to justify if King George II had died earlier than he did. Embarrassment was no excuse for abandoning legitimacy and orthodoxy, but the
argument for logic was still vulnerable to emotion. Perhaps for that
reason it did not have a universal appeal.

More than half the Greek exiled Government reacted in a body
towards the eight signatories of the document which precipitated the
crisis, leaving Tsoudheros almost alone beside the King. The KKE had
chosen its ground and time with skill. By a master-stroke of political
blitzkrieg, it had isolated in the glare of a lightning flash the one subject
on which all its rivals had to agree against the established régime; it had
thrust into outer darkness every dispute which separated the rest of the
Greek political world from itself, and it split the exiled authorities in
two like a rotten tree. This had been made possible by tactical exploitation
of the unresolved conflict between the two schisms that rent Greek political life. Democratic republicans, such as composed a half of the resistance
delegation and more than a half of the exiled Government, were perpetually torn between the rival antagonisms of anti-Communism and anti-
Monarchism. August 1943 was one of their recurrent crises. The triangle

[1]See p. 132.

of forces was open to two resolutions, according to the strength of the alternative attractions to which the men in the middle were exposed: either their democratic feelings would repel them from the Communists, or their republican feelings would repel them from the Monarchists. But only one of the contestants was trained and ready. By their skill in playing upon the latter feelings and allaying the former, Tzimas and his companions closed the republican ranks before anyone had time to think of closing the democratic ranks. Tsoudheros' Government, already potentially divided between republicans and royalists, came close to disintegration.

For the first time the constitutional problem of Greece became crystallised, even if its other problems remained obscure. If the republican members of the exiled Government resigned, as they immediately wished to do, only two possibilities lay open. Either an entirely royalist Government or an entirely republican Government must follow: for no republican could, after such a climax, have conscientiously consented to take office under a King who had boldly refused to accept the ultimatum presented to him. The EAM/ELAS delegates were ready with a proposal for a new Government if Tsoudheros should fall: they had taken soundings before they left Greece, and even selected their future enemy Papandhreou as Prime Minister. They waited confidently to be called upon.

The Government which held office when the delegation arrived from the Greek mountains was the delicate outcome of a compromise. The compromise could not be repeated if it resigned. To prolong the compromise was only possible if the resignations could be prevented; if the delegation were quietly restored to the Greek mountains, and the whole episode were forgotten. The choice between prolonging the compromise and accepting either of the uncompromising alternatives unfortunately rested not with any Greek authority but with HMG, to whom the King and his Government naturally turned for advice. The British authorities, they argued, had brought these obstreperous individuals out of Greece; the British authorities alone could put them back; the British authorities were the only channel of communication with occupied Greece, and the only source of Allied counsel available to the Greek exiles; the British authorities must decide, and bear the whole responsibility for the decision.

The responsibility was accepted almost too readily, at the expense of a valuable opportunity. That no official consultation of the American authorities in Cairo took place was an unfortunate omission for various reasons; the chief was that American officers were about to join the BMM in the Greek mountains. The American equivalent of SOE, known as OSS (the Office of Strategic Services) and commanded by General Donovan, who as a colonel had toured the Balkans in 1941, had recently set up headquarters in Cairo. The fact that it was not consulted at this time bred suspicion, especially as some of the dissident members of

Tsoudheros' Government (notably Sophoklis Veniselos) were privately in touch with American officials, as well as with five American Senators, who were then in Cairo in the course of a tour of the theatres of war throughout the world. Despite these opportunities and dangers, the British authorities made their decision alone: the six delegates must return to Greece, and the Greek Government must remain in office.

The way the decision was executed was easier to criticise than the decision itself. It was difficult to guess in detail what would have followed if any other decision had been made, but the probabilities were clear. The proposal that three portfolios of the exiled Government should be held inside Greece, presumably by members of the resistance organisations, was the most reasonable idea that emerged from the upheaval: but it would not have been finally acceptable even to the delegates who put it forward, except as part of their wider plan, which had already been rejected. It might well have been more fully debated; even if the debate could have led nowhere, it would at least have forestalled a later grievance. But every prospect, other than the decision which was eventually made, appeared to the responsible authorities to lead directly towards disaster. If the Government of Tsoudheros had collapsed in August 1943, it must have been succeeded by a Government dominated by EAM, in virtue of their self-assumed leadership of the republican cause; or by a Government of extreme royalists, who would at that time (whatever may have become the case since) have represented practically no active element in Greek life. The eventual result of either alternative would have been a repressive authoritarianism, either of the KKE or of the monarchist right as the case might be: in fact, the crisis of 1944-5 would have come a year earlier, perhaps with the opposite result. Neither Communist nor neo-Metaxist dictatorship could be considered acceptable; no other possibility could be foreseen in the circumstances

The trouble was that the truth had been brought to light by the wrong people: the unrepresentative nature of the King's Government had been exposed by the no less unrepresentative dexterity of the Communists. Faced with the choice between the two, the British authorities instinctively decided that the right action was no action. The hard-won compromise of a predominantly republican coalition under a titular monarchy was plainly preferable to an irreversible settlement which could only develop through violence into a new authoritarianism of one of the extremes. What may emerge from the dilemma before the eyes of the historian is not that the wrong choice was made, but that the dilemma ought never to have been allowed to occur. If the gulf between the exiles and their fellow-countrymen in Greece had not widened steadily during the two preceding years, the Communists would not have been able to exploit it with such suddenness in August 1943. Holding the exiled Government together at all costs may have been the only way to make the best of a bad job: but the job was still bad, and the best of it was poor enough. Given the circumstances, the British authorities could hardly have decided otherwise. Whether the circumstances need have been given is part of a wider question; but whether the decision, once taken, was wisely executed is a question of more immediate importance.

The tactics of the Communist delegates had everyone on edge. Once it had been agreed that their ultimatum must be rejected and the exiled Government must be restrained from disintegrating, only one idea ruled the minds of those who had been so rudely awakened from their dogmatic slumbers: to dismiss the delegation as soon as possible. The recalcitrant ministers of Tsoudheros were persuaded not to resign; the provocative delegates were required to return to Greece. It was hoped that by the end of August the crisis would be over, at least for the time being. But the resistance delegation, while on their way back to the aerodrome for their return journey, prevailed upon Tsoudheros himself to ask the British authorities for a respite. The ostensible reason was that they had not had time to complete their military discussions with GHQ, Middle East. This was true, if only because the KKE component of the delegation had insisted, in reversal of the plan concerted before their arrival in Egypt, on provoking a political crisis before proceeding to military discussions. The initiative in pressing for a postponement of their departure came again from the three Communists. That Tsoudheros and the British authorities successively gave way was symptomatic of the indecision which prevailed. The six delegates therefore remained in Egypt until the middle of the following month. In the meantime three of the principal British personalities concerned (Brigadier Myers of the BMM, his immediate superior in SOE Cairo, and his adviser from the Foreign Office, Major Wallace) set out for London to explain the crisis.

The unwilling postponement did not undo the harm which the abrupt dismissal had caused. The conviction fostered among the delegates by their Communist members, that the British authorities now intended to reimpose the monarchy upon Greece willy-nilly, was strengthened by the suspicion that Brigadier Myers, whom all of them trusted, had vanished from the scene for good. This suspicion, by an instinct characteristic of Greek sensitivity, became a certainty in their minds even before it became true. They were convinced of it before the end of August, although his deputy[1] was not officially appointed to succeed him until the beginning of December. During the interval a confusion of intrigue and suspicion permeated Anglo-Greek relations; but the single thread of

[1] Myself, hereafter referred to successively as acting commander of the BMM and commander of the AMM. In case it is of more than autobiographical interest, it is worth adding that on this and three subsequent occasions I formally (but unsuccessfully) sought to be released from this responsibility.

decision which stood out from the tangle was that King George II declared his intention to abdicate if Brigadier Myers returned to Greece. His insistence, amid so much uncertainty, was perhaps decisive.

Brigadier Myers was alone, except perhaps for one or two colleagues in SOE Cairo, in being aware of the complexities of thought on both sides of the gulf. The delicate intricacy of the King's position did not reveal itself on the surface. It might not at first sight have seemed to make much difference whether, on the liberation of Greece, he returned thither with his Government or not, provided that the fate of both was duly submitted to the people's will; and that had already been categorically promised. But the order of events was crucial. To put the return of the King first, the election of a new Government second, and a plebiscite on the constitution third, would have given the King, in the eyes of his enemies, an unfair advantage to be unscrupulously exploited; to reverse the order would have given, in the eyes of his friends, the same advantage to his enemies. No permutation of the possibilities could have given an impeccably fair result, for suspicion and antagonism had already gone too far. The principal result of the impact of ideas which took place in August was that both sides accused each other, and both suspected the British authorities, of bad faith and ulterior motives. The atmosphere of Greek politics in an Egyptian summer made it easy to believe almost anything of almost anybody.

The six delegates' reprieve merely postponed the transfer of the crisis back to the mountains from which it had come. It did not aggravate the trouble, for the delegates achieved nothing further to consolidate their spectacular début; nor did it ease the situation, for the potential dangers in the Greek mountains still remained. But this was not easily seen in Cairo, where the mountains were still a closed book. A tendency crept over the Anglo-Greek authorities to act as if the crisis would be over as soon as they were rid of the guerilla delegation. It was impossible that any such crude identification of symptom and disease should become explicit; but it appeared to be tacitly implied in the conduct of the period; and the uninformed observer had only appearance to go by. Superficially it looked as if the Greek authorities hoped to dispose of the problem by passing responsibility to the British authorities, and the British authorities by getting rid of the troublesome delegation back to Greece. However wise the motives, this tendency to underrate the importance of what went on in Greece, so long as tranquillity was restored in exile, appeared to be exemplified in several incidents of the time.

On the Greek side, one of them was the decision to send Bakirdzis back to the mountains with the guerilla delegation. Bakirdzis had made no trouble in the Middle East, but his reputation was dangerous. Since he was a friend of Kartalis and Psaros and had spoken of a wish to form a guerilla force, he was sent back to Greece with no positive instructions, but simply to be rid of him from Cairo. Another example was the appointment of Sbarounis to be Varvaressos' under-secretary immediately after his arrival from occupied Greece, where his last appointment had been Financial Adviser to Tsolakoglou. The attitude to collaboration implied thereby was a sign of complacence which the underground in Greece was not likely to ignore; but it was tacitly assumed that what went on in Greece under the occupation had no real existence.

On the British side the same appearance was created by the suppression of almost all information about the delegation's visit. No report on the crisis was transmitted to the acting commander of the BMM, nor were the vital facts communicated to the Press. In the former case, silence correctly but rather forcibly exemplified the principle that the BMM was not concerned in politics. The latter case was more serious, because it was from this date that the trouble with the Press began. It could not be suggested that the British authorities failed to appreciate the importance of the Press; rather perhaps HM Ambassador knew newspaper-men too well. The result in any case was that public opinion was left mainly uninformed, and partially misinformed. There thus took place none of that interaction between official policy and popular pressure by which democratic processes are fulfilled; after another year, there followed anger and confusion. Meanwhile a false sense of security re-enveloped the Greek world of Cairo. The constitutional problem was returned to cold storage; the gratifying prospect of Italy's capitulation occupied every mind. Like a parcel returned unopened, the crisis which had come from the Greek mountains in August was sent back in September. It almost came to be forgotten that the parcel contained a time-bomb.

(b) *In the Greek Mountains.* The guerilla delegation returned to Greece by the same route on the night of 16th-17th September. With them in the aeroplane were Gen. Bakirdzis (on his way to join EKKA), Ioannis Peltekis (on his way back to Athens), and the first two American members of the AMM. They were not accompanied by either Brigadier Myers (who never returned) or Major Wallace (who only returned a year later). It was hoped that the history of Greek resistance would be resumed where it had left off a month earlier; but the hope was delusive. What followed was not a period of tranquil stock-taking, but the climax in October of the KKE's first attempt to seize absolute power in Greece. The motives for this attempt may be summed up under three general headings: the expectation that the war was about to end; the acquisition by ELAS of an enormous increase in fire-power; and the belief that the British authorities would forcibly impose an unwanted régime on Greece. These three motives may be taken in turn.

The end of the war was expected from week to week throughout 1943 in Greece. Repeated disappointments did nothing to damp the volatility with which it recurred time after time. Without some such wishful thinking to keep them going, the Greek population could hardly have survived their ordeal. The technical difficulties of forcing the Allies' advantages to a speedy consummation were mercifully hidden from the peasant, the guerilla, and the man in the street. But the growth of the belief was not only a matter of ignorance and of temperament, for it was shared by the astute politicians and military experts of the underground, who were sufficiently confident by October 1943 to act in a decisive way. For men reading the omens in the remote darkness of enemy occupation, the belief was not unreasonable: the events of 1943 had given it some substance, as a brief war-diary of that year will show.

In January 1943 Tripoli had fallen to the British Eighth Army, and the German Sixth Army had surrendered to the Red Army at Stalingrad. At the end of the month Mr. Churchill met the Turkish President and Prime Minister at Adana; an event which naturally resurrected the perennial rumour that Turkey was about to come into the war on the Allies' side. The Germans laboured desperately to spread dissension in Eastern Europe. They accorded their official approval to Mihailovitch in Yugoslavia, and everywhere harped on the Soviet menace. They uncovered mass-graves of Poles in the Katyn forest, and of Rumanians near Odessa, to lay at the door of the USSR. Their efforts underlined their bankruptcy. The puppet rulers of Italy, Hungary, Croatia and France were summoned to meet Hitler in rapid succession during April and May; none the less, the collapse of the eastern front appeared to be presaged by the withdrawal from it during the year of Italian, Hungarian, Croatian and Rumanian troops. The Germans announced a new plan for a Balkan bloc, but the few details that emerged showed that it was only a last attempt to hold down the ubiquitous disturbances. Except Yugoslavia, all the south Balkan countries exposed the weakness of the New Order by recurrent collapses of their collaborating Governments. Rallis succeeded Logothetopoulos in Greece, Bozhilov succeeded Filov in Bulgaria, five successive Governments ruled Albania during the first half of 1943. The Serb and Croat puppets remained precariously in office only because no substitutes could be found. In July the ominous name of Tito was proscribed in a German order for the first time. Agitations for the union of Cyprus and the Dodecanese with Greece were launched. Within the space of four summer months, North Africa was cleared of the Axis; Sicily was occupied; Rome was bombed; Mussolini fell; King Boris mysteriously died; Italy was invaded; Mihailovitch rounded on the Germans and attacked shipping on the Danube; Badoglio capitulated unconditionally; bombs began to fall on the capital of every state on the side of the Axis. It was enough to intoxicate a less exuberant character than the Greek.

German precautions in Greece intensified the heady atmosphere. Five

Greek generals, including Papagos, were carried off to captivity in Germany for fear of what they might do in Athens; Security Battalions were lured into the field to fight the multiplying guerillas; convoys of German troops were constantly on the move. When the King proclaimed the impending liberation of Greece, and the Aegean islands were occupied by Greek and British forces, hope trembled on the brink of certainty that the expected day had come. Time after time it dropped back, only to rise again. Each time the conduct of EAM/ELAS could be read as a barometer of Greek expectations. After Tripoli and Stalingrad, they attacked Saraphis; after Tunis and Bizerta, they attacked Psaros and outlying units of Zervas; after Sicily, they attacked PAO in Macedonia, ES and EOA in the Peloponnese; after the capitulation of Italy, they launched a general civil war. These are not statements of cause and effect; they are contemporaneous symptoms of parallel trends. Momentary recoils followed each disappointment; but even after their crowning decision of October 1943, disappointments were still counterbalanced by new flowerings of hope. The invasion of Greece did not come, and the Aegean islands were recaptured by the Axis; but the Allied Foreign Secretaries met at Moscow in October, and their leaders met at Teheran and Cairo in December; it seemed impossible that nothing should come from that. Every Greek mind followed the same groove, with the KKE in the van. Everything was seen in terms of Greek affairs, from a Greek view-point, for the single purpose of the liberation of Greece.

The crucial event which sprang from this crescendo of delusion was the culminating attempt by the KKE to seize control of the Greek mountains, by attacking EDES in October 1943. The preceding outbreaks of smaller scale were merged by this action into the general conflagration of civil war. It is therefore not surprising that the most convincing of the portents seeming to presage the end of the war, should have occurred immediately before that attack was launched. This portent was the capitulation of Italy, which has the additional interest of showing the first important example of the working of the JGHQ in the absence of the principals. Like the Security Council of the United Nations, which might almost have been modelled on it, the JGHQ could only work if all its members wished it to work. Its decisions were reached by compromise, and executed only if they happened to suit its participants. Because it did not completely fulfil the conception either of the BMM or of EAM/ELAS, its destiny could not be certain until one or the other decisively prevailed: until, that is, political ambitions became genuinely subordinated to military operations, or until EAM/ELAS successfully absorbed their rivals and forced the framework of the JGHQ to coincide with that of ELAS GHQ. As long as EAM/ELAS were represented chiefly by Saraphis, who still had to win his spurs from his new masters by obstructing his old allies; and as long as EDES, EKKA and the BMM were each represented by subordinate officers,[1] whose principal anxiety was to mark time on the positions reached by their superiors before them; for so long there was no hope of a permanent solution for any delicate problem. It was with precisely such a problem that the tottering power of the Italians immediately confronted the hardly less unstable committee which presided over the National Bands.

The collapse of the Italians had been visibly approaching for some time. Although the dismissal of Mussolini had been decided on the assumption that both Fascism and the war against the Allies would continue, his successor Badoglio immediately abandoned the former, and by August was ready to abandon the latter. Secret communications were in progress between Italy and the Allies on the highest level. Formal negotiations were thereby authorised on a lower level between the JGHQ and the Italian Commanders in Thessaly; they had actually begun before the six delegates left for Egypt. Before their return, the negotiations were completed, and approximately twelve thousand Italians had transferred their arms to the side of the Allies. This appeared to be a triumph for the National Bands, but the reality behind the appearance was less satisfactory. The episode revealed, even to the Italians, the incompatibility and lack of confidence between the guerilla leaders. Negotiations had been opened separately by each of the organisations composing the JGHQ, with the object of acquiring as many weapons as possible for themselves. No success had been achieved, nor had the JGHQ begun to function in co-ordination, until the day on which the unconditional surrender of Badoglio's Government became known over the wireless. Within twenty-four hours General Infante, commanding the Pinerolo Division in Larisa, had offered to transfer the command of his force to the Allies' representatives in Greece; as such the members of the JGHQ were at last compelled to act in unison, for fear that none of them would snatch anything in time from the grasp of the Germans if they did not.

The first meeting of General Infante and the JGHQ took place on 11th September. Infante's only considerations were that his conduct should be approved (though it could not be authorised) by his High Command in Italy, and that any agreement should be guaranteed by the acting commander of the BMM on behalf of the Allies. He made it clear that he would enter into no agreement with the guerilla leaders alone. They, on their side, were primarily interested in acquiring as many Italian weapons as they could before the Germans intervened. Consequently they were disposed to agree to almost anything with Infante, but almost nothing with each other. It happened that the majority of the

[1]These were Lt.-Col. Ghikopoulos, Col. Mavrommatis and Col. Ravtopoulos successively for EDES; Major Papathanasiou for EKKA; and myself as acting commander of the BMM.

L

Italians under General Infante's orders lay in the vicinity of ELAS units, and very few in the vicinity of EDES or EKKA. Saraphis claimed on behalf of ELAS the right to all their weapons. Since their equipment included almost every kind of weapon from artillery downwards, with a fire-power such as no Greek guerilla had yet dreamed of, their disposition was important. Neither Infante nor EDES nor EKKA would voluntarily have resigned them into the hands of ELAS; Saraphis knew that the BMM would not have acquiesced either. It was therefore decided that the Italian troops should come over to the guerillas with their weapons; that they should retain them so long as they proved themselves willing to fight the Germans; and that only such surplus weapons as could not be manned by the Pinerolo Division should be handed over to the guerillas, to be divided proportionally between them. The surplus was not important; ELAS took delivery of it on behalf of the other organisations, none of whom ever saw their share. What was important was the fire-power which still lay in the hands of the Italians. None of the Greek organisations had given up hope of acquiring it, but only EAM/ELAS were able, by reason of their predominance in the area of the Italian surrender, to devise an effective plan of seizure.

A chain of coincidence favoured EAM/ELAS in this matter. Thessaly was the one area in Greece where their monopoly had remained practically unchallenged since the dissolution of Saraphis' independent force. Although there were isolated units of EDES in embryo as a consequence of the "National Bands" Agreement, no force but ELAS was adequate to receive the enemy's surrender. Thessaly was also the one area of Italian occupation whose commanding general was brave enough to transfer his allegiance. That was due largely to the chance that he had served in London and Washington as Italian Military Attaché, and knew where his sympathies lay. But the transfer of the Pinerolo Division would still never have taken place if there had been no BMM, or if the BMM had refused to guarantee the terms of the surrender. The acting commander of the BMM was asked by General Infante to guarantee that the terms set out in the Instrument of Surrender[1] would be observed by the guerillas. As a member of the JGHQ, he could only have refused to do so at the expense of denouncing the good faith of its other members, and allowing the Pinerolo Division to surrender instead to the Germans. There was, in fact, no alternative, although there was already suspicion that EAM/ELAS would not respect the terms they signed.

The signature of the Instrument of Surrender on 12th September, 1943, turned the Pinerolo Division into the first actively co-belligerent Italian formation in Europe. It deserves emphasis because it illustrates all the three motives to which the culmination of the KKE's first campaign can be attributed. In the first place, it fostered the belief that the war was about

[1] See Appendix D for the text.

to end. The belief was underlined immediately afterwards, when German troops began to leave Greece for the north in great numbers. The guerilla system of intelligence failed to grasp that these movements were partly a bluff to trap themselves, and partly a redistribution throughout the Balkans necessitated by the loss of the Italian garrisons of Albania and Yugoslavia. The Albanian puppets, perhaps deceived by the same token, seized the opportunity of declaring themselves neutral, and shortly afterwards expected a seat in the Allied Control Commission of Italy; but they performed the transformation less dexterously than the Bulgars a year later, emerged from it without gaining anything, even attention. Besides creating this general deception, the Italian surrender assured the KKE, in the second place, of an enormous increase in the fire-power of ELAS, as soon as the units of the Pinerolo Division could be manœuvred into convenient positions for disarmament. By presenting ridiculous excuses for scattered dispositions, by insinuating Communist propaganda among the bewildered Italians, by borrowing specialists and weapons that were never returned, the commanders of ELAS from the first set about preparing the Pinerolo Division for despoliation when the time was ripe. At the end of September it had ceased to exist except on paper, and was ready for the step which gave the KKE their second motive for launching the civil war of October. At the same time the attitude of the British authorities, as revealed to EAM/ELAS by the episode of the Italian surrender, gave them the third of their motives. The last was one of several related symptoms.

From the beginning of the negotiations, some weeks before the Italian surrender became a fact, the EAM/ELAS members of JGHQ had noticed in the acting commander of the BMM a propensity to take the side of anyone but themselves in any dispute that arose. First it was EDES or EKKA; then it was Sarandis, the Nomarch of Trikkala, who acted as the Italians' go-between; then it was General Infante himself. They could infer that this was not a personal matter: it was because the intentions of EAM/ELAS directly contradicted the intentions of the British authorities. The BMM had categorical instructions from General Wilson to acquire every possible Italian weapon; to reserve to itself the responsibility for reallotting them; and on no account to allow the whole booty to fall into the hands of ELAS. The Commander-in-Chief distrusted the purposes to which EAM/ELAS would put such a windfall of fire-power, the equivalent of which could never be made up by the usual resources at British disposal. It was uncertain at the time whether aeroplanes could be adapted to drop artillery, or even heavy mortars and machine-guns; although something was later achieved in supplying all of them, it never reached the magnitude of an entire division's equipment. Since General Infante would not surrender to guerillas alone, and only British consent could secure the windfall, it was a reasonable condition that the distribution should rest in the same hands as the allotment of air sorties. Theoretically, that meant in the hands of the JGHQ; but the discretion of the BMM was easily exercised to adjust supplies by air to fit military requirements. It was not so easily exercised in the case of equipment that was already assembled before their eyes in an adjacent area of Greece. The instructions given to BMM therefore led to long and acrimonious arguments. They ended in the compromise described, which EAM/ELAS were already conspiring to frustrate, and left a sting which permanently poisoned their relations with the British authorities. The same result emerged from almost every debate of the JGHQ during the same period.

The pin-pricks of this mutual suspicion occurred daily. They were generally trivial, but one other example besides that of the Italian surrender deserves attention. The purpose of the "National Bands" Agreement had been to allow new forces to take the field against the Germans, unmolested by ELAS and led by whom they chose. To facilitate operations, their commands were to be incorporated with the subordinate commands of ELAS, and with an appropriate BLO, in Joint Headquarters subordinate to and modelled on the JGHQ. In the case of the existing forces of EDES and EKKA, it was difficult for EAM/ELAS to evade this provision. But in the case of forces new to the field, the subordinate commanders of ELAS were instructed to contend firstly that such forces could not be admitted to a JHQ until they existed in the field; secondly that until they had been admitted to a JHQ, they had no right to exist in the field, and could legitimately be attacked.[1] While the "National Bands" Agreement was being signed, EAM/ELAS were already applying this rule to three of their minor rivals: Athos Roumeliotis, who had actually signed the first draft of the Agreement; ES and EOA in the Peloponnese, which never survived to have a chance of signing it; and PAO, the resurrected form of YVE in Macedonia, which signed the final draft of the Agreement only to have its adherence disallowed by EAM/ELAS. The suppression of Athos Roumeliotis was regretted by no one, and condoned by the BMM; he had never served any useful purpose, and was legitimately regarded by the KKE as a deserter from ELAS. But the BMM earned disfavour in the eyes of EAM/ELAS by the obstinacy with which it defended their Peloponnesian and Macedonian rivals. Both were accused of collaboration with the Germans; both were forced into positions in which they had almost no alternative but to do so: both presumed upon the support of the BMM

[1]This argument is not presented, as it might seem, in conscious irony. It exactly reproduces the kind of arguments that the KKE put forward; though they took care not to put them both forward through the same spokesman, at the same time, in the same context. Communist logic is full of such pairs of mutually incompatible arguments; but their incompatibility, in terms of formal logic, is only apparent when they are constated. Those accustomed to Communist logic are too shrewd, and those accustomed to formal logic are often too polite or puzzled, to do this at the right moment.

to behave provocatively towards EAM/ELAS. Yet neither could be abandoned by the British authorities without sacrificing the principles of the "National Bands" Agreement. The KKE could find only one explanation of British obstinacy in supporting these minorities: that they were to be used, along with EDES and EKKA, to back the reimposition on liberated Greece of the exiled King and Government. The idea that the BMM was only concerned to enforce the terms of the "National Bands" Agreement seemed unplausible.

Such was the state of suspicion when the six delegates returned from Egypt. To the visible sympathy which the BMM had shown successively towards EDES and EKKA, towards General Infante, towards ES and EOA and PAO, towards anyone in fact but EAM/ELAS, there was now added complementary news of the antipathy with which the proposals of the delegation had been received by the Anglo-Greek authorities in Cairo. The first reassembly of the JGHQ in its entirety (with the exception of Brigadier Myers, who had already in effect been relieved of his command) was marked by a tirade from Saraphis against the disloyalty of his colleagues outside EAM/ELAS. Hostility towards Greek rivals was near boiling-point. Doubts of British faith were fed by small errors of the BMM. The most serious lay in the handling of the principal newcomers in the aeroplane by which the delegation returned: Bakirdzis, Peltekis and the Americans. No information had come in advance that Bakirdzis and Peltekis were to be on the aircraft, nor any clear instructions about the American cavalry officers with them. Because Bakirdzis expressed an inclination to form a guerilla force in his native Macedonia, it was suggested to him by the BMM that he might take command of all forces there if ELAS, EDES and PAO would accept him. Because Peltekis was destined to resume his subversive activities in Athens, he was immediately sent back there without consulting EAM/ELAS. Because the senior American had in advance been appointed as liaison officer to a cavalry unit of ELAS, no suggestion was made that he should be treated as a member of the JGHQ, nor was it his wish. But EAM/ELAS resented these decisions. They knew, as the BMM did not, that Bakirdzis and Peltekis were already ripe to move insensibly in their own direction, and that American policy towards Greece was already far enough apart from British policy to make the insertion of a wedge between them comparatively easy. The small errors therefore contributed to large results. The night of 16th-17th September restored the six delegates to Greece, and transformed the BMM into the AMM, under conditions which were ominous for the future.

By the end of September 1943 the leaders of EAM/ELAS were convinced, like most other Greeks, that the occupation was about to end; they were assured, with reasonable luck, of obtaining the entire equipment of the Pinerolo Division; they believed that the British authorities were preparing to frustrate their political aims by force as soon as they returned to Greece. All three motives combined to urge them to decisive action. They showed their mood by the judicial murder of several heroes of the Gorgopotamos operation, as well as of a group of men from the village of Molos in Roumeli, who were accused of collaboration with the Germans but vainly pleaded membership of EDES; British supplies to ELAS in Roumeli were accordingly suspended under the terms of the "National Bands" Agreement. They gave the next hint of their intentions by asking the BMM to pay in advance the entire allocation of sovereigns to which they were entitled for maintenance up to the end of the year. The failure of this *ballon d'essai* did not hinder their plans. The opportunity was fortuitously provided by the events of the end of September. The Allies had reoccupied some of the Aegean islands; the exiled Government had sent Sophoulis, a cousin of the aged Liberal leader, to Samos as its official representative; the Germans were moving troops northwards. Liberation seemed imminent. On 29th September the expected crisis came: a warning order was issued to the JGHQ to prepare for crucial operations against six major aerodromes in Greece. Connecting this order with the apparent withdrawals of the Germans, EAM/ELAS concluded that the allied forces were about to return to Greece. They refused to co-operate in the plan. A few hours later, but not before they had shown their hand, they learned that the inference was incorrect: the purpose of the operations was to relieve German pressure upon the Aegean islands, which the allied forces were already in danger of losing. The plan proposed that against one of the six aerodromes, Larisa, not the guerillas but the Pinerolo Division itself should be used. The Pinerolo Division had already ceased to exist except on paper,[1] but the misconception suited EAM/ELAS. They reversed their position, promised to engage the other five aerodromes, and urged General Infante to the impossible assault upon Larisa. They had thus made and retrieved a small miscalculation; but the general future seemed clear. Despite the momentary shock, EAM/ELAS were still convinced that the German occupation was about to end; they executed the rest of the plan accordingly.

From 1st October events moved too fast to be controlled, but in the direction required by the KKE. An abortive attack was launched by a mixed force against Larisa. EAM/ELAS made use of Infante's pre-occupation with this operation to complete their preparations against the Pinerolo Division, which was already reduced to units below the strength of companies, spread over a front of nearly a hundred miles. No attacks were made against the other five aerodromes, except by one or two Allied officers, because the guerillas had other business in hand.

[1]That this was unknown to SOE Cairo was a good example of incomplete understanding between its staff and the BMM, for which the latter was to blame.

Communications which had taken place between Infante and Zervas, and between Zervas and Red Cross representatives acting for the Germans, were linked by EAM/ELAS into a Fascist conspiracy against themselves. Incidents of minor friction, such as occurred daily between the guerillas without consequence, were seized upon as *casus belli*. On 8th October ELAS attacked units of EDES in Thessaly, and enlarged its attacks against ES, EOA and PAO. On the same day Colonel Ravtopoulos, the senior EDES member of JGHQ, was recalled by Zervas. On 10th October the attack on Larisa aerodrome misfired. On 12th and 13th October ELAS attacks upon all rivals, except EKKA, became general throughout Greece, and the remaining EDES members of the JGHQ were placed under arrest. Elsewhere on the 13th a New Zealand officer was killed by an ELAS bullet. Italy declared war against Germany on the same day; Infante took the opportunity to ask EAM/ELAS that his division should be concentrated, to take over a separate sector against the Germans. On the morning of 14th October EAM/ELAS acceded to this request, and disarmed them all in the afternoon. Neither the "National Bands" Agreement nor the Italian Armistice was ever formally denounced. ELAS GHQ continued during the winter of 1943 (as again in December 1944) to protest their implicit obedience to the orders of GHQ Middle East (except such orders as were issued under "obvious misapprehension"), while they set about destroying their rivals.

The equipment of the Pinerolo Division, especially the mountain artillery, was rushed across the Pindus range to be used by Aris Veloukhiotis against Zervas, and a local truce was arranged with the Germans. The timing of the whole operation seemed masterly: the KKE apparently had Greece in its grasp at the moment when the German occupation was about to end. ELAS GHQ even proclaimed that the British authorities had ordered them to attack, because their rivals were guilty of collaboration with the Germans. It seemed likely that this proclamation would have its effect before it could be denounced; if the plan succeeded in a few days, it would not matter what the British authorities replied. But within two days a graver miscalculation was revealed: the Germans were not leaving Greece after all. Having successfully bluffed the intelligence system of every guerilla organisation, and the grape-vine telegraph of the entire country, they turned into the mountains from east and west, and rent the resistance to ribbons at will. In the chaos that followed it seemed doubtful whether any organisation could survive.

By the middle of October it was plain that the plans of the KKE had miscarried; but nearly three months passed before they would acknowledge it. The Germans reoccupied the Aegean islands and the mainland lines of communication which the Italians had abandoned.

Greek resistance was diminished by the elimination of all the rivals to ELAS except EDES, which nearly succumbed to combined attacks of Aris Veloukhiotis and the Germans, and EKKA, which remained precariously neutral. But hatred of EAM/ELAS threw up other rivals, some of whom gave up resistance as hopeless and resigned themselves to collaboration. Andon Tsaous appeared in Eastern Macedonia; the minor armed collaborators of the Germans were enabled to expand into the relatively formidable forces of Poulos, Khrysokhöou and Mikhalagas in West Macedonia, and into the Security Battalions in southern Greece.

The discredit of EAM/ELAS, which fed this opposition, was increased by allied denunciations. The BBC, which had hitherto warmly supported ELAS, now named Aris Veloukhiotis as a war criminal: a charge which he did his best to justify by seizing and assaulting British and Greek members of the AMM. In the House of Commons Mr. Churchill, with *prima facie* justification, accused ELAS of murdering a British officer. Although the guilt was reduced on investigation to culpable negligence resulting in accidental death, nevertheless the shock offset the charge against PAO, which EAM/ELAS had widely advertised, of trying to kidnap another British officer. On 22nd October General Wilson broadcast an appeal for unity, in which he blamed unspecified guerillas for turning their weapons on their compatriots; leaflets dropped by aeroplanes over Greece categorically fixed the blame upon ELAS.

Only the most formidable accusation of all was omitted. It had accidentally been revealed to the acting commander of the AMM that the Red Cross representatives, whom the Germans sent into the mountains to obtain a truce with the guerillas, had failed with Zervas, but succeeded with a formation of ELAS.[1] The decision by higher authority not to advertise this folly may have been prompted by the embarrassing entanglement of a British officer in equally unorthodox negotiations with the Germans in Athens.[2] But even without this addition to the indictment, it was known throughout Greece that EAM/ELAS had forfeited the confidence of its British allies, and reduced the resistance movement to its lowest ebb.

(c) *Among the Exiles.* The discredit of EAM/ELAS was a matter of satisfaction to the Greek authorities in exile, who had formed an unfavourable opinion of the whole resistance movement and an underestimate of its significance.[3] Once the six delegates from the Greek

[1]See page 78.

[2]See page 39. Conceivably this may account for the story published in *Pravda* in January 1944, that Ribbentrop had lately met a British representative in a neutral capital to discuss a separate peace.

[3]Ten months later, when the civil war was over, a Greek cabinet minister's private secretary asked me if there was any way of starting it again.

mountains had been sent back, the Government of Tsoudheros quickly recovered. The republican ministers forgot their wish to resign and turned to less disruptive matters: the capitulation of Italy furnished enough business to drive the recent nightmare out of their heads.

There were diplomatic problems arising from the new relation with the Italians, and administrative problems arising from the temporary liberation of several Aegean islands. The two became interlocked by reason of the fact that some of the islands in question had previously belonged to Greece, and some to Italy. Tsoudheros clarified the diplomatic problem by broadcasting on 9th September, that his Government had agreed on the terms of the Italian armistice before it was signed; and on 14th October, that the admission of the Italians as co-belligerents against the Germans had also been accepted, though reluctantly, by the Greek Government. He left open the right to press claims against Italy later, especially on the Dodecanese islands. Two of these, which were among the first of the Aegean islands to be liberated, had spontaneously declared their adherence to Greece; but Tsoudheros was not permitted to instal a Greek administration anywhere but in Samos and other islands which belonged to Greece before the war. The younger Sophoulis and the elder Tsigantes were sent to Samos as civil and military representatives of the Government respectively, but the Dodecanese had to wait until March 1947 before a Greek administration took control of them for the first time since the Byzantine Empire.

Disappointment that the Dodecanese were not immediately placed under Greek sovereignty was mollified by the inclusion of a Greek member (as well as a Yugoslav) in the Allied Control Commission for Italy, and by the contemptuous indifference with which the Allies received the Albanian puppets' declaration of neutrality and their claim for similar representation in the ACC. Ioannis Politis took up the Greek appointment in November; almost at once, the whole Greek world heard with satisfaction a denunciation of Count Sforza for his part in depriving Greece of the Dodecanese thirty years before. But the rescue of Mussolini by German parachutists in September, and the recapture of the Aegean islands in October, were set-backs to the optimism with which the Greeks in exile, like their compatriots under the occupation, were awaiting the end of the war.

Attention was then turned to Moscow, where the first conference of the Foreign Ministers assembled on 18th October. The day before, a meeting of the Pan-Slav Committee gave them a calculated hint by acclaiming Tito and denouncing Mihailovitch; but there were other more welcome signs of the times in Moscow. A new Turkish Ambassador to the USSR had been warmly received, perhaps as a sop to western prejudice. Democratic notions of religious toleration appeared in the establishment of a Council of Affairs to keep contact between the Soviet

Government and the Russian Orthodox Patriarchate, and of an Ecclesiastical Administration of the Moslems of Central Asia. As both the Patriarch and the Mufti were aged, these concessions might also be interpreted as examples of authoritarian technique: so might the first appearance of Stalin in the uniform of Marshal of the Soviet Union, when he received Mr. Eden on 21st October. But the mood of the time favoured a kindlier interpretation; allied observers looked to Moscow with agreeable anticipations. Distracted by the spectacle, the Greek Government in exile at first paid little attention to the civil war in the Greek mountains.

Even when it was noticed, its implications were not at first appreciated. It might be assumed that the Germans' counter-attack would help to draw the quarrelsome guerillas together again; it might be hoped that the Moscow conference would result in Soviet intervention with EAM. There was even some gratification in Egypt at the spectacle of thieves falling out, wasting each other's energies and resources, before coming to rest in a deadlock of mutual exhaustion. There was some justification, though not until several months had passed, for all these states of mind. In the meantime only two interventions were attempted. The exiled King and his ministers broadcast on 28th October, the anniversary of Italy's attack on Greece, a series of appeals for unity among the Greeks; these included assurances that the day of deliverance was approaching. On 24th November Sophoklis Veniselos, the Minister of Marine, broadcast another appeal for unity, and another promise to the Greek people of freedom to choose its own "representatives and government" on the day of liberation. Part of these declarations was stale and barren; part was delusive. Two months of silence in which they were the only punctuation, showed that the essential point had not been grasped. The policy which culminated in the "National Bands" Agreement had been based upon the assumption that the German occupation would come to an early end, at the latest before winter, and that ELAS would continue to be dependent upon British aeroplanes for arms and ammunition. In the course of October 1943 both these assumptions had become invalid, and the plan of the KKE stood revealed. Yet the Greek authorities in exile continued to behave as if nothing in the remote and barbarous mountains could have any real significance.

CHAPTER IV

INTERLUDE

NOVEMBER 1943—FEBRUARY 1944

"It was when the nearest of kin were no longer at peace
That there was talk of 'dutiful sons';
Not till the fatherland was dark with strife
Did we hear of 'loyal henchmen'."

Attributed to LAO-TZE.

THE Greek exiles were not to blame for having no policy towards the KKE. The more extreme among them would have argued that they had a policy, which the British authorities frustrated. They had opposed the creation of a resistance movement in Greece, and wished to denounce it once it was in being. They argued that the British created and sustained EAM/ELAS, and deprived the legitimate authorities of their control over Greek affairs. The fallacy of this argument has already been exposed: the truth was, on the contrary, that only British intervention had forestalled the monopoly of the KKE and enabled any other political elements in Greece to survive at all. If the British authorities had ignored Greece throughout the occupation, there would still have been a resistance movement, numerically no less strong: but it would have been exclusively in the hands of the Communists, instead of shared with other political elements. The less extreme among the Greek exiles would have argued that the British authorities had erred in the opposite direction, by preventing them from coming to terms with EAM/ELAS in August 1943. They had been ready to resign from Tsoudheros' Government, in order to enter into a new coalition with EAM and its colleagues, and the British had prevented them. The fallacy of this argument lay in their own instability. They had taken for granted, on the word of a vocal minority, that the future of Greece depended upon an undemocratic act of violence against the constitution, which would have placed Greek sovereignty in the hands successively of EAM, of the KKE, and of the USSR. There can be no controversy with those who think that this would have been a good thing: my purpose is to undeceive those who do not understand that it would have happened, and to account for the actions of those who thought, rightly or wrongly, that it would have been a bad thing. The moderate republicans of

Tsoudheros' Government, who were at that time still among the unen-
lightened, would have been just as indignant with the British authorities
a year later, if they had been allowed to resign and surrender, as they
were at being restrained.

The reason why the Greek exiles had no practicable policy to meet
the Communist policy lay not in any folly of their own, but in the
impossibility of a policy. Neither Greek nor British nor allied policy
was any longer capable of being reframed to meet the problem which
had shown itself in August 1943: it could only have been met years
before, because it was not a Greek but a Balkan problem, and in a sense
a world-wide one. On a narrower scale, it can be called the problem
of resistance throughout Europe, provided that resistance is recognised
as part of the larger problem of foreign occupation: and foreign occupation as part of the larger problem of world war: and world war as part
of the larger problem of the international conflict of independent sovereignties. In its narrow scope, the crux of the problem was the use of
resistance for political ends. If a general fault may be charged to the
account of the Anglo-Greek authorities, it was not an attempt to distort
the Greek resistance from one political end to another, as their critics
have argued, but a failure to realise in time that it was being used for
political ends at all; a failure, in fact, to take it seriously. When that was
fully realised, control had already passed out of their hands. They had
no more choice in the new question, whether or not the resistance
movement should be stopped, than they had had two years before in
the old question, whether it should be started. Once the Communists
had taken the lead, the best that the allied authorities could hope to do
was to mitigate the consequences. The late summer of 1943 was an
opportunity for verifying that conclusion.

It is questionable whether the military value of guerilla movements
in the Balkans justified their continued existence after August 1943.
Irregular tactics had paid dividends in the earlier stages of the war, when
the Allies were behind the Germans in organisation and equipment.
When they were battling for time to set their machinery of total warfare
in motion, every pin-prick was worth while. A handful of commandoes,
saboteurs, franc-tireurs or guerillas could do damage out of proportion
to the expense involved. Greece provided an instance in 1942 at the
Gorgopotamos viaduct, the destruction of which, at negligible expense,
cut Rommel's principal supply line for six weeks during the battle of
North Africa. But by August 1943 the Allies had passed to the offensive;
numerical and material superiority made victory in the long run certain;
the value of guerilla campaigns ceased to bear any proportion to the
disasters which they brought upon the civilian population, and the
political troubles which they laid up for the future. But it was not possible
to close them down, because the foregoing arguments were irrelevant

to the purpose for which Balkan Communism had launched its contribution to resistance. Disasters to the civilian population and political troubles in the future were, if anything, welcome to the Communist Parties of the Balkans, since a suffering and discontented population was a potential reinforcement of Communism. Considerations based merely on the war effort against the Germans were indifferent to Balkan Communists, since the Germans were certain to be evicted in any case. If the British authorities, urged on by the Greek authorities, had decided in August 1943 to close down their missions and supplies to the National Bands in Greece, they might have been justified by military considerations; but the only effect upon EAM/ELAS would have been to hand over to them unchallenged control of the country. It was a mistake to perpetuate the myth that the Balkan guerillas still contributed indispensable aid to the war effort: having decided in Yugoslavia that backing Mihailovitch was no longer worth while, the correct inference should have been that no guerillas were worth while, not that Tito was worth adopting in his place. But these were mistakes of secondary importance; whether they had been made or not, the course of the resistance movements in the Balkans was set. ELAS had already integrated relations with the LNC of Albania, with Tito's lieutenant Tempo in Yugoslavia, with the Macedonian SNOF, and with the partisans of Bulgaria. The political implications of these connections were already crystallised. In the summer of 1943, when HMG chose in Yugoslavia the one policy that was certain to expedite the policies of Balkan Communism, the decision only hastened the evil day; it might have been postponed, but could not at that stage have been averted.

These wider considerations make it impossible to blame the Greek authorities in exile for having no constructive policy to meet the threat implied in the civil war of 1943: but it was unwise to behave as if nothing was happening. From the middle of October to the latter half of December 1943 no further allusions to the civil war were publicly made beyond the few that have been recorded. The state of popular knowledge on that subject was summed up by the London *Times'* correspondent in Ankara, when he commented on the divergences between the guerillas on 1st November: "Many of (their) reciprocal charges are certainly unfair and exaggerated; they are the result of that deplorable state of mind which labels as 'Fascist' anybody opposed to social upheavals, and as 'Communist' any person favouring social reforms. The immediate consequence of this sharp division among the Greek people is . . . the weakening of the movement of resistance against the Germans, but it may also lead, after the liberation of Greece, to civil war between the rival factions." Comparing this balanced judgment with the *Times'* reports on the same theme a year later, it is easy to see the effect of the suppression of vital evidence over a prolonged period. Because the Anglo-Greek authorities persisted in concealing what was going on, it was assumed by public opinion, and especially by the Press, that they had something discreditable to conceal. As usual, suspicion fastened upon the relations of HMG and the King of the Hellenes. The crucial implications of the civil war were thus obscured by the trivial question of the King's position, on which almost every possible permutation of diplomatic vocabulary had already been expended.

On 9th November in the House of Commons Mr. Churchill denied having given any undertaking to the King of the Hellenes. He added that "until the Greek people can express their will in conditions of freedom and tranquillity, it is the settled policy of HMG to support the King of the Hellenes, who is at once our loyal ally and the constitutional head of the Greek state." The perennial interest in Greece of HMG's critics was thus momentarily staved off, without any mention of the more important topic of the civil war. Two days later chance distracted their attention to a crisis in the Lebanon, which occupied the rest of November. By the time public interest was ready to revert to Greece, it was again possible to occupy it almost entirely with the King's matter. On 11th December a letter was published, dated 8th November, from King George II to his Prime Minister, stating that "when the long-desired hour of liberation for our country strikes, I shall examine anew the question of my return to Greece, in agreement with the Government and in the light of the political and military conditions of the time and the national interest." This revised definition of the King's position coincided with a report from Greece that fighting between ELAS and EDES, which had died down, was beginning to flare up again. The coincidence created the impression that the King's matter was the issue at stake in an otherwise unimportant brawl, and clouded the truth behind a delusion that Zervas was fighting in defence of the monarchy. The desire to minimise the importance, and even if possible to conceal the existence, of the civil war in the Greek mountains thus contributed to the efforts of Communist propaganda to misrepresent its nature. Instead of a struggle precipitated by ELAS to impose the KKE on Greece, it became fantastically transformed in the public eye into a struggle precipitated by EDES and the British to reimpose the King.

Still hoping that it would peter out into a deadlock, the exiled Government postponed resolution a little longer. On 14th December Tsoudheros held a Press conference from which allusions to the civil war were again almost excluded. He announced the aims of his Government under five headings, of which only the last touched on the crucial topic. The first was to prepare for the King's return; the second was to bring about the co-operation of politicians in exile and those in Greece as soon as the country was liberated; the third was to develop a Balkan union; the fourth was the economic security of the Balkans; the fifth was the final welding of Greece's internal unity. He described the King's decision of 8th November as "that of a great patriot"; he added that the Greek situation was clear "save for the spectacle of guerillas in conflict with each other." That meant that it was not clear at all, but the exiles were in a mood to be thankful for small comforts. In that mood it was even possible to set off against each other the two most recent actions of the Soviet Government in Balkan affairs. In November Tito had set up an Executive Committee of National Liberation, a Legislative Council, and a Partisan Assembly in the mountains of Yugoslavia, and a Military Mission of the Red Army had been accredited to him; but at least in the following month M. Novikov, the new Soviet Ambassador to Greece, had presented his letters of credence to King George II in Cairo. It could be hoped that this might be a prelude to Soviet intercession with EAM, especially when Allied solidarity was being reaffirmed at Teheran and Cairo. On December 17th another appeal for Greek unity was broadcast, this time on a non-political basis, by Admiral Dhemestikhas: but when that too failed the exiled authorities realised at last that they had to grapple seriously with the problem.

As a display of fighting, the civil war had not been impressive; that fact had helped to delude the exiles about its importance. The cost of killing a man was incalculable: it had taken several thousand rounds at slightly more than extreme range even to frighten one. Most of the casualties were hostages; a characteristic of this type of warfare which pointed to the more important fact, that it should be measured in terms of political bitterness rather than military effectiveness. That was why the KKE had persisted after its immediate objective could be seen to have been missed. Every rival, except the neutral EKKA, was eliminated in turn; Zervas was driven back into a small area of Epirus, where his force was kept in being by liberal supplies from British aeroplanes. EAM/ELAS, whose supplies had been almost entirely cut off as the penalty of aggression, were unable to give the knock-out blow. Their plan could only have succeeded if their conquest of the mountains had been followed, as they expected, by the evacuation from Greece of the Germans, leaving them a political vacuum to supplement their military hegemony. When it was plain that the Germans were not going after all, it was also plain that the whole plan had broken down; but not until the middle of December was failure admitted. When the Greek mountains had passed through more than two months of chaos, from which only the Germans profited, EAM/ELAS at last expressed their willingness to make peace. This decision came immediately after two simultaneous symptoms of Allied policy: the appointment of the acting commander of the BMM, whom EAM/ELAS had hoped to see removed, as substantive commander of its successor, the AMM; and the arrival in Greece of Major Wines, the first American to make the AMM a Mission that was allied in fact as well as in name. The desultory struggle had been prolonged beyond its usefulness in the hope that some intervention, perhaps American, perhaps Russian, would oblige the Greek and British authorities to abandon their support of the rivals of EAM/ELAS. A moment had come at the beginning of December when Zervas' position was so desperate that the Commander of AMM had reluctantly recommended such a course, as the only hope of making further resistance to the Germans possible, even on terms chosen by EAM/ELAS. This was a decisive moment in the history of British relations with Zervas, because hitherto the military motive for supporting him had predominated over the political; but now the former had all but disappeared. Although Zervas' military power could be resurrected, the motive for doing so must henceforth be nakedly political. Nevertheless the recommendation of the AMM was not accepted. A few days later the American attitude seemed to be made plain by the arrival of Major Wines. A few days later still the KKE realised that, at least for the time being, the game was up. They asked for the mediation of the Allied authorities to negotiate terms with Zervas on 19th December. Two days later Tsoudheros made his first practical attempt to meet the problem.

Broadcasting from Cairo on 21st December, in the name of General Wilson as well as the Greek Government, he stressed two new points in a fresh appeal for unity. They were the first points he ever made in terms current not among the exiles, but among the guerillas, whose leaders had been warned to listen to the speech and to present their comments. The first point was that men guilty of collaboration with the Germans should be expelled from the resistance organisations. The second was that if the guerillas could not unite, they should disband and go home. The first point pleased EAM/ELAS, who interpreted it as directed against Zervas; the second infuriated them. Psaros and Zervas offered little comment; the former being formally neutral in the civil war, the latter being always ready for any settlement that might suit the Allied authorities. Neither referred to collaborators, since Psaros was not accused and Zervas had a vicarious uneasiness on behalf of some of his followers. On the basis of their combined comments, Tsoudheros prepared a second broadcast for 31st December. But before he delivered it, Zervas attacked ELAS in an effort to regain lost ground before an armistice should supervene. EAM/ELAS interpreted this, added to his silence about collaborators in EDES, as a breach of faith both on his part and on that of the AMM, whose liaison officer at Zervas' HQ was accused of directing the operations. The only intervention of the AMM in reality was to halt Zervas' advance at what seemed to be the best operational boundary between EDES and ELAS; but the latter were in no mood to believe this. Tsoudheros' second broadcast, therefore, which should have been followed by the submission of formal terms for negotiation by both parties, did not have the expected result. Although the speech referred to messages of support which the British Foreign Secretary and the American Secretary of State had sent to Tsoudheros, it also contained charges against EAM/ELAS of dictatorial methods. It was followed by a long silence, while Aris Veloukhiotis mounted a counter-attack against Zervas.

Until the counter-attack was ready, no pressure moved the leaders of the KKE, although many things happened that might have mollified them. On New Year's Day, 1944, not only King George II but even Moscow Radio appealed for unity in Greece. On 12th January a Soviet Note was handed to the Greek Ambassador in Moscow supporting the establishment of a united front of Greek guerillas. In the same month a royal decree deprived members of all collaborating governments of Greek citizenship. As if to point the moral, *pour encourager les autres,* the collaborating Minister of Labour was assassinated in Athens a few days later. Tsoudheros broadcast again, warning the Security Battalions to desert by 31st January on pain of being treated as traitors. All this had no effect, except on Ioannis Rallis, who broadcast a curious reply implying that the King had abdicated, and incongruously appealing for an end to internal strife. The Security Battalions extended their activities; the silence of EAM remained unbroken. Rumours spread that EAM was forming a shadow government under Professor Svolos, in support of which the Greek armed forces of the Middle East were about to revolt. The rumours were truer than was believed at the time, but they did not affect the KKE's immediate plan: they were prepared to come to terms for the moment, once Aris Veloukhiotis had again chastised Zervas. His counter-attack began in the latter half of January, and simultaneously EAM/ELAS put forward three conditions for a truce. The first was that each force should retain the positions which it occupied at the moment of the cease-fire. The second was that Zervas should denounce those members of his organisation who had collaborated with the enemy. The third was that negotiations for the formation of a united guerilla army should begin at once. The terms were transmitted to Zervas by wireless through the AMM and Cairo; under military pressure from ELAS and diplomatic pressure from the AMM, he accepted all three. Aris Veloukhiotis delayed the cease-fire by a series of tricks until he had driven Zervas back to his minimum area; the truce finally took effect on 4th February.

An armistice conference attended by EAM/ELAS, EDES, EKKA and the AMM occupied the rest of February. Its importance lay only in the interpretation of the third term of the truce; agreement was quickly reached on lesser points. A joint denunciation of the Security Battalions was signed on 19th February[1]; Zervas' repudiation of Gonatas, Tavoularis, Voulpiotis and other members of EDES as collaborators with the Germans was accepted; minor jockeying for position on the

---

[1]The text is given in Appendix E. This document, which was never officially heard of again, is discussed on page 98.

M

line between the two forces persisted. But none of these things had the same importance as the question of a united guerilla army. It was the intention of EAM/ELAS that this should be a single guerilla army, under a single command, responsible to a single cabinet minister in Greece, representing a single coalition government. By an error of telegraphic transmission, the delegates of EKKA and EDES[1] arrived at the conference unaware of the breadth of this intention. The EAM/ELAS delegates[2] emphasised in a telegram to Tsoudheros that they regarded the conference not as the last stage of the civil war, but as the first stage in the reorganisation of his Government. Tsoudheros replied that as soon as the guerillas had settled the civil war, he would be ready to discuss a new coalition with them. The British and American representatives[3] at the conference were instructed to confine the discussion to military matters; and in consonance with that policy, the British representative, who had at first been appointed to represent the Greek Government as well, was limited to the representation of the Greek High Command.

It was impossible to confine the armistice conference to military matters. The Greek resistance was founded on politics; the civil war had political roots and political consequences. Every theme of discussion was debated in political terms, even when they were disguised in military language. The very notion of a united army had political implications; for an army implied a commander-in-chief, responsible to a war minister, responsible in turn to a cabinet. The delegates at the conference could not even discuss a coalition of their forces without some resignation of independence, which was intended by EAM/ELAS and feared by the rest to mean absorption in the framework of ELAS GHQ. They could not discuss a commander-in-chief without considering the political backgrounds of the candidates. Of the two men who might have been acceptable to all the guerillas, General Plastiras was in exile in France, and General Othonaios was too infirm to leave Athens; but neither would have been acceptable to the exiled authorities. No other was seriously discussed, though the names of Bakirdzis, Mandakas, Manettas and Sariyiannis were put forward, in addition to Saraphis, Zervas and Psaros. Above all, they could not discuss the theme that was uppermost in every mind, without going beyond their terms of reference: namely, the proposal of the EAM/ELAS delegates that the guerilla organisations should form a committee among themselves, with the provisional status of a government and the function of negotiating a coalition with Tsoudheros. The suggested title was "Preparatory Governmental Committee." The shadow of Tito's Committee of National Liberation

---

[1] Kartalis and Pyromaglou throughout; Psaros and Zervas for a few days each.
[2] Petros Roussos and Saraphis.
[3] Myself and Major Wines.

darkened the conference table; the delegates of EDES and EKKA knew that they were being offered a last chance of adhering to a shadow government which EAM intended to form in any case, with or without them. But being debarred by the instructions of Tsoudheros and the Allied authorities from discussing any but military subjects, the conference devoted the greater part of its sessions to a philological debate on the comparative significance of the epithets "united" and "single," in qualification of the new army which they had no intention of forming.

The Allied representatives made only intermittent attempts to bring the other delegates back to the point. They believed that the longer the conference went on, the less likely the civil war was to break out again. The dissolution by the civil war both of the "National Bands" Agreement and of the JGHQ was not unwelcome to them, since both had outlived their usefulness; the fact that almost no mixed areas were left, containing intertwined organisations of various complexions, was to the advantage of operations against the Germans. Such operations were believed to be imminent; indeed, a plan transmitted to the AMM by SOE Cairo envisaged the liberation of Greece before the end of April 1944, and assigned a harassing role to the guerillas. But this prospect did not add to the urgency of the proceedings in February, because in the first place the suggested date of liberation was determined partly by the desire to distract attention of the guerillas from each other, and in the second place all of them privately promised their co-operation to the AMM before the Armistice Conference began. The AMM was therefore content with the resultant situation, and glad to let everyone have his say at length, in the certainty that nothing unacceptable to the Allied authorities was likely to be unanimously acceptable to the guerilla delegates. At the end of February, as a consequence, none of the controversies had been settled. The conference broke up after signing at the Plaka Bridge (which spanned the river dividing EDES from ELAS) an agreement that amounted to no more than an indefinite prolongation of the armistice.[1] The crucial clause was a secret provision binding all three organisations to facilitate the return to Greece of Allied troops; for this was the necessary condition of all subsequent agreements and of the eventual restoration of a recognised government from exile. That was not a little, since the agreement was freely negotiated; but it did not meet the ultimate purposes of EAM/ELAS.

The one certainty which emerged from the dissolution of the conference was that EAM/ELAS had in mind a new political project. The "Preparatory Governmental Committee" was plainly no mere *ballon d'essai*, but a plan of deadly seriousness. The Greek authorities in exile were at last becoming aware of the intention and its importance. The

[1]The text is given in Appendix F.

promise which Tsoudheros had given, to open negotiations for a new coalition when the civil war was formally terminated, was honoured as soon as the Plaka Agreement became known. Even earlier the suggestion that, when Greece was liberated, a regency under the Archbishop of Athens might be a desirable compromise, had been mooted among the Greek authorities. King George II left Cairo for London in the middle of February, leaving Tsoudheros' hands free for the negotiations. Complicated arrangements were put in train to bring a host of Greek politicians from Athens and the mountains together with their fellows in Cairo. The indications were that at last a serious attempt was to be made to solve the problem which had been shelved in the preceding August. How that was to be done, after the steady deterioration which had taken place in the interval, is a question which Tsoudheros might have found difficult to answer. But he was not called upon to do so after all: before the political migration had got under way, chaos was come again.

CHAPTER V

THE SECOND ACT

"One of the laws is very peculiar and surprising: it deprives of the franchise anyone who remains neutral in a civil war."

PLUTARCH, *Life of Solon.*

THE second act, which covers the second attempt of the KKE to win absolute power, is distinguished by a new characteristic. For the first time the nature of the political struggle was clear; not to the public opinion of the world, since the facts were still withheld from the Press, but at least to the contestants. At last the political world in exile became aware that they were not, as they had supposed, playing the old game of Monarchists versus Republicans, or Populists versus Liberals, but a new game, too frightening in reality to be called a game, of Communists versus the Rest; at last the Rest realised that if they failed to win the new game, they would never be able to return to the old one. Their complacency was additionally shaken by Mr. Churchill's speech of 22nd February, in which was heard for the first time a hint that came to be bitterly repeated a year later, that the British authorities were becoming fed up with the antics of the Greeks. They learned momentarily to draw together against the menace to their political survival; not at once, nor unanimously, but at least with growing alertness. Irresponsible republicans were still prepared to make reckless gambles in April 1944, on the assumption that the old game was still in progress, even after the KKE changed all the rules in March; but they were in a diminishing minority, and their irresponsibility was known. The true issues crystallised before the eyes of all but the most obstinate among the Greek exiles, as verified reports were canalised into Cairo not only from Greece, but even more disturbingly from all over the Balkans.

In Albania the LNC, the equivalent of EAM/ELAS, was in a state of civil war with both its Nationalist rivals, the Legality (Legitimist) Movement supporting King Zog and the Balli Kombetar, which was driven (like ELAS' rivals) into collaboration with the Germans. In Yugoslavia Tito was not only at war with Mihailovitch, but through his partisan Assembly had repudiated the exiled Government and King, and through his Committee of National Liberation had demanded representation in UNRRA. In Bulgaria guerillas were in the field under the inspiration of the Communist Dimitrov, with the result that in Eastern Macedonia and Western Thrace the only Greek Nationalist movement, newly inspired to energetic activity by Andon Tsaous, was oppressed in equal proportions by the Germans, by EAM/ELAS, by the occupying Bulgars and by the Bulgarian partisans. It is possible that about the turn of the year a representative of the KKE met an officer of the Bulgarian occupation to discuss the future of Macedonia.[1] Bulgarian troops had already occupied Florina, Kastoria and Edhessa, which lay within the area affected by such discussions. The rest of West Macedonia was exposed to the danger of SNOF, the organ of the slavophone autonomist movement, which even the KKE found beyond control. Communism was spreading fast in the Balkans, for all the usual reasons and several irrelevant ones, such as admiration for the successes of the Red Army and disillusionment at the British failure to hold the Aegean islands. In January 1944 Molotov announced a proposal by the Soviet Government to grant certain concessions in foreign policy and defence to the independent sovereignty of some of the Soviet Republics. German propaganda, with some plausibility, interpreted the proposal as a device to facilitate the entry of the East European states into the USSR: it was noticeable that the first three states to benefit by the measure were those lying on the most probable routes of Soviet expansion to the west and south-west, Byelorussia, the Ukraine and Armenia. In March the Red Army entered Rumanian Bessarabia, having already penetrated the 1939 frontiers of Poland and accorded *de facto* recognition to a government of its own choosing. These lessons were before the eyes of the Greek Government even before its local storm broke. Most of them drew the inference that Greece was exposed to the same threat. Apart from the few exceptions who will appear in the following paragraphs, the exiles then abandoned the old game and grimly prepared for the new. The departure for London of the principal object of controversy in the old game, the King of the Hellenes, symbolised the change of purpose and cleared the decks for action.

As awareness grew and determination stiffened, the task confronting the KKE became more complex. Unexpected reactions necessitated variations of tactics; one gambit after another was discarded. The period from the beginning of March 1944 to the end of the year makes up a single act in the drama for a reason which the narrative will make clearer: that it comprises a single, undeviating campaign of the KKE, extended through a greater length of time than had been foreseen, to exploit the political vacuum which the departure of the Germans was expected to leave behind in Greece. But although the theme of this chapter is thus single, it falls into four distinct phases as the manœuvres of EAM/ELAS and the counter-manœuvres of the rest successively shifted the balance of the struggle. In the first phase, the KKE made a new attempt at political

[1] See Appendix A, para. (g).

and military *blitzkrieg*, which almost succeeded, but finally failed before a toughened opposition. In the second phase the KKE retired, puzzled and divided, to lick its wounds while the initiative passed to its opponents. In the third phase the KKE returned to the contest with a new policy of political infiltration under the guise of co-operation. In the fourth phase the KKE reverted to the conclusion that the game could after all be won by a knock-out; and tried, and failed again. By the end of that last phase of the second act, the opportunity was past and another interlude of false security was the necessary consequence. The four phases will be examined in turn, in enlargement of this analysis, as part of a single theme.

1. *MARCH—MAY* 1944.

In 1944 the KKE was faced by the same problem as in 1943, but in an acuter form. Although numerically its membership, and still more its penumbral following, had increased, it was still a minority in Greek life. Since it could not win and retain political power by constitutional means, two alternatives only were open to it: armed violence or political infiltration. From the periodical variations of Communist strategy, it can be argued that both policies had their advocates, whose views from time to time prevailed and succumbed within the political bureau of the KKE. Aris Veloukhiotis favoured the revolutionary policy of armed violence; Siantos probably favoured the milder policy of infiltration. Both policies had been tried in 1943, and neither had succeeded. Since no third possibility presented itself, the only course in 1944 was to make preparations for either or both again. But the difficulties had grown; improvement of tactics was needed if either strategy was to succeed.

The obstacle to armed violence was the growth of armed opposition. The civil war brought a decisive change in the order of battle in Greece. The Peloponnese had been cleared of ES and EOA; central Greece had been cleared of Athos Roumeliotis and the outlying units of EDES; northern Greece had been cleared of PAO. But the armed opposition had taken a new form. There now existed not only the remnants of rival organisations that were theoretically on the same side as ELAS against the Germans, but also an augmented opposition that was openly (though reluctantly) on the side of the Germans. The civil war had given fresh strength to both kinds of opposition. In the mountains, by clearing out of existence the mixed areas in which different groups of guerillas coexisted under the terms of the "National Bands" Agreement, the civil war had left in their place a number of hard cores which were smaller but tougher than before. The toughest was Zervas, whom the civil war had reduced to a minute area of north-west Greece, but one which at least he had to himself. Although it was not convenient in size or shape, nor strategically important in position, he had been enabled to drive ELAS entirely out of it, just as ELAS had driven his forces entirely out of the rest of Greece. The next toughest was Andon Tsaous, who had taken advantage of the KKE's preoccupation with PAO to establish himself impregnably east of the River Strymon. The combined hostility of ELAS and the Bulgarian partisans, whose liaison was conducted by the Greek Communist Rhodhopoulos (alias the Bulgarian Communist Radev), failed throughout the winter and spring to shake his grip. Less tough than Andon Tsaous, but still not contemptible, was Psaros in southern Roumeli. More dangerous than any of these were the forces armed by the Germans to fight ELAS, since they occupied the vital areas of the plains, barring the way between the organisations in the mountains and their objectives in the towns. The Security Battalions, the armed villagers of Mikhalagas, the forces of Poulos and Khrysokhöou, all owed their prosperity to the excesses of EAM/ELAS; all expected as a result to enjoy the favour of the Allies. This was the gravest problem which exercised the Communist leaders of 1944. It led to repeated efforts to secure Allied intervention on their side, but hatred of the KKE had nourished it too effectively to be extirpated.

The obstacle to political infiltration was grounded in a similar appreciation of the KKE'S policy. No politician above the horizontal line had any longer any doubt about the meaning of EAM. It had been the best contrivance that the KKE ever devised, but its independent usefulness was over. The fact that EAM was in function, though not in structure, simply another name for the KKE became well known to every participant in the political contest before 1944 was half way out. Communist diplomacy therefore needed to create a new coalition, bearing the same relation to EAM as EAM to the KKE: a bigger and better nutshell was needed to house the same kernel at the centre. Whereas EAM and ELAS had been devices for drawing recruits towards the KKE from below, what was now in their minds was a more ambitious device for drawing recruits towards the KKE from above: from the respectable and professional classes, and from the newer generation of politicians. Negotiations towards this end had begun before the end of 1943, and rumours of them had leaked out in January, 1944. But the task had become abnormally difficult since the disguise fell from the KKE. Eager democrats like Professors Svolos and Angelopoulos, able soldiers like Generals Mandakas and Bakirdzis, seasoned politicians like Askoutsis and Hadzimbeis, were not to be fooled into mistaking the identity of the KKE, even though a few simpletons and buffoons like General Grigoriadhis and the Bishop of Kozani had been hoodwinked. Svolos had been cautiously associated with some leaders of EAM since 1942; Mandakas and Askoutsis had both had experience of resistance in Crete, where it matured earlier than on the mainland, before moving to Greece, the former voluntarily in 1944, the latter by deportation in 1941; Bakirdzis had been the earliest and most successful of all secret agents in the underground. Men of such experience could only be won to the new coalition which the KKE envisaged if they believed that EAM/ELAS intended to turn to the democratic ways of patriotic Greeks. It was not hard for the KKE to put on this act, as they had successfully done six months before; but now it had to be even more carefully timed.

The required hypocrisy was easier than the timing. The essence of the timing was to reach the tactical climax at the moment when a political vacuum should be created by the transition from German occupation to Allied liberation. Just as the German Army would launch its attack at the weak point of junction between two Allied armies, so the KKE aimed their attack at the weak point of transition between two foreign tenancies. Their first attempt had reached its culmination at the moment when the Italians capitulated and the Germans were expected to withdraw. Their second attempt was calculated to coincide with the withdrawal of the Germans, which was reasonably certain before the end of 1944. The difficulty was to be sure of the date more precisely; the vacillations of KKE policy during the first half of the year were largely reflections of this uncertainty. As the negotiations with the new proselytes matured, the Communists became daily more anxious to probe the Allies' programme of operations. Plans had been roughly adumbrated between the AMM and the guerillas for their final operations against the German withdrawal, even before Brigadier Myers left Greece; almost daily through the winter ELAS GHQ would ask the AMM when these plans were likely to mature. Upon this information depended the timing of their own operations, and the development of their courtship of Svolos and his companions. At last in January the information came; Greece was expected to be liberated in April, 1944.

The Allied calculation was wrong again. Perhaps it was not so deliberately delusive as it had been the previous summer; but it was in the minds of the military planners that the earlier the date specified to the guerillas, the easier it might be to distract their attention from fighting each other to fighting the Germans. That principle had worked in July 1943, but two important changes had since taken place. The first was that the Balkans were no longer scheduled to be liberated by an Anglo-American invasion from the south, but by a Russian invasion from the north-east; Greece, although excluded from the Soviet theatre, was not to be actively liberated but passively allowed to drop off German-occupied Europe. The second change was that Greece was no longer a country in which a handful of guerillas prevented the Germans from total occupation; on the contrary, a handful of Germans and second-rate satellite troops now prevented the guerillas from total occupation. These two changes diminished the psychological success of the revived plan. When the AMM explained that the purpose of the operations required of the guerillas was to harass and delay the retreating Germans, the Political Adviser of ELAS GHQ (at that time Dhespotopoulos) pertinently asked what advantage to the Greeks would accrue from harassing or delaying an enemy whom they were as eager to be rid of as he would by then be to go. On the other hand, the news helped to bear out other indications of the time, and so to determine the policy of the KKE in more important respects. April was not *prima facie* an improbable date for the German evacuation of Greece. It was the earliest month in which large-scale movements could be undertaken to regroup German forces into a narrower ring for the defence of Europe. The Red Army was on the borders of Rumania, and straws floated in every wind of the Balkans. The arrogance of Tito, the restlessness of Bulgaria and Albania hinted at their expectations. Collaborators were tottering. Pavelitch in Zagreb and Neditch in Belgrade had both tried to resign; Bozhilov in Sofia had been warned to change his policy, in a letter signed by the revolutionary Georgiev and the former Minister of Agriculture Bagrianov, both of whom were moving back into prominence. The Greek Communists speeded their negotiations to fit the tempo of the time. Since April was a plausible date for the Allies' return, the KKE acted in March.

On 26th March, two days after Tsoudheros had publicly expressed the hope that the armistice between the guerillas would endure, it was announced that a body calling itself the "Political Committee of National Liberation" (known by its Greek initials as PEEA) had been set up in the mountains. This was the Preparatory Governmental Committee, which had been proposed by EAM/ELAS at the Plaka Conference, under a new name and without the participation of EDES or EKKA. A significant exception to their abstention was General Bakirdzis, who suddenly re-emerged without notice as temporary president of PEEA. He was repudiated by EKKA, and soon relegated to an obscurer position by EAM, when Professor Svolos arrived in the mountains to assume the presidency; but like many of the others who flocked to join PEEA in executive and administrative positions, Bakirdzis continued his effort to bridge the gap between the KKE and the rest of the political world; his opportunity to prove his sincerity came decisively several months later in Salonika.[1] His first colleagues in PEEA were a nice balance: Mandakas, Tsirimokos, Gavrielidhis and Siantos; of whom only the last three belonged previously to EAM, and only the last two to the KKE. When Svolos, Angelopoulos, Hadzimbeis, Askoutsis, Stratis, and a host of civil servants and labour leaders of EEAM, of whom very few were Communists, reached the mountains in April, the enlarged breadth of PEEA put the KKE in a still smaller minority. Hope revived all over the Greek world that political stability was attainable without revolution.

[1] See page 218.

The new names raised the political quality of the resistance movement to a new level. Like Tito's Committee in Yugoslavia, moreover, the composition of PEEA gave appropriate weight to those areas of the country where independence of outlook and distaste for central government were strongest: Bakirdzis and Svolos were both Macedonians; Mandakas and Askoutsis were both Cretans. Their moral position was further strengthened by the abolition of the post of Political Adviser in ELAS; by the conduct of elections to give PEEA the backing of a representative parliament in the mountains; and by the appointment of Professor Svolos to lead their delegation to Egypt. The strength of these three buttresses, though unequal, was cumulative. The political advisers, it was true, reappeared as ADCs or seconds-in-command; the polling took place with the knowledge that no one would vote against an official candidate; but against Svolos there could be no cavil.

The happy timing of this enterprise was attested by the reactions of the Greek world at home and abroad. Its implications were seen by most, though not all, of the Greek authorities, who now began to pay the penalty of having failed in the past to put the issues clearly before their people. Nevertheless, politely non-committal telegrams were exchanged between Bakirdzis and Tsoudheros, emphasising the importance of forming a government representative of all opinions. The British authorities were embarrassed. In the USSR, the Tass Agency and Tiflis Radio attacked Tsoudheros' Government as reactionary and unrepresentative. Among the ordinary Greek population, the enthusiasm with which the announcement of PEEA was received varied almost in direct proportion to their distance from its seat. In the mountains it was received with indifference; in Egypt with acclamation, culminating in demonstrations in Alexandria and Cairo on 25th March, the National Day of Independence.

The reactions in the Cabinet and the armed services were Tsoudheros' most anxious concern. On 31st March a group of officers from the army, navy and air force called on him to demand his resignation. On 2nd April his Minister of Marine, Sophoklis Veniselos, spoke on the necessity of reaching political understanding with the guerillas and other organisations, "even if certain personages must withdraw to make it easier." The next day Tsoudheros resigned, and by 6th April mutinies were in progress in the army and navy. Simultaneously came the news that PEEA and Tito's Committee had agreed to exchange representatives. The King of the Hellenes was recalled from England; Veniselos was asked to form a Cabinet, and declined. Tsoudheros agreed to carry on until a new Government could be formed. Tsoudheros and Veniselos both telegraphed to PEEA and received assurances on 9th April from the KKE and EAM that they intended to work for national unity. On 11th April the King arrived in Cairo, and made a fresh proclamation on the following day. He declared that after the liberation of Greece, its régime would be decided by a free vote; that he himself, like every citizen, was at the disposal of the people; that a representative Government outside Greece, composed largely of Greeks from the occupation, was needed at once. He did not add, for obvious reasons of security, that representatives were already on their way: a fact which might have made a difference if it could have been known before Tsoudheros was driven out of office. On 13th April Veniselos agreed to form a Cabinet, from which Tsoudheros was excluded. The most important new appointment was not political: Voulgaris became Commander-in-Chief of the Navy. On 17th April the new Government announced that EAM and EDES had agreed to send representatives to Cairo to discuss the formation of a Government of national unity. But in the mountains they were already lining up against each other again, and the fear of a new civil war had persuaded the AMM to call another conference of the guerillas, at Koutsaina in West Thessaly.

The fear was justified from an unexpected direction; while the conference was assembling, on that same 17th April, ELAS attacked EKKA, murdered Psaros and scattered his force. Those of the 5/42 Regiment who could escape, joined the Security Battalions in Patras; those who could not, succumbed. When the last conference of the guerillas met at Koutsaina without the representatives of EKKA, whom ELAS detained on their way, Dhespotopoulos triumphantly arrogated to EAM/ELAS the credit for having annihilated EKKA in Greece and brought down Tsoudheros in Cairo. It only remained, he seemed to imply by these words, to dispose of EDES and Veniselos. The Koutsaina Conference, which had been called to complete the work of the Plaka Armistice by defining the boundaries between ELAS, EDES, and EKKA, therefore served no purpose except that of clarifying the menace of the KKE both in Greece and in Egypt. ELAS refused to compromise on the only agendum, their boundary with Zervas, and hinted at a renewal of force. Zervas stood his ground as always; ELAS withdrew once more from the bloody prospect of a fresh war in the mountains. But in Egypt Veniselos was a weaker antagonist. When PEEA, EAM, ELAS and the KKE demanded separate representations at the forthcoming conference in the Middle East, the unreasonable demand was feebly accepted. The mutinies persisted unchecked, until Admiral Voulgaris, with passive support from British guns, ended the naval mutiny on 22nd April, and British troops disarmed the 1st Greek Brigade two days later. Allied war correspondents in Cairo took the opportunity to present a protest against the censorship of their despatches in Cairo; but the authorities were too deeply engaged to notice it. The trouble was not over: on 26th April Veniselos resigned. He was succeeded by one of the earliest of the politicians who arrived from Greece for the forthcoming political discussions: the Social Democrat George Papandhreou. On the 27th Papandhreou announced a programme of eight points, which later became the Lebanon Charter.[1]

This episode appears at first sight to bear out Dhespotopoulos' claim to full credit for all the anarchy and confusion; but the evidence is not conclusive. Although agents of EAM/ELAS were responsible for exploiting and consolidating the breach in the political and military structure of the Middle East, it is still not certain that they themselves made the breach. The committee of officers which demanded the resignation of Tsoudheros was not composed of agents of EAM: they were over-enthusiastic democrats of the same kind that had caused the previous mutiny in 1943. The intervention of Veniselos bore the classic stigmata of a republican outburst of the familiar kind; the reaction of the King of the Hellenes was just as familiar. The usual formulae and clichés were brought out of store in the usual style of high-minded hopefulness, as if neither side were aware that the old game of politics had been replaced by the new struggle for survival. The hot-heads of the armed services had not grasped it either; it was rumoured that their ringleaders were encouraged, as a gambit in the political game, by two of the service ministers themselves. But even if Veniselos, as Minister of Marine, and Karapanayiotis, as Minister of War, had allowed themselves to be blinded by traditional grudges, there were others in authority who had not. The ranks of the awakened were steadily reinforced from occupied Greece. The return of the King from London seemed symbolically to reinstate the old game; but the arrival of Papandhreou with a new picture of occupied Greece, and the failure of Veniselos to control the mutinies which made him Prime Minister, had opened most eyes to the facts. Newcomers from Greece for the projected conference mainly confirmed Papandhreou's presentation of the case. He received telegraphic support from Mr. Churchill, and Mr. Churchill received telegraphic support from President Roosevelt: but the Soviet Government declined on 5th May to intervene in any way. When the representatives of PEEA, EAM, ELAS and the KKE (Svolos, Angelopoulos, Stratis (of EEAM), Askoutsis, Porphyroyennis, Saraphis and Petros Roussos) arrived in the Middle East they found themselves obliged, by the intensity of feeling which the mutinies had provoked, to denounce them in telegrams to Mr. Churchill and President Roosevelt. Papandhreou's position was thus indirectly strengthened. But some of the Liberals, still bent on the old pastime, refused to serve under him; so no Cabinet was formed before the general conference took place. It was not until the political delegates had assembled from all over the Greek world, at a mountain resort in the Lebanon on 17th May, that the gulf between the old

[1]See Appendix G for its terms.

delusions and the new reality was revealed to the shocked participants in a starkness that could no longer be ignored by any of
them.

April and May 1944 thus constitute a landmark in the political history
of Greece. At the beginning of April some of the Liberal Republicans
were still sufficiently blind to play into the hands of the KKE, merely
to score a point or two in the only game they knew. This put the EAM/
ELAS leaders in the mountains in a stronger position than they had
expected. When they sent their delegates to the Middle East under
Svolos, they had been prepared to bargain from strength, but not from
the overwhelming political and military strength which the weakness
of Veniselos in Cairo and the unchallenged annihilation of EKKA in
the mountains had subsequently given them. Their mood hardened
while Svolos' party was actually on its way: but space and time intervened against them. Intercommunication was slow at all times; during
the conference it was suspended between the delegates and those whom
they represented. So while the mood of EAM/ELAS hardened at home,
that of their delegation became softened by their first contact with the
rest of the Greek world. Svolos, whose self-imposed role was to be the
half-way point at which the Communists and the rest would meet, found
that he had not reached half-way himself. The period of Veniselos'
weakness was in the process of transition to Papandhreou's determination, precisely while the attitude of the EAM/ELAS leaders in the mountains was moving back to intransigeance in response to its appreciation
of the political and military success in April. When Svolos and his companions reached Egypt, they were out of rhythm with both sides; but
the hardening of the political world in Egypt was more tangible than
that of their colleagues in the mountains, which they could hardly even
suspect. So the initiative passed to Papandhreou. In the interval of
Veniselos' brief tenure of office, the Greek political world had woken up.
The eventual measure of its alertness was that when Veniselos next
tried to precipitate the same crisis (in August), his gesture was hardly
noticed; already by the latter half of May the four days of debate in
the Lebanon were enough to destroy what delusions remained. That is
why Papandhreou, as chairman of the conference, was able to telegraph
to Mr. Churchill that the constitutional question had ceased to exist.
His meaning, although in the circumstances he could not explicitly
say so, was that no Greek could waste time on a controversy which had
been shown to be relatively trivial, when it was seen beside the threat
to Greece's national independence. Papandhreou's other expressions of
opinion in May were less flattering to his political wisdom; but that
was because his language was constrained by a political purpose. The
Lebanon Conference, which in fact performed the service of clarifying
the issue between the KKE and the rest of the Greek world, had for

diplomatic purposes to be represented as having performed the miracle
of restoring Greek unity.

The Conference from 17th to 20th May was used as a forum for
the interchange of home truths, from which EAM/ELAS emerged
with their head bloody but unbowed. From Liberals of every trend,
from Populists and National Populists, from EDES and Kartalis, the
ghost of EKKA, from Kanellopoulos and Papandhreou himself, the
representatives of PEEA, EAM, ELAS and the KKE learned what
responsible Greeks thought of them. The conduct of ELAS was denounced
especially by Kartalis, who had already been on his way to Egypt when
the 5/42 Regiment of EKKA was attacked and his friend Psaros murdered. The gulf between ELAS and its rivals was plain when EDES
and EKKA agreed to be embodied unconditionally in the National
Army, and ELAS refused. Saraphis failed even to make the specious
point that the remnants of EKKA had already been embodied in the
Security Battalions; he fell weakly back upon the excuse that ELAS
could not consent to being embodied in the National Army "because
of the military requirements of the British." Everyone knew the real
reason, that ELAS already owed allegiance to a rival Greek Government;
the same awareness permeated every stage of the debate. It seemed hardly
possible that the antagonistic groups could join in a coalition government after what had been said across the conference table; still less that
they could subscribe unanimously to the eight points reiterated in
Papandhreou's final speech, which constituted the Lebanon Charter and
the programme of his Government.[1] Yet both things happened. The
terms of the Charter were made acceptable to the rival groups by the
insertion in controversial clauses of a phrase to the effect that the facts
were in dispute. Agreement on a coalition was achieved by battering the
delegates of PEEA, EAM, ELAS and the KKE into a mental daze in
which they were hardly responsible for their actions.

This first counter-offensive against the KKE resulted in the announcement on 24th May of a new Government under Papandhreou, in which
most of the delegates to the Lebanon Conference were to be included;
but because the nominations of EAM and its satellites were not available,
the names of the ministers could not be specified. Pleasure was expressed
none the less in the House of Commons by Mr. Churchill and Mr.
Eden. After two weeks of waiting, under the impulse of the great events
of 5th and 6th June in Italy and France, the formation of the Cabinet
could no longer be delayed. It was agreed by the political leaders concerned that the King's letter of 8th November amounted to an undertaking to take his Government's advice about his return to Greece; it
was agreed also that all of them were left free by the fifth point of the
Lebanon Charter to retain their own views on the constitutional question.

[1] Summarised in Appendix G.

On these terms the new Government was formed, and the names were announced. Sophoklis Veniselos was Vice-Premier; EDES, EKKA, and most of the political parties of Egypt and Athens were represented; five vacancies were left for EAM. Kartalis, as Minister of Information, was sent soon afterwards to London (accompanied by the poet Sepheri-adhis) to represent the Greek Government's point of view, with marked but only temporary success. A more immediately important mission, however, was that on which Saraphis was sent back into Greece, to explain the conduct of the delegation of which he was a member. In the eyes of the KKE in the mountains, despite the pressure of their democratic colleagues, there was nothing to explain. The signature of the Lebanon Charter and the agreement to serve in a Government under Papandhreou were both repudiated.

2. *JUNE—AUGUST* 1944

The delegation of PEEA, EAM, ELAS and the KKE was left in an embarrassing predicament. All except Saraphis were obliged to stay in the Middle East, unable to explain themselves satisfactorily to either side. To Svolos, Angelopoulos and Askoutsis, who had hoped to form the bridge between democracy and Communism, this was galling; to Porphyroyennis and Petros Roussos, both members of the KKE, it was politically disastrous. Porphyroyennis returned to Greece soon after Saraphis; but the rest clung hopefully to their positions. Although Svolos' personal prestige rose with the prolongation of his stay, especially among British observers below the highest levels of authority, he was spared nothing in his official capacity. He was called as a witness at the court-martial of the mutineers, who claimed to have risen in the name of PEEA, although he had already repudiated their action. He was treated to the outspoken comments of the British as well as the Greek authorities on the conduct of PEEA. He was helpless to intervene while his colleagues in the mountains, whom he had come to represent, bombarded the new Government with telegrams contradicting the policy which he had pursued. Throughout June the Greek world, Svolos not least of them, waited in bewildered suspense.

On 7th July the receipt of two telegrams from the mountains was announced. The first, signed by Porphyroyennis and Saraphis, alleged breaches of the Lebanon Charter by Papandhreou's Government. The second, signed by Bakirdzis, Siantos and Hadzimbeis, submitted new conditions for the entry of PEEA into the Government and proposed a new protocol to the Lebanon Charter. Papandhreou explained in a broadcast that the crux of the dispute was the position of ELAS, which EAM demanded should be excluded from the command of the Greek National Army; and that the new terms required a Cabinet of fifteen members, including seven nominated by EAM. The Cabinet rejected the terms; on 13th July Svolos announced that he and his companions were returning to Greece. Before the end of the month a new ultimatum from PEEA and EAM, demanding the resignation of Papandhreou, was also received and rejected. Although hope was not abandoned that there would be a change of heart, Papandhreou was obliged to complete his Cabinet with others. He could at least be given credit at once for two results of his patient efforts: he had brought together Populists and Liberals (as well as other parties) in a single administration, which had not been achieved before in any real sense, and was not again until the still more disastrous year of 1947; and he had effectively based his government on the last Greek elections of 1936, which made it at least more representative (to the extent of a few months) than Mr. Churchill's contemporary coalition in Britain.

The reasons given for EAM's refusal to honour Svolos' commitments were unreal. The fact that one of their telegrams was signed by Porphyroyennis and Saraphis, when they returned to the mountains from their unfortunate mission, was a transparent device to save face. The fresh demands were absurd, and could not have been put forward with any doubt of their reception. The real reasons for the reversal of policy have therefore to be found elsewhere. The fundamental fact has been pointed out: that even while Svolos and his companions were committing themselves at the Lebanon Conference, their minds were already out of tune with those who had sent them. Subtle and rapid fluctuations were perpetually in progress, both in Egypt and in the mountains; it was psychologically as well as physically impossible for any individual precisely to register and respond to all of them. Svolos had spent only a few days in the mountains before he left on his mission; he could hardly guess at the intricacies of mentality which prevailed there. During July he was not one but two moods behind his colleagues in the mountains. He had left Greece at a time when EAM/ELAS gave promise of being in a mood to bargain: to drive a hard bargain, certainly, but to reach one and stand by it. On those terms he had accepted his mission. Barely had he left the seat of PEEA when the events of the second half of April seemed to put the game into the hands of EAM/ELAS; but Svolos, adjusting himself to the mood of the Middle East, actually made more concessions instead of fewer. Becoming aware of the discrepancy soon after the Lebanon Conference, he modified his language accordingly. On 13th July, before returning to Greece, he joined in the abuse of Papandhreou and spoke of having been treated "like an accused person." His colleagues in the mountains were already entering yet another new phase, which again manifested itself in a stubborn refusal to be co-operative; but it seemed to have a new basis. They were still defiant, but not so markedly with the defiance of conscious strength; rather with their backs to the wall. The most likely explanation of the new phase of

N

conduct between June and August is that the leaders of the KKE were for the first time experiencing fear.

It is only possible to guess at the motives of a Communist Party; the suggestion that the KKE momentarily lost its nerve in the summer of 1944 is therefore no more than a guess. But it is known that the party was always potentially divided on methods and principles. There were members who believed in violence and members who preferred political infiltration; members who wished to adhere undeviatingly to the Moscow line, and members who thought first as Greeks. The events of April and May aggravated dissension between these points of view, especially since the KKE had just exposed itself afresh to the arguments (if not the influence) of democratic Greeks by enlarging the coalition from EAM to PEEA. The violent policy of April could be seen in retrospect to have yielded only partial success. In Egypt Tsoudheros was gone, but Papandhreou was in his place; in Greece Psaros was gone, but Zervas was still there; not to mention Andon Tsaous in East Macedonia, and Security Battalions or their equivalents almost everywhere. The reactionary thugs of X under Colonel Grivas were first dimly heard of at this time, but these ranked among the lesser menaces to the Communists. A desperate attempt to secure the removal of the Commander of the AMM, whom the KKE confusedly regarded as the fountain-head of policy, failed in May. Even worse for EAM/ELAS, there were beginning to appear rudiments of an *Allied* policy: although the British and American authorities in Egypt were still easy to split, the leaders of the AMM in the Greek mountains spoke with one voice. The progress of the war was equally disturbing. While the collaborators and the rivals of the Partisans were crumbling into impotence throughout the Balkans, in Greece they were stronger than ever. The impending evacuation of the Germans had again failed to mature when it was expected. The penetration of the Red Army into the Balkans was known to be delimited in advance, by Allied agreement, at the northern frontiers of Greece. The outlook for the KKE was thus less bright than that of the rest of Balkan Communism. To these misfortunes were now added three fresh dangers: the unification of almost all anti-Communist politicians by Papandhreou; the supposed intention of the British authorities to declare war on EAM/ELAS; and the rejuvenated power and hostility of all ELAS' surviving rivals. The first of these has already been shown as the result of the Lebanon Conference; the last two, which are interrelated, became unmistakable soon afterwards.

While EAM was being urged to participate in the new-found national unity, the British authorities were considering, under pressure from Papandhreou, a plan which amounted to a declaration of war upon ELAS. It was the intention of the plan, having first extricated the AMM from Greece, to denounce EAM/ELAS publicly as an enemy of the

Allied cause. A strong battery of arguments was, with eventual success, arrayed against this policy: the chief of them was that it would not weaken EAM/ELAS, but throw the country to their mercy; the least was that it was impossible to extricate the AMM either in time or alive. What is important in retrospect, however, is not that the plan was good or bad, since it was finally rejected, but that it became known to EAM/ELAS. When or how it became known cannot be ascertained; it is enough that eighteen months later the KKE Press in Athens was able to print the texts, distorted but substantially genuine, of several telegrams exchanged on this subject. One of the telegrams which fell into the hands of the KKE contained a counter-proposal of the AMM that the few Allied troops in Greece (amounting to less than 400 of all ranks) should not be removed but reinforced. The suggestion was based on the principle that the presence of Allied troops would help to keep the guerillas from fighting each other, and their steady infiltration into the mountains would expedite the process of liberation from within, both by harassing the Germans' retreat and by instantaneously replacing them. The Plaka Agreement had already sanctioned such infiltration. But EAM/ELAS inclined to the inference that the intention was to import troops to attack ELAS. Although this interpretation was rendered ludicrous by the smallness of the force suggested, nevertheless the correspondence as a whole was bound to impress EAM/ELAS, even from the barest hints, with a contradiction between the secret planning of military policy and the official process of political conciliation. The British authorities were in fact only debating an alternative plan to meet a breakdown of the policy of conciliation; the alternative never went beyond the stage of hypothesis. (That no decision had been taken was shown by the continued infiltration of British and American troops in small numbers while the debate went on; among them was the representative of the Foreign Office, Major Wallace, who returned to Greece at long last in July, only to lose his life a month later before he could contribute an opinion.) But having lost its character of secrecy and being misinterpreted as categorical, the hypothesis could only breed mistrust. It helped to hold together the non-Communist politicians in PEEA and EAM who were otherwise inclined to criticise Communist policy. Given that the British authorities appeared to be following two contradictory policies, EAM/ELAS and PEEA had no hesitation in deciding which was the real one.

Their conclusion appeared to be borne out by the British attitude to their rivals, on both sides of the fence which separated resistance from collaboration. Zervas was treated to supplies in excess of his immediate needs, which were small because he had been ordered to abstain from major operations, and disproportionate to his strength, which was barely a quarter of ELAS: about 10,000 to 40,000. This liberality only partially redressed the heavy preponderance which ELAS had enjoyed in the previous year; but the suspicion that it was due to political motives drew strength from the fact that the British and American Commanders of the AMM were unaware that it was taking place. The same discrimination was applied to the only other relic of independent resistance, Andon Tsaous in the far north-east. Even the Security Battalions, in the judgment of EAM/ELAS, enjoyed British favour. The joint denunciation of these and other collaborators which had been signed in February,[1] had not been published; no attempt by the KKE to extract a definition of British policy towards them had succeeded. The fact that former adherents of PAO, EDES, EKKA, ES and EOA (all ex-favourites of the British authorities), had by this time found harbour in the Security Battalions, increased the suspicion. The inference that the British were prepared to use anybody to suppress EAM/ELAS seemed plausible in July, when Zervas, without protest by the AMM, launched an attack on the 24th Regiment of ELAS, which bordered his area to the south. The function of the 24th Regiment was to make it impossible for Zervas to carry out operations against the Germans; on military grounds Zervas' measure was justified, after repeated attempts at a reasonable settlement, by the plea that the 24th Regiment served no useful purpose and prevented EDES from doing so. Simultaneously, for military reasons of the same nature, Zervas expelled the collaborating Turko-Albanians from their native district of Chamouria, where they had persistently interfered with operations on the northern borders of his area. ELAS and the Albanian partisans at once espoused their cause, disregarding the military background to Zervas' action; the political implications, to which alone EAM/ELAS gave weight, added to the conviction that the British authorities were intent upon using Zervas to destroy ELAS.

In these circumstances an uneasy division of purpose could be detected among the adherents of PEEA, both inside and outside the KKE. Inside the KKE, the apostles of direct action under Aris Veloukhiotis were openly spoiling for a new fight; the apostles of political infiltration under Siantos were wondering whether to persevere. Outside the KKE, the apostles of conciliation under Svolos were equally wondering whether to exert what little influence they still had in favour of unity, or to resign themselves to the growing conviction of bad faith on the other side. Two things were common to them all. The first was a fear that Greece was being left behind the rest of the Balkans in the race to achieve what they all called, with however little mutual agreement on the details, progress and social reform. While everything that they indiscriminately labelled as reactionary was as strong as ever in Greece, everywhere else it was tottering. In Rumania Antonescu had already put out peace feelers, and in Bulgaria Bagrianov had succeeded Bozhilov

[1]See page 177 and Appendix E.

with the same intentions. In Yugoslav affairs an agreement had been reached between Tito and Shubasitch, which pointed towards the triumph of the former and the annihilation of everything that Pavelitch on the one hand, and Neditch and Mihailovitch on the other, stood for in the southern Slav world; one after the other Serb and Croat members of the exiled Government resigned in protest, some against its virtual surrender, some against its continued existence. In Albania the last of the puppet Prime Ministers had taken office for the express purpose of establishing his country's neutrality, while Enver Hoxha (whose LNC was now known as FNC, having changed from a movement to a popular front) was making sure that there would be no rivals in pursuit of power when the Germans left. The stagnation of Greece in contrast to this Balkan effervescence was disturbing to all trends of thought within PEEA.

To it was added a second unifying emotion: the Greeks' dislike of being treated as if big powers were made up of big schoolmasters and small nations of small boys. The effect of scolding one group and trying to appoint prefects out of another was equally to draw the schoolboys together against the schoolmaster. When Svolos found his delegation treated as "accused persons," it reminded him that he was a Greek and a patriot; he may well have remembered that in the titles PEEA, EAM, ELAS and even KKE, whatever the other letters stood for, the Es stood for "Greece" and "National." The notion that British policy could use ideology to split the KKE and its satellites came up against the oddly misplaced spirit of nationalism, and was rebuffed. The apostles of direct action, of political infiltration, and of conciliation, thus found themselves unexpectedly drawn closer together within PEEA by anxiety and resentment; a situation which the first of the three, suffering least of all from confusion and bewilderment, were the readiest to exploit. In this mood PEEA continued to assail the authorities in Cairo with petulant ultimatums which they knew could not be accepted. Intransigeance had hardened into defiance. They were no longer bargaining from strength; they were no longer bargaining at all.

3. AUGUST—NOVEMBER 1944

At this moment of irresoluble deadlock a *deus* intervened literally *ex machina*. On the night of 25th-26th July a Russian aeroplane took off from an Anglo-American base in Italy on a flight authorised for training purposes. During the night it landed in Yugoslavia near Tito's GHQ and embarked ten members of the Soviet Military Mission. Flying to Greece, it dropped two of them over Macedonia and landed the rest on the mountain aerodrome in Thessaly which had been constructed a year before for the evacuation of the guerilla delegation to Egypt. The operation, conducted with skill and security as well as bad faith, became known to none of the other Allies until the eight members of the Soviet Mission to ELAS, under Colonel Popov, reached ELAS GHQ on the morning of the 26th. On that date the British and American ALOS in command of the AMM were both out of Greece reporting to their respective Governments, and their substitutes were both absent on a visit to Zervas' territory. The Russian intervention in Greece could not, therefore, have been better timed for the purpose of causing consternation; but its more important effect was different. It was a mutual disappointment of both the Soviet Mission and EAM/ELAS, from which British policy (even to a limited degree Anglo-American policy) momentarily emerged as *tertius gaudens*.

The arrival of the Soviet Mission, and especially its method of arrival, showed the Soviet Government's distrust of the information on which British policy was based. Already on 5th May the Soviet Government, simultaneously in London and Moscow, had formally refused to join HMG in any pronouncement on political matters in Greece. Throughout the summer M. Novikov, Soviet Ambassador to the exiled Government of Greece, had persisted in disbelieving the account of Greek affairs reported by British representatives in the country. A curious chance had offered the British authorities the opportunity of confirming their account. A group of Russian prisoners, including a regular officer, had escaped from a German camp in Greece, and taken refuge successively with ELAS and with the AMM. In written accounts of their experiences they testified that they had been treated worse by ELAS, who had tried to force them into fighting Zervas and had put them in a concentration camp when they refused, than by the Germans. Although the evidence of escaped prisoners, who were by Soviet convention legally dead, would not have impressed M. Novikov, he could hardly have denied its validity; but unfortunately the documents were mislaid in Cairo until after the opportunity had passed.

What was important to the Soviet authorities, however, was that their arguments were weakened by lack of any direct information. They were evidently convinced that the British authorities would not allow them to send observers to Greece, in spite of the open admission of their mission to Yugoslavia: they already thought in terms of those rigidly exclusive spheres of influence which later became separated by an iron curtain. They therefore adopted a subterfuge, which was dismissed by M. Molotov in reply to HMG's protests with a shrug of indifference, as a matter too trivial even to have been referred to his level of authority at all. What followed was an example of the principle that the best thing to do with people who criticised British policy in Greece during the German occupation was to send them there. ELAS, who had expected the Soviet Mission to bring manna from heaven, found Colonel Popov unable even to supply his own party with vodka, let alone ELAS with gold, arms and ammunition. On the other hand, the Soviet Mission, which had expected to find an army of at least the same kind, if not the same magnitude, as Tito's partisans, found a rabble thinly veiled by an elaborately centralised command. Living mainly at ELAS GHQ, they could not even observe the distant units which, with the sympathy and confidence of ALOS who had them virtually under command, were really doing what the mass of ELAS was only pretending to do: fighting the Germans. Colonel Popov and his companions, therefore, only saw those features of EAM/ELAS which the KKE expected to impress him most, and which in fact impressed him least. Neither on the military nor on the political level does it seem likely that a favourable report on EAM/ELAS went to Moscow. The Soviet Government was at that time more concerned over the successful prosecution of the war against Germany than over Balkan ideologies. Circumstantial evidence suggests that EAM/ELAS suffered an abrupt shock as a result.

Within a fortnight of the Soviet Mission's arrival, for reasons which cannot have been unconnected with it, PEEA gave ground to the extent of offering to send five (no longer seven) representatives to serve under a prime minister other than Papandhreou, whom they still attacked for his "actions, omissions and pointless statements." Having first assured himself of his Cabinet's confidence, Papandhreou replied offering the Ministries of Finance, Communications, Agriculture, National Economy and Labour. In the middle of August, when no reply had been received, a last appeal was sent to PEEA, with the approval of Papandhreou's Cabinet, over the signatures of the Liberals Veniselos and Sakalis, and the Agrarian Mylonas. Almost at once PEEA announced its readiness to join Papandhreou's Government on exactly the terms which it had been denouncing for the last two months.

As if by a magic wand, the angry, anxious, bewildered obstinacy of the early summer was translated into goodwill. Almost for the first time, PEEA was really unanimous. The anger of the apostles of direct action, the anxiety of the apostles of political infiltration, the bewilderment of the apostles of conciliation, melted back into harmony. The phase of unstinted co-operation, the Indian summer of the well-meaning, of Svolos and Bakirdzis and the administrative officials below the highest levels of PEEA, lasted from the beginning of August to the end of October. It extended through the period during which almost the whole of the Balkans were liberated from the Germans, while the same sequence of convulsions, which had shaken south-east Europe to its foundations in a few weeks of 1941, was repeated in reverse. Against the background of an historic summer, in which Rome and Paris were liberated; in which Hitler barely survived a revolutionary plot; in which Tokyo was bombed, and Warsaw rose in revolt; in which American opinion became so convinced that the war was about to end that periodicals offered almost no market for stories referring to it: the commotion stirring the microcosm of the Balkans can only be indicated by a pattern of dates.

On 2nd August the Turkish Government severed diplomatic relations with Germany (without, however, declaring war until the following February). A few days later Mr. Churchill met Shubasitch and Tito in Italy, to congratulate them upon their recent agreement, while King Peter's Government crumbled in a succession of resignations, and Mihailovitch was formally repudiated. In mid-August another Soviet Military Mission, two strong, arrived in Albania from Greece, and Enver Hoxha's succession became assured. On 23rd August Antonescu's Government was dismissed by King Michael of Rumania, who appointed General Sanatescu for the express purpose of making peace with the Allies. Three days later Bagrianov's Government ordered the disarmament of all foreign troops on Bulgarian soil, thereby inviting the Germans to leave. On 30th August the Red Army captured Ploesti, and entered Bucharest the next day. In the first week of September events followed each other at a speed beyond the capacity of any contemporary observer to follow, especially in Bulgaria. The importance of the Bulgarian development to the Greeks lay in the fact that East Macedonia and West Thrace had been virtually incorporated in Bulgaria; some Greeks believed that EAM had privately agreed to work for the recognition of the *fait accompli*. Every Greek therefore watched Bulgaria intently in the autumn of 1944; some watched the former colleagues of PEEA just as intently at the same time. To their surprise, both passed the test with credit.

On 1st September Bagrianov resigned. He was replaced by Muraviev, who severed diplomatic relations with Germany. By 5th September the Germans were on their way out of Bulgaria, but not fast enough to suit the Soviet Government, which declared war on Bulgaria for the first time. Within twenty-four hours, Muraviev asked for an armistice. On 6th September the Red Army reached the Danube at Kladovo, and two days later crossed the Yugoslav frontier. That same day, 8th September, Muraviev's Government declared war on Germany and resigned. It was succeeded by the "Fatherland Front" under Georgiev, the successive modifications of which have persisted ever since. The Red Army was tumultuously welcomed in Sofia, but without the agreement of the Western Allies it was still technically impossible for the USSR to grant Georgiev's Government an armistice. Bulgaria was thus formally at war with all the remaining belligerents in Europe on both sides; but although this anomaly was not terminated *de jure* until 28th October, when the Bulgars had at last satisfied the Western Allies by withdrawing from Greek territory, nevertheless the Bulgarian army was already in action against the Germans on a considerable scale by the middle of

September. This astute transfiguration set the pattern which most of Germany's satellites tried to follow, though not all succeeded.

Coats were turned daily at this time. A Finnish armistice delegation reached Moscow on 7th September. On 15th October, the day on which a similar Bulgarian delegation arrived, the Hungarian Government also asked for an armistice: this was granted only in January 1945, on condition that the Vienna Award was annulled and that Hungary declared war on Germany. The Rumanian Government had failed to anticipate the Soviet occupation of Bucharest, and paid the natural penalty of being replaced by a body bearing the familiar and revealing title of "National Democratic Front" before an armistice was granted. By the middle of October Allied Control Commissions had come into being, at least on paper, in Bucharest and Sofia. On 20th October Belgrade was liberated by the arrival of the Red Army and Tito, and Valona by the departure of the Germans and the arrival of Enver Hoxha a few days later. On 25th October the last Albanian puppet resigned. The following day Tito and Shubasitch met on Yugoslav soil for the first time. It was observed from the first that the Governments of Yugoslavia and Albania now resembled each other "to the minutest particulars," which left no room for surprise when they entered into a customs union two years later. Tirana was freed in November: in Yugoslavia the advance of the Red Army, supported by Yugoslav and Bulgarian partisans, proceeded slowly but surely. But none of these causes of Communist satisfaction compares for felicity with the contrast between the villainous record and the providential reward of Bulgaria. This is the point of contact at which the wider commotion of the Balkans impinges again upon the relatively gentler evolution of Greek affairs over the same period. The Bulgarian armistice was the first test of the sincerity of the Greeks who had been incorporated from PEEA into Papandhreou's Government.

Up to this point the new reconciliation, which had sprung into operation when the Soviet Mission reached the seat of PEEA, met no major embarrassments: no breakdown had occurred, because nobody wished it. Papandhreou and his colleagues were under pressure from the British authorities to avoid it: within PEEA the apostles of conciliation under Svolos, and probably the Communist apostles of infiltration under Siantos as well, had consistently worked for a coalition; even the bellicose wing of the KKE had to submit to the fiat of the Soviet Government, which may be presumed to have been transmitted through the Soviet Mission. None but trivial obstacles remained to be overcome in the next month; almost all the news was good. The King of the Hellenes returned to London. On 17th August Papandhreou announced that Greek troops were in action in Italy, blotting out the memory of the mutiny by service which culminated in the capture of Rimini. During the next few days Papandhreou visited Italy to meet Mr. Churchill, an occasion that was marred only by the impossibility of informing his Cabinet, for reasons of security. He returned to Cairo on 26th August to find Veniselos, Rendis and Mylonas offering their resignations in protest. The setback was remedied on 1st September by the addition of a liberal (the younger Sophoulis) and two Populists, who improved the balance of the Cabinet; the incident was forgotten the next day, when six representatives of EAM and its satellites were sworn in. The fact that they had been escorted from the mountains by the British brigadier currently commanding SOE Cairo, who had spent a week of goodwill visiting ELAS GHQ, caused the six representatives almost as much satisfaction as the generosity of Papandhreou in giving them one more post than he had promised. True to their distinctions, they insisted that they represented three different bodies: Svolos and Angelopoulos (Minister and Under-Secretary for Finance) and Askoutsis (Communications) represented PEEA; Tsirimokos (National Economy) represented EAM; Zevgos (Agriculture) and Porphyroyennis (Labour) represented both EAM and the KKE. To outsiders this seemed silly, like much of their recent conduct; but there were favourable signs. Only two of the six were Communists; and Svolos announced the dissolution of PEEA, on the ground that it had completed its mission.

Goodwill appeared to mount daily. General Wilson broadcast a last warning to Greeks collaborating with the Germans, that they should desist "while they had time"; words which satisfied a long-felt wish of EAM/ELAS. On 5th September Mr. Cordell Hull, the American Secretary of State, expressed pleasure at the formation of the Greek coalition. The next day Papandhreou made a broadcast and gave an interview to the Press, before his Government left Egypt for Italy in preparation for their return to Greece; from these together four points emerged. The first was that his Government, basing itself upon the Lebanon Charter, aimed to liberate and rehabilitate Greece, and to safeguard the sovereignty of the Greek people. The second was a fresh threat to the Security Battalions that any members who did not desert would be treated as criminals. The third was that order would be maintained in liberated Greece, so that the people could freely decide on "the constitution, social order and government that they desired." The fourth laid down Greece's claim to Saseno from Italy, to Korytsa and perhaps Valona from Albania, and to part of Mount Rhodhopi from Bulgaria. The Dodecanese were taken for granted; no mention was made of Cyprus, to avoid embarrassing His Majesty's Government: but the hope was privately expressed to HMG that Bulgaria should not be accepted as a co-belligerent, nor allowed to leave troops on Greek soil. Since Papandhreou was the spokesman, neither Svolos nor his colleagues were called upon to commit themselves; but the time for them to do so was coming, and they were ready.

The Greek Government was transferred to the neighbourhood of General Wilson's GHQ at Caserta, but one member after another was dispatched on the errand of infiltration into Greece in the wake of the retreating Germans. Covered by the "Iron Ring" of Crete and the outer islands, the German retreat was proceeding fast in September. Papandhreou announced the liberation by the guerillas of several towns in Thessaly: which meant that the guerillas walked in a few hours after the Germans walked out. The Government was already represented in Athens by Zevgos and Tsatsos; General Spiliotopoulos was appointed Military Governor of Attica with the reluctant consent of EAM/ELAS, who regarded him as a collaborator. Kanellopoulos was present in the Peloponnese, to share with Aris Veloukhiotis the honours of liberation. Makkas was established as the Government's representative in the Ionian islands, Bourdharas in the Aegean, Lambrianidhis and Porphyroyennis in North-East Greece, before the end of September. On 28th September the two guerilla generals, Zervas and Saraphis, who had been brought out of Greece for the occasion, signed an agreement at Caserta[1] with General Wilson, Mr. Macmillan (the British Resident Minister), and Papandhreou. Under its terms all their forces were placed under the Greek Government, and simultaneously by the Greek Government under the orders of the British general commanding the Allied Forces for the liberation of Greece. Lieut.-General Scobie had been appointed to this command, with an American brigadier-general as his deputy. Although Dhespotopoulos had been sent to control Saraphis at Caserta, EAM/ELAS proved goodwill by accepting all the clauses, including an operational boundary with Zervas less favourable to themselves than that which they refused at Koutsaina. The agreement completed the work, begun at Plaka seven months earlier, of ensuring that the return of the Allies (and with them Papandhreou's Government) should be unchallenged by EAM/ELAS. Without the Plaka Armistice, the Lebanon Conference would have been impossible; without the Caserta Agreement it would have been fruitless.

Zervas and Saraphis returned to Greece to harass the German withdrawal and to co-operate in the maintenance of order. Both did their individual best: Zervas with as much success as the strategic limitations of his corner of North-West Greece allowed, and Saraphis with as much success as his political directors allowed. The bulk of ELAS concentrated upon the task of occupying the principal towns, and a part of EDES did the same, to forestall ELAS where it was open to them to do so. Vengeful fanatics of both organisations behaved atrociously to their political opponents in the process: EDES especially in Preveza (where ELAS forestalled them, but obeyed Gen. Scobie's order to withdraw), and ELAS throughout the

[1]Text in Appendix H.

Peloponnese, especially in Kalamata. Nevertheless two things must be noted in their favour. The first is that not only the forces of EDES (as goes without saying) but also the forces of ELAS, and its civil arm EP, were willing to co-operate with the incoming authorities in the maintenance of law and order, provided that they were used as the instruments of law and order, and not treated as the menace against which law and order had to be maintained. The second is that those individual units of both organisations which lived in the fighting zone, accompanied and virtu-ally commanded by sympathetic ALOS, fought well against the Germans in intimate co-operation with the British, Greek and American units which made up the army of liberation. In spite of them all, Greece was liberated because the Germans left, not because they were driven out; the difficulty was even to keep contact with their rear-guard. The Allied forces were often a day behind them, detained partly by problems of supply and communication, partly by the enthusiasm of their welcome. British and guerilla troops entered Patras on the night of 3rd-4th October, Athens a week later, Salonika by the end of the month. Only the iron ring of the islands (principally Crete and Rhodes) remained in German hands another seven months. Papandhreou entered Athens with his Government and General Scobie and HM Ambassador, but without the King or any figure of the resistance, on 18th October, two days before the Red Army and partisans entered Belgrade. The last Germans left Greece on 1st November, harassed by a handful of ELAS and British troops. The transports of liberation were enjoyed to the full, but its problems had hardly begun. The one solid ground for hope was that, thanks to the agreements of Plaka and Caserta, a generally acceptable Government had reached Greece at all.

Papandhreou's Government appeared to start well. The Prime Min-ister's first speech on Greek soil, delivered in Constitution Square in Athens on 18th October, pleased the right by asserting Greece's claims to Northern Epirus (at present known as Southern Albania) as well as the Dodecanese, and by insisting that all armed forces be reorganised into the National Army. It equally pleased the left by declaring that the police and gendarmerie must be purged and reorganised; the war profiteers and "the few traitors" must be punished; and by announcing the early conduct of a plebiscite and elections for a Constituent Assembly, and for local mayors and municipal councils. The last words showed the Government's attention to provincial affairs; but nothing was said of elections in the trade unions, which the KKE was already anticipating, under cover of the new General Confederation of Labour (formerly EEAM). Papandhreou's intention in his first speech was to avoid con-troversy: but tranquillity was not easily won. Athens was in a ferment of Dionysiac joy, which the demagogues were busy converting into ideological passion. Demonstrations and counter-demonstrations, slogans

and counter-slogans in red and blue paint, political songs of all complexions, often set to the same tunes, propaganda and counter-propaganda
through megaphones at street corners, all these had violently broken out.
The organisers were the KKE for the left, and X, which had just emerged
from ambiguous obscurity into ugly fruition, for the right. Papandhreou
reconciled the ostensibly opposing claims of "Popular Democracy" and
"Greater Greece" in the synthesis of "Greater Greece under a Popular
Democracy." Dialectically this showed that the slogans of right and left
did not verbally conflict; but the furious debate up and down the streets
of Athens, under the windows of the embassies, of General Scobie's
headquarters, and the Government offices, continued for deeper causes.
It was questionable, in the Bedlam that Athens became in October and
November, whether the coalition Government could retain its unity
over the heads of its turbulent supporters. Miraculously, it seemed to do
so, even under the pressure of formidable problems.

The immediate problems can be summed up under six heads, following the chronological sequence in which the severity of each asserted
itself[1]: Relief (I), Finance (II), Political Crime (III), Foreign Relations
(IV), Public Order (V), National Defence (VI). The constitutional question,
in the absence of the King, was hardly raised even indirectly, so truly did
Papandhreou seem to have spoken when he declared it defunct in May.
The first of the six problems was the most urgent, for Greece was again
near the brink of starvation which had actually been crossed in 1941.
UNRRA was preceded in Greece by an Anglo-American organisation
under Major-General Hughes known as Military Liaison (abbreviated to
ML), one of whose many functions was to organise the first stages of
relief. Its success depended on the co-operation of the Greek Government
and workers; but the partial destruction of the Piraeus harbour by the
Germans, the total interruption of road and rail communications, and
repeated strikes organised by EEAM, made the work slow and difficult.
The Minister of Labour, being a Communist, might have been expected
to control the workers, but his loyalty was divided between his party and
his Government. As a Communist, he was ready to countenance, if not
inspire, strikes on the familiar grounds that discontented workers and
hungry citizens were the best material for his ideology: as a minister, he
was equally ready to end strikes as soon as they had served their purpose.
Nevertheless, by the middle of November 130,000 tons of supplies of all
kinds, as a monthly average, were being unloaded in Greece, and routes
were already opened up for their delivery by road to the provinces. From
this point the first problem passed into the second, Finance.

A mission from the British Treasury accompanied Papandhreou's
Government in an advisory capacity. Inflation had become so appalling
in the latter period of the German occupation, that the average civil

[1] Since these categories will recur, they are here numbered for reference.

servant could barely buy one cigarette with a month's salary. To restore the currency, a British Military pound was put into circulation with a fixed value of 600 drachmas, and transactions in gold were made illegal. This measure was announced by Svolos, who shared with Angelopoulos the Ministry of Finance, the second major department under the control of former members of PEEA. They announced that the wages of State employees would be fixed at an average equivalent to seven shillings a day; that a purchase tax would be imposed on luxury goods, and a heavy tax on war profits. None of these proposals ever became effective, and inflation crept back. The process was lubricated by the sovereigns let loose in Greece during the occupation, which had gravitated to the extremes in whose hands they were most dangerous: the industrialists and the Communists. Many of the valuable goods imported by ML, being unaccustomed luxuries to those for whom they were intended, passed straight out of their hands into the black market. Svolos was only saved from the stigma of failure by the ease with which the blame could be transferred to the confusion of the times and the failure of other departments. At least he was sincerely doing his best; nor was there any dissension within the Government on financial policy. The exception which proved this rule was a farcical debate in the Cabinet on the propriety of continuing to describe Greece as a kingdom on its bank-notes.

On the third problem, especially the crime of collaboration, there was also formal agreement. The Security Battalions had been disarmed during the progress of the Allied forces through Greece; almost all were under detention to await trial. The exceptions were those who had been massacred by the orders of Aris Veloukhiotis, or the few who had escaped; to these must be added, in Macedonia, the armed villagers of Mikhalagas, whom British representatives could not persuade to surrender so long as ELAS were in their neighbourhood. While the small fry awaited their fate, it was announced that a Special Military Tribunal would try ten major criminals on a charge of high treason. These included Tsolakoglou and Rallis, but not Logothetopoulos, who had escaped to Germany; they also included Colonel Lambou, Chief of the Special Security Police, and Colonel Plitzanopoulos, Commander of the Security Battalions. General Pangalos, who had helped to inspire the formation of the Security Battalions, was put under arrest, for protection rather than indictment. Cries of "Vengeance!" and "Guilty men!" were roused against them to the point of hysteria by the agitators of EAM/ELAS, who still feared that they would evade justice. They sought to keep the matter before the public eye by organising faked funerals, with supposititious corpses of alleged victims, and hired widows howling through the streets of Athens, in alternation with demonstrations demanding "What the people wants!" and "Popular Democracy without the

King!" All these slogans, brilliantly devised and interlaced, confused the volatile minds of the Athenian crowds, most of whom were only out for a lark, and exasperated the Anglo-Greek authorities. But there was no indication that any attempt would be made to evade the punishment of collaborators. Apart from legal quibbles, this matter caused no dissension within the coalition in October and November.

The fourth problem, that of foreign relations, carries this survey almost to the danger-point at which divisions between PEEA and the rest within the Cabinet might be expected to show themselves. The labels which they attached to each other, as satellites of the USSR on the one hand and of Britain on the other, began to be legible. The dissension involved the conduct of the war as well as inter-Allied relations. The northern border of Greece was the southern limit of the Balkan theatre of the Red Army; but at least the tips of three tentacles had extended across the frontier. Across the Albanian frontier there was already a traffic in both directions, by which a unit of Albanian partisans had been placed under the command of ELAS as a gesture of goodwill, and a prominent Albanian collaborator, formerly King Zog's Prime Minister, had been handed over by ELAS to the FNC. Across the Yugoslav frontier lay the incalculable force of SNOF, one of whose commanders, Gotchev, had twice mutinied from the command of ELAS. The affiliation of the slavophone Macedonians was instinctively closer to any Yugoslav authority than any Greek, even if both happened to be ideologically identical; for what mattered to the Macedonian was not ideology but his personal vendetta with the Greeks. As if to point the moral, Radio "Free Yugoslavia" had opened up broadcasts in the Macedonian language from 22nd September. To nationalistic Greeks no more distinction could be drawn between SNOF and Tito than between Tito and the USSR.

Still more menacing was the tentacle which lay across the Bulgarian frontier: the test case of the sincerity of Svolos' colleagues, to which reference has been made. When the Bulgarian Army became transformed, in one night of early September, from a formation of the German occupation into a formation of the Red Army fighting the German occupation, the problem arose of Bulgar troops in Eastern Macedonia and Western Thrace. These areas lay outside the theatre of the Red Army, under whose command the Bulgars suddenly claimed to have passed. The natural solution was that they should withdraw from Eastern Macedonia and Western Thrace into pre-war Bulgaria, thus disembarrassing the Allies of a problem in military etiquette, and the Greeks of a detested incubus. But the Bulgars could plead both military and political excuses for remaining. The military excuse was that they were needed to hold a front against the Germans on the River Strymon; the political excuse was that there was no visible authority to take over the administration of territory which had for three years been virtually part of Bulgaria. Both excuses had some basis, and in sustaining both the symbolic figure of Radev reappears.

That the Bulgarian Army was penetrated by organised disaffection, even while still nominally allied to the Germans, is proved by the efficiency with which it changed sides almost in a body, and by the facility with which it absorbed the Bulgarian Partisans into its ranks. The transition was facilitated by men like Radev, who was a partisan commissar one day and a regular colonel the next; being a Greek by birth as well as a Communist by conviction, he was also a valuable link with the KKE. Thanks to the triple role of such men, the Bulgarian occupation enjoyed the advantage of being the only force in north-east Greece, once it had completed its about-turn, that could both fight the Germans and maintain order effectively. EAM/ELAS were not interested in the former task; their Communist leaders were ideologically pre-disposed to share the latter with the new Bulgarian administration. It has been argued, from the inadequate evidence of a document attributed to one junior commander of ELAS,[1] that there was a categorical agreement to allow the Germans to withdraw unhindered. The probability is that EAM/ELAS would not have been so foolish as to commit this to writing; they and the Germans each knew what suited the other without explicit agreement. The Bulgarian Army, on the other hand, became more than formally enthusiastic about fighting the Germans. The new Minister of War invited a representative of the AMM to Sofia to concert operations. Since the forces of Andon Tsaous were not sufficient by themselves to hold the Germans, it was agreed that the Bulgars should support them with heavy weapons. EAM/ELAS were invited to participate in the plan, but preferred to denounce the ALOS responsible for it as collaborators, while they themselves acquiesced in the Bulgarian civil authority so long as its activities were principally directed against nationalist Greeks. When the Army Corps of ELAS, which General Bakirdzis had been appointed to command with Markos Vaphiadhis as his political adviser, occupied Salonika at the end of October, a Bulgarian Military Liaison Mission was already attached to it. But the readjustment did not diminish EAM's attacks on Andon Tsaous and the AMM, although Bakirdzis himself carefully refrained from participating in them. This was the chaotic state of affairs to which the representatives of Papandhreou's Government and the Allied Command were introduced on their arrival in October. The fact that one of the Government's representatives was the Communist Porphyroyennis, and the other was Papandhreou's personal Under-Secretary, Lambrianidhis, added spice to the *farrago*.

The Greek world watched anxiously to see what would happen.

[1] See App. A (g). But EAM certainly tried to negotiate an independent *surrender*.

There had been rumours of agreements between the KKE and the Bulgars, that part of north-east Greece should remain in Bulgarian hands and another part should join the autonomous state of Macedonia which was the darling of Balkan Communism. The rumours were publicly denied time and again, at least once by Svolos, himself a Macedonian. General Wilson himself denied the existence of any such agreement undertaken by any authority; it was one of the prerequisites laid down by the western Allies for an armistice with Bulgaria, that all Bulgarian troops should first leave Greek soil. Nevertheless the rumours persisted, even to the point of specifying the date on which the KKE would proclaim Macedonian autonomy in Salonika. It is possible that some such agreement had been made earlier in 1944 between the KKE and the Bulgarian authorities, who were engaged in reinsurance on the highest level from an early stage. That no attempt was made to implement the agreement, if it existed, was probably again due to the intervention of the Soviet Government, whose primary interest was still to beat Germany. The attitude of the Red Army in the Balkans to the ideological frenzies of the local Communists had been noticeably cool. Instead of enjoying the expected sweets of liberation, the Bulgars found themselves swept away by the Red Army to fight Germans in Yugoslavia and Hungary, losing in the process their first casualties of the war. The Soviet Government was not disposed either to waste valuable manpower or to antagonise Britain at such a critical moment by leaving the Bulgars to make trouble in Eastern Macedonia and Western Thrace: the time for that would come later. In response to Soviet insistence rather than a reformed sense of duty, the last Bulgarian troops left Greece on 25th October. Radev withdrew to Sofia and Andon Tsaous to Athens. Greek Nationalists and Communists watched each other with the same tense hostility as before, but superficially tranquillity was restored to northern Greece. The Albanian battalion of FNC partisans disappeared; Gotchev's battalion of SNOF was allowed to maintain its refusal to serve under ELAS, and to revert to the command of Tito's lieutenant, Tempo, in Yugoslavia. The frontiers of Greece and her neighbours were temporarily tidied up. Such were the wishes of the Soviet Government; the Communist Parties of Bulgaria, Macedonia, Yugoslavia, Albania and Greece had no alternative but to acquiesce. On 28th October the Bulgarian armistice was signed. From the Greek point of view, the satisfaction of being rid of the Bulgarian occupation was almost equalled by the relief of finding the sincerity of PEEA vindicated.

The cohesion of Papandhreou's Government, having survived the first four obstacles which have been discussed so far, disintegrated soon afterwards over the remaining two; so it is important to see what the sincerity of PEEA meant at this stage. It meant that all the six ministers who had joined Papandhreou from PEEA were co-operating in principle with

o

their colleagues in the task of rehabilitating Greece, but not all for the same reasons. Sincerity was a word of different connotation to the three elements concerned. To the bellicose element of the KKE, it meant no more than the necessity of submitting to the line indicated from Moscow. They executed the official policy with loyal efficiency, but not without the hope that it would be changed to the policy, which they believed in without respect to circumstances, of revolution and bloodshed. In deference to their predilections, the cauldron of turmoil was kept quietly simmering, a little below boiling-point, in readiness for any eventuality. To the diplomatic element of the KKE, who believed in using the method of intrigue and infiltration within a constitutional system, sincerity meant continuing along the same slow path as before, towards absolute power by patience and subversion: an easy task, because for the moment the Moscow line coincided with their own. They believed that they had only to wait for the prize to fall into their lap; but if the party-line altered, they were ready to co-operate just as sincerely in the opposite policy. To the third element of PEEA, the high-minded democrats led by Svolos, sincerity meant the same as it meant to the British authorities; they were for the moment happy in the delusion that their policy had prevailed. Of the six men who had joined Papandhreou from PEEA, none had thereby given up his particular objectives and principles, but for the moment the same policy happened to suit them all.

How it might have worked out, as co-operation merged successively into penetration, into subversion, and finally into assumption of power, can be inferred from the similar process which matured more rapidly in the trade unions. The parallel is illuminating. The central committee of EEAM had accompanied PEEA into the mountains in March 1944, and there transformed itself under Theos, Kalomoiris and Stratis into the new General Confederation of Labour, in opposition to the collaborating body of the same name in Athens. Having agreed to take over the Workers' Centres collectively when the Germans left, the Communist group in EEAM anticipated the agreement by seizing all of them independently in October. In deference to protests by Kalomoiris and Stratis, Theos then proposed that elections should be held under a truce within EEAM. The terms were that its component groups, the Reformists and the Communists, would present joint lists and instruct their followers which candidates to prefer. From this arrangement proportional directorates should have emerged throughout the country; but Theos failed to instruct his followers accordingly, and as a result Communist candidates obtained majorities everywhere. At that stage Kalomoiris and Stratis considered breaking with Theos and dissolving EEAM. Events developed too fast for them, however, and in November and December they found themselves swept along on a stronger tide than they could withstand, just as Svolos and his associates did in the political storm.

But comparison of the two trends shows that Communist policy had developed more rapidly in the trade unions than in national politics. The former indicates what might have come later in the latter. The stage in political infiltration which would have corresponded to the manipulation of the elections in the trade unions had not been reached in November. But the comparison helps to clarify the connotation into which the word "sincerity," in application to the motives of PEEA, might have evolved. It may not look very sincere in the end; but that the word was originally applicable is shown by the simplest fact of all. If EAM/ELAS had been determined to seize power by violence on the liberation of Greece, the capital was waiting empty for them to do so on the day the Germans left.[1] They could only have been evicted, if they had so decided, by a costly invasion, which Allied pressure and public opinion would have made impossible. By no conceivable calculation could a better opportunity be expected to recur. That they did not seize Athens in October, before General Scobie's forces arrived, is a final proof of their sincerity in the sense defined.

The British authorities recognised the symptoms and adapted their plans accordingly. The re-entry of British troops into Greece was carried out on a peaceful basis. Apart from skirmishes with the German rearguard, no fighting took place in the process of liberation; it was assumed throughout General Scobie's headquarters that no more shots would have to be fired. Warnings of the possibility that EAM/ELAS were preparing an alternative plan were discounted; the fact that the warnings emanated principally from sources connected with SOE Cairo did not commend them to the new British authorities in Athens. It was probably true, at the time when the warnings were rejected, both that EAM/ELAS had an alternative plan in preparation (as any military headquarters would) and also that they were still bent on co-operation. The latter was the prevalent assumption of the British military authorities. They dispersed their supplies and manpower accordingly in a manner which suited the administrative task for which they had come to Greece, and was not adapted to fighting. They underestimated the fire-power which ELAS had available, by a misjudgment for which their sources of intelligence were to blame.[2] They interpreted the signs of the times to suggest that EAM/ELAS did not intend to precipitate a fight. On the evidence, they were right: the people who miscalculated were EAM/ELAS when they changed their minds.

[1] Even before the Germans had left Athens, it had been entered successively by Lt.-Colonel Sheppard, Lt.-Colonel Macaskie, and Colonel Jellicoe with a handful of men. These three, although remarkable men, did not constitute an insuperable obstacle to the immediate seizure of Athens by ELAS.

[2] One of the sources was myself: after two years of intimate acquaintance with EAM/ELAS, I was entirely deceived.

In considering why they did so, there is no further need to consider separate motives for each of the three elements of PEEA. The group led by Svolos ceased to have a mind of its own once it had become committed in September, and vacillated to and fro in hopeless confusion throughout November and December. The two groups within the KKE again became actuated by the same motive: the apostles of patient penetration came to believe what the apostles of revolutionary bloodshed had always believed, that there was no way to power after all but force. The only important question is why the KKE changed its mind. That the forces of liberation under General Scobie were smaller than had been expected is not decisive. The KKE would not have refrained from seizing Athens before they arrived *merely* because they were expected to be large, nor tried to do so after they arrived *merely* because they turned out to be small. The military factor was only the condition which made success likely or unlikely; it was not the reason why the attempt was made. In general terms, the reason can only have been that the policy of infiltration through co-operation was seen to be doomed to failure. But that only pushes the problem a stage farther back. If the KKE concluded that the Anglo-Greek authorities were not after all going to allow the game to be played into their hands, then they must have suspected some change of policy. There was in fact no such change of policy: what, then, made the KKE suspect one?

The answer must be tentative; but probably a great part of it can be summed up in the inter-play of personalities. Almost all the characters enumerated in Chapter II were now on the stage together. Allied policy, which had been expressed in Greece during the last months of occupation by one Englishman and one American speaking with one voice, had now ceased to be expressed with one voice and ceased to be allied. The trouble lay not in mutual antagonisms, although such did exist, but in multiplicity. The decisions of the Greek and British authorities alike, singly and jointly, were the product not of responsible individuals but of committees. Committees delay and compromise; Communists are trained to read between the lines and to drive home wedges. Within the Cabinet they had no difficulty in reading the signs: for once, Papandhreou was finding it harder to keep Populists and Liberals loyal to him than to conciliate the PEEA group. Among the British authorities, the grains of sand were harder to detect, but they made themselves felt: none of the authorities quite disagreed with each other, yet none of them quite agreed. The hopes of EAM/ELAS had been pinned rather upon the military than the civil component of the British authorities, but after the liberation of Athens the soldiers in whose sympathy they trusted seemed to lose influence over policy. First Greece had been transferred in August from the Middle East Command to the Central Mediterranean, leaving the work of winning confidence to be done all over again, under the additional handicap of impending changes in the latter command. Next, the liberating British forces under General Scobie had been warned not to attach importance to what they might be told by the AMM and SOE Cairo, both of which now disappear from the scene.[1] This suited the leaders of EAM/ELAS in so far as they regarded some of the ALOS, especially the commander of the AMM, as their enemies; but it also deprived them of the sympathy of other ALOS and the good offices of the brigadier commanding SOE Cairo, whom they had come to regard in a brief acquaintance as their best friend. In the late summer the game had appeared to be swinging their way: they had captured the goodwill of the Press and of public opinion throughout the Allied world; the immediate return of the King to Athens had been prevented; the democratic members of PEEA had favourably impressed the Allied authorities, especially the Americans. But during the first weeks of liberation, although none of these advantages had been lost, they were offset in the judgment of EAM/ELAS by mounting evidence that the Anglo-Greek authorities, especially the politicians and diplomats, had after all made up their minds to frustrate them. Neither Soviet nor American representatives in Athens showed any inclination to put pressure on the British authorities for their sake. General Scobie startled them by the forcefulness of his personality. The objects for which they were struggling, under the new guise of political co-operation, seemed to be in danger; it was this fear that again gave the bellicose element in the KKE the upper hand over the apostles of peaceful penetration. Policy was transformed back into revolutionary violence by degrees which can most easily be followed in the development of the problems in categories V and VI (Public Order and National Defence). The most significant thing about their development is that it registers a steady deterioration of relations exclusively between EAM/ELAS on the one side and the Anglo-Greek authorities on the other, without any trace of outside intervention. Neither the

---

[1]In thus abruptly taking farewell of the AMM, I feel obliged to add a summary judgment on its work; but because bias is inevitable, I cannot include it in the text. The strategic value of the AMM has been attested by the Commanders-in-Chief under which it served; of that I am no judge, nor is it relevant here. Of its diplomatic value, I consider this simple justification certain: that but for the AMM, the Greek people would have had no *choice* in its future, however desirable that future might have been. If there had been no AMM in Greece from 1942, the Communists would have been in total control of Greece when the Germans left. The western Allies must then either have left Greece to be *forcibly* incorporated in the USSR, or fought their way back into Greece in order *forcibly* to restore the old régime. The AMM handed over Greece relatively intact in October 1944 to settle its own future under a government unanimously recognised, with the help of Allies unanimously welcomed: on 12th October, 1944, no sane observer could have controverted that conclusion. Of responsibility for the decisions taken after that date and their consequences, the AMM alone must be entirely acquitted, because it was entirely excluded. On the other hand, though this has no historical relevance, I cannot pass over the personal sense of unfulfilled obligation towards the Greek people with which I gave up its command.

Soviet Government nor the American Government plays any part in this scene, beyond the occasional murmurs of voices-off.

4. *NOVEMBER* 1944—*JANUARY* 1945

The problems of Public Order and National Defence were interrelated. When Papandhreou entered Athens, the distribution of armed forces, both civil and military, was unfavourable to his Government if trouble should break out. Those that could be counted loyal in all circumstances were the police and gendarmerie in Athens; Zervas' force in north-west Greece, based on Ioannina; the *Capetanioi* of Andon Tsaous in north-east Greece; and the small British force under General Scobie. The last established a divisional headquarters in Salonika, a brigade headquarters in Patras, battalions and companies here and there, and almost nothing but administrative services in Athens, where small naval and RAF units supported them. For the sake of completeness, three other groups must be mentioned, only to deduct them from the total. These were the private army of X, which had grown steadily since the liberation of Athens; the Security Battalions, which had been disarmed, but would have been glad to show their loyalty to the new Greek authorities as well as the old; and the armed villagers of Mikhalagas, who were still waiting in the neighbourhood of Kozani for a British force strong enough to accept their surrender and protect their lives. None of these could be used for any lawful purpose. The rest of Greece was in the hands of EAM/ELAS, who occupied the towns, the villages and the provinces not only with combatant troops of ELAS, but also with their private police force, EP. General Spiliotopoulos, the Military Governor of Attica, was reported to have bluffed EAM/ELAS with threats of the large forces available to him, but apart from the above there were only two limited sources from which he could draw: the Sacred Squadron under Colonel Tsigantes the elder, which was in the Aegean islands; and the Greek Brigade in Italy, now known from its first victory as the Rimini Brigade. The latter was transferred to Greece and enthusiastically welcomed in Athens by all but EAM/ELAS on 10th November. Such was the situation when the Cabinet began to discuss the future of all these forces.[1]

Papandhreou's first proposal on public order was that the gendarmerie should be purged and EP dissolved by the end of November; both should then be replaced by a National Guard. For national defence he proposed that all the guerillas should be demobilised and given "moral

---

[1] The story of this phase is given in more detail in Richard Capell's *Simiomata* and Byford-Jones's *The Greek Trilogy*; but even those do not claim to be more than personal accounts. An American, W. H. McNeill, gives a painstakingly impartial account in *The Greek Dilemma*; but his version of earlier events, like that of Byford-Jones, is misinformed. The *history* of December 1944 still cannot be written. I attempt only a brief and tentative reconstruction of motives.

and material rewards"[1]; four classes should be called up into the new
army in December; regular officers from the forces abroad or from the
guerillas should be absorbed into it; officers commissioned by the
guerillas should be given special facilities for training. The call-up of
the 1936 class began on 24th November. The PEEA ministers expressed
no immediate reservations about EP and Papandhreou, construing their
silence as consent, published this decision; but they never considered
themselves bound by it. More explicitly, they demanded the demobilisation of the Rimini Brigade. The presence of the latter in Athens, where it
served no military purpose comparable to the need for it in Italy, was
provocative, even if unintentionally;[2] Papandhreou therefore agreed that it
should be given "generous leave." He further proposed that General Scobie
should be in charge of the demobilisation of the guerillas, to guarantee
that it should be conducted fairly and that it should be completed by
10th December. Meanwhile he made several concessions to EAM/ELAS.
General Spiliotopoulos, whom EAM/ELAS regarded as a collaborator,
was replaced as Military Governor of Attica by Colonel Katsotas.
General Othonaios, whom the guerillas had theoretically agreed
upon as their C-in-C in February, was made C-in-C of the new
national army. He was offered Saraphis as his deputy, and Vendiris
was removed from the post of CGS at Othonaios' request.
Lambrianidhis, who had returned from Macedonia to be Under-Secretary
for War, was removed from his post in response to accusations of indis-
cretion in drawing up the list of officers who were to supervise the
call-up in the provinces. He was replaced by General Sariyiannis, a
nominee of EAM/ELAS, who brought the representation of PEEA in
the Government up to seven.

    These concessions did not go far enough to allay suspicion of the
plan for demobilising ELAS and EP. No objection was raised by Zervas,
who began preparing EDES for demobilisation in the last week of
November. Several members of the Cabinet threatened to resign if
demobilisation did not take place by 10th December. But when General
Scobie met Zervas and Saraphis in Athens on 22nd November to discuss
the demobilisation, it was plain that Saraphis was not authorised to sign
such an order to ELAS unless the entire Government, including the
PEEA members, signed a decree of demobilisation. The problem passed
back to the Cabinet, which had not yet committed itself on paper. At
a series of meetings of the Cabinet, Papandhreou saw that no draft
decree proposed by himself would be accepted by his Communist

[1]The promise of rewards was never honoured, even for those guerillas who obeyed the
Government's orders.
    [2]Since the arrival of the Rimini Brigade in Athens was in my opinion the most important
single factor contributory to the loss of faith by EAM/ELAS, it is right to add that I had
categorically advised against it three months earlier.

colleagues, who already had the remaining representatives of PEEA under their control at least to the extent of their *veto*. Papandhreou therefore invited the PEEA members to draft the decree; it was submitted to the Cabinet and approved on 28th November. Its essential provisions were four: firstly that ELAS, ELAN, and EDES should be demobilised by 10th December, with the exception of a brigade of ELAS and a proportionate unit of EDES (which neither Zervas nor his representative in the Cabinet had required); secondly that the military forces of the Middle East should be demobilised on their return to Greece, except the Rimini Brigade and the Sacred Squadron; thirdly that those demobilised should surrender their weapons; fourthly that the gendarmerie and EP should hand over to the National Guard, which was in process of formation and into which some of them would be absorbed, on 1st December in some districts, and 17th December in others. Papandhreou with difficulty persuaded the other members of his Cabinet to accept the PEEA draft; but on the following day the PEEA members themselves refused to sign it, and Zevgos presented an amended draft on behalf of his colleagues. The principal differences were two: firstly the demobilisation of the Rimini Brigade and the Sacred Squadron were additionally demanded; secondly the clause prescribing the surrender of weapons was deleted. The retention under arms of EP was not demanded, although this had previously been the principal point of dissension. Papandhreou's colleagues refused to accept the amendments; the full Cabinet never met again.

From that moment the revolution was decided. It only remained to wait for the occasion of its outbreak, which all parties saw coming. EAM/ELAS, who already had an Army Corps Headquarters in Athens under General Mandakas, moved reinforcements towards the capital. They were more heavily armed than they had been during the occupation, since the Germans had left behind many dumps within their reach, knowing even without explicit agreement to what use they would be put. Mortars and artillery were registered on key-points in Athens, but no shot was yet fired. The first act of defiance was the refusal of EP to hand over its duties to the National Guard on 1st December. On the same day Zevgos published an article in *Rizospastis* declaring that the time for negotiation was past, and only arms could settle the issue. ELAS GHQ was formally reconstituted, as a symbol of open repudiation of the Government's authority. Papandhreou, who had hitherto taken no action beyond making a speech on 29th November in which he accused the KKE of "inciting the people to civil war," treated EP's refusal as rebellion. He called a meeting of the Cabinet for the same evening without notifying the PEEA ministers. The original six resigned during the same night, reluctantly followed a few days later by General Sariyiannis, who already had the reputation of a collaborator and did not wish to add to it that of a Communist. On 2nd December the Cabinet met again without the seven PEEA members, and approved a decree dissolving ELAS, ELAN, EP and EDES. All regular officers were ordered to report to the Ministry of War, to which all weapons and ammunition were also to be surrendered. These two decisions technically put the entirety of EAM/ELAS in the wrong, whatever they might do thereafter except surrender; but many members of ELAS, who were subsequently penalised for disobeying them, would have been willing to conform if they had been free to do so. In protest the KKE, to which the initiative of EAM and PEEA as a whole had now passed, announced their intention to hold a demonstration on 3rd December and a general strike on 4th December. The Cabinet first permitted and later forbade the demonstration, which took place none the less; simultaneously the strike began, twenty-four hours before the time announced. During the morning of Sunday, 3rd December, the revolution broke out. When the crowd of demonstrators in Constitution Square closed with the police, several policemen fired into them, which was exactly the object for which the KKE had assembled them there. According to some accounts the crowd fired back; according to others it actually fired first, and had already thrown hand-grenades through the windows of political enemies before it ever reached Constitution Square. The truth can perhaps never be known, since Athens had been so accustomed to random shots and spasmodic bloodshed in the last few weeks that the historical starting-point is hard to fix. But what precisely happened is no more and no less important than any other ostensible *casus belli*: if the conflict had not come about in that way, it would have come about in another. Papandhreou broadcast that night, fastening the blame upon the Communists. He was right, but his police had enabled the KKE, in the eyes of most of the Press and the world, to put him in the wrong. In the words of a greater policeman than any in Athens, "it was worse than a crime; it was a blunder." Colonel Grivas launched X into the fight, thus adding another trump to the KKE's hand; and the ostentatious funeral of the victims of Sunday furnished them on Monday with a Roman holiday after their own hearts.

The British forces under General Scobie were not yet committed; nor was the Rimini Brigade, which was confined to barracks in Athens, nor the Sacred Squadron, which remained in the Aegean islands. The first assault of ELAS as it moved into Athens to avenge the blunder of Constitution Square was directed against the police. But it was obvious that they intended to seize the whole of Athens; the minimum that could be held against them was mutinous disobedience to orders. The Cabinet, under whose orders Saraphis had placed ELAS at Caserta, had decreed the demobilisation of ELAS and the replacement of EP by the National Guard. General Scobie, under whose operational command Papandhreou had placed all troops at Caserta, made a proclamation on 1st December undertaking to protect the Greek state from unconstitutional violence, and issued an order to ELAS on 4th December to withdraw from a defined area of Athens by midnight of 6th-7th December. On 2nd December Mr. Churchill issued a statement in London supporting General Scobie's first proclamation, and in the early morning of 5th December ordered him to take command of Athens for the purpose of restoring order. During the course of that day, in which all available forces became committed to hostilities against ELAS, General Scobie explained at a Press conference the grounds which justified his intervention: that an attempt was being made to achieve a political object by armed force, and that ELAS and EP were technically mutinous troops. The first point might be open to logical cavil, but the second was unanswerable.

During the five weeks which intervened before EAM/ELAS admitted defeat, General Scobie's forces nearly succumbed. They had to be strongly reinforced by units from Italy, under the operational command of Gen. Hawkesworth, to whom the credit for the battle of Athens principally belongs. Fighting under General Mandakas with a determination which few of them had ever shown against the Germans, ELAS at one time held almost the whole of Greece but for a few square miles of Athens. The provoked error of the police had strengthened ELAS materially as well as morally: it had inculcated in the small American contingent in Athens (as well as the still fewer Russians) a spirit of neutrality with a benevolent bias in favour of EAM/ELAS; it had helped to swell the ranks of revolution with many simple Greeks who believed, as the KKE told them, that the opposition was confined to the police, the collaborators and the Security Battalions. The holocaust of executions which OPLA perpetrated against innocent hostages eventually reversed the balance of emotion; but that did not become known until weeks later. EAM/ELAS started with the odds in their favour.

The tiny British units, which had been deployed in the provinces to maintain order and administer relief, were obliged to withdraw, sometimes with casualties, from every area except Salonika and Patras, where relations were carefully maintained between the British authorities and ELAS. Salonika in particular, where another outbreak of revolution might have sealed the fate of Athens, was miraculously saved by the tact of the British Consul-General and divisional commander, and by the good sense of General Bakirdzis in command of ELAS. Even the fanatical Markos Vaphiadhis, political adviser to ELAS in Salonika, recognised the insecurity of his party's moral position. An EAM/ELAS demonstration on 17th December passed off almost without notice; the local leaders of ELD and the Socialist Party announced their secession from EAM. But the party's physical power in the north did not slacken. A conference during December was attended by Communist representatives from

Bulgaria and Albania; ELAS could use Albanian territory to pass from Macedonia to Epirus against Zervas; men were sent freely across the frontier to Yugoslavia for further training in partisan warfare. There is no evidence that foreign troops helped ELAS, apart from casual German deserters and northern Greeks of ill-defined antecedents; but none were needed: ELAS was enough for its task. The remaining forces of Mikhalagas and Andon Tsaous were quickly wiped out. Between 18th and 30th December Zervas' troops were driven out of north-west Greece, by force of circumstances which have been stated in Chapter II[1], and evacuated by the Royal Navy to Corfu. By New Year's Day the legitimate authorities had been ousted from every part of Greece except a part of Athens, together with Salonika, Patras, Corfu and some of the Aegean islands (the rest of which were still held by the Germans). In the meantime, however, the military defeat of ELAS had gradually been made certain, and political provisions had been made by the Anglo-Greek authorities to consolidate their approaching victory.

Within the responsible circle of the Greek and British authorities, the initiative had passed entirely to the latter, just as their opponents' initiative had passed entirely to the KKE. The KKE had a policy but no principles; the British authorities had principles but no policy. The intention of HMG was still to ensure liberty and tranquillity for the Greek people to determine their future by democratic methods: "Holding the ring" was one of the catch-phrases of the day; another was "The ballot, not the bullet." But these words did not constitute a policy in the face of two political extremes, represented under arms by ELAS and X, neither of which believed in democratic methods. Throughout November, and still more in December, British policy gave to the outside observer an impression of Machiavellian cunning, and to the intimate eye-witness an impression of groping conscientiously in the dark to find something that might not be there.

The danger in November had lain in the need for haste. It was almost impossible to persuade coalition ministers to agree on anything without discussing everything else under the sun for several days, but Greece's rehabilitation demanded immediate decisions on all the problems which have been outlined. Yet hasty decisions could not serve the interests of Greece in the long run, because those concerned would not carry them out, even when they had signed them, unless it happened to suit them. If the Government had been left to set its own tempo, progress would have been slower but surer: all but the hard core of the guerillas might eventually have drifted back home on their own initiative; relief might have been delayed, but no factious exploitation of the delay would have been possible so long as all parties remained in the Government; political mistakes might have been made, but responsibility for them would have

[1]See page 81.

been shared by all, including the KKE. As it was, more haste meant less speed. Precipitation led to decisions which convinced EAM/ELAS of the bad faith of the Greek and British authorities. The provocative presence in Athens of the Rimini Brigade, whose maintenance under arms when ELAS was to be demobilised seemed to have only one meaning; the absence of the Russian and American representatives from consultations affecting Allied relations; the ignorance in which the ordinary British troops were left of every issue at stake,[1] the exclusion of the PEEA ministers from the Cabinet summoned on 1st December; the disregard of the Press, who sympathised with EAM/ELAS almost to a man: all these were effects of precipitate conduct, which might in themselves be easy to justify, but left too many opportunities for malicious criticism after the event.

In December, after the fighting had broken out, there could be no policy beyond a determination to win the fight; but there were also new complications. The events of the war far away from Greece seemed to conspire to make the task more difficult. The German break-through in the Ardennes underlined the fact that British troops, who were needed on other fronts, were fighting Greeks who called themselves allies. In the Balkans the Russians were able to point to battles against the real enemy, in which even Bulgars were taking a prominent part, but not a single Greek or Englishman. A political crisis in Italy, during which Mr. Churchill was said to have intervened to prevent Count Sforza coming to power, seemed to confirm by an ominous analogy HMG's meddlesomeness in the internal affairs of other countries. The resistance forces of France and Belgium were passing through the same phase as those of Greece at the same time: the fact that in France they were incorporated in the regular army, whereas in Belgium they were recalcitrantly disbanded, seemed to the critics to be directly attributable to the contrast that in Belgium operational responsibility rested with a British general, whereas in France it did not. Finally, the approach of the Yalta Conference increased the importance of reaching a settlement as quickly as possible.

These embarrassments were rubbed into the wounds of the British authorities by the House of Commons; by the annual conference of the Labour Party; by the Press of the Allied world, with the London *Times* in the lead; and even by the American Secretary of State and some members of Mr. Churchill's Cabinet. Mr. Churchill defended his Government's conduct with vigour and justice, but with regard only to the narrower aspects of the crisis in Greek affairs. His justification of HM Ambassador and General Scobie was unanswerable. Of the rest of the British authorities in Athens no justification was needed; the worst that could fairly be said was that there were too many of them, with minds

---

[1]For example, in the regimental magazine of a unit that was engaged against the rebels in Athens, I have read the statement that the "civil war" was between ELAS and EAM.

and energies that moved at different speeds. During the crucial weeks of November none of them had done less than might have been expected; nor had any of them, as crises demand, done more. Responsibility lay in more masterful hands. The revolution was the fruit of two years' work by the KKE, aided by the follies and complacency of their opponents; but the threat which the revolution constituted to Allied unity and the British coalition, was the fruit of two years' concealment of the truth. The anger of a misinformed public, whipped up by an embittered Press, was added to the catastrophes of December 1944. In this dark gloom the British authorities groped for a policy.

In the diplomatic fluctuations which accompanied the fighting, the Communists can be seen calculating principally on long-term objectives, especially as their immediate hopes declined, while their opponents concentrated upon the day-to-day problems of restoring order. This was logical, since the KKE had the positive goal of absolute power, and the British authorities the negative goal of ensuring fair play; though neither "positive" nor "negative" here has a pejorative sense. The events of December and January demonstrated this logic. On 8th December, when British troops had been engaged for three days, Saraphis addressed a telegram to General Scobie protesting against the conduct of Papandhreou's Government and British intervention. ELAS were in a strong position, not only militarily but politically. A question in the House of Commons on 5th December had revealed the critical mood of the Labour Party, and a debate on an unofficial amendment to the Address, moved as a vote of censure, was about to take place on 8th December. Nevertheless General Scobie replied to Saraphis the next day in terms of repudiation. The debate in the House of Commons ended on 9th December in the rejection of the amendment, although disquiet appeared even within Mr. Churchill's Cabinet. EAM/ELAS, who still looked like crushing the hastily gathered opposition, took advantage of the uneasiness to send Porphyroyennis to General Scobie on 11th December to propose terms. General Scobie anticipated his proposals by demanding firstly the withdrawal from Athens of ELAS and secondly the surrender of civilians fighting in support of ELAS.

While EAM/ELAS debated their reply, the Anglo-Greek authorities debated the next political steps to be taken. Papandhreou had wished to resign at the beginning of the revolution, but agreed to remain in office because no alternative Prime Minister could be found except Sophoulis, who was over eighty and far more bitter against the KKE than any member even of the existing Cabinet. On 13th December, however, General Plastiras arrived in Athens from his exile in France. The suggestion that he should become Prime Minister under a Regency of the Archbishop of Athens was debated round the narrowing circle of the capital that was still free. It won the approval of almost everyone concerned, with the significant exceptions of the King of the Hellenes, who boldly wished to return himself from London, and Papandhreou, who insisted that talk of a Regency merely obscured the true issue of the Communist menace. It was true that the KKE was already appealing to Sofia and Belgrade, and perhaps even through Colonel Popov to Moscow: Papandhreou's objection may therefore have shown a more far-sighted apprehension of the problems than any other Greek on the same side; but the immediate need for a Government and a head of the state predominated among the rest. This preoccupation was intensified by a visit to Athens of Mr. Macmillan and Field-Marshal Alexander, the Resident Minister and the new Supreme Commander of the Mediterranean theatre. Optimism revived as better news came from Salonika, and perennial rumours of the disintegration of EAM spread again. The moderate Socialists, such as Svolos and Tsirimokos of ELD and the Reformist group in EEAM under Kalomoiris and Stratis, wished to secede, but were not able to do so at present; they were too paralysed to help towards the cessation of hostilities. There was in fact little but wishful thinking to comfort the British authorities in mid-December. The King remained stubborn about the Regency; the RAF headquarters were captured by ELAS; the fighting spread to involve Zervas in disaster in north-west Greece; the Conference of the British Labour Party passed a resolution on 13th December regretting the policy of HMG; the new American Secretary of State, Mr. Stettinius, made critical remarks about British intervention in Italy and Greece. It is not surprising that EAM/ELAS continued to be intransigent.

On 14th December their reply to General Scobie put forward terms of their own, one of which accepted the condition that ELAS should withdraw from Athens. The other terms demanded the withdrawal of the Rimini Brigade and Sacred Squadron from Athens; the disarmament of the gendarmerie and Security Battalions; the confinement of British troops to tasks defined in the Caserta Agreement; and the re-formation of a Government of national unity. The references to the Sacred Squadron and Security Battalions were based on obvious misconceptions; the invocation of the Caserta Agreement was also mistaken, as General Scobie was able to prove by publishing its terms. But the attitude of the KKE implied in this communication was not entirely surprising nor unreasonable. It was rejected, however, as providing no basis for discussion, on the ground that it ignored the second of General Scobie's conditions. Perhaps if the British forces had been on top at the time, instead of fighting with their backs to the wall, the answer given on 16th December might have been different. The KKE might have done well to study the British idiosyncrasy of regarding all terms as unreasonable when they are in danger of defeat. Instead they disregarded General Scobie's reply and drafted a new communication on 18th December, which repeated their proposals in a more diffuse and argumentative manner. This document was not received by General Scobie until 22nd December; before it could be answered the arrival in Athens of Mr. Churchill and Mr. Eden on Christmas Day shifted the level of dispute.

Greece recognised the personal intervention of the British Prime Minister and Foreign Secretary as bearing the marks of a spectacular climax; but the marks were superficial, and only served to disguise an anti-climax which had almost no effect upon the course of events. Militarily the tide of battle was already turning in favour of the Anglo-Greek authorities. Politically the situation remained unaltered on the day of the two great visitors' departure. All that had happened in the meantime was a vast conference on 26th and 27th December, which was adjourned *sine die* after two sessions. The conference was attended by five different groups under the chairmanship of Archbishop Dhamaskinos. The British authorities were represented by Mr. Churchill, Mr. Eden, Mr. Macmillan, Mr. Leeper, Field-Marshal Alexander, and General Scobie; the Greek world on the first day by Papandhreou, the elder Sophoulis, Kaphandaris, Maximos, Dhragoumis and Plastiras, all of whom had participated in the recent debate about the Government; on the second day additionally by Kanellopoulos, Mylonas, Sophianopoulos, Gonatas, Alexandhris, Periklis Rallis, Stephanopoulos, Theotokis and Tsaldharis, of whom the first five bracketed the Liberal Centre, and the last four were Populists; EAM/ELAS by Siantos, Partsalidhis and Mandakas; the Allied world by the United States Ambassador, the French Minister and the commander of the Soviet Military Mission. Of this imposing collection, in which to some minds even passive collaboration seemed to be symbolised by Gonatas, the first and last groups withdrew after a few introductory remarks, leaving the Greek politicians by themselves with little idea what they had been summoned to discuss. Although they represented every possible opinion, few of them had recovered from the political coma in which they had slept since 1936. The EAM/ELAS delegates took the opportunity to put forward new conditions of peace, which were for the first time preposterously and deliberately unacceptable. They demanded up to half the seats in the Cabinet, including the Ministries of the Interior and Justice and the Under-Secretaryships of War and Foreign Affairs; the demobilisation of the gendarmerie, the Rimini Brigade, the Sacred Squadron, and the new National Guard; a plebiscite on the Constitution in February, and elections for a Constituent Assembly in April. They provoked the reaction that they wished. General Plastiras refused to discuss the terms, and the Populists left the room. The only point of agreement was the desirability of a Regency; but it was plain that the KKE was resolved on a fight to the finish. They realised that the USSR was not coming to the rescue; their imminent victory was already turning into imminent defeat: so the most likely explanation of their intensified intransigeance is that they preferred total defeat to the consequences of a peace negotiated by concession. Capitulation after a fight to the last round would serve their political purposes better in the long run than the obligations of an unfavourable compromise. In this spirit they prolonged the fight after its objects were lost, while Mr. Churchill returned to London to persuade King George II to acquiesce in the Regency of the Archbishop of Athens.

On 30th December it was announced that the King was resolved not to return to Greece until he was "summoned by a free and fair expression of the national will." The next day the archbishop took the oath as Regent, and accepted Papandhreou's resignation. General Plastiras took office on 3rd January with a predominantly republican Cabinet, of which the most significant member was Sophianopoulos as Minister for Foreign Affairs. Sophianopoulos was known to be friendly to EAM, and liked to be thought to enjoy the confidence of the USSR. Within a few days of his appointment EAM sent to General Scobie an offer of new terms, which represented a slight recession from their earlier demands, followed soon afterwards by a delegation headed by Zevgos. General Scobie, having consistently maintained his two original conditions, replied by withdrawing the offer of an armistice on such easy terms. He was justified by EAM/ELAS' disregard of international law in treatment of prisoners and seizure of hostages; but his strength lay in the altered position of the battle. Athens and Piraeus were cleared by 5th January; British patrols reached a point more than twenty-five miles north of Athens two days later. With the approval of the Regent, General Scobie invited a delegation of ELAS to discuss new terms. On 10th January Partsalidhis and Zevgos arrived for the purpose, accompanied by two staff majors; thereby indicating that in the view of EAM/ELAS capitulation was a political process in which soldiers performed only technical functions. A truce was signed on 11th January, providing for a cessation of hostilities at one minute after midnight on 15th January, followed by a progressive withdrawal of ELAS forces. Despite the protests of the Regent, of General Plastiras and of HMG, EAM/ELAS refused to release Greek hostages, on the ground that civilians captured in Athens while fighting on their side had also been treated as hostages and deported to Egypt. This matter, together with the future of ELAS itself, was left for settlement by a subsequent conference, which was to be convened on 25th January. British troops re-occupied the remainder of Greece without hindrance; they found General Bakirdzis particularly co-operative when they entered Salonika on 17th January. The conduct of HMG was justified by the publication of documents from the Foreign Office[1]: by speeches in the House of

[1]"Documents Relating to the Situation in Greece," Cmd. 6592, January 1945.

Commons from Mr. Churchill on 18th January and from Mr. Eden
the next day; and by the report of a TUC delegation, which arrived in
Athens under Sir Walter Citrine on 22nd January.[1] The population of
Athens showed its feelings by its greetings of Mr. Churchill and Mr.
Eden on their way back to England from Yalta in February. To most
Greeks it seemed that a nightmare had ended; to a few it seemed that
their ambitions had been frustrated. Yet some, whose dispassionate per-
spicacity rose above the turmoil of Athens at the turn of the year, saw
that both feelings were beside the point. A firm obstacle had halted the
course of Greek history; but it was only a matter of time before Greek
history flowed round it or over the top.

---

[1] *What We Saw In Greece*: Report of the TUC delegation, Feb. 1945. This delegation
conscientiously sought its information from sources which it thought least likely to suffer
from instinctive bias against the left; for instance, it consulted the rank and file of the British
troops rather than General Scobie's staff officers. It was unfortunate for this high-minded
purpose that there was a good deal more bias against EAM/ELAS among the former, who
had just fought them at grimly close quarters, than among the latter, who had not.

CHAPTER VI

INTERLUDE

JANUARY—APRIL, 1945

"I am convinced of this great truth, that to save a revolution you must stop it going too far."

Attributed to THIERS.

THE second interlude marks another change in the character of this story. The difference is that between the materials of history and current affairs. From the viewpoint of 1948, the events which go to determine the motives and trends of 1941-4 belong to the immutable past, even if they may not all yet be ascertained. From the same viewpoint, the events which go to determine the motives and trends of 1945-6 are not yet closed. Reconstruction must be all the more tentative. But certain trends can already be detected which no historian of Greece is likely to dispute. The principal two, of which the others are derivatives or corollaries, are those defined in the preface as the subjects of this survey. The extensive relation of Greece as a source of Allied discord, and the intensive relation of mutual hatred between Greeks, both became henceforth fixed *foci* in the evolution of Greek affairs; other signs of the times which derived from them had still to establish their permanency. Examples of the latter are the alignment of British armed force with the extremists of the right, and the alignment of many Greek Liberals with the extremists of the left. These phenomena were only the fortuitous outcome of events, to which many parallels can be drawn from past history. That there was nothing in the order of nature to make permanent the uneasy bedfellowship between the British Army and the forces of Royalist reaction can be deduced from an analogy: when Greek and British forces last fired upon each other, the cause lay in a very different intention of the Allied authorities in the first World War, to coerce or expel King Constantine. On the other hand, the gravitation of the Liberals towards the extreme left, which began after the failure of the December Revolution, might be foreseen to be just as ephemeral as the same phenomenon ten years before, when even the name of Greece's greatest statesman became incorporated in the incongruous compound of "Veniselocommunism." But the two new characteristics which came into being as a result of the occupation and resistance, the external and internal facets of ideological discord, are branded more deeply on the body of the Greek nation. The nature and first effects of these are the theme of the next two chapters.

Their nature can be summarised from the foregoing narrative. Its starting-point was Greece united under the late King George II in 1941; formally united by the régime of the Fourth of August, and to some extent really united by the war. But unity had been imposed at the expense of three unsolved problems: communism, constitutional cleavage, and foreign relations. These three problems were inter-related, since the Communist leaders owed their primary allegiance to a foreign power, the USSR, and used the constitutional cleavage to split and weaken their rivals of the old political world. The German occupation gave them their opportunity, and years of experience underground, where Metaxas had driven them, gave them the ability to take it. The old political world was weakened and made ripe for disruption by the same things which made the Communists strong. They had submitted to the anæsthetic of Metaxism; the occupation split them along new lines of division which cut even across the constitutional cleavage. Some escaped to Egypt; some collaborated with the Germans; some slept on; only a few saw in the occupation the same opportunity as the KKE, to assume an active role in reshaping the destiny of their country. These few were naturally the less conservative, since those who had no quarrel with the current way of life, whether under German or British influence, saw no cause to do anything but await liberation. Resistance to the Germans was therefore led by a small section of the community in which the KKE predominated. A large proportion of ordinary Greeks was attracted to them by patriotic propaganda, with no understanding of their political purposes. Within this resistance movement, the Communists' political purpose was to win power and use it to incorporate Greece in a Soviet Federation of the Balkans: the political purposes of the others were hazy and vaguely republican at first, but gradually solidified, as they realised the purpose of the KKE, into an effort to obstruct it. At the same time, the static majority of the old political world became hardened into a still firmer hostility towards the KKE. Being out of touch with the world of resistance, the Greek politicians of Athens, Cairo and London tended to identify the underground with its most vocal element, so that when the KKE brought discredit upon themselves, the whole world of resistance was compelled to share it. The anti-Communist miscellany, by a later and derivative reaction, became similarly dominated by the most vocal element in their heterogeneous make-up: the militant Royalists, who were alone able to pit force against force by reason of their strength in the armed services. In the conflict of these extremes, the democratic centre swayed to and fro by revulsion and reaction, becoming identified by public opinion with whichever extreme they happened to be nearer at any given moment. Greece thus became divided into two mutually irreconcilable worlds, each comprising a hard core and a floating population. The conflict within this microcosm was reproduced by the circumstances of the war in the macrocosm of world power. The allegiance of the hard core on one side to the USSR induced the other side to direct its hopes towards Britain and the USA. Circumstances persuaded both Governments to accept this loyalty, though the USA delayed longer about doing so than Britain. The chief circumstances were a fear that the KKE would stifle democracy in Greece, as December, 1944, confirmed; and that if the USSR obtained an outlet to the Mediterranean Sea through puppets in Greece as well as in Bulgaria and Yugoslavia, their presence would threaten the security of the Suez Canal (which principally exercised the British in 1945-6) and the oilfields of the Middle East (which principally exercised the Americans in 1947). The local quarrel thus reflected the wider division of the great powers: the reflection was cast back and forth and multiplied in an infinite series, as in two confronting mirrors. The Germans in occupation of Greece were a temporary screen between them; but since the screen was withdrawn and they were left face to face, there has been no hope of any termination of the series. That is how the theme stated in the preface came into being: how it developed remains to be seen.

The first effect of the confrontation in December, 1944, was the re-assertion of right by the intervention of British might. This was clearly stated, though with the exaggeration of shocked ignorance, by the report of Sir Walter Citrine's TUC delegation in February, 1945. But right was interpreted by interested Greeks in another sense; to both factions it meant the triumph of the Right. Because the British Army had forestalled a plot of the extreme left, it was assumed that they were the instruments of a plot of the extreme right. No one took seriously the suggestion that they had intervened to restore equilibrium, since the fearful experience of December, 1944, had left no one in the mood for moderation. The centre was as bewildered as before; only the extreme right, in whose name X had tried to take part in suppressing the revolution, was ready to exploit the blunder of the KKE. The British authorities had refused the assistance of X, but the impotence of the centre left them in the end with no alternative to the services of the political right. The history of 1945-6 becomes the record of their growing ascendancy; the precise reversal of the trend of events under the occupation. There is a parallel between the two trends, because the wilder adherents of the right imitated the methods of the left, from whom they learned the arts of infiltration, propaganda and unofficial thuggery. By expanding their control over the armed services and police, and by exploiting the financial power of the industrial world whom the revolution had scared into their arms, they made a mockery of the moderate governments, which the British successively supported in the hope of staving off the extremes, and brushed aside as an absurd hypocrisy the British passion for dispassionateness. Even under republican administrations, the Royalist right crept back into authority: Vendiris and Spiliotopoulos into the highest positions in the army; Dhimitratos into the trades unions; Zervas, repudiating both his anti-monarchism and his abjuration of politics, into a dubious reputation as the founder of the National Party of Greece and the power behind the right-wing coalition EME. At the end of 1945 the right was as dominant in Greece as the left had been at the end of 1943, almost entirely because of the blunder of December, 1944. But there were two important defects in the parallel. One was that the political leaders of the right, unlike those of the left, did not seek to exploit the excesses of their irresponsible supporters; they were simply unable to control them. The other was that whereas during the ascendancy of the left, the rest of the political world had watched in helpless apathy, during the ascendancy of the right, the KKE were neither helpless nor apathetic, but calmly engaged upon their preparations for the third round.

There was a period of recoil from defeat before they put an active policy into motion again; a hesitant interim, like the aftermath of an earthquake, which lasted from the armistice in January to the fall of Plastiras in April. Yet even at a time when no one was sure what ought to happen next, practised discipline gave the Communists an air of self-confident arrogance. They approached the conference which succeeded the armistice with the manner of conquerors; their trade union representatives met Sir Walter Citrine at the end of January as men with a legitimate grievance. After Sophianopoulos had been appointed (with Periklis Rallis and Makropoulos) to represent the Greek Government in the conference summoned to meet at Varkiza on 25th January, nearly three weeks passed before the delegates of EAM/ELAS presented themselves. In reply to the Regent's invitation of three Communist representatives and one military expert, they insisted on preserving the formality of coalition by including Tsirimokos of ELD in their delegation. After stubborn argument, they gained their first point by compelling Plastiras' Government to receive Siantos, Partsalidhis, Tsirimokos, Saraphis and two staff officers in Athens on 1st February. They continued to stand their ground in the opening sessions at Varkiza, which coincided with the conference at Yalta. Siantos' preliminary demands were the inclusion of the KKE in the Government and a general amnesty; but these were only bargaining points. After many days' debate an agreement was signed on 12th February, in terms not unfavourable to defeated revolutionaries.[1] In the light of future events, the most important provisions can be seen to have been those for the demobilisation of ELAS, ELAN and EP

[1] See Appendix I for the text.

(including the surrender of a specified number of weapons); for the release of hostages and the partial amnesty of political crimes; for the lifting of martial law, coupled with the suspension of certain articles of the Constitution (including that forbidding arrest without warrant, which remained in force only in Athens and Piraeus); for the purge of civil, armed and security services; and most important of all, for the conduct under Allied supervision of a plebiscite on the Constitution and elections to a Constituent Assembly (in that order) before the end of the year.

The effect of these clauses was to leave the extremes of left and right free to make trouble on their own terms. The left, having to surrender a specified number of weapons which was still less than their total stock, tacitly assumed the right to do what it liked with the rest. The right, armed with the suspension of *habeas corpus* and the vindictive indiscipline of the newly formed National Guard, was free to pursue personal vendettas against anyone who could be represented as a Communist. The cycle of revolution and counter-revolution, persecution and retaliation, breakable only by an act of enlightenment which no Greek politician had the courage to take, was thus given another spin on its way. Without the safeguards of good faith, the Varkiza Agreement was sterile; but like the Lebanon Charter before it, it was rashly welcomed as conclusive.

When the Varkiza Agreement had been signed, Greece became a backwater again. The high tides running in the great outer world, and even in the narrower Balkan world, passed Greece by for several months. In the greater world, public interest was concentrated on the Yalta Conference, especially on its controversial settlement of the Polish problem. As the Red Army approached the Oder line and Eisenhower's armies crossed the Rhine, the end of the war became more important to the world than the domestic troubles of Greece. Turkey and Egypt, as well as several South American states, hastened to declare war on Germany and Japan in time to secure places at the forthcoming conferences of the United Nations in San Francisco. Having filled the headlines of the Allied Press for several weeks, Greece became almost forgotten in the wider importance of these events, except when Mr. Churchill and Mr. Eden revisited Athens on their way home from Yalta; and momentarily when Sophianopoulos used his position as head of the Greek delegation at San Francisco to vote with the USSR, and against the USA and Britain, in favour of admitting Argentina to the United Nations. Even Sophianopoulos' sycophancy passed unacknowledged by the Soviet Government, which sustained the pose of indifference to Greek affairs that Stalin had adopted at Yalta, by informing the Greek Ambassador in Moscow that it did not intend to send an Ambassador to Athens for the present. Soviet propaganda similarly ignored Greece, and turned its vituperation upon Turkey; this was the preliminary to the denunciation of the Turko-

Soviet Treaty of 1925 on 19th March. Throughout the summer Turkey continued to be the principal target of Soviet interest, which alarmed the western Allies by its attention to the Straits, and the Greek Government by its attention to the Dodecanese. Since it was common ground that Italy was to lose the Dodecanese, whose strategic value was an equal temptation to the USSR and Turkey, it was a matter of urgency to reassert Greece's prior claim. It was done unofficially by the publication during March of telegrams from three of the islands proclaiming their union with Greece, and still more demonstratively by a visit of the Regent to Rhodes in May. These incidents momentarily recalled Greece to the public memory; but for most of the spring of 1945 the Allied world left the Greeks to bury their dead, while it finished off the war in Europe.

Even in the narrower world of the Balkans there were more pressing interests. The controlled Press of Yugoslavia had avoided showing interest in the Greek revolution, apart from an attack on Papandhreou's Government for "terrorising the Macedonians" in November 1944, and one bitter editorial in *Politika* at the end of December. At the beginning of 1945, the Albanian, Yugoslav and Bulgarian Governments were more concerned to consolidate their own position than to worry about Greece. Being all derived from resistance movements of the extreme left, they were able to assimilate their policies to each other; but Yugoslavia was handicapped, as the others were not, by the relics of a rival régime in exile, which still enjoyed the sympathy of the western Allies. The handicap was steadily worn down during 1945. In January King Peter dismissed his Prime Minister, Shubasitch, but was obliged a few days later to reappoint him, with a mandate to go to Belgrade and join Tito in a Government under a Regency Council. Although Peter remained King in name, his last flicker of freedom died when he lost the argument over the constitution of the Regency. The new Government of Tito and Shubasitch was sworn in on 5th March. Its most significant feature was the appointment of a special minister for each of six regions composing the Yugoslav federation, including the elastic ambiguity of Macedonia. This step was perhaps designed ultimately to facilitate the expansion of the federation to include Albania and Bulgaria on equal terms, just as the partial decentralisation of the USSR had been designed on a similar principle a year before. The tightening of local bonds between the three countries naturally followed. Albanian and Bulgarian troops were fighting the Germans in central Yugoslavia, alongside Tito's partisans and the Red Army. A Yugoslav Military Mission arrived in Sofia, and a Slav Congress assembled there in March to proclaim the importance of Pan-Slav unity. On 28th April Yugoslavia resumed diplomatic relations with Bulgaria; in May Tito recognised the Albanian Government under Enver Hoxha. These steps began the process which turned Albania, Yugoslavia and Bulgaria into a group of uniform puppets, acting with one will and speaking with one voice. It is beyond the scope of this work to trace the process in detail; but it must be kept in mind, as a background to the affairs of Greece, that the country's northern frontiers were in effect from the beginning of 1945 the southern frontiers of the USSR.

Some months passed before all Greeks became aware of this background to their daily life. The period of Plastiras' Government was an interlude of trivialities, marked by few events of internal importance after the Varkiza Agreement, and almost none of external importance after the second visit of Mr. Churchill and Mr. Eden. In the latter category only two deserve mention: the arrival of three members of the TUC, Messrs. Tewson, Feather and Papworth, to supervise elections in the Greek trade unions; and the signature on 1st March of an agreement between the Greek Government and UNRRA, which took over duties of relief and rehabilitation from ML during the next three months. The principal events of domestic importance arose from Plastiras' preference for government through personal henchmen, especially fellow-officers from his republican past. In appointing them, he failed to notice that many had ceased to be republicans during his long absence; fear of Communism had driven them towards the King. There were protests when he placed the police and gendarmerie of Athens under the Military Governor of Attica, for the importance of separating the civil arm from the new National Guard (which temporarily combined certain functions of both police and army) had already been seen. When Plastiras took the further step of appointing General Vlakhos as Under-Secretary of the Interior, with a seat in the cabinet and independent control over public security, Periklis Rallis resigned the post of Minister of the Interior in protest. Plastiras proceeded to the more monstrous folly of appointing General Gonatas, whom many regarded as guilty of collaboration with the enemy, to be Governor-General of Macedonia; but the time was not ripe for this rehabilitation, and the appointment had to be cancelled on the intervention of the Regent. The disunity of the Cabinet became more marked when Sophianopoulos went to San Francisco in April to present a policy out of accord with Greek opinion at home. From this confusion the personality of the Regent stood out alone in the eyes of most Greeks.

The Regent grew daily in moral stature, and fortunately surrounded himself with more able men than his Prime Minister could command. Through his secretaries, the lawyer Yiorgakis and the poet Sepheriadhis, he was able to keep contact with the political left and the cultivated world of Athens; through his friend Lt.-Col. Macaskie[1] he was on intimate terms with HM Embassy. His visits to Salonika and Mesolonghi in March, foreshadowing the more important visit to the Dodecanese in May,

[1]See page 38 for Lt.-Col. Macaskie's past history in Greece and his relation to the Regent. In 1947 he became *The Times*' correspondent in Athens: an appointment which went far to wipe out the memory of *The Times*' attitude during the winter of 1944-5.

confirmed his popularity and still more his significance as a symbol of hope. The reaction of public opinion from the violence of the Communists had reached a midway point, beyond which the extremes of Royalist fanaticism were only in distant view. Sophoulis voiced a fairly general opinion when he announced that the Liberal Party would favour the establishment of a "Kingless Democracy". The King of the Hellenes himself restrained his impatience, and confined his broadcast on Independence Day, 25th March, to generalities based on the need for political unity. Greece seemed to be preparing to settle down under the Regency, with the acquiescence of both Royalists and Republicans. The Regent's position was strengthened by indications of mutual good faith between the extreme left, who surrendered more weapons than they had agreed at Varkiza, and the established authorities, who repatriated the harmless supporters of ELAS from Egypt as fast as transport could be made available. Only the KKE insisted, for tactical reasons, that justice had not been satisfied. In March EAM presented a memorandum to Mr. Macmillan, listing violations of the Varkiza Agreement by Plastiras' administration, and demanding a representative Government and an inter-Allied commission to examine the situation in Greece. A month later the Regent dismissed the Government of Plastiras, for reasons ostensibly connected with the publication in the right-wing press of an indiscreet letter from Plastiras to the Greek Ambassador at Vichy in 1941. The real reason lay neither in the past indiscretions of Plastiras nor in the protestations of the Communists, but in the fact that the Regent, having measured his own strength and popularity against the inadequacy of his Prime Minister, had decided that a more reliable Government was needed. It was characteristic of the time that his new Prime Minister, Admiral Voulgaris, who had suppressed the naval mutiny a year before, was as devout a Republican and as firm an opponent of the KKE as his predecessor. Even Sophianopoulos (who was still absent at San Francisco) temporarily retained his post as Foreign Secretary. Nevertheless the press of the extreme left, having denounced Plastiras for several weeks as a tool of the Regent, and the Regent as a puppet of the British, now began to denounce both for dismissing him.

The protests of the KKE were made for the record rather than in fulfilment of a considered policy. They had shown skill in salvaging some assets from the defeat of January; but the defeat had been more disastrous than they cared to admit, and behind the bluff of face-saving there were doubt and recrimination. A purge of the party resulted in the reconstruction of the Political Bureau, in which Petros Roussos lost his place among its six members, and his wife Khrysa Hadjivasiliou gained hers. Simultaneously the formal disintegration of the EAM coalition was carried a stage further when the formation of a new party called ELD/SKE (Popular Democratic Union/Socialist Party of Greece) was announced on 18th April, under the presidency of Professor Svolos. Askoutsis, Tsirimokos and Stratis, all of whom had been associated with PEEA, belonged to the new party. Its independence of the KKE fell short of its promises; it won neither the respect of the political world nor the fear of the Communists. They had greater reason to fear other things: the wrath of Moscow, which was invariably visited upon failure, and the danger of internal disruption. These were two aspects of the same fear, since the line of internal cleavage was drawn between those who regarded Soviet policy as sacrosanct and those who aimed to cultivate an indigenous variety of Marxism. Although Siantos, who had led the party throughout the war, favoured the latter policy, the balance was tipped by the news that his predecessor, Nikos Zakhariadhis, whom rumour had reported dead, was alive in the German concentration camp at Dachau. Zakhariadhis had been the nominee of Moscow as Secretary-General of the KKE; instinctive discipline left no doubt that he would resume his leadership unchallenged. The party waited anxiously for his return throughout the month following the fall of Plastiras, unwilling to commit itself to decisions on policy in the meantime, but knowing well what the decisions would have to be.

The abyss into which the KKE had betrayed itself, as well as Greece, is illuminated by the process of elimination which left the Communists with only one possible policy and no alternative choice. For three years they had worked faithfully for a Soviet policy in the Balkans, alternately by armed violence and diplomatic intrigue. Their purpose had been to achieve the Sovietisation of Greece by attaining political power themselves. A variety of methods lay open to them; all of them had been tried to exhaustion; and all had failed. They were now reduced to one humiliating course, the reversal of all that had gone before. Having failed to bring about the incorporation of Greece in a Soviet Union of the Balkans through the achievement of their own power, they had to fall back upon the achievement of the latter as a consequence of the former. Their status dwindled from that of Mussolini to that of Quisling; from being acknowledged satellites to being a fifth column. During the two years which elapsed between the fall of Plastiras in 1945 and the passage of the American loan to Greece and Turkey in 1947, the work of the KKE in Greece was confined to a calculated effort to destroy the state. Their purpose was to bring about the downfall of each successive Government of the country, to foment rebellion and disorder, and to facilitate the imposition from without of what they had failed to achieve from within. Nothing helped them so much as the disrepute into which they had dragged down the whole resistance movement. By insisting that every member of it was tarred with the same brush, the more relentless adherents of each Greek Government (with one exception) helped

to swell the ranks of the KKE's fellow-travellers with reluctant democrats. The injustice of their fate blinded well-meaning sympathisers of
the left to the vices of those with whom they shared it. The tragedy
thus took on the Sophoclean horror of innocence suffering for kindred
guilt. This third act was formally inaugurated by the dismissal of Plastiras
in April; but its first effectual episode was the return to Athens of Nikos
Zakhariadhis in a British aeroplane at the beginning of June.

CHAPTER VII

THE THIRD ACT

*"Multiplicity of authority is not a good thing:
Let us have a single authority and a single King."*
HOMER, *Iliad II. 294-5.*

FOR a party aiming at the disruption of the state, Greece presented a target almost entirely composed of bull's-eyes in the years 1945-7. The marks at which the Communists could aim may be summed up under the same six heads as before; for none of the measures taken by Papandhreou had survived the revolution, and no useful steps had been taken by Plastiras. The six categories of Relief (I), Finance (II), Political Crime (III), Foreign Relations (IV), Public Order (V), and National Defence (VI), therefore still apply. The last three, and to some extent the first three as well, came to overlap so intimately that the distinction is academic; but it serves the interests of orderly narrative. In addition the constitutional question, which Papandhreou had laid temporarily to rest, was resurrected by implication in the appointment of the Regency, and more directly by the last clause of the Varkiza Agreement, where it was correctly subdivided into plebiscite and elections. But these did not constitute a separate problem so much as a political framework within which the real problems were argued out; each politician offering judgments on the latter in terms of the solution of the constitutional question to which he happened to be predisposed. The material and administrative problems summed up under the above six heads remained much the same throughout the period of this chapter; so did the uses to which the KKE put them; but the political approach of the rest of the Greek world passed through a succession of phases. In the first, the period of non-political government, the problems were treated on their merits, even if without success. In the second, the period of unelected political government, they were treated largely in terms of the general framework set round them by the constitutional question. In the third, the period of elected political government, the two subdivisions of the constitutional question were successively disposed of (but not solved) without regard to the fact that the material and administrative problems remained almost untouched under any of the six heads. The sections of this chapter will correspond with those three phases.

1. *Service Government, April* 1945.

The Cabinet of Admiral Voulgaris was called a Service Government because its membership was drawn from the armed and civil services and the professional classes. Its non-political character was rounded off by the resignation in July of Sophianopoulos, who had remained Minister of Foreign Affairs after Plastiras' resignation only in order to complete his mission to San Francisco. He was replaced, on a principle which British custom regards with suspicion, by a professional diplomat, Ioannis Politis, who had hitherto represented Greece on the Allied Control Commission in Rome. The principle was unavoidable, if only by elimination: for an elected political government was impossible until elections became technically possible; an unelected political government could have no democratic basis; and a political coalition had been tried already without success under Papandhreou. There was no further alternative: all Voulgaris' ministers were therefore specialists, who were politically neutral, but happened to be mostly republicans. The ablest, who also had the most difficult tasks, were Varvaressos as Minister of Supply and Vice-Premier; Costa Tsatsos (the brother of Papandhreou's minister, and like him an intimate friend of the Regent) as Minister of the Interior, with Katavolos (a former adherent of EKKA) as his Under-Secretary; and Zakkas as Minister of Labour. Of these, Varvaressos was the keystone of the Cabinet. The confidence of the western Allies in him was important, since he had the task of administering the supplies of UNRRA, the principal inter-allied mission in Athens. Many of the other departments had British Missions[1] to help them in 1945; notably the three armed services, the police and gendarmerie, and the Ministries of Finance, Transport and Justice occasionally; and the Government as a whole enjoyed constant advice from British MPs; but these were not, as UNRRA was, indispensable conditions of Greece's survival. Varvaressos was therefore also the principal target of the two minorities to whom the downfall of a government of predominantly republican moderates was a vital interest: the industrial capitalists on the right, and the Communists on the left.

The motives of each were different. The former wished the swing of the pendulum away from the left to go further, not to be halted midway at liberal republicanism. The Communists wished to bankrupt every alternative government in turn, whatever its relative position on the pendulum's curve. Their methods were also different, though the effect was as if they worked in alliance. In sabotaging Varvaressos' efforts to solve the related problems of categories I and II (Relief and Finance), the Communists operated rather against the former and the industrialists against the latter; but the operations fortuitously dovetailed. As a result,

[1]None of these had any connection with the British (Allied) Military Mission to the Greek guerillas, which disappeared from the scene before the Revolution.

the phase of relief, which should have passed into the phase of rehabilitation during 1945, had still not done so in 1947. The Greek people learned to their cost what it means when the same state of affairs happens to suit both extremes. Labour discontent and financial chicanery held back the Greek economy from recovery. Strikes and the black market were the means; but a major contributory factor was also the destruction of communications, which were worse than at any time for forty years. The psychological gulf between Athens and the provinces, as well as the physical gulf between the government and its subordinate instruments, facilitated the deliberate sabotage of reconstruction.

Varvaressos' plan for economic and financial reconstruction had as its bases simply price control and planned taxation. Neither of these is a revolutionary idea by western standards; nor, as ideas, were they revolutionary in Greece. But the peculiarity of Varvaressos was that he actually intended to control prices and collect taxes. The brave intention was not wisely executed: he talked down all opposition, some of which was reasonable, and ignored all obstacles, some of which were insuperable. A small but recurrent obstacle, for example, was the presence in Greece of British servicemen (and some Americans) with much larger sums to spend than the average Greek. Their competition for consumer goods helped to force prices up to levels which made life impossible for the Greeks. When inflation reached intolerable proportions, servicemen suffered in their turn, and had to be allowed special rates of exchange until the drachma was periodically revalued. But the services' pay, being based on sterling or dollars, rose proportionally, and the same spiral was set going again after a brief stability. That was a minor example of Varvaressos' difficulty; the major difficulties lay in the fact that the industrialists controlled most of the gold in Greece, and the KKE most of the labour.

The glut of gold was a legacy of the occupation. Since the people had learned from four years' experience to have no confidence in the drachma, control of gold meant control of prices; many months passed before another government wrested control of it from the industrialists. An outstanding example of the character of Greek industrialists was the millionaire Bodossakis Athanasiadhis, who fancied himself as the *Eminence Grise* of Athenian politics; having once had many public men in his pay, including Voulgaris and Zervas, he had some reason for the fancy. To such men, who used gold in their private transactions, the inflation of the drachma was not merely no inconvenience, but actually an advantage in meeting Varvaressos' taxes. The Communists, who held almost the only other large stock of gold, enjoyed the same advantage, to which they could add the special asset of a vested interest in popular misery. The KKE thus had the best of both worlds: they could sabotage Varvaressos' schemes by restraining Greek labour from the work that was essential to reconstruction, and simultaneously draw political dividends from inflammatory propaganda based on the consequent suffering. The supplies of UNRRA could not be distributed, nor the few natural resources of Greece exploited, without the co-operation of the workers in their own interests. The splendid capacities of Greek labour have often been proved; never better than by the feat of opening Salonika harbour to shipping with almost no modern equipment, within a few weeks after the Germans had sunk forty-three ships along the quayside. But the Greek trade unions had as much power to promote inflation by restricting labour as the industrialists had by manipulating gold and embezzling UNRRA supplies. Justifying themselves on the ground that the industrialists were doing the latter (which was true, but not the whole truth), the KKE saw to it that the trade unions did the former. The control over Greek labour which that implies was not absolute; but for practical purposes it was enough.

A brief summary of events since the revolution will help to clarify the current position of the KKE in the trade unions. The political tangle within the syndicalist movement had been complicated under Plastiras, by the addition to the rivalry between Communists and Reformists of a new group under Hadjidhimitriou, to whom Plastiras' Minister of Labour entrusted the reconstruction of the General Confederation of Labour. When Kalomoiris and Stratis returned to Athens, reassured by the Varkiza Agreement and the intervention of Citrine, they were equally disgusted with Theos and Nepheloudhis, whose Communist thugs had murdered some of their followers, and with Hadjidhimitriou, who represented no reality in the life of Greek labour. But the adherents of the former still controlled most of the workers' centres in northern Greece, which they had seized after the liberation; and the adherents of the last controlled those of Athens and Piraeus, where they had been arbitrarily installed. The intervention of Citrine induced all parties to agree to fresh elections, which Messrs. Tewson, Feather and Papworth came from London to supervise; but for obvious reasons the Communists were in no hurry to conduct them in the north, nor Hadjidhimitriou in the capital; and after weeks of frustration with small success, the TUC representatives retired. A still sorer point to the Reformists was the composition of the Directorate of the General Confederation, which could only be determined by ministerial appointment until all subordinate elections had taken place. Before Citrine's intervention, Hadjidhimitriou held all the seats, and refused for many weeks to concede any rearrangement which would give him less than an absolute majority. Theos threatened to form a rival General Confederation, the framework of which was actually constituted in ERGAS (the Workers' Anti-Fascist League) by tempting away a few of his rivals' followings. But the enterprise petered out; ERGAS became recognised as synonymous with the Communists, when at last the patient efforts of Stratis and Kalomoiris induced Hadjidhimitriou to accept less than an absolute majority in the Directorate of the official General Confederation.

This minor success was facilitated by the fall of Plastiras' Government and the intervention of a more understanding Minister of Labour under Voulgaris. But no lasting effects came about, because there followed an internal revolt in Hadjidhimitriou's group, by which he lost the leadership to the equally irresponsible Makris. Zakkas, the new Minister of Labour, went on trying vainly to fill the vacuum until a legitimate Directorate should be elected, by appointing a succession of coalition directorates: but neither extreme would agree on their proportions. Compromise after compromise was tried and rejected; elections proceeded with dilatory haphazardness; the indiscretions of Makris and the consequent tantrums of Theos and Nepheloudhis protracted indecision throughout the duration of Voulgaris' Government; all that remained certain was that neither extreme wished harmony to be restored. From 20th September, when the last of the provisional directorates which Zakkas was prepared to nominate lapsed without a successor, anarchy supervened. It was remarkable, however, throughout 1945 that even if the Greek trades unions had no legal head, someone was in control of them for the purposes of obstruction. The KKE hardly troubled to disguise that it was they, under the guise of ERGAS, who exercised this partial control. Strikes broke out spasmodically all over Greece, especially in the north and the tobacco-growing areas, without ever attaining the generality which a representative, instead of a factional, leadership would have imposed. As the workers became aware that they were inflicting hardship on each other, the proportions of their stoppages diminished. But they were enough to show (especially when civil servants came out as well) that even if the Communists had only a partial control over the country, the Government had still less. Relief was thus incompletely effectual: for that part of its task which consisted of turning over bulk supplies and equipment to the Government was feeding an almost bottomless well; and that part which consisted of personally administering help in the provinces was hampered by local politics. The divorce between the Government and the governed, whether they were industrialists or Communists or the victims of both, broke Varvaressos' plan and led to his resignation at the beginning of September. Voulgaris announced that his policy would continue, but he spoke only from wishful thinking. The collapse of the economic plan was the symptom of a complete failure of government. It was only the most unmistakable of many.

The inter-connection of the problems can be seen in the nodal position of one department, the Ministry of Justice. The minister was involved, directly or indirectly in each of the six categories under which the Government's problems have been listed. In Relief and Finance (I and II) he was involved through his duty to investigate irregular traffic in sovereigns and UNRRA goods, which sometimes implicated his colleagues in the Cabinet; he was even involved in trade union elections through his representatives, who had to validate or (more often in the circumstances) invalidate them. Political crime too, in the strict sense of the third category, was his special concern; but because crime was a more complicated term than six months earlier in the first flush of liberation, and because all its associations were primarily political, the minister found himself involved in every other issue as well.

He was responsible, for instance, for prosecuting both collaborators and Communists: two comprehensive and embarrassing tasks, which stirred every controversy that lay before the Greek people, and were unequally handled. The courts trying collaborators ruled that the charge of forming Security Battalions could have no place in the indictment, because their intention had been only to maintain law and order "against criminal elements." The storm provoked by this ruling was aggravated by the leniency of the sentences passed on each of the admissible charges of collaboration, although the leniency was easy for the disinterested to understand. In the mood of the time Communism seemed a worse crime than collaboration; and collaboration, unlike capital punishment, admitted degrees. At some degree the charge of treason could apply to everyone who had any commerce whatsoever with the Germans, no matter how high-minded his motives. It had been applied to Generals Gonatas, Sariyiannis and Spiliotopoulos; to Ioannis Peltekis, Angelos Angelopoulos and Sbarounis; even to the Archbishop of Athens himself. It was applicable to subordinates and associates of ELAS, EDES, EKKA and PAO (not to mention the more disreputable resistance groups), even if their leaders were not incriminated. These graduations of criminality made it invidious to impose the death penalty on any defendant. Although it was imposed on Tsolakoglou and others, it was at once suspended; Rallis was only sentenced to imprisonment for life.

The KKE thus acquired another grudge against society, which they could share with the innocents of the resistance movement. To emphasise the unequal severity of the law, they also shared with the same class all the available accommodation in the state gaols. Since arrest without warrant, and without even formal indictment, had become permissible outside Athens and Piraeus, the gaols overflowed with so-called Communists held for vaguely specified crimes. The overcrowding of the prisons was thus another of the problems in which the Minister of Justice was involved, with the help at various times of two different British Missions. The proportion of men held for crimes committed in December to men held for collaboration (more crudely, the left and the right) was enormous. In many cases there seemed to be little hope of ever bringing them to trial.

Q

A partial solution for both problems was found in the formula of "decongestion of the prisons," which mitigated the nuisance without conceding the principle of amnesty. By increasing the number of courts, releasing those charged with offences up to (and including) the December revolution who had not been tried within six months of arrest, and restoring Article 5 of the 1911 Constitution, which forbade arrest without warrant, the minister eased his burden. But the KKE did not want all their followers released. In gaol they could conveniently work upon their fellow-prisoners to ensure that, however many might mistakenly have been arrested as Communists, the mistake should be rectified before they came out. They had their material concentrated for indoctrination in the right mood; they had a grievance, which they did not wish to lose, for exploitation in the press. Zakhariadhis challenged arrest himself, by publishing an article in the Communist newspaper *Rizospastis*, alleging that Greek troops were being concentrated against the Albanian frontier. The Public Prosecutor instituted proceedings against him, thus providing at his trial a forum for the political world of Athens, which badly needed a substitute for Parliament and made full use of it under the pretence of giving evidence; but the court had more sense than to imprison the Secretary-General of the KKE, and it was not until he had gone into hiding in May, 1947, that a Greek court proceeded to the empty farce of sentencing him *in absentia*. As a political martyr and incumbent of the chair of propaganda at the Communist University which the Averoff Prison had become, he would have undone even the feeble policy of "decongestion." The episode was only important as evidence that Greeks still possessed a freedom to write and say what they liked, which was unparalleled in Eastern Europe. But the irresoluble paradox remained, that it was questionable whether the occupants of the gaols were better inside or out. Many were comparatively harmless victims of the suspension of *habeas corpus*; many were professional agitators whose field of action was wherever they happened to be; rather fewer (and those not always easy to identify) were indictable criminals. Decongestion was as futile as amnesty was controversial. The Ministry of Justice had become the archetype of a department whose task was beyond its control. This in turn was a symptom of the general disintegration of order.

The impact under which law and order were disintegrating was a resultant of the forces in categories IV—VI of the Government's problems. Public Order (V) was no longer an isolated problem: it was interconnected with that of Foreign Affairs (IV), since one of the principal threats to public order arose from across the northern frontier of Greece; and also with that of National Defence (VI), since the other principal threat to public order arose from within the Greek armed forces. The names under which the Greek people became aware of these threats were still the KKE and X; but the realities had grown in intricacy. Both left and right had expanded their connotation at the expense of the centre, which in theory still comprised the majority of Greek opinion, but in practice, ground between the upper and the nether mill-stone, was in danger of extinction. Before the end of 1945 the growth of the two extremes had threatened to swallow up every politically conscious Greek. The disputes typified by the KKE and X had nearly become the entire content of Greek politics.

The KKE narrowed its membership by the purge which followed the revolution, but widened both its penumbral following and its political scope. The indiscriminate persecution of Greeks connected with the resistance movement, by petty officials pursuing vendettas, had given it many more potential voters, at least in its guise of EAM. The return of Zakhariadhis had defined its party line, even if it had not eliminated internal disagreements. The restored Secretary-General, being less aware than his predecessor of domestic Greek feeling, was correspondingly more sympathetic to Soviet policy. The co-ordination of policy with other Balkan Communists was no longer in doubt, nor was the intimacy of the KKE's affiliation to Moscow. The party emerged from its ordeal more compact, efficient, and determined. Its thugs and bandits, including Aris Veloukhiotis, stole back into action. It no longer disguised its habit of looking northwards for guidance, as well as for the infiltration of armed support; but it still found the thin mask of EAM useful for expressing its purely Greek policies. Zakhariadhis' first public pronouncement after his release supported Greece's claim to the Dodecanese and Cyprus, but suggested that claims in the north would endanger Balkan peace and co-operation. The outcry against this pronouncement so embarrassed the KKE that a revised policy was drafted by which the party, "while maintaining its reservations," would bow to the opinion of the majority. Thereafter the Communists took care when speaking in the voice of EAM to agree with most of the territorial claims of the Nationalists, and to confine more controversial items (such as that Northern Epirus was not worth the trouble of a fight) to the utterances of the KKE. The two Communist dailies, *Rizospastis* and *Eleftheri Elladha*, consistently echoed the Yugoslav *Borba* and the Soviet *Pravda*; but Svolos, having theoretically disowned the KKE while still in practice supporting EAM, used his paper *Makhi* to insist that Macedonia must remain Greek. The distinction of two voices proved a valuable investment. It was even found convenient with one of them to disown dissidents like Aris Veloukhiotis, who had denounced the Varkiza Agreement; but generally the Communists found themselves "unable to restrain" the resentment of the Greek people, while at the same time EAM pleaded for moderation, orderliness and common sense.

A parallel development took place on the right. X remained the hard core of its violent activities, and had the same relation as the KKE to the accretions of its outer rind. It enjoyed the sympathy of some senior officers; although there is no evidence to connect Zervas with it in 1945, his former adherents helped its work, when they returned from Corfu to Epirus, by completing the expulsion of the Chams; other professional soldiers similarly found that its mood chimed with their own. To its satellites in the armed forces it was able to add SAN (the League of Young Officers), whose existence as a monarchist pressure-group was first asserted by Tsoudheros in April; it seemed to be admitted when Voulgaris issued an order of the day to the armed forces, warning them against political activities. This warning, of course, applied equally to Communist activities in the forces; but although the KKE had made strenuous attempts to penetrate the services, its success there, except at the lowest levels, was negligible compared to the political activities of the right. Another of X's affiliations was to the small groups of bandits that began to take the field in opposition to the remnants of ELAS, especially in the Peloponnese and Thessaly, under the fanatical leadership of Manganas and Sourlas respectively. They came to be loosely described as right-wing because their purpose was to help exterminate ELAS; but vendetta played a larger part than politics in their formation. The political parties of the right therefore professed to have no control over them or X, just as EAM professed to have no control over Aris Veloukhiotis. The campaign of the Greek authorities against Manganas and Sourlas was less enthusiastic than against Aris Veloukhiotis; indeed when the last met his death in a skirmish on 16th June, 1945, the "bandits of the right," if they were not in at the kill, certainly gave help in tracking him down. Their object was to co-operate with anyone in fighting the KKE, even with a government which they hoped to see replaced by a more extreme authority; their co-operation naturally outdid it, for instance by system-atically smashing printing-presses working for the KKE in provincial towns, although the Government officially permitted a free press. Their determination was strengthened by a conviction that the majority of the civil and armed services sympathised with them. Although the Government did its best to restrain vendetta, it largely shared that conviction, which the events of December, 1944, had made probable. Indeed, it could hardly have been otherwise; nor could the Government do anything, short of abdication to the KKE, to alter it.

Another complication was added by the existence of three distinct forces claiming the principal responsibility for national security; the police (together with the gendarmerie in the provinces), the National Guard as organised under Plastiras, and the army. Theoretically there was no overlapping of their functions, since the National Guard was a temporary body from which the gendarmerie was to take over in September, 1945, and the army was only responsible for the security of the frontiers. In practice their functions were made to overlap, in the first place by the uneven rate at which the reorganisation of the gendarmerie matured in different parts of the country; in the second place by the infiltration of sources of internal trouble into Greece from across the northern frontiers. The point and degree at which they became the concern of the military and civil arms respectively was a nice one, which the KKE was ready to exploit. There was thus some misunderstanding between the gendarmerie and the army, added to the contempt with which both regarded the National Guard. Many of the last, recruited in haste under Plastiras, inadequately trained and equipped, vindictive and ill-disciplined, appeared to combine unpleasant characteristics of ELAS and the Security Battalions. But they, like most of the Greeks whom they persecuted, were only the tools which helped to destroy public order. The hands belonged to cleverer men.

In this respect again Voulgaris' Government was handicapped by a fortuitous identity of interest between the extremes. Both hoped to profit from disorder: the right by overthrowing the service Government and replacing it themselves; the left by breaking up what was left of the Greek state in order to facilitate foreign intervention from the north. The effort of the former was straight-forward and blatant. The latter were more subtle; only inklings of the design could be detected. The opposing sides proclaimed their respective allegiances by implication during May, when the right used King George's Name Day to organise nationalistic demonstrations, and EAM used VE-Day to send greetings to Stalin. The left scored handsomely over the right in this round, for St. George's Day passed off with moderate enthusiasm; but Stalin sent EAM a polite reply, which was more than the Regent and Prime Minister received on the same occasion. The superiority of the KKE in making use of an opportunity for advertisement appeared again in June, in another parallel between the flamboyant return to Athens of Zakhariadhis and the unheralded return of General Papagos and his four companions from the same captivity. The result of the British General Election in July gave the left an even more brilliant opportunity; though when the expected revolution at the Foreign Office failed to take place, the opportunity soon passed to the right. But this jockeying for position in the public eye was a trivial pastime compared with the more important issues raised in the summer of 1945. When Tito failed to consolidate his attempt to seize Trieste in May, and the determination of the western Allies to save it from Slav occupation became evident, it was not hard to guess that attention would be turned to Salonika, the only other major port in the Mediterranean to which the Soviet satellites could construct a plausible claim.

The agitation began in July. As soon as the frontiers of Yugoslavia had been adjusted by the restitution of Kossovo from Albania and a corner of Macedonia from Bulgaria, all three turned their attention southwards. A violent campaign broke out in their newspapers, faintly echoed by the *Rizospastis* and *Eleftheri Elladha*, against the Greek Government's persecution of the Turko-Albanian Chams and the Slavophone Macedonians. The right-wing press of Athens retaliated by accusing the Albanians, Yugoslavs and Bulgars of exterminating their Greek minorities. Each accused the other of plotting armed onslaught across the frontiers, although impartial observers visiting the menaced areas could find no evidence of imminent conflict and little of maltreatment. But it was certain on the one hand that Greece had no armed forces worth the name with which to threaten anyone; on the other hand that the Red Army had increased its strength in Bulgaria, and that Tito's Government had developed a predilection for sending military missions to repatriate Yugoslavs from neighbouring countries that had none. One such mission had reached Albania; another unsuccessfully invited itself to Greece. When this was refused, the Yugoslav Government addressed a note to the Greek Government, in language which was once the accepted harbinger of war, denouncing imaginary violations of the frontier, and cruelties against the Slavophone population of Greece, which were less wholly imaginary but still not within Tito's competence. Shortly afterwards the Albanian Government presented a note containing similar charges in less unrestrained language: they concerned unauthorised landings in Albania across the Corfu strait, and the discrimination of Zervas' Epirote adherents against the Chams. To both the Greek Government replied with dignity and effect, but the right-wing press, replying with less dignity, damaged the effect. The troubled area of Macedonia was visited during the summer by the Regent, the Prime Minister, Svolos and Zakhariadhis; but even the last provoked no incident. The impression that the trouble was largely manufactured by politicians in the capitals seemed to be confirmed by the arrival in Athens of a deputation of Macedonian Liberals, to inform their leaders, Sophoulis and Kaphandaris (who had amused their old age by stimulating the agitation to embarrass the Government), that the country was no longer interested in political issues, in comparison with the task of reconstruction. But the instigators of the trouble, both in Athens and Belgrade, were still only warming up.

The agitators of the right were probably correct in believing that their antagonists were privy to a plot against the integrity of the northern frontiers: that was demonstrated in 1947. But their methods of combating it made matters worse. Their newspapers demanded the immediate occupation of Northern Epirus and part of Bulgaria, if necessary with British troops for want of others. Their control of the National Guard was morally stronger than the Government's, thanks to the methods by which it had been recruited. Their influence in the army through X and SAN was scarcely less, and in the gendarmerie and police about the same. These were used to oppress Greeks associated with the resistance movement by official means; armed bandits supplemented the oppression by unofficial means. The result was a numerical accession to the left; at the same time the irresponsibilities of the right-wing press lent colour to the accusations of Tito and the KKE. A British Police Mission did its best to eradicate the inclination of minor officers of the civil arm to take the law into their own hands, but found itself baffled by the fluidity with which such officers slipped through their grasp and changed places without notice, often contrary to express agreement. Imperfect communications left irresponsible subordinates with too free a hand. In June the first step in the right direction was taken by the divorce of the gendarmerie from military command; but even within the Ministry of the Interior they were subject to the co-ordinating activities of an army officer, General Ananiadhis, whose position resembled the controversial appointment of General Vlakhos under Plastiras. All the British Missions impressed upon all the Greek services the importance of eliminating the principle of changing appointments for political reasons with every change of Government; each successive Government agreed that the principle must be eliminated, with effect from their own surrender of office to their successors. The state of Greece in 1945 was one for laughter and tears, but the world had few of either to spare.

Greek affairs were a sideshow in comparison with the events that commanded the attention of the world month by month in 1945. The dates show for themselves how little space there could be in the headlines for Greece. In April Hitler and Mussolini perished; in May Germany surrendered unconditionally; in June British and French troops became engaged in an outbreak in the Lebanon, which almost threatened to repeat the story of December in Athens; in July the "Big Three" met at Potsdam, interrupted by the startling result of the General Election in Britain; in August the atomic bomb ended the second World War; in September the four principal Foreign Ministers met in London. None of the powers could give Greece more than a divided attention; the USSR scarcely showed even that. Britain continued to pour money and missions into the country, but it was already becoming plain that British resources were limited: the election of a Labour Government shook Greek confidence, which had already been undermined by the revelation in December that the British were something less than supermen. British influence had nearly shot its bolt in Greece: having devoted huge expense to holding the door open for democratic processes to take their course, against attempts by the extreme left to slam it in 1944 and by the extreme right to slam it in 1945, the British taxpayer was ready to give up. The USA, not yet ready for the plunge, confined their commitments to acceptance of the invitation at Varkiza, that they

should participate in supervising the elections, and to the abortive suggestion that a commission representing the four principal powers should
examine the situation on the frontiers. Otherwise the United States
Government had only the non-committal responsibility of participation
in UNRRA, to which their contribution vastly outweighed any other
country's, but theoretically without political implications. The interest
of the USSR in Greek politics was even less at the visible level. The
Soviet Government expressed disapproval of electoral supervision as an
unwarrantable interference, although it had accepted the principle at
Yalta. Two more probable motives were the fear that the other powers
would claim the right to intervene in other Balkan elections; and the
probability that the Greek left would be defeated in fairly conducted
elections, leaving the USSR, if it were one of the guarantors, with no
ground for complaint. The Soviet Government therefore maintained
its pose of indifference. Stalin ignored the greetings of the Regent and
Prime Minister on VE-Day, declined to send an ambassador until
November, and left Soviet propaganda in the hands of the Tass Agency,
the Soviet Film Corporation, the Greco-Soviet Cultural League, and
the Yugoslav *Chargé d'Affaires*. French concern was extended only to a
special interest in the syndicalist movement and an agreement to join
the USA and Britain in supervising the elections. But the political world
of Athens, habituated to being world news in 1944, continued to behave
as if it occupied the centre of the stage in 1945. To the Greeks, for
instance, almost the only importance of Germany's surrender in May
lay in the release from enemy occupation of Crete, which was expediti-
ously re-occupied without serious disturbance, and Rhodes, which still
remained to be acquired. Political activity in Greece was similarly conducted from a self-centred point of view.

The political agitations of the summer were in substance efforts to
exploit the Government's administrative troubles, in the various categories that have been discussed, for which some of the agitators were
themselves chiefly to blame. But the form which the agitations took
was the comprehensive one of political controversy, as if changes in the
Government or settlement of the constitution would end all administrative difficulties. An elected Government and a ratified constitution were
essential pre-conditions of stability and order; but to insist on them as
panaceas at a time when the mere condition of electoral registration
made them technically impracticable was plainly an interested manœuvre.
It was the Government's dilemma that stability could not be assured
until an elected Government had the moral power to enforce it, nor
could such a Government be elected until stability was assured. This
logical *impasse* was not the Government's fault, but its enemies did not
hesitate to exploit it. The KKE kept up a running fire of abuse; so did
the extreme right, for reasons which were opposite in form and identical

in content. The Republican centre joined the attack for reasons of personal ambition, although such political sympathies as Voulgaris' ministers had were not far from their own. In July, and often thereafter, the quintet of Sophoulis, Kaphandaris, Plastiras, Mylonas and Tsoudheros (who had come out in new colours since he no longer owed allegiance to the King) became a familiar sight on the steps of the Regent's house. The purpose of their mission was to recommend a representative Government, five members of which they were ready to nominate at a moment's notice.

The force of these contrary impulses added up instead of subtracting from each other. The Regent felt obliged to conduct discussions to meet the agitation, which was particularly directed against the Ministers of Justice and the Interior, and the Under-Secretary for War. But none of the agitating groups would serve in the same Cabinet with each other. In August a simple compromise was reached to the satisfaction of nobody. Five ministers and two under-secretaries (including all the victims of agitation) were replaced, and the service Government continued. But Sophianopoulos had already resigned in July, and Varvaressos followed him in September. With the loss of its two strongest and most controversial characters, Voulgaris' Government became more homogeneous; but it was the homogeneity of nonentity, and its days were numbered. The monarchists continued to denounce the Regent as the tool of the Republicans. The Republicans continued to demand a representative coalition. The Communists continued to demand the resignations of both Voulgaris and the Archbishop, and the formation of a coalition from which they were content to be excluded: not for altruistic reasons, but because they did not wish to share responsibility for the political chaos, which they foresaw as a necessary step to their own power. Voulgaris wished to resign, but was dissuaded by the Regent.

A respite was gained when the Regent was invited to England in September. It was hoped that he might return not only with the promise of a loan in sterling and the present of Cyprus and the Dodecanese, but also with a solution of Greece's political problems. Accordingly the agitation diminished for a few weeks, and the Regent went confidently to London. It seemed opportune that his visit coincided with another conference of the four Foreign Ministers; but all hopes were dashed. No Greek delegation was invited to the Foreign Ministers' conference on the terms of the Italian peace treaty; no loan was adumbrated; no undertaking was given on Cyprus or even the Dodecanese. M. Molotov refused to meet the Regent in private, and made hostile remarks about Greece at a press conference on 18th September. The meeting of the Foreign Ministers overshadowed the visit of the Regent. He returned to Greece by way of Paris, bearing nothing but a GCMG and a new scrap of paper proposing a new salvation.

The document which the Regent carried with him from London dealt simply with the one issue to which the political controversy had been narrowed down by exhaustive discussion: the relative order of the plebiscite and the elections. The Varkiza Agreement ordained a plebiscite on the constitution first, followed by elections within the year 1945. The latter provision was already impossible for technical reasons, since electoral registration had been delayed by disorders and four times postponed. But the former provision was the crux of the controversy. The prevailing belief, which had grown out of the December revolution but had not yet become clear at the date of the Varkiza Agreement, was that if the plebiscite took place first, confronting the Greek people with a plain choice between monarchy and republic, they would identify the latter with its noisiest apostles, the KKE. The monarchy would therefore win a majority for reasons irrelevant to its own merits: the vote would be a negative vote against Communism, but would have a fortuitously positive effect in favour of the King.[1] It would then be only a question of time before a reaction set in, when the people realised that their votes had been determined not by the pull of desire but by the push of aversion; and the perennial cycle of constitutional revolutions would be initiated afresh. If, on the other hand, the elections took place first, there would be (in general terms) three choices instead of only two open to the electors: the monarchist parties of the right, the republican parties of the centre, and the extreme left. If the republicans of the centre proved themselves capable in the meantime, they might be able to command many floating votes which would otherwise have been cast at the plebiscite for the King out of fear of Communism. If the Republican centre emerged victorious from such an election, then the plebiscite could follow in a calmer atmosphere, since a vote for a Republican constitution would no longer be identified with a vote for Communism.

This argument, which naturally appealed to the Greek Republicans, also pleased the Regent and HMG. Critics might argue that the former was influenced by the possibility of prolonging his Regency; but those who knew him were convinced that his motives were disinterested, as he seemed to show by offering his resignation at the same time. They might also argue that HMG had reversed its policy of forcing the King back on his people, and just as unreasonably turned against him. Although this argument appealed to the King's entourage, it was no less misconceived than the earlier conviction which it replaced; for at no time was the policy of HMG either to re-impose the King or to exclude him, but only to leave the Greek people free to make its own decision. In 1944 that policy had appeared unduly favourable to the King merely by

---

[1] The first time I heard the remark, which became common in 1945-6, that: "I am a staunch Veniselist Liberal, so I should vote for the King to keep out the Communists," was at the height of the KKE's ascendancy in March 1944.

reason of the ascendancy of the left, which tried to anticipate the ballot by presenting a *fait accompli*. In 1945 the exact reverse can be seen by substituting in the foregoing sentence "unfavourable" for "favourable" and "right" for "left". No modification of principle was made in this policy when Mr. Bevin took over the Foreign Office from Mr. Eden in July 1945; the course of events in Greece, not the General Election in London, gave an illusion of change. The specious contradiction is thus easily resolved in logic, and was so resolved by Mr. Noel-Baker in the House of Commons on 17th October.

British relations with Greece had in fact reached a point at which non-intervention was indeed "a metaphysical term indistinguishable from intervention." To refrain from intervention at this stage would have amounted to positive action in favour of the King of the Hellenes, since the past interventions of HMG, together with other influences, had set in motion a decisive trend of events in the King's favour. The one impartial course now open to HMG was to halt that trend, to redress the unfair balance and to relieve the Liberal Republicans of the disadvantage with which Communist excesses had fortuitously burdened their cause. This could only be done by one last intervention, to reverse the order of plebiscite and elections laid down in the Varkiza Agreement. HMG, although reluctant to intervene at all so soon after inheriting the problem from Mr. Churchill's Government, was thus obliged to accept the difficult principle that their only course truly consistent with a policy of non-intervention in Greece was to make this last intervention in the interests of impartiality. HMG's motives were naturally misconstrued both at home and in Greece. At home, even those who understood the motives involved, generally ascribed them to the resultant of a tension between the Socialist Foreign Secretary's supposed determination to intervene against the King of the Hellenes, and his permanent staff's supposed determination to succour the King by preventing any intervention. The absurdity of this misconception of the relation between a minister and his department, neither of whom could have had the least personal bias about King George II as such, is exposed by the foregoing account, which shows that the reluctance to intervene must naturally have lain in an overwhelming degree with the new ministry rather than with its established staff. In Greece on the other hand misinterpretation took a different and indigenous form. The proposed intervention was seen exclusively in terms of Greek politics, where there is no such thing as impartiality. It was assumed that the reversal of the last provision of the Varkiza Agreement was a partisan intervention by HMG on behalf of the left and against the right; it was therefore welcomed by EAM because it put off the return of the monarchy, denounced by the right for the same reason, and coolly received by the Liberal centre, which was already doubtful of its chances in early elections.

The proposal was embodied in a declaration signed by M. Bidault and Mr. Byrnes as well as Mr. Bevin, and published on 20th September,[1] the day after the Regent's departure from London. The suggestion was that elections for a "revisionary assembly" should precede the plebiscite, which should not take place till tranquillity was restored. It involved no personal change of front on Mr. Bevin's part, since he had made the same proposal at the Labour Party Conference during the December revolution. It involved a gratifying assumption of initiative on the part of France and the USA; both had hitherto suspected British motives, but they could no longer do so when the Foreign Office manifestly put the King's personal interests in the background. All three governments, now equally involved in responsibility for the elections, instructed their representatives in Athens to support the Regent in impressing upon the leaders of the moderate parties that this was their last chance to stave off the extremes; that only by leaving the constitutional question in abeyance could they save Greece.

The gambit failed. Mounting inflation, increasing disorder, over-flowing prisons, confusion in the electoral registers, threats to the northern frontiers, disappointment at the dismissal of Greece's national claims, all combined to convince every politician that no compromise could be an effective substitute for his particular panacea. The political game went on where it had been left off. The fall of Voulgaris' Government was initiated by the resignation of his Minister for War on 28th September. More negotiations for a Coalition Government began, and broke down by 5th October. On that date Voulgaris announced that the elections would be held on 20th January; he made no reference to the plebiscite, thus implying acceptance of the Foreign Secretaries' proposal. Two days later Sophoulis announced that the Liberals would abstain from the elections, on the ground that circumstances would not permit them to be fairly held under Voulgaris' Government; on the same day the Populists announced their abstention as a protest against the post-ponement of the plebiscite. Between the devil and the deep sea, Voulgaris resigned on 9th October.

For the rest of October, administration practically ceased to exist while the politicians lobbied the Regent, the ambassadors and each other. Four attempts to form a new Cabinet failed before Sophoulis was given the task, with the express proviso that he must include Populists. On 11th October the atmosphere of Athens was so explosive that all demon-strations were banned the following day, which was called (by an antici-pation of nearly three weeks) the anniversary of the German evacuation of Greece. Mr. McNeil, the Foreign Under-Secretary, announced in the House of Commons that British troops would oppose any attempts either by the right or by the left to seize power by violence. His words

[1]See Appendix K for text.

were interpreted as a warning to X, which was reported to be mobilising in Athens. The tension increased when Sophoulis confessed failure and resigned his mandate on 13th October. Tsoudheros and a little-known professor called Dhimitrakopoulos (Voulgaris' Minister of Public Works) successively tried and failed to fulfil the same task. On 17th October the Regent personally presided at the Council of Ministers, from which only Voulgaris and his Under-Secretary were absent. He explained that his assumption of the duties of Prime Minister was a temporary measure to continue the administration while a permanent solution was found; but it harmed his prestige, and did not lessen the tension.[1] The return to Athens of Exindaris and Sophoklis Veniselos, both of whom had kept out of politics for some time, raised hopes of a solution; but almost any news, true or false, raised hopes, which vanished twenty-four hours later. After nearly a month of crises the task of forming a Government was entrusted to Panayiotis Kanellopoulos, who took office on 2nd November with a nondescript Cabinet that was not quite "political" nor quite "service." A week later the economic and financial programme of his Government was announced; but he had no time to implement the policy (which won the approval of the British Financial Adviser), nor even to formulate a policy on the controversial topics of amnesty and elections. On 20th November he was called upon to resign.

The new intervention which brought about the downfall of Kanellopoulos so abruptly was the arrival in Athens of Mr. Bevin's Under-Secretary, Mr. McNeil, to study the conditions for a British loan. His mission was not specifically political; but it became obvious that in the prevailing circumstances, financial help was throwing good money after bad. At Mr. McNeil's suggestion, the Regent summoned a meeting on 20th November of all former prime ministers and the leaders of all parties that had provided governments of Greece. The definition excluded only the Communists, the Socialists and a few minor splinters; but the exclusion, which completed the political ostracism of the KKE, created a new grievance, besides committing the tactical error of freeing them from responsibility for the welfare of their country.

The agenda of the meeting covered three points: the formation of a broad Coalition Government; the adoption of a specific programme of reconstruction with the help of HMG; the conduct of elections not later than March, 1946, and of a plebiscite on the constitution not earlier than March, 1948. The Regent was authorised to quote the support

---

[1]The most brilliant of Athens' many satirical weeklies, *Laoutsikos*, published a dialogue purporting to portray the Regent's discussions on the formation of his Cabinet. It was decided that the principal posts should be shared between the Regent, the Archbishop and the Prime Minister; the remainder should be allotted to Papandhreou, which happened to be the surname of the Archbishop as well as of the ex-Premier. Athens would have been shocked by this irreverence before October.

of Mr. Bevin for this programme. It was rejected outright by the Populists, and accepted by Sophoulis, who agreed to form a Government in his capacity as elder statesman rather than as leader of the Liberal Party. But the Regent found himself again between two fires. In order to extend the coalition as widely as possible, he insisted that Sophoulis must include Papandhreou in his Government, despite the resistance of the former and the willingness of the latter to withdraw. The Populists, perhaps exacerbated by announcements of the British and American Governments' conditional recognition of Enver Hoxha in Albania, and of the Soviet Government's appointment of Admiral Rodionov as Ambassador in Athens, demanded the resignation of the Regent for exceeding his mandate in agreeing to the postponement of the plebiscite till 1948. In London the King of the Hellenes gave a statement to the press reserving the right to reconsider his conduct in view of the new policy. On 21st November the archbishop resigned his appointment. He was persuaded with difficulty to withhold his resignation until he had sworn in Souphoulis' Government without Papandhreou; some days later he was persuaded by the British and American Ambassadors with less difficulty to withdraw it altogether. Thus constitutionally the situation remained unchanged, but politically government by specialists had given way to government by professionals. An important stage in Greece's progress had ended in almost total failure.

2. *Unelected Political Government, November* 1945

Despite the confusion in which Voulgaris' Government ended, its successor had reasons for hope. Sophoulis brought into the Cabinet with him most of the traditional following of the Liberal centre, including Kaphandaris, Rendis and Mylonas. To them he grafted the principal representatives of the non-Communist resistance, including Kartalis, Pappas, Peltekis and Petimezas, besides sending two others of the same class, Pyromaglou and Yiorgakis, to official appointments outside the capital. It does the last two credit that they accepted, for few Greek politicians believe themselves alive outside Athens; it does Sophoulis credit that he thought appointments outside the capital sufficiently important to deserve first-class men. He was still more successful in excluding Papandhreou, who had moved a little away from his former republicanism, as well as in including Tsoudheros, who had recanted his former loyalty to the King at about the same time, and Sophianopoulos, who returned to the Ministry of Foreign Affairs. His Cabinet was therefore political without being confined to his own party; in order to emphasise this character, Sophoklis Veniselos was elected to deputise for him as leader of the official Liberals. Sophoulis therefore had the advantages without the embarrassments of political support. He could also claim the support of HMG, which Mr. McNeil had promised before returning to England to expedite financial assistance. EAM too had pledged its support on the basis of Sophoulis' undertaking to restore the prestige of the resistance movement and destroy the power of ex-collaborators.

Even the seasons gave him a better chance than his predecessor. April, when Voulgaris took office, is the hungriest and most restless month of the Greek year; November is the most contented. In April the old harvest is consumed, and the new one not yet gathered; the melting of the snows opens up the mountains to brigandage and the frontiers to invasion; bed-bugs, fleas, lice and mosquitoes hatch out, to spread irritation, typhus and malaria; provincial politics emerge with them from hibernation. In November these movements go into reverse; in 1945 even frontier disputes had their close season. Meteorology had yet another political role. It was argued that climatic conditions made elections in January impossible; but it was also argued that the fairest elections ever held had taken place in January 1936, perhaps for that reason. It was already technically impracticable to hold the elections on the date announced by Voulgaris; but there was still good reason to hope that Sophoulis' Government would be able to make a good job of them by March. The meeting of Messrs. Byrnes, Bevin and Molotov at Moscow in December gave the hope, as usual, an optimistic impetus.

The Government started well. Confronted with the same series of problems as its predecessors, some of them in an aggravated degree, it might claim in its first three months at least to have pegged them to a halt, and in some to have registered progress. In the task of relief and reconstruction, UNRRA had never known a better Minister of Supply than Kartalis; nor in the related problem of economics had the Financial Adviser known a better Minister of Co-ordination than Tsoudheros. The two ministers went to London shortly after Mr. McNeil, accompanied by the American head of UNRRA and two officials of the British Treasury. They returned in January with a financial agreement that promised to end the disastrous inflation, which had carried the sovereign to the value of 183,000 drachmas at the turn of the year. The agreement provided for a loan of £10,000,000; for the cancellation of Greece's debt to Britain of £46,000,000, outstanding since 1941; for a revaluation of the drachma at 20,000 to the pound sterling; most important of all, for the despatch of a new Economic Mission with executive powers, and the inclusion of a British and an American representative with three Greeks on a Currency Committee, to have absolute control over the issue of bank-notes. While this agreement was being negotiated, the American Government announced a loan to Greece of 25,000,000 dollars through the Import-Export Bank, and two months later another of 10,000,000 dollars earmarked for the purchase of US Army supplies left behind in Europe.

These assets were partially offset by the unsympathetic reception of Greece's claims at the UN Conference on Reparations in Paris, whose allocations the Greek Government at first refused to ratify. The refusal was soon withdrawn: Greece could not afford to be haughty until her own house was put in order. Tsoudheros set about this with a determination equalled only by Varvaressos, and with better sense of realities. An important step was taken to control the circulation of gold. In December 1945, a law had been passed making it illegal to traffic in gold and foreign exchange; another had provided machinery for the correct use of credits and the observance of currency regulations. But in the industrialists' stranglehold over Greece's finances, such legislation expressed only wishful thinking. Kartalis and Tsoudheros returned from London with a better weapon: a quantity of sovereigns sufficient to enable the Bank of Greece to undercut the black market by selling sovereigns at the official price. This was only an interim measure until financial stability was restored; but at least it created such an interim, which had not yet been allowed to exist, for as long as the sovereigns lasted.

Even the sabotage of reconstruction from the opposite extreme was prevented for a short time. The syndicalist anarchy which followed the expiry of Zakkas' efforts on 20th September evoked the intervention of the World Federation of Trade Unions, whose French representative, Saillant, visited Athens in December. Under his chairmanship an agreement was reached to carry out fresh elections, from which a new Directorate of the General Confederation emerged, under the Secretary-Generalship of the Reformist Paparhigas, by the beginning of March. This advance was witnessed by another TUC representative, Mr. Bagnall. The Directorate was predominantly left and strongly influenced by ERGAS; but at least the no less troublesome and far less representative group of Hadjidhimitriou and Makris was deprived of its hegemony. Although Sophoulis' Government was not left immune from the threat of strikes, it could claim a reasonably fair settlement of the syndicalist problem; some of the results appeared in the progress achieved by the new Minister of Supply during his short tenure. In categories I and II the record was good.

Sophoulis' Government also started well in confronting the two domestic problems of political crime (III) and public order (V). During 1945 membership of the resistance movement had come to be regarded as a political crime, and collaboration with the Germans against Communism a political virtue. Whatever the rights and wrongs, the plain fact was that an ex-guerilla was as likely as not to be found in gaol, and an ex-member of the Security Battalions as likely as not to be found in the uniformed services.[1] Sophoulis met part of the problem by an amnesty, which was long overdue, for all political offences, all crimes committed by way of resistance to the enemy, and all other crimes except murder committed between 27th April 1941 and 12th February 1945: that is, from the date of the Germans' entry into Athens to the date of the Varkiza Agreement. All prosecutions and sentences for the so-called crimes of resistance, not excepting the murder of members of the Security Battalions, were explicitly withdrawn. But Sophoulis did not feel strong enough to take further measures against the ex-collaborators, especially those that had filtered back into the armed services, because of the objections of the British Missions to any purge of the forces on political grounds. To this principle Sophoulis paid lip-service; although some of his ministers made secret changes against the advice of the British Missions, he himself was content for the moment to leave well alone. At least the worst of the evils had been removed when the National Guard was relieved of its duties shortly before he took office.

The problem of national defence (VI) was in the same position as that of public order. Although the spheres of influence of the army on the one hand, and the police and gendarmerie on the other, were left clear-cut by the withdrawal of the National Guard, the same tug-of-war between political elements within them went on. Discrimination against ex-members of the underground and in favour of ex-members of the Security Battalions seemed to Sophoulis' ministers to be the same thing as discrimination against Republicans and in favour of Monarchists. The temper of the times favoured anyone against the Communists, and inclined to identify all forms of Republicanism with the KKE. In combating this propensity, Sophoulis again found himself handicapped by the insistence of the British Missions upon political neutrality; but his War Minister, General Manettas, achieved one notable success in winning the assent of the British Military Mission to the removal of General Vendiris from the post of Assistant Chief of the General Staff. This was the most important appointment, in the Government's view, for the purpose of ensuring the loyalty to it of the principal armed service. In the related problem of foreign relations (IV), for the first month of its power Sophoulis' Government came near to enjoying the bliss of those who have no history. The one significant event was the auspicious arrival in Athens of the Soviet Ambassador, Admiral Rodionov.

From all these six points of view the position of Sophoulis' Government had become, partly by circumstances and partly by its own efforts, easier than that of its predecessors. Its early troubles were comparatively

[1] A long list of ex-officers of the Security Battalions in the army and gendarmerie was presented (through myself) to the appropriate British Missions in July 1945; but it proved impossible to substantiate the charges, since the Courts had already declared them void against the collaborating ministers; or even to investigate them, since documentary evidence could only come from the services concerned, where the accused were already entrenched.

R

small. EAM renounced its support of the Government as early as 11th December, and demanded its own inclusion in a new coalition; it thus took away something that Sophoulis had never asked for, did not want, and had not expected to retain. At the beginning of January Theos published a manifesto threatening strikes, which broke out in most of the major towns a few days later. They did not become general, because Greek workers were tired of being exploited to suit the political advantage of the KKE: by 9th January all workers in the public utilities of Athens had returned to work, leaving the strength of the Government unimpaired. The immediate results were hardly more serious when the extreme right put similar pressure on the Government with the same purpose from the opposite direction. Disturbances in the Peloponnese culminated on 19th January in the seizure of Kalamata (where the KKE had behaved atrociously fifteen months before) by armed members of X under Manganas. The Government proclaimed martial law; the rebels withdrew into the hills with hostages, fourteen of whom were reported to have been murdered. Within three days order was restored and the surviving hostages were released. The resultant effect was not to shake the Cabinet, but to strengthen Sophoulis' argument to the British Police Mission that the civil arm could not be relied on to prevent disturbances, so long as it contained officers politically disloyal to the Government. Not long afterwards ominous reports came that left-wing bands were being re-formed in Macedonia; but it was unlikely that these could take action before the winter was over.

Sophoulis' personal position was attacked more seriously from within his own party, when the time came to make an official pronouncement on the elections. In early December British, American and French representatives, who had been invited nearly a year before to supervise the elections, arrived in Athens; this made it necessary to do something about holding them. Sophoulis was obliged by his undertaking to the Regent to announce that they would be held in March 1946. He took advantage of the fact that in Greece elections can only be held on Sunday to choose the latest possible date, 31st March. The Allied representatives, who were in process of forming themselves into the Allied Mission for Observing the Greek Elections (AMFOGE), also required to know the method by which the elections would be conducted. Sophoulis chose proportional representation, on the formal ground that the law prescribing it at the elections of 1936 was still in force; it was also the only method likely to give small parties like his own a chance. A decree was put before the Regent fixing 31st March as the date, PR as the system and 300 (later raised to 354) as the number of seats. This decision infuriated the Populists, who were already anticipating victory on any system, but a bigger victory by majority vote; just as a section of the Liberals under Sophoklis Veniselos was infuriated by the early date, which gave them insufficient time for reorganising their political machinery. The result was a split within the Liberal Party. Sophoklis Veniselos (who had long been toying with the right wing of the centre, such as Papandhreou and Kanellopoulos) drew together with the Populists in an electoral coalition. It was an agreement of a kind which had long been thought desirable by detached observers, who feared that the restoration of the old political game between Populists and Liberals would only facilitate the Communist revival. But the motives of Veniselos and his colleagues were less high-minded. They had nothing in common, except that all of them, for different reasons, were annoyed with Sophoulis, and all of them favoured elections by majority vote. On this understanding they came together with the Populists to exert pressure against the electoral decree. For some time it seemed likely that the Regent would refuse to sign it, in order not to antagonise the right; but when at last the decree was published, the new coalition broke up. These intrigues had no effect on the Government, because it was not a party government; but they split the tiny fragment of the Liberals still further, and made the electoral victory of the Populists more likely.

At the age of about eighty-five[1] Sophoulis had no personal grounds to worry about the distant future which these manœuvres affected. He denounced Veniselos' action, thus accepting the schism of the Liberal Party, but his Government was strong enough to survive such minor storms. His whole duty consisted in ensuring the free and fair conduct of elections so that he could hand over a relatively stable situation to an elected successor. But before that could be done two storms of a different order of magnitude, one external and one internal, broke over Greece and nearly swept his Government away altogether. The first was a complaint by the Soviet Government, at the first meeting of the Security Council of the United Nations, that the presence of British troops in Greece was a danger to the peace of the world. The second, which was not unconnected with the first, was a violent campaign which convulsed the country, against the conduct of elections in March at all. In both storms Sophoulis stood firm, not without buttressing; but his cabinet partially disintegrated under the successive shocks.

The decision of the Soviet Government to bring the Greek situation before the Security Council, under Article 35 of the UN Charter, caused more serious agitation in Greece than among those principally concerned. From the Soviet point of view, the decision was a *ballon d'essai* designed to balance the similar invocation of Article 35 against themselves by the Iranian Government. Something more than a balance was sought by the addition of a Ukrainian complaint against the British policy in Indonesia, and a Yugoslav complaint against the retention of a Polish

[1] He was born in Samos under Turkish rule, which kept imperfect records.

army in Italy; but these were only variations on the central theme, with which they stood together and ultimately fell. From the British point of view the intervention was satisfactory, since the debate on the Soviet complaint not only brought the American Government into the open, but ended in the defeat of the complaint; it also gave HMG an opportunity to promise the withdrawal of British troops after the Greek elections. From the point of view of the UN Organisation, the incident was an unexpectedly successful inauguration of the Security Council; it set a standard which was promising at the time, even if the promise was not later sustained. But from the point of view of Greece's domestic politics, it was a disaster. The approach of the elections, which the Soviet Government had refused to supervise, suggested the suspicion that one of the purposes behind the complaint was to frustrate or influence them. If that were so, the Soviet Government committed a tactical blunder, but perhaps won a strategic success: at the expense of present failure, it could hold in view the more remote object of steadily worsening the internal situation of Greece, in order to justify future intervention. In either case the immediate result was to assure the already probable victory of the right-wing parties at the General Election.

This result emerged from the dilemma in which the Soviet intervention put Sophoulis' Government. By contending that British troops in Greece were an instrument of political pressure, M. Vishinsky obliged the Greek Government either to agree or to deny it. Since British troops had come to Greece by agreement with a previous Government, which had never been questioned, still less repudiated, Sophoulis could not instruct his representative at the Security Council to agree with Vishinsky. On the other hand, he himself privately attributed the growing ascendancy of the right to the presence of British troops, and his inability to control service departments to the intervention of British Missions. Despite this embarrassment, he sent Sophianopoulos to London to rebut the Soviet case. Sophianopoulos felt the same embarrassment more personally, because his reputation as a friend of the Slav powers was at stake. Having arrived in London, he refused to present the Greek case in accordance with his instructions. Sophoulis dismissed him from office, appointed Rendis in his place, and instructed the Greek Ambassador in London to support the British case until the new Foreign Minister could arrive. The upshot in London was a motion accepted *nemine contradicente* that the matter was regarded as closed; but the upshot in Athens was another step towards the extinction of the moderate centre and the disintegration of Sophoulis' Government.

By reminding Greece that the USSR was still interested in Greek affairs, the incident gave fresh ammunition to the agitators of the right. A year had passed since the Communist revolution, during which the moderate republicans had, in the view of public opinion, been given almost too favourable a series of chances to prove themselves. Plastiras, Voulgaris, Kanellopoulos and Sophoulis (all declared republicans) had successively failed, because it suited both the right and the left that they should fail. The KKE planned that every government in turn should fail, until there remained no alternative but foreign intervention in their own favour. Such intervention could not come until British troops withdrew; they would not withdraw until an elected Government took office. Since the KKE had no hope of electoral success, it was a matter of satisfaction to them that the Populists were likely to win the elections: their victory would simultaneously establish the condition prerequisite for the withdrawal of the British, and exhaust the last alternative that remained to be tried before democracy could be declared bankrupt. The extreme right followed the same argument up to the penultimate stage: they agreed that they were themselves the last alternative before the deluge, but they were convinced that they could hold it off. The same desperate struggle was therefore in progress as in the summer of 1936; but this time the electors were more alive to the issues, or thought they were. Having learned in December 1944 what Communism would mean to them, and having seen throughout 1945 that moderate Republicanism lacked the forcefulness to save the country, they had made up their minds long before March 1946 to vote for the right. They may have come to their conclusions for the wrong reasons; they may have blamed the centre for things that should have been blamed on the upper and nether millstones. A certain degree of blindness to exact realities of detail was endemic below the horizontal line, because the political game was largely conducted by individuals whose claim to speak for parties was a fiction: no Liberal or Populist voter below the horizontal line was ever consulted, for instance, about the agreement[1] made by Sophoklis Veniselos and Tsaldharis in January 1946. What mattered to the electors was not the fact, but what they believed to be the fact. Such beliefs were themselves the facts which settled the elections before they took place.

When Sophianopoulos allowed himself to be dismissed rather than obey his instructions, the Greek people saw simultaneously the logical impossibility of the centre and the dilemma of their country's position in the world. The latter was only the former writ large; and because the people saw them so, they were so. The debate in the Security Council brought into focus the certainty that externally Greece had to choose between the USSR and the western democracies; the dismissal of Sophianopoulos brought into focus the certainty that internally Greece had to choose between the Communist left and the monarchist right. Neither certainty left any alternative choice; the two fitted into an exact perspective, like pictures in a stereoscope. There was nothing new about

[1] See p. 259.

the principle underlying the facts.[1] What was new was the coincidence which simultaneously illuminated the internal and external facets of the principle just before Greece's first election in ten years. From that moment social and administrative issues vanished from the electoral platform, leaving two clear-cut alternatives, which could be expressed in various ways without varying their significance: right versus left, Monarchy versus Communism, Balkan sovietisation versus western democracy, Britain and the USA versus the USSR. These issues, and these alone, were alive when Greece moved into its pre-electoral turmoil in March 1946.

The extreme left admitted that the issue in these terms could not be in doubt by announcing their intention to abstain, although they permitted their adherents to register in case anything should change their minds at the last moment. Although abstention was technically illegal by Greek law, Sophoulis was debarred from saying so by the fact that he had incited his own followers to commit the same offence under Voulgaris' Government. On 8th February EAM demanded representation in the Government as a condition of participation in the elections. On 17th February the KKE issued a denunciation of all the familiar wrongs; with the addition of a demand for the union of Cyprus with Greece, which looked inconsistently like vote-catching. They succeeded in disturbing public opinion. Many members of Sophoulis' Cabinet thought that elections conducted without the extreme left would be profitless. They argued that it was essential for the future stability of Greece to include the KKE in the legitimate political life of the country, if only for fear of their machinations as political outlaws: "Stalin finds some mischief still for idle hands to do." In pressing Sophoulis to postpone the elections so that EAM might agree to participate, they may have been influenced by the hope that their own electoral chances would in the meantime be strengthened. But both hopes must have proved delusive. The KKE would never have allowed EAM to take part in elections which must, however long they were postponed, have resulted in a victory for the right unless they were manipulated; nor could the chances of the centre have improved, however many purges of the services and the electoral machinery took place, after the climactic demonstration of their impotence in which the past year had culminated. The mind of the Greek people was made up; perhaps temporarily, perhaps for the wrong reasons: but certainly nothing except fraud could have prevented the victory of the right at the polls in 1946.

Sophoulis shared the wish of his colleagues to postpone the elections, if only for a month, on the grounds that printers' strikes had delayed the publication of electoral registers and that law and order were not yet adequately restored; but his hands were tied by his mandate from

[1] My own attention was first drawn to it by Pyromaglou in 1942, almost exactly in the form stated here.

the Regent, and by the arrival in force of the American, British and French observers who made up AMFOGE. To the other arguments against postponement was now added the technical impossibility of retaining the observers (who were mainly military personnel due for demobilisation) beyond the middle of April. It was almost certain that if the elections were postponed, the Allied Governments would not supervise them. To the dissident members of Sophoulis' Cabinet, this objection was irrelevant: so was the pledge which he had made in taking office. Ten ministers and under-secretaries, including Kaphandaris and almost all the resistance representatives, resigned before the middle of March. Sophoulis replaced them with the impassive courage of hopelessness, and extended the closing date for nominations to 20th March, in a last effort to bring in the left. Svolos and Sophianopoulos announced their agreement with EAM in abstaining. Through Professor Yiorgalas of EPON and Karvounis, editor of *Eleftheri Elladha*, who were on a mission to London, EAM demanded a postponement of six months; even X demanded an extra week, ostensibly to prepare a list of candidates, actually to ensure that grievances were not a monopoly of the left. HMG announced its reasons for advising against postponement, and reiterated its intention to withdraw British troops as soon after the elections as conditions allowed. Sir Reginald Leeper and General Scobie were replaced by successors during the same month, as if to emphasise that British policy did not depend, as critics argued in Athens, London and Washington, on personalities. The participating parties, consisting of the Populists and their satellites, the right centre of Papandhreou, Kanellopoulos and Veniselos, the official Liberal Party under Sophoulis, the Agrarian Party of Mylonas, and the Nationalist groups of Zervas and Gonatas, announced their electoral programmes; almost no difference could be detected among them, except an explicit reservation by the Populists on the postponement of the plebiscite till 1948. The constitutional question thus became recognisably the only controversial issue at stake: the elections were to prejudge the future of the monarchy in exactly the way that the three-power declaration of September 1945 had tried to avert. The failure of the centre to furnish the substance of a third choice, supplemented by the resurrection of the Soviet bogey in January, had nullified the subtle segregation of the political dilemma into elections first and plebiscite afterwards. Tired of trying to steady the pendulum half-way, HMG bowed to the phenomenal will of the Greek people.

Once it was certain that the right was going to win, it was also certain that it would win by a large margin. The enormous majority which the Populist Party and its satellites won on 31st March did not prove, as its enemies maintained, that the elections were conducted by fraud or duress; nor did it prove, as its supporters maintained, that the

Greek people were solidly behind them. It exemplified the familiar principle that most Greeks will in their own interest vote for the side that they know is going to win. This consideration was reaffirmed with a wealth of statistical accuracy by the scientific methods of AMFOGE. But it could have been stated just as certainly before the voters went to the polls. The certainty took excitement out of the polling; 31st March passed with the calmness of confidence on one side and resignation on the other. Apart from one clash in Macedonia, no armed violence took place; no physical coercion was exercised to compel or prevent voting. The expected lobbying for the formation of a new Government began on 2nd April; the expected denunciation by EAM followed two days later. But the last word on the elections lay with AMFOGE, and there can be no quarrel with its verdict:[1]

"The Mission finds that the proceedings of election day were orderly and satisfactory. The registration lists in large areas contained irregularities but there was no significant amount of illegal voting. Intimidation existed, in some degree, from both extremes and was even on occasions given countenance by members of the gendarmerie, but it was not extensive enough to affect seriously the election. The practice of deliberate abstention did not reach large proportions. The Mission therefore concludes that notwithstanding the present intensity of political emotions in Greece conditions were such as to warrant the holding of elections, that the election proceedings were on the whole free and fair and that the general outcome represents a true and valid verdict of the Greek people."

The conclusion was reached by way of scientific proof, not by way of subjective impressions. The method was devised by the American contingent, which shared full responsibility in Greece for the first time. The principle of AMFOGE was therefore of greater importance than the content of its report. In relation to the vital facts of the Greek situation, its report was true in one sense and irrelevant in another; but its importance lay in the alignment of anti-monarchist America with left-wing Britain in endorsing a triumph of the monarchist right in Greece. The two Governments also agreed to supervise a revision of the electoral registers before they were used again in the plebiscite. The French Government, by withdrawing from this further responsibility, left the British and American Governments in sole partnership to confront the Soviet Government across the battlefield of Greece. Each side had in Greece its external proletariat of satellites, to echo its voice and anticipate its intentions: each satellite comprised a hard core drawn from above the horizontal line, unscrupulously controlling a variable accretion drawn by circumstances willy-nilly, with imperfect comprehension and

[1] Quoted from the Report of the Allied Mission to observe the Greek Election, page 23: (Cmd. 6812, dated 10th April, 1946).

little love for either side, from below that line. The same scene was crystallising out of the confusion which succeeded the liberation of every occupied country; only the ascendancy of the rival roles differed. The archetype of the scene had been set in Spain in 1936; ten years later its development was not very different.

3. *Elected Political Government, April 1946.*

It follows from the last paragraph that the political events of the next year in Greece have small intrinsic importance, and little space need be devoted to them for their own sake. Greek cabinets were no longer their own masters, partly because their decisions were only a microscopic reflection of events in the outer world, partly because they were subject in execution to the whims of irresponsible supporters (above, but only just above, the horizontal line) and petty officials over whom, with the best will in the world, the Government had little control. The goodwill and sincerity of the political leaders of the right were clear, but the mood of public opinion in Greece and the outside world was against them. The insubstantiality of the intensive development of Greece's history can be read in the fluctuations through which its executive passed without any visible effect on the life of the ordinary Greek. Within a year of the elections, Greece had three Prime Ministers and five Governments (two of them identical); even the fortuitous complication of three different heads of state had no more and no less effect than the political vagaries of the right. Up to the spring of 1947, when the American loan brought the third act to an end, Greece had had thirteen Prime Ministers (including a King and an Archbishop) in the six years since the death of Metaxas, even if the count excludes collaborators and those who were invited to form Cabinets but failed. Since Tsoudheros occupied three of those six years, the remainder averaged three months each. This was not only a symptom of instability but a guarantee that the Government's control of its functions must progressively decline. In 1946 the progress quickened to a gallop.

Soon after the triumphant anti-climax of the elections, the victorious right felt the frustration which afflicts an army advancing to assault abandoned positions. Although the official Liberal Party under Sophoulis had won forty-eight seats, the effective opposition was excluded from Parliament by an act of political violence on the part of the left, which seemed like suicide but might turn out to be more like murder. The Populist Party confessed its awareness of moral insecurity, as well as administrative impotence, by the changes of composition which its Cabinet passed through. On 4th April it formed a Government which included politicians of the right centre, such as Veniselos, Papandhreou and Kanellopoulos, under the chairmanship of a political neutral whom it would be absurd under any other system to call Prime Minister: a judge called Poulitsas. The reason was that the Populist party had not yet succeeded in electing a leader. When it did so, not without opposition, Tsaldharis moved up from the Foreign Ministry to the Presidency of the Council on 17th April. His principal rivals, Theotokis, Mavromikhalis and Stephanopoulos, took office under him; Poulitsas vanished back into obscurity within a fortnight. Veniselos, Papandhreou and Kanellopoulos resigned with him, and all three declared not long afterwards that they would prefer a republic to a monarchy; Veniselos even rejoined the official Liberal Party under Sophoulis in the end, so that for the time being this trio's wheels had come full circle. In the meantime the Populists committed the Government on the one issue about which they had no doubts. They put administrative problems aside, arguing that structural problems were antecedent to them. Their principle, speciously logical but fatally ambitious, was that they could not consider how Greece was to be governed until its framework, constitutional and geographical, was fixed. Despite the expressed wishes of HMG that the question of the monarchy should be left in abeyance and that the Archbishop of Athens should continue his Regency, it was announced on 4th April that Parliament would meet on 29th April (less than the customary six weeks after the elections), to debate the constitutional plebiscite. The Archbishop offered his resignation on the ground that his task was finished, but allowed himself to be persuaded to withdraw it until the plebiscite. Royalists were quickly restored to all operative posts, especially the Army (where General Spiliotopoulos became Inspector-General of the Forces and General Vendiris returned as Chief of the General Staff) and even the trade unions (where the Metaxist ex-Minister Dhimitratos re-entered the complicated field). In return for the compromise which retained the Regent in office, the newly constituted Government of Tsaldharis put off the opening session of Parliament to 13th May. When it assembled, the Regent himself announced that a bill would be presented fixing the date of the plebiscite for 1st September; on 13th June Mr. McNeil announced the acquiescence of HMG in the House of Commons.

Beyond this determination to restore the King as soon as possible (which was stressed by defining the subject of the plebiscite not as "the constitution" but as "the return of King George II"), the Government showed no constructive policy, but only praiseworthy hopes. Tsaldharis' first statement, on 17th May, confined foreign affairs to the satisfaction of Greece's national claims, which had been submitted to the Council of Foreign Ministers in Paris; and divided domestic affairs (apart from the monarchy, which took first place) into economic stability and internal security. The earliest approach to the former was a hint that Greece needed another foreign loan. Towards the latter Tsaldharis' Government first made a few tentative steps, such as the closure of X's offices in the provinces and the arrest of Manganas; and then a bold leap by passing (against many abstentions in Parliament) a Security Law of great severity. *Habeas corpus* was again suspended, and arrest without warrant permitted. The Government intended to apply this measure impartially; the proportion of prisoners with right and left affiliations became far less unequal than in 1945: but the Cabinet had difficulty in controlling its own adherents, who wished only to enforce the rigour of the law against political opponents. The effect was therefore seen not against the instigators of disorder but against the small fry and those who had no interest in disorder at all. Typical victims of the vengeful spirit of the times were Saraphis and Bakirdzis, who were exiled to Aegean islands; Svolos, Angelopoulos and Kokkalis, who were deprived of their professional appointments; the bishops of Kozani and Elis, who were removed from their sees; and the thousands of anonymous adherents of ELAS, whose position is typified by the story of Nikolaos Beis in Chapter I[1]: whereas the like of Siantos and Zakhariadhis, having nothing of which the state could despoil them, were untouched. The cure was worse than the disease. Public order continued to deteriorate; inflation was held off only by the sale from the Bank of Greece of quantities of sovereigns varying from five to seventeen thousand daily. A totally unreal budget was presented on 7th June, showing an estimated deficit of 175,430 drachmas. No issue seemed to be real to Tsaldharis, except the restoration of the King, and the acquisition of personal prestige by presiding over the Cabinet to which the Dodecanese should be entrusted. In the last week of June he set out for Paris and London in quest of the consummation of these two triumphs.

But Greece's problems no longer admitted separation. The six categories under which they were divided in 1944-5 had become in 1946 no more than six names for the same problem: the survival of the Greek state. Material and economic reconstruction (I and II) had hardly begun; political crime and civil disorder (III and V) were multiplying; the condition of foreign relations and national defence (IV and VI) had become alarming. By concentrating public attention first upon an election that settled nothing, then upon a plebiscite that was a foregone conclusion, little was contributed towards the survival of the Greek state against the manifold threats; by directing attention towards Greece's national claims, the Government only set in relief the fact that it could not manage what it already had. Without a policy to meet all the threats, the Cabinet could not successfully combat any of them; for they were being used against it as the several instruments of a single policy. That policy was designed on the classic model of the Nazis: to exploit internal unrest derived from administrative failure in the primary interests of intervention from without, as a means to the secondary end of usurping power. The operation was timed, in the same way as the two previous

[1] See page 58.

attempts of the KKE, to coincide with the withdrawal from Greece of the only armed force capable of frustrating it. The date on which British troops would withdraw had not been announced; but it was foreshadowed by their concentration and steady reduction.[1] The readiness of British acquiescence in the early date of the plebiscite implied the same conclusion. The approach of the final vacuum kept the KKE almost too obviously ready for action during the summer of 1946. One feature of their activity was the adoption by the extreme left of the leading role in agitating for the incorporation of Cyprus with Greece; for if the British were about to leave the latter a vacuum to be occupied by Soviet satellites, it would be convenient that the former should fall with it. But this was incidental: the principal activity of the KKE was the preparation of the mainland for foreign intervention.

Guerilla warfare of a kind hardly distinguishable from that of 1942-4, except by a more fanatical determination, was already bursting into life here and there in the summer of 1946. The Ministry of Public Order announced on 8th June that "roaming Communist bands had created a desperate situation in Macedonia." With characteristic folly, the armed extremists of the right played into the hands of the KKE by retaliating in kind in the Peloponnese, thus distracting attention from the vital area in which alone internal disorder could be attributed to foreign intervention. But since British troops would not withdraw before the plebiscite, the KKE had no temptation to extend the scope of disorder until September. The Government could draw encouragement from EAM's order to its supporters to participate in the revision of the registers which AMFOGE had recommended, and from the collapse of the attempt by ERGAS to organise a general strike on 19th June in protest against the Security Law. When Tsaldharis returned from abroad, with a promise of the Dodecanese given at the second meeting of the Foreign Ministers in Paris, and with high hopes derived from commercial talks with HMG in London, the Government felt sufficiently secure to allow a temporary relaxation of its measures against the Communists. The relaxation was valuable for the sake of appearances at the time of the plebiscite; but hardly had the results been announced on 5th September, showing nearly seventy per cent of the poll in favour of the King, when two days later the rigour of the law was reimposed. Martial law was proclaimed in Northern Greece to combat the new guerilla movement. Disrespectful remarks about the King were declared to amount to lèse majesté, for which the statutory penalties were brought back into force; a prosecution was initiated against Zakhariadhis for making a speech considered to be "an incitement to disorder"; and army officers who

[1]No formal notification of withdrawal was given to the Greek Government until 5th August, 1947; and even that made no substantial difference, since big reductions had already long been in progress, and yet British troops were still to be found in Greece in 1948.

had been associated with ELAS were sent into exile without trial. But the first class of Greeks to suffer severely from the Government's ferocity was the General Confederation of Labour.

The first action taken against the Directorate of the General Confederation, which had been in office since March, was technically legal, though it was not tactfully executed. A decision of the Supreme Court on 26th June had retrospectively invalidated two of Zakkas' decrees of the previous year, on the ground that the minister had exceeded his constitutional rights by intervening to appoint provisional Directorates.[1] The court was concerned with juridical correctness, and had to disregard the difficulties which Zakkas had conscientiously tried to disentangle. From the point of view of Tsaldharis' Government the usefulness of the decision lay in the invalidation of all conduct of the nominated Directorates, which the new Minister of Labour extended to cover the subsequent elections themselves. In August the General Confederation was declared to be illegally constituted. Its directorate was forcibly deprived of office and replaced by a new body, in which Makris' followers were restored to their dominating position, by an act of ministerial intervention far more inexcusable than any by Zakkas that the Supreme Court had invalidated. In September the Government went still farther. By virtue of the resurrected Security Law and the invalidation of the elections, left-wing leaders of the trade union movement were arrested in many parts of the country, in some cases on the formal ground that they refused to surrender office. In the north, where the strength of ERGAS was greatest, directorates of the Workers' Centres were imprisoned wholesale. The onslaught upon the left wing of the syndicalist movement was justified by the simple logic that the KKE was the source of Greece's internal disorders, and ERGAS was an appendage of the KKE. The same logic might have been used to visit the sins of X upon Makris' following; or the Government might have been softened by the conspicuous ineffectiveness of ERGAS in organising general strikes. But Tsaldharis' Minister of Labour was not susceptible to reason. It needed the intervention of another British Labour representative, Mr. Braine, to secure the release of some of the trade unionists, and of yet another, Mr. Tewson again, in 1947, to reopen the question of elections. Even so, the position of the trade unions at the end of this survey was in principle no different from that which Sir Walter Citrine had found two years earlier.

It needed the still more powerful intervention of King George's return to impress upon the Government the folly of multiplying enemies by condoning indiscriminate persecution. The King arrived back in Greece on 27th September, aware that some forty per cent of the electorate had either voted against him or abstained from the ballot,

[1]See page 240.

and that in Piraeus, Salonika and Crete an absolute majority of votes had been cast against him. He had conducted himself with circumspection even when the huge majority of 1935 had restored him for the first time: in 1946 the need was ten times greater. His first act, in accepting the formal resignation of Tsaldharis, was to invite him to form a broader Government. This attempt, which was renewed at intervals during the remainder of the King's reign, failed upon the refusal of Sophoulis' Liberals to serve under Tsaldharis. Veniselos, Papandhreou, Kanellopoulos, and even Zervas, would not accept office under him unless he gave up the ministries of Foreign Affairs, War and Economic Co-ordination to other hands than Populists. A fortiori no wider coalition could be expected. The result was that the same Cabinet resumed office on 2nd October. But the King could not accept a failure which exposed him to the persistent accusation of owing his position to a powerless and factional Government. On 21st October the Cabinet again submitted its resignation, that another attempt might be made to widen its range. After a week, the negotiations between the political leaders again failed. The King summoned a conference under his own chairmanship, which resulted in another deadlock by 2nd November. Two days later Tsaldharis formed another Government of substantially the same composition. By this time the disintegration of its authority over the northern Greek provinces, which was the principal cause necessitating its reformation on a broader basis, had reached a degree which a statement by the Foreign Office in London could characterise on 25th September as "rather serious, amounting to a small-scale civil war." This was the outward sign of an inward corruption, and each fed the other. Administrative failure and political persecution led to public disorder, which in turn intensified failure and invited persecution; the confusion of Greece's northern borders and the affiliations of the persecuted element combined to contaminate internal unrest with foreign infusions. By concentrating attention upon the former, helped by the tactlessness of the Government, the KKE was able to camouflage the latter, and to represent the outbreak of the new guerilla war as a domestic affair in which the right lay, if not on their side, at least on that of their fellow-victims.

As if to emphasise the grievance, disturbances in the north rose to a new climax in the week of the King's return. Communiqués published by the Government and the guerillas were unreliable, but it was certain that Dheskati, on the borders of Thessaly and Macedonia, was occupied by the guerillas in the last week of September. This was the signal for a general outbreak, whose centre of gravity shifted gradually northwards. In November Skra, on the Yugoslav frontier, was captured by the guerillas; a few days later a train was raided near the Turkish frontier. The guerillas did not attempt to hold captured positions against the

Greek Army when it went into action against them; both sides were thus able to claim the attainment of their objectives. Foreign opinion was further confused by the dual character of the fighting, which was represented by the Government as instigated by foreign intervention from the north and by the KKE as springing from the dissatisfaction of the ordinary Greek at persecution by the ruling party. The foregoing paragraphs have shown some justice in the latter view, though the blame lay with over-zealous subordinates rather than Cabinet ministers. The KKE was at pains to discredit the former view by periodically diverting disturbances from the extreme north to areas such as the Peloponnese, where foreign intervention could hardly be argued, as well as by the customary devices of propaganda. Nevertheless, the Government succeeded in amassing evidence of intervention from Yugoslavia, Albania and Bulgaria. The Greek representative to the United Nations was accordingly instructed on 30th November to request investigation on the spot by a mixed commission. Tsaldharis himself set out for New York the next day to present the Greek case. On 4th December a memorandum was addressed to the Secretary-General invoking Articles 34-5 of the Charter. It specifically charged that the guerillas were being trained and armed on foreign soil, that they were crossing the frontier under the protection of the Yugoslav, Albanian and Bulgarian authorities, and that Greek fugitives from justice were being harboured in those countries with a view to subversive activities against the Greek Government. On 20th December the Security Council unanimously approved the dispatch of a commission representing all states that were members of the council, with powers to conduct investigations in any part of Greece, Yugoslavia, Albania and Bulgaria.

The ferocity of the debate which preceded this decision foreshadowed the ultimate division of the UN Commission between the two points of view, both of which contained truth. It was certainly true that the Greek Government had brought trouble on its own head by its domestic policy; it was also true that the Governments of Albania, Yugoslavia and Bulgaria were seeking by encroachment and intrigue to expand their frontiers southwards. Which of these truths was logically prior was as unascertainable, even by a commission of eleven different nationalities, as the relative priority of hen and egg.

The bridge between the two truths, linking them into one composite policy aimed at the disruption of the Greek state, was the KKE; this can be read in the espousal by the KKE of the foreign cause in every controversy between Greece and her neighbours throughout the year. The controversies took place sometimes exclusively within the inner orbit of the Balkans, sometimes in the outer orbit of the great powers; but the two orbits were concentric, the national alignments were identical in either case on opposite sides of the lines of cleavage, and in every case the line bisected Greece. The consistent adoption by the left-wing Press of the side opposed to the Greek Government in purely international controversy cannot have been accidental, and must weaken the force of its simultaneous contention that the quarrel from which sprang the new guerilla war was purely domestic.

The events of 1946 sharply defined the gulf fixed across the Balkans between Greece on the one side, with Turkey as her only friendly neighbour, and the rest of the Balkans on the other; with the result that the relation between Greece and the western democracies necessarily became of the same order as that between the rest and the USSR. The last attempt which gave any hope of closing the gulf was made at Moscow in December, 1945. The upshot of that meeting of Messrs. Byrnes, Bevin and Molotov, so far as it concerned the Balkans, was a decision to recommend the inclusion in the Rumanian and Bulgarian Governments of two members from the opposition parties; but no reference was made to Greece. In the case of Bulgaria, where elections had taken place in November under the shadow of disapproval formally expressed by the United States Government, negotiations to fulfil the recommendation were declared to have broken down in January. The announcement was made in Moscow, where Georgiev had conducted the talks with the opposition in the presence of M. Vishinsky. In the case of Rumania, where it had been suggested that elections should take place in addition to the broadening of the Government, the latter condition was formally satisfied in January; but the former was not met until the late summer, and even then was far from satisfied in the opinion of the western Governments. In Bucharest and Sofia the Allied Control Commissions watched in impotence, divided like the macrocosm which they reproduced into the Soviet point of view on one side, and the Anglo-American on the other. The relations of the British and United States Governments with the Balkans thus entered upon a new phase marked by the same frustration and indignity as those with Spain under Franco. Recognition of the Rumanian and Bulgarian Governments amounted to no more than remaining on speaking terms for the purpose of exchanging acid notes. Yugoslavia and Albania occupied a slightly different position in the same category, indirectly because neither had been at war with any of the United Nations. Tito's Government, which Britain and the USA had done even more than the USSR to instal in absolute tyranny, was too strong for the former to exercise diplomatic pressure upon it when they changed their minds. Enver Hoxha's Government, which had not yet reached a maturity at which diplomatic language and usage were profitable, could in practice only be treated as a puppet of Tito's. This relationship was confirmed by the signature in July of a twenty-year treaty of mutual assistance, and in November of a customs and currency union, as well as by an exact concurrence of policy in religious and political persecution in both countries. Against Yugoslavia, therefore, the western powers did not direct the same criticism of its internal affairs as they did against Bulgaria and Rumania; to Albania, although they accorded it formal recognition, they sent no formal diplomatic representation. These were only superficial modifications of a single relation, which was basically identical between the western and Balkan Governments. That it extended *de facto* to the whole of Eastern Europe was emphasised by Tito's visits in March to Warsaw and Prague, where pacts of mutual co-operation were signed with Poland and Czechoslovakia; and by the visit of the Hungarian Prime Minister to Moscow on a similar but less equilateral mission in April. The homogeneity which had been the vague and distant goal of the Czech-Polish Agreement in 1941 and the Greco-Yugoslav Agreement in 1942 was being impressed upon Eastern Europe from another direction and in a different pattern. The British Government, which had sponsored those agreements, and the Greek Government, which had participated, were both absentees in 1946.

The schism of the Balkans became progressively more clear-cut as every successive act of hostility or provocation between any member of the eastern combine (consisting of the USSR, the Balkan Governments, and the left opposition in Greece) on the one side and any member of the western combine (consisting of the USA and Britain, the moribund oppositions in the Balkans, and the elected Government of Greece) on the other side, infallibly evoked a unanimous response from each of the combines as a whole. This was verified in theory at every conference of the year: at the Council of Foreign Ministers in Moscow in December 1945, in Paris by stages in the summer of 1946, and in New York in November; at the Peace Conference in August 1946, and at every meeting of the General Assembly or Security Council of the United Nations. It was more grimly verified in practice. Examples were the trial and execution of General Mihailovitch in July: the shooting down of American planes by Tito's Air Force in August; the recall of the Yugoslav Minister to Greece in the same month; the failure of Greece to obtain adjustments of her northern frontiers in the peace treaties; the resurrection of the Greek question in the Security Council by the Ukrainian delegation in September, and by the Greek Government in December; the disastrous damage to ships of the Royal Navy by mines in the Corfu Strait in October; the infringement of diplomatic privilege by the Bulgarian Government in the process of calling in Bulgarian currency in March, 1947; the recall of the Soviet Ambassador to Greece a month later; the Hungarian *coup d'état* in June; above all, the "Treason Trials" in the autumn throughout Eastern Europe. In each case the attitude of the USSR was identical with that of the Balkan Governments concerned, and was echoed by the Press and propaganda of the

KKE in Greece. In each case the converse occurred on the opposite side, so that the USSR could point to the solidarity of the western combine in justification of the solidarity of its own. This dichotomy of international interests makes it *a priori* improbable that the internal schism of Greece, which manifested itself in the new guerilla war of 1946-7, could have been (as left-wing propaganda represented it) a purely domestic affair. The internal history of the UN Commission, which arrived in Athens in January 1947 to investigate the situation on the frontiers, confirmed the improbability. If the new guerilla war was an indigenous protest against domestic tyranny, it was incredible that at almost every point of the investigation the self-same international dichotomy should have emerged. When the Greek rebels, under the familiar leadership of Markos Vaphiadhis, Lazanis and Kissavos, were protesting that their rebellion was not supported by Albanian, Yugoslav or Bulgarian encouragement and help, it was singular that the only members or attached officials of the UN Commission who entirely confirmed their point of view (apart from the USSR and Poland) were the Albanian, Yugoslav and Bulgarian representatives.

It was difficult to *prove* that the disorders in northern Greece were instigated from abroad in collaboration with the KKE: it was also almost impossible to *doubt* it. The KKE had learned its lesson from experience with SNOF, and especially with Gotchev, too well to allow its forces in northern Greece to be flooded again with uncontrollable hordes of slavophone Macedonians, to whom all Greeks alike were anathema and ideological orthodoxy was secondary. Outside help, if it existed, was restricted to impersonal reinforcement, on which evidence was more difficult to gather. The inadequacy of Tsaldharis' Government had reinforced the guerillas with a reluctant accretion of simple Greeks, drawn from the category which had been the victim of unreasoning discrimination since the revolution of December 1944. It was therefore, by a confusing mischance, just as easy to argue that the latter was the crucial fact which the former irrelevantly obscured, as to argue that the former was the crucial fact which the latter irrelevantly obscured. In this dilemma the British authorities found themselves too embarrassed to take decisive action; HMG could not forget that its predecessor had found almost the whole world against it when it had done so two years before. Consequently the Greek Government met a downright refusal when it asked Britain in November 1946 to supply arms for the protection of civilians in northern Greece. The Greek Government allowed the distinction between official and unofficial means of combating the guerillas to become hazy; the irregular adherents of Zervas and Andon Tsaous were permitted to resume their vendetta against ELAS under a semi-official guise. But the British authorities could not condone such measures; their position was already sufficiently vulnerable to malevolent criticism by reason of the part played by British Missions in training the regulars engaged. Moreover, under the impact of the domestic crisis of the winter 1946-7, HMG had at last to admit that it could no longer fulfil its commitments in Greece.

By this time, however, one of the bitterest critics of 1944 had shifted ground. President Truman had sent a special observer, Mr. Mark Ethridge, to the Balkans before the end of 1945, on a mission similar to that of Colonel Donovan for President Roosevelt in 1941; he was later appointed American member of the UN Commission to investigate the Greek frontiers in 1947. Next, Mr. Paul Porter was sent to make financial investigations. These two interventions marked a turning-point. Alert Athenian politicians, applying such simple and conclusive tests as that of the size, quantity and opulence of motor-cars rolling through the streets, were already convinced that Britain's day was ending and America's dawning. Those who had devoted years to proving that they were practically natives of Claridge's now turned their energies to proving that they were practically indistinguishable from Southern Democrat senators. In the summer of 1946 a firmer American policy in the eastern Mediterranean emerged to justify them. In August, when the Yugoslav Government was showing an inclination to frustrate the international-isation of Trieste, the United States Navy suddenly multiplied its strength in the Mediterranean to a formidable force, which paid extensive visits to the principal ports, including those of Italy, Greece and Turkey. In December another American interest in the Middle East was stressed by the conclusion, with the approval of the British and American Govern-ments, of an agreement between the Standard Oil Company, the Socony Vacuum Oil Company, and the Anglo-Iranian Oil Company, including a provision for joint investigation of the possibility of constructing a pipe-line from the Persian Gulf to the Mediterranean. The Greek Govern-ment read the omens. While the external aspect of Greece's problems was publicly referred to the intervention of the United Nations, its internal aspect was privately referred to the one power, in default of Britain, which now appeared to have both the means and the incentive to save the country from disintegration.

The simultaneity of these two appeals signified the dual loss of control over the internal and the external affairs of the country; it also showed that the Government recognised the inseparability of the two. The problem of Greece's survival had two aspects, as indivisible as hill and valley. One was the problem of averting collapse from within; the other was to prevent it being crushed from without. These two dangers were interlocked: if one was realised, the other would be also; they could only be nullified together. Having failed to mitigate either by itself, the Government was obliged, even at the expense of confessing failure, to enlist help for both from abroad. It acted correctly in addressing its two appeals, since the problem of external interference was a proper matter for the international tribunal of the Security Council, and the problem of domestic bankruptcy was a private matter that could properly be referred independently to the one country capable of meeting it. Although there was nothing irregular in the Greek Government's procedure, it put the USA in a dilemma hardly less embarrassing than that of Britain. In the first place, the State Department had no respect for Tsaldharis' administration. In the second place, American public opinion had not been pleased by the restoration of King George II. In the third place, the inescapable coincidence of the Greek appeal for domestic help with the frontier investigation made any American action on the former look like prejudgment of the latter. The first embarrassment was removed in January 1947 by the substitution for Tsaldharis' Government of a slightly broader administration under the elder statesman Maximos, the Populists' equivalent to Sophoulis; the second was removed in March by the death of King George II, which brought his less controversial brother Paul to the throne. The Americans might have been fairly satisfied with the new Government, at least as a step in the right direction: for although Maximos was weaker even than Tsaldharis, who remained Foreign Secretary, and although the ex-revolutionaries Zervas and Gonatas were included, nevertheless there were hopeful signs in the exclusion of the Populist arch-intriguers Theotokis and Mavromikhalis and the inclusion of the vigorous trio of the right centre, Kanellopoulos, Papandhreou and Sophoklis Veniselos. With the new King no reasonable man could quarrel, still less with his charming, brave and imaginative Queen, Frederika, though extreme republicans might eventually find cause to do so. But the third embarrassment was irresoluble: nothing could make an American loan to Greece appear as anything but a hostile act to the USSR and its satellites.

The logic by which American opinion was helped over this hurdle can be put simply. Under present leadership and in present circumstances, the USSR could not afford a war, and the western powers (whose initiative now lay with the USA) would not provoke one. The "present" during which the world should therefore be safe from war could not be chronologically defined in terms of leadership, but in terms of circumstances it might last as much as fifty years. Although the prospects were therefore reasonably good, there were many things short of war that could happen in the meantime to the detriment of the west. Soviet dogma still held that capitalism must lead to war; Soviet policy must be expected to continue aiming at the construction of just such buffer-states as the west had previously constructed against the USSR, with the buffers pointing in the opposite direction. The encroachments necessary to consolidate these buffers would continue just as far as the western powers let them. Since there was no danger of unprovoked aggression from the west, encroachment from the east need only be limited by western reaction, and could always be halted short of war. The task of American diplomacy was therefore to state the limits before it was too late; before Stalin repeated the tragedy of Hitler. The task seemed easier than it had been before the second World War, because the USSR could not conceivably want a war, as Germany plainly had. Whereas Berlin had been ruled by homicidal maniacs, Moscow appeared to be ruled by cool and hard-headed men aware of their risks and responsibilities. If this argument was correct, it was only necessary to make clear in advance where the expansion of the Soviet buffer-head must stop, before the USSR or its satellites had tried to find out by probing for a vacuum. The vacuum left by the Germans in most of Eastern Europe had already been filled, and could no longer be regarded as a practicable field of operation for a new diplomacy. Greece, which was with Turkey the one remaining area open to experiment, was about to be left a vacuum by Britain's imminent withdrawal on both economic and military fronts. HMG had informed the United States Government that their economic commitments to Greece must expire on 31st March. British troops in Greece were diminishing to the strength of less than a brigade, which was maintained only as a counter to the continued presence of Soviet troops in Bulgaria. The intensification of the guerilla war appeared to aim at decisive action, perhaps coupled with the re-establishment of a free government in the mountains, to coincide with the British withdrawal. President Truman therefore decided, as Mr. Churchill had decided three years before, that if a foot was not put down then and there on the northern frontier of Greece, it might never be possible to put it down anywhere. It was announced on 28th February, 1947, that negotiations for a loan to Greece and Turkey of £100,000,000 were in progress in Washington. Within three months it was an accomplished fact.

The association of Turkey with Greece as a beneficiary of this policy (to the extent of twenty-five per cent.) helped to define it in larger terms as amounting to what was called the "Truman Doctrine": that the eastern Mediterranean was an American sphere of interest. In Turkey, which had little need of a loan, the purpose showed itself as more nakedly political than in Greece, which had great need. The American Government made two belated attempts to soften the impression of power politics. The first was to refer the proposed loan (after it was announced but before it was ratified) to the Security Council of UN. Failure to do this earlier had been regrettable, not only because the UN Secretariat felt affronted, but also because the treatment of Greece's internal and external troubles needed the co-ordination of a common authority; the loan as well as the frontier problem needed the attention of the Security Council: the solution, like the problem, had to be ambivalent. UN's endorsement was given in spite of Soviet opposition.

But Soviet opposition was more successful in frustrating the American Government's second attempt to dilute the significance of the Truman Doctrine. When the Secretary of State tried in June to enlarge it into the so-called "Marshall Plan" of continental aid to Europe as a whole, the USSR together with its satellites boycotted the plan, and thereby forced it back into the same anti-Communist mould from which the Truman Doctrine had emerged. This definitive schism between the USA and the USSR left world opinion agreed on only one point: that rightly or wrongly the USA had inherited the historic role of Britain, especially in the eastern Mediterranean.

The immediate effect in Greece was to anticipate the vacuum on which the KKE was depending. The next phase in the guerilla rebellion reflected the confusion of its motives. While the UN Commission was investigating the disturbances in Greece, guerilla activity was reduced to a degree consonant with the claim to legitimate grievance. Between then and the ratification of the American loan, the rebellion expanded to a new level of violence, as the guerillas multiplied their activities and the Government launched a series of drives to exterminate them. With the help of a new and fairly generous amnesty, Government troops at first scored some successes; but much the same result would have been brought about anyway by the American intervention alone. By declaring Greece an American sphere of interest, the Truman Doctrine encouraged the rebel rank and file to desert, and showed their political advisors that persistence could only logically culminate in war between the USA and the USSR. The belief that the Soviet Government was not yet ready for such a culmination generated a tendency above the horizontal line as well as below to give up the effort, at least for the time being.[1] Part of those above the line (including the Secretary-General of the KKE, Nikos Zakhariadhis) retired into hiding; part of those below took their chance of desertion or surrender. But these were not all: fanatics continued audaciously to plan a "free government" in the Macedonian mountains, and trouble was kept simmering both spontaneously and deliberately. It continued spontaneously, as brigandage and vendetta naturally continue in the Balkan mountains, especially among young men who had been taught by the western allies themselves that it was heroic to sabotage authority. It was revived sporadically by its initiators to test the strength of American reaction and to provide guerilla training. But what was lacking was the conviction of urgent, immediate, historical purposefulness: all these were hesitant and negative reactions. More positive consequences must be sought on higher levels.

The Americans had at last followed the British Labour Party and almost

---

[1] Markos Vaphiadhis even put forward terms on which he was "prepared to come to an understanding," in the form of a letter to *The Times*, published on 10th September, 1947; but his quaint adoption of England's most individual convention had no effect whatever.

all the rest of Mr. Churchill's critics (except, of course, Communists and fellow-travellers) in realising that the issues were indeed as he had stated them: they also followed the rest in not admitting it. Like all who criticised British policy in 1944-5, and subsequently adopted it themselves, they argued that their opinions had been right all along, and had only changed because the facts changed. But in thus objectifying their subjective transformation, they deceived themselves. They had at last realised that the issue in Greece lay not between republicanism and monarchy, in which their mission was to counterbalance British support of monarchy, but between communism and western democracy, in which their mission was to counterbalance Soviet support of communism. What they still needed to realise was that this had been the case ever since 1941: that the latter issue had been the primary one all the time, and that the secondary character of the former had only been concealed by the KKE's skill and its opponents' folly. The significance of the USA's change was rightly interpreted by Mr. Churchill.[1] Although no American official ever admitted it, the truth was that if HMG had not acted as it did under violent American criticism in December 1944, there would have been no Greece left for the USA to save in 1947. Indeed, so far as political events in Greece can be ascribed to the protecting power, American policy went much farther in the same direction within six months than British policy had dared to go in six years. Under the American aegis things began happening in Greece at once which the British authorities had perhaps dreamed of, but never dared attempt. For instance, the elected governments of Maximos and Tsaldharis were successively turned out, to be replaced in September 1947 by a Liberal-Populist coalition under Sophoulis, whose parliamentary following was a tiny minority; the Communist press was then suppressed in October; a joint Greco-American staff was formed to fight the guerillas in November; the right to strike was abolished in December; and finally, after the proclamation of a "free government" under Markos Vaphiadhis in the mountains on Christmas Eve, the KKE was outlawed at the end of the year. Each of these actions enormously exceeded every corresponding intervention that the British had once attempted and the Americans once castigated. In fact, they carried to a logical conclusion the principle that, as Greek opinion was too volatile to be ascertained, what mattered was to satisfy public opinion at home. In this policy, which is called "imperialism" by those who are not for the moment practising it, there was implicit a tacit apology by the USA to Britain; but it was never made explicit. Thus far examined, the Americans' own frame of mind was itself negative.

What the American intervention amounted to positively was an act of crystallisation, such as had last taken place in the Balkans in 1941. May 1947 thus ended the third act as definitively as April 1941 had opened

[1] Articles in the *Daily Telegraph*, 12th and 14th April, 1947.

the first; in comparison with it, the report of the UN Commission (as much a foregone conclusion, or rather two contradictory foregone conclusions, as that of AMFOGE) was merely an epiphenomenal confirmation. The true significance of the American intervention can be seen in the Soviet reaction, which was to divert its energy to marshalling its settled resources and consolidating those that were still imperfectly settled. Hungary, Rumania and Bulgaria were enfolded in a closer embrace by the USSR; but Greece had temporarily to be left alone until it became clear whether the American intervention was as determined as it made out. Greek Macedonia might remain an exception, since the USSR counted it not as part of Greece, but as part of the Balkan resources that were to be consolidated and marshalled; it was a useful no-man's-land, equivalent to Spain in 1936: but the open attempt on the main body of Greece had to be put off. How long it had to be put off depended only on one consideration; the fear that American obstinacy might turn a minor Balkan disturbance into a third World War before the USSR judged the time ripe. It was already clear in 1947 that once the fear was removed, or the time became ripe, the restraints would be let slip. How long it might be before that happened was anybody's guess.

The Truman Doctrine, combined with the Marshall Plan in the interpretation which Moscow forced upon it, therefore ended a chapter not in the sense that it made war inevitable, nor in the sense that it incontestably guaranteed Greece's survival, though it made one or the other more probable; but rather in the sense that at last it precisely clarified the issue in Eastern Europe into a contest between the western system headed by the USA and the Soviet system of the USSR. This general schism was most exactly reflected in miniature by the sensitive mirror of Greek affairs; a natural symbol of it was the dichotomy of the UN Commision, when it finished its work, into those members who asserted, and those who denied, that there had been violations of Greece's northern frontier. But the sum of the whole matter as far as Greece was concerned lay not in such words and symbols. It lay rather in the simple fact that the USA had replaced Britain. This third act could therefore be seen to have ended in exactly the same way as the previous two: in the reoccupation of the expected vacuum by a third party at exactly the moment when Communist policy was preparing to inherit it from its previous occupants. The KKE had thus been baulked successively by the Germans, the British and the Americans. But Communism can be patient as well as precipitate; and there was nobody else left to baulk it.

CHAPTER VIII

CURTAIN

". . . they are fighting each other within a hermetically sealed conveyance. The fight for a better seat, for a broader view, for a little more comfort is rather meaningless, as they are being carried by it relentlessly towards the same terminus."

EMERY REVES, *The Anatomy of Peace.*

THE whole of this chapter is guesswork, but some of it is probable. It is presumable as a start that if the American Loan is to be seen in history as another interlude in the sense previously used in this survey, then it will be seen as the last in that sense. There is no candidate except the USSR and its satellites to inherit the vacuum that would recur if the USA were to withdraw defeated from their task in Greece. Besides this awareness, the United States Government entered upon its responsibility with the record of previous errors to guide it. Among mistakes preventable by external decision, the study of the preceding period would suggest to them the following: the acceptance by the British authorities of responsibility for decisions that should have been taken exclusively by Greek Governments, especially those of Tsoudheros and Papandhreou; the acquiescence in the discrimination of successive Greek authorities against the Resistance Movement; the depreciation of Greece's currency by the uncontrolled infiltration of gold during the German occupation; the mystification of the Press and public opinion of the world about Greek affairs during the war; the unresolved conflict of policy between short-term strategy and long-term diplomacy. None of these could be classed as faults of malicious intention: it should be clear by now that British intentions were wholly beneficent, if only because beneficence happened to coincide with expediency. Among misfortunes not preventable by external decision, however beneficent, might be counted various manifestations of the shortsightedness of successive Greek Governments living mentally in a dead past: the folly of leaving the KKE to monopolise most of the worth-while causes which should never have been subjects of political schism, such as the enfranchisement of women and the official replacement of the obsolescent *katharevousa* language by the current demotic[1]; the misguided effort to suppress

---

[1]There is much inconsistency on these subjects: for instance, the Populists officially favour the enfranchisement of women, but do nothing to implement it; the KKE favours demotic, but often uses *katharevousa*.

political problems by military means (such as had been proved bankrupt already by the German occupation); the perpetuation of the domestic cycle of political victory . . . reprisals . . . revolution . . . defeat . . . counter-reprisals . . . counter-revolution . . . political victory, as the accepted sequence of Greek history since the first World War; the tactlessness with which each Government allowed itself to be put morally in the wrong, as Papandhreou's was by the police in Constitution Square in December 1944, and Tsaldharis' was by the court in Salonika which condemned a fifteen-year-old boy to death in 1947. Such items have only to be listed to make it plain that they are nowhere near the heart of the problem; but the expertness of the KKE in exploiting trivialities made it important to avoid them.

Although the Americans were, if anything, less well equipped than the British to sympathise with the psychological complexities induced in the Greek mind by suffering, terror and insecurity, they started with advantages besides the experience of others' mistakes and misfortunes. Three of the most valuable were that American intervention could be expected to bring to the fore new kinds of Greeks; that Greece became assured of a longer respite than before; and that the American outlook upon Balkan affairs might in some important ways be less parochial than that of its predecessors. The first two go no nearer to the roots of a solution than the items gathered into the last paragraph to the heart of the problem. But in the third it may be legitimate to see the kernel from which the future may emerge. It would be optimistic, though not necessarily mistaken, to depict that future as a solution of the Greek problem in the sense desired by Greece's friends; but at least an examination starting from this point may yield clues for historical prediction, while the first two points can be used as guidance to the short-term prospects.

The first two advantages ascribed to the American intervention correspond to two irremediable handicaps of the preceding phase: the paucity of suitable Greeks to evolve a ruling class, and the lack of time to rebuild the Greek state on sound foundations. These are restatements of the two themes laid down in the preface. The lack of a class recognisably destined to rule was the outcome of the succession of dictatorship, war, occupation and revolution, which had soured the creative rivalry on which democracy is based into irreconcilable antagonism. The restless sense of a race against time to restore Greece was similarly the outcome of revolution and the fear, engendered by the rivalry of the great powers, that it might be repeated. Under these pressures British influence in Greece had failed to inject creative vitality into Greek politics, or even to find time to realise such potentialities as it found. The left centre of the resistance movement, perhaps the best of the new blood, only found its way into the political life-stream four months before the elections, whose arresting effect upon Greece's renascent system was then a foregone conclusion. During the first two years of liberation, Greece barely survived by living from hand to mouth in daily apprehension; but the American intervention in 1947, if it was as determined as it seemed, promised a margin of security that could at last be measured in years instead of weeks. It not only gave a new amplitude to the ordinary Greek's vision of the future; it also enlarged his vision of the political field. Greeks had many different conceptions of the meaning of the USA. To some, Americans were practically the same thing as Englishmen; to some they were all Lincolns or Roosevelts; to some they were all Fords or Rockefellers. In the upper levels of Greek authority, only the first conception had played an important part during the period of British influence; but now other ideas were certain to rise to the surface, all of them dynamic, not static like their idea of England. The great hope of the American intervention was that a new leaven of creative inspiration, such as had not been experienced since the youthful ferment of Eleftherios Veniselos, might enter into the flat brew of Greek politics.

But Greece would still not survive if success were confined to these relatively narrow limits. The universe of discourse is still too small, as an analogy may help to show. If an aeroplane is diving out of control, its prospects are not improved merely by reducing engine-speed, or merely by interchanging the seats of some of the passengers and some of the crew. Those, in other terms, were the immediate effects of the American intervention; and the coincidence of the death of King George II made about as much additional difference as if the principal VIP happened to fall out of the aeroplane in the course of its dive. The task which American policy had to undertake was to regain control of the aeroplane and pull it out of its dive. To this task all the problems and prospects so far mentioned were irrelevant. History would not judge the petty trivialities going on inside the aeroplane: it would record that the aeroplane did or did not finally crash. This was the test in which the third characteristic of the American intervention offered either the one hope of Greece's survival, or at least the clue to the historical reasons for its failure.

It has been represented as a weakness of British policy towards Greece that it was not a Balkan policy; though that is not a criticism, because circumstances debarred it. That has been the basis common to every chapter of this survey. The faults and successes that have been recorded lay within the constricting compass of a closed circle of impossibility, from which neither for good nor for evil was British policy able to break loose. Greece belonged, ever since it was created in 1832, to an obsolescent order of magnitude which has not yet been replaced by a higher and more viable level of sovereignty. The nineteenth century redrew the map of Europe on the principles of liberal nationalism, which the peacemakers of 1919 and 1946, with few exceptions, accepted as sacrosanct. Greece was a creation of those principles, though her frontiers have yet to remain firm for any consecutive period of fifty years. It is impossible to study those frontiers, or any other conceivable frontiers of Greece, whether in terms of geography, strategy, ethnography or bare human comfort, with any sense of satisfaction. It is impossible to share the life of the Greek people without a sense of something radically preposterous. The top-heavy administration; the contrast between the capital and the provinces; the gulf between the two peoples that occupy them; these and countless other incongruities attest a faulty principle of construction. The fault is that even the limited statehood which was the goal of Greece's creators, and which their creation had barely begun to approach even under the guidance of Eleftherios Veniselos and the coercion of Metaxas, was an historically antiquated notion when it was first applied. It assumed the inviolability of Balkan separatism, which has been the curse of the Balkans ever since.

Criticism of Balkan separatism evokes in a philhellene mind the converse notion of Balkan federation, which has more horrible associations still. An example of the Greek reaction was the answer of the London Greek newspaper *Hellas* to the suggestion of the *Sunday Times* early in 1944 that a federative solution was needed for the Macedonian problem: "What kind of federation could be conceived for sharing an indisputably legitimate property between the owner and an intruding bandit?" The allusion to Bulgaria was justified; but the emotion implied is one that makes solutions impossible. The same emotion prevents the solution of internal problems by arguing that every offence committed by one side against the other must be punished when the positions are reversed. Set in these terms, neither of the problems stated in the Preface could ever be solved. The offence of Bulgaria was inexcusable; so were the offences of ELAS: but at some point, if the vicious circle is ever to be broken, the inexcusable has to be excused. The important point for history is not who is right or wrong, but who will be the first to give up legitimate grudges? On the domestic level, the essential principle is that it is more important to achieve tranquillity than to be in the right. On the international level, the essential principle was expressed in the noblest contribution to political philosophy made in this century, when Edith Cavell explained shortly before her judicial murder that "patriotism is not enough."

That principle will not be understood in the Balkans so long as it is interpreted to mean that patriotism is wrong. It means nothing of the sort: it means that the present order of national sovereignty is too exclusive. The principle has been elaborated by many men since, significantly most of them Americans. Their argument is based upon the historical progress of societies to successively higher levels of organisation by the partial resignation (or enforced abandonment) of lower orders of sovereignty. The subsumption of lower orders of sovereignty into a higher order, which is called federàtion, does not entail the destruction of patriotism, but only of nationalism; it is specifically not a total subsumption of all powers, but only of those which jeopardise the relations of neighbouring communities having independent sovereignty. This is not a theory but an observed fact. A Texan and a Scot are just as patriotic to-day, but not as nationalistic, as if they were still allowed to raise private armies and issue private currencies. What they have learned from resigning a part of their sovereignty is that patriotism is not enough. The lesson still remains to be universally practised at the higher level to which they have passed. The nations of the world have reached different levels, and therefore different degrees of understanding of the lesson. In quantitative terms, the highest level yet reached is occupied only by the USA and the USSR, which are already powers not only of a different size and strength, but of a different order of magnitude from Britain or France or Greece. Nations are uneasily aware that they cannot speak on equal terms until they reach the same level. The obstacle, which is again observable, is that such transitions from lower to higher orders of social magnitude are always resisted: even if they are created without force, they may still need force to prevent them falling apart. Bloodshed was needed to create the federal unions of Switzerland and South Africa, as well as to preserve those of the United States and Canada. The example of Mr. Churchill's offer to France in 1940 showed that even imminent disaster may not be enough to bring about the voluntary resignation of sovereignty, and weakened the force of his revival of the principle in 1947. The fate of such a statesmanlike enterprise among politically mature societies augurs ill for south-east Europe.

This is no place to argue the merits of the principle, least of all to advocate them to the sensitive suspicions of the Greek people. Both the general and the particular cases have been argued already by experts.[1] The important point here is not that such a federation of south-east Europe is a good or a bad thing, but that whether we like it or not, it is coming about. The Union of Southern Slavs was already in 1947 an almost accomplished fact, in a different sense from the Serb hegemony between the wars; partly because it was a federation, and not the rule of a dominant race; partly because it was already absorbing Albania and perhaps Bulgaria. The Greek nationalist can justify his abhorrence of being additionally included on two grounds: that he is not a Slav, and that the manifest destiny of his country is not riparian, like that of the Danubian states, but maritime. He is right on both points (which could

---

[1]Generally, by Emery Reves in *The Anatomy of Peace*; with particular reference to south-east Europe, by Hugh Seton-Watson in *Eastern Europe, 1918-41*: as well as many others.

also be made by an Albanian), but it seems unlikely that history will let him get away with it. The ethnographical argument is a lost cause which, in terms of anthropological time, may soon be defunct; in the heterogeneous mixture of the Balkans, it is doubtful whether it has any but a specious validity now. The geographical argument can be reversed to suggest that the characteristics of Greece and the rest of the Balkans are complementary; an argument that acquired an increased appeal to the rest, which urgently need a maritime outlet, when Tito failed to win Trieste in 1945-6. The incorporation of Greece in the USSR, terrible though it would seem to all philhellenes, would in fact be neither more nor less logically incongruous than that of Finland or Rumania. But whatever the justice of the Greek nationalist's cause, he has taken his stand plumb in the path of history. The maxim on which the successive Balkan Ententes were precariously balanced, that the states of south-east Europe cannot survive alone, has already been proved upon the bodies of all but Greece and a fragment of Turkey. Familiarity with the geography, economics and ethnography of the area leaves the conviction that the proof cannot halt there.

The conclusion will be repudiated by most Greeks, as well as most English philhellenes. The significant fact is not the repudiation but the coincidence of those two points of view. There have been innumerable friends of Greece in England, as well as of England in Greece: I have never heard an Englishman expressing dislike (as distinct from criticism) of Greeks without feeling certain that he himself was to blame. But at the risk of forfeiting the right to the title of philhellene, I must add that the unreasoning sentimentality of Anglo-Greek friendship has often done Greece harm. It is one thing to be drawn towards Greece by bonds of admiration for an unparalleled antiquity, by the fellow-feeling of a maritime people, by community of heroic suffering in war after war for over a century: but it is another thing to allow these sentiments to sanctify a narrow nationalism which argues that Greeks are a chosen race, exempted by the privilege of British sympathy from the need to meet their neighbours on equal terms. Because the Greek peasant is nice and the Bulgarian politician nasty, it does not follow that Greece must always be right and Bulgaria always wrong; any more than the converse would follow from the converse premiss. But the Englishman, brought up on Jack the Giant-killer, has a natural admiration for the Greek who has so often played the role of Jack, against the Turkish Giant, the Teuton Giant and the Slav Giant in turn. The same sympathy which drew Englishmen to the support of Greek nationalism drove them also to submit to the nascent nationalism of Egypt, India, Palestine, the Arab States and the Near, Middle and Far East in general, immediately after the second World War had signalled the approaching end of the nation-state. It is because such sympathies are second nature to the Englishman that Greece has felt encouraged, throughout its protection by Britain, to stand in the path of history. Because the sovereignty of Britain, considered in isolation from its dependencies, belongs to the same order of magnitude as that of Greece, and because the political life of Britain is itself torn apart by the same schism as Greece, it has been impossible for the former to help the latter take its place in that new order of society which is coalescing in south-east Europe.

This is another way of restating the thesis that Britain had no Balkan policy. During the war Britain could not have had a Balkan policy, because the diverse circumstances of the Balkan states did not permit uniformity except by the procrustean methods of the USSR. Britain could not afford a Balkan policy, partly in the sense that in 1942 it was imperative not to offend the USSR, and partly in the sense that since the war it has proved impossible to remain a first-class power on a third-class income. But in any case temperament and tradition disqualified the mind of British authority from pursuing such a federative solution with the enthusiasm of conviction against the trend of circumstances. The idea certainly crossed British minds: it was apparent in January 1942, in the most hopeful episode covered by this survey[1]; but it was soon buried in oblivion, only to be resurrected by unofficial cranks. Britain had, generally speaking, a sentimental weakness, a political weakness and an economic weakness in favour of Balkan separatism. The USSR had none of these weaknesses; that is the reason why the USSR would have beaten Britain in Greece in the long run. But what mattered in 1947 was that the USA had none of these weaknesses either. The voices of their President, their Secretary of State, and their public opinion all proclaimed their freedom from them.

The first and third of these voices were sometimes inclined in 1947 to speak in tones resonant of the idolatry of the dollar and the witch-hunt against Communism. Overtones in them even hinted that, from the view-point of the USA, neither quantitatively nor qualitatively, neither geographically nor culturally nor materially, was Britain itself very remote from the Balkans. The relation thereby implied in the long run between Britain and the United States would resemble that between Austria and Germany's Third Reich. But there was another point of view in the USA: Secretary Marshall spoke in tones more truly characteristic of America. In his first public speech after taking office, he said[2]: "I doubt seriously whether a man can think with full wisdom and deep conviction regarding certain of the basic international issues to-day who has not at least reviewed in his mind the period of the Peloponnesian War and the downfall of Athens." By narrowing his vision to focus on a minute point of the remote past, he widened it to a universal conspectus.

[1]See page 122.
[2]At Princeton, March 1947.

The importance of the parallel on the lips of an American Secretary of State is that the century covered by those events, like the twentieth century, terminated a lower order of magnitude in the known hierarchy of sovereignty by forcibly subsuming it in a higher order. The Peloponnesian War was the death-blow of the Greek city-state, just as the second World War was of many, if not all, the European nation-states. The independent sovereignties of the city-states were subsumed in the higher order of sovereignty of Macedonia and later of Rome. In the impending transfiguration of the nation-state, there were in the first half of the twentieth century only two sovereignties belonging to the higher order replacing it, the USA and the USSR; but there is no reason to despair of creating others. What would be a cause for despair would be a failure to recognise what is happening, such as was the fate of Greece under British guidance in the 1940s. It is not encouraging to infer the parallel from ancient Greece in this respect: for the two greatest minds of the ancient world, Plato and Aristotle, not only failed to observe the extinction of the city-state which was taking place around them, but hymned its virtues as sacrosanct, everlasting and in principle beyond improvement. Secretary Marshall suggested, though he could hardly have said outright, that the USA did not suffer from the same delusion about the nation-state, when in a speech in June 1947 he enlarged the conception of the "Truman Doctrine" into a project of "continental aid" on principles similar to Lease-Lend for Europe as a whole.[1] It was significant that both these important speeches were addressed to universities.

The American mind, in fact, does not suffer from the limitations of the European in this respect. It has grown up among new ideas, taking the new order of sovereignty for granted as part of its heritage even without its Secretary of State's adjuration to study the downfall of the city-state. When the American loan was passed in May 1947, American opinion was only potentially ready for its responsibilities, and only half-aware of their extent; but it was conscious of an historic mission. It was no more likely to set about encouraging gallant little Greece to stand up to big bullying Bulgaria than to set about encouraging gallant little Wales against big bullying England; it might just as well encourage Mercia to stand up to Wessex or Oklahoma to Texas, and it knew it. But valid principles do not always fit awkward facts; the facts in south-east Europe in 1947 were very awkward. The likelihood that intuition, habit and temperament would guide the USA to draw out the essential principles of unity latent in south-east Europe, rather than to treat Greece parochially as an isolated problem, only threw into relief the contrasting fact that nine-tenths of south-east Europe had already had its latent unity drawn out and hammered into uniformity on another anvil. The application of western principles to the task having been anticipated

[1] At Harvard, 5th June, 1947.

by that of Soviet principles, it was hard for the United States Government
to devise a method impervious to hostile misconstruction. In blunt
terms, the USA were salvaging the last "free" remnant of south-east
Europe (Greece and a fragment of Turkey) to use as a bridgehead for the
northern expansion of economic imperialism; for the American policy
might as well not start as not expand. Realistic Americans did not deny
the fact, though they would repudiate the terminology. Seeing that it
was the only alternative to the sovietisation of south-east Europe when
British interests withdrew, they might argue that it would be historically
justified so long as it was not merely obstructive; so long, that is, as the
policy was positively Balkan and constructive, not negatively Greek and
parochial. But the justification carried with it the risk of war, just because
of the non-parochial essence of the policy.

The question was whether the USA alone could achieve a policy
which Britain alone had been unable either to afford or even to conceive.
An Anglo-American policy would have been preferable to a purely
American policy in 1947, just as it would have been to a purely British
policy in 1942; for almost all Greeks would have acquiesced in a joint
policy, and none would have been able to play off the USA and Britain
against each other. This principle was implicit in Mr. Churchill's speech
at Fulton, Missouri, on 5th March, 1946, but like his conception of a
voluntary federation of Europe, it came too late. There was a danger that
a unilateral policy might fail again for the same reason as before; at
least, a greater danger than if the American policy had come into being
earlier, and had consisted of participation in a joint responsibility instead
of assumption of the whole. The inference that joint responsibility was
the intention even in 1947 can be read into the request that most of the
British Missions should not yet withdraw; but it was obvious, when the
material responsibility had changed hands, that the moral responsibility
must eventually follow it, if only to exempt American intervention from
the familiar charge of "pulling Britain's chestnuts out of the fire." It
would then be no mitigation of the peril if Britain's habitual slogan, "too
little and too late," were simply replaced by the USA's "too late and
too much." It was perhaps impossible that an integrated Balkan policy,
which could not be achieved in 1942, should be achieved five years later,
when most of the Balkans were already lost and the principle of Anglo-
American integration was itself disintegrating. If that had to be conceded,
the question was whether 1947 was not too late for any Balkan policy
but preparation for war.

The danger, although real, could be discounted as far as the question
of Greece *simpliciter* was concerned. No war was going to break out
merely *because of* the American policy to Greece, even if one should
happen to start *in* Greece. No third World War would be confined in
its origins to the Balkans, nor to any other parochial quarrel. The character

T

of such a war, if it came, could already be seen in 1947; it would be a religious war. Portents of the impending recrudescence of religious war were visible, though certainly not inexorable. Balkan Communism was already preparing for it, as it prepared for every possible contingency without taking any for granted. The supreme capital of international Communism was also preparing for it, though with calmer and more deliberate steps than its satellites. If anything, the influence of Moscow may have been rather one of restraint, for the Communism of Moscow had already undergone the metamorphosis of maturity, whereas that of Sofia and Belgrade had by 1947 only reached the stage of militant effervescence which characterised the Bolshevik revolution of 1917. The Kremlin, indeed, like the Vatican in Europe's last religious wars, has shown itself ready to serve long-term ends by short-term alliances with ideological enemies; and again like the Vatican, it has suffered internal schism as a result. It might even carry the parallel to the point of war on its own fellow-worshippers: but the contradictory tactics would always tend to the one strategical objective. By more direct methods, Communism *in partibus infidelium* pursued the same ends, with a general respect for the dictates of Moscow harnessed to the more exuberant fanaticism of proselytes. Sustained by the fervour of a supra-rational faith that they alone were in step with history, the Balkan successors to the Third International worked to generate the mystical aura of a crusade about their eruptions of violence; to undermine mundane loyalties by spiritual appeals of a higher order; especially to create their private martyrology and hagiography. (The canonisation of Aris Veloukhiotis would at least seem to history no more extraordinary than Gibbon's account of the transfiguration of George of Cappadocia into St. George of Merry England.) But what is questionable is whether the necessary fervour exists on the other side: for it takes two religions to make a religious war. The desultory counter-canonisations of Goering and Mihailovitch, perhaps even of William Joyce to keep Horst Wessel company, and the demagogic counter-propaganda of militant anti-Communism throughout the world lack the spark of faith. The worship of the American way of life has not yet the necessary spiritual depth. The USA have set themselves to lead the world: but the negative character of the American reaction to ideological conflict is still typified in the anecdote of Huey Long's answer to the question, whether he thought America would turn Fascist: "Sure, but we'll call it anti-Fascist." That is to say, American opinion still has to make up its mind what it is *for* in foreign affairs, instead of only what it is *against*. Anti-Communism, unqualified by positive character, has been one of the best allies of the Third International abroad. In viewing the prospects of a conflict between the USSR and the USA, Stalin might well rest satisfied in the conviction that the latter would run out of dollars before the former ran out of doctrine.

These uncertain issues would be determined on a wider stage than that of Greece, or even of the Balkans. Events there would be symptoms, not causes, of conflict on a higher level. War is in any case the last and crudest vehicle for exporting Communism. The American policy in Greece could safely be elaborated into its widest and boldest implications in the certainty that the third World War, if it came at all, would not come merely because of that policy; and that if it came at all, it would involve the Middle East just as surely whatever was done or left undone in the Balkans. The important difficulty for American administrators in that particular area, considered in detachment, was not the choice between appeasement and aggression, but the technical problem of deploying the American way of life from the Greco-Turkish bridgehead into the sovietised Balkans. There were certain obvious opportunities that could only be exploited on an American scale with American resources by American genius: for instance, the reorganisation of riparian life by the application of the principles of TVA to the Danube; and the elimination of the social and physical prerequisites of brigandage and guerilla warfare by lavish expenditure upon schools and motor-roads. But the example of UNRRA was not encouraging to such enterprises: care would be needed to prevent tough and skilful governments from exploiting American aid, as before, to their own credit and to the intensification of their own control. From the view-point of 1947 it could only be seen that the USA had an historic opportunity, and certainly the means and perhaps the genius to use it. But if the opportunity were used simply to prop up Greece and Turkey on a subsidy of dollars, then the effect of American intervention would last exactly as long as the dollars. As soon as American public opinion became tired of the sordid transaction, or as soon as a major slump hit the USA, Greece would be back where it was when the operation started; ripe once again for the USSR to pluck. This was perhaps the alternative assumed by the Soviet Government, which may therefore have given itself little uneasiness at the prospect of the Truman Doctrine. If Mr. Marshall's wider vision were to be frustrated in that way, the future course of Balkan history could be easily predicted in another direction.

The evidence in 1947 suggested that if American policy were to amount only to temporary stabilisation, not to permanent creativity, then a return to authoritarianism in Greece was inevitable. Dictatorship of the right was probable as a start; dictatorship of the left was probable as a sequel. There were portents of the former before the American loan. One was the appointment of Zervas, an expert in the technique of private armies, as Minister of Public Order. Another was the absolute majority of the Populists and their allies in Parliament, enabling the right to move towards dictatorship under the mask of democratic processes, without the painful necessity which had constrained Metaxas to dissolve Parliament before he could establish his authority. By the same token, the extreme left was freed from the shackles of parliamentary responsibility, to plot subversive instead of legitimate opposition. Since a dictatorship of the right could only survive by American acquiescence, the sequel seemed likely to be the incorporation of Greece into the Soviet Federation of the Balkans under a Communist dictatorship, as soon as the next and last vacuum should be created by the withdrawal of American support. In the estimation of Balkan Communism, it could probably be taken for granted that American support, however large in scale, would only be temporary in duration. Since Balkan Communism was prepared to wait indefinitely with the patience of true faith, the conclusion must, by the premises of this paragraph, be justified in the end. Thus while the immediate prospect for Greece would perhaps be a repetition of 1936, the ultimate prospect would in any case be a repetition of 1453. In this "gale of the world" Greek politics could achieve nothing. At no point in the sequence would the republican centre play any relevant part, except that of catspaw: nor the monarchy, except to provide, with familiar artificiality, a convenient figurehead to the right and a convenient target to the left. That is why none of the political deaths of the years 1945-47—the two Rallis, Kaphandaris, Zevgos, Bakirdzis, George II, Siantos—made the least political difference to the trend of Greek history: nor had any political death since those of Veniselos and Metaxas. Events had gone too far to wait on personalities. This conclusion, it seemed, could only be falsified by an internal breakdown of Communism.

Such a breakdown is not impossible, though it seems more likely to occur after the conquering career of the internationalist doctrine has reached its widest extent, at least in Europe. If Communism did conquer Europe, not by war but by ideological penetration, there would be a prospect of schism within the creed. The accidental primacy of Russia in the practical application of Communism would hardly survive the complete sovietisation of Europe. Western democracies would not long submit to the doctrinal dictation of Slavs in Moscow once they had absorbed the true faith, any more than Constantinople or Geneva in past centuries would submit to that of Rome. It might thus be possible for western Europe, having first succumbed to Communism, to emerge triumphant with the benefits of federal unity, which it is less likely to achieve by any other predictable means; and with an indigenous variant of the faith which could erect against the Muscovite dogma something like the moral force of Lutheranism contending with Roman Catholicism, instead of (as it now has) something like the moral weakness of Mithraism contending with Christianity. The emergence of indigenous variants of Communism after conversion has already been proved possible in China, and would surely be possible in western Europe; what is good in Communism might thus survive the police-state which has usurped its name. But it is questionable whether this prospect could comfort Greece, whose future is menaced by a two-pronged fork; Communism is only one prong, and its twin is the proximity of the Slav races. The domination under which Greece would come in a total sovietisation of Europe would be Slav in character; in any subsequent European schism, geography alone would condemn Greece to the far side of the cleavage.

Those are the possibilities. Of the two long-term alternatives, that sovietisation would absorb Greece into the rest of south-east Europe and that Americanisation could expand from the former into the latter, the evidence assessable at the date of the American loan suggested that the former was perhaps the more probable: but it would be absurd to deny any degree of probability to the latter, when the United States Government had undertaken its task with open eyes. Of the other possibilities suggested in this chapter, that of a third World War and that of a right-wing dictatorship in Greece, both were from the historical view-point comparatively transient and secondary, since either would serve in the end as a step towards one of the long-term possibilities. For this purpose, a short term must be reckoned in years, or at most in decades: a long term in decades at least, or perhaps in centuries. The evident irresolubility of the two schisms, or rather of the intensive and extensive aspects of the one schism, which this survey depicts and its title symbolises, seems to ensure that one or other of the long-term possibilities will come about soon rather than late; but even if the schisms were to be resolved, some such outcome in south-east Europe appears likely. Paradoxically, the long term is easier to calculate than the short: like trying to read a complicated and fluctuating graph, it depends on the scope of the eye or the power of the lens. The general curve of its mean slope can be detected from a distance, but the irregular fluctuations of which it is made up are apt to be misleading, and even, under magnification, to suggest a precisely contrary trend. There will be many such fluctuations before the final trend reveals itself: there may be temporary relaxations and constrictions of Soviet unco-operativeness on the visible level, as well as ups and downs of American policy and its execution. History will judge the American intervention in the Middle East not with the facile finality of current observers, misconstruing momentary irregularities of the graph, but by the long-term results which will show themselves in its mean slope. When history examines these graphs, it will perhaps see the years which form the subject of this survey only as a kink in the curves representing successive interventions in the history of the eastern Mediterranean. It is too early to guess where the kink will appear: at the end of a British curve; at the beginning of a soviet curve; in the middle of a western curve; or somewhere almost lost in the vast curve of the eastern Mediterranean world itself. The year of the American loan was even too early to detect the direction its mean slope would take; but the uncertainty was at least better than the long-term certainty which it replaced. Although it did little to reduce the complex variety of immediate possibilities, it did Europe the service of increasing the ultimate possibilities from one to two.

NOTE ON EVIDENCE

The sources of this book are almost entirely British, and practically none of them can be listed bibliographically. Many of them are oral, some are unpublished diaries and reports, and a considerable proportion are stored only in my own memory. On behalf of the last, I apologise for any errors that may be detected. The military background, which I have taken for granted, has been made the subject of a detailed study by Colonel E. C. W. Myers, CBE, DSO, which I have had the good fortune to read; but it has not yet been published; nor has any other book in English containing useful material on this period.

I have avoided all Greek sources, since both hearsay and written evidence in Greece suffer from defects. Hearsay evidence is contaminated not only by exaggeration (which is not a unique fault) but also by a desire to please the inquirer by telling him what he wants to hear. One instance will illustrate both points. In the spring of 1943, all Greece knew that the relations between the BMM and EAM/ELAS were bad. The BMM was therefore regaled with accounts of Communist atrocities. It was decided that one specimen case, the murder of a village priest in the district of Trikhonis, should be investigated by a British officer. He conducted a court of inquiry, at which one witness after another described in increasingly horrible detail the circumstances of the priest's death. EAM/ELAS at last announced that they had a new witness to produce on their side. He turned out to be the priest whose death was the subject of the inquiry.

Written evidence from Greek sources suffers from a similar lack of critical spirit. The use of forged documents to discredit political opponents has frequently been mentioned; only one such document can be unreservedly accepted as genuine, since it was accidentally presented by the men whom it incriminated.[1] Other examples, of varying degrees of reliability, will show how this sort of evidence was used.

(a) The earliest notable instance was the evidence adduced by EAM/ELAS in March, 1943, to prove that Saraphis (then a renegade from their ranks) was in collusion with the Italians. The documents were widely canvassed and regarded as damning; but they were never published, and no one ever saw them. The Commander of the BMM repeatedly asked various leaders of EAM/ELAS to show him the incriminating documents; although one of them claimed to have the documents in his pocket at the time when he was asked, they were never produced. The reason was that Saraphis was expected to repent and to be admitted into ELAS as its Commander-in-Chief, which could hardly be done if the evidence against him were published. The news of his conversion spread so slowly round Greece, that he was still being denounced in Epirus after he had been rehabilitated in Roumeli: it would have been still worse if the damning documents had been published. From personal acquaintance with Saraphis, I should say that these documents were either damning and forged, or genuine and innocuous; but it is possible that they never existed at all. In any case, EAM/ELAS had set a dangerous precedent, which was soon to be used against themselves.

(b) Later in March, 1943, Zervas presented to the BMM a document purporting to record a decision by the KKE to "proclaim the dictatorship of the proletariat and declare war upon the Greek people" in that month. Although this was an unplausible document, and although EAM/ELAS repudiated it with a good deal of credibility,

[1] See page 78.

Zervas allowed it to be published in his clandestine press. It was the sort of document which would convince nobody but those who had already made up their minds about EAM/ELAS.

(c) The KKE countered this revelation after a discreet interval by publishing a letter, alleged to have been abstracted from Zervas' correspondence, in which an agent of EDES in Athens wrote to him deploring the collaboration with the Germans of which other members of EDES in Athens had been guilty. This document was used to prove that Zervas himself was in collusion with the Germans; but obviously it proved nothing of the sort, because if he were collaborating, there would have been no point in deploring to him the collaboration of others. Since it was admitted later that members of EDES in Athens had collaborated with the Germans, and since the document, strictly interpreted, did not serve the purpose for which it was used, there is some likelihood that it may have been genuine. A fabricated document would have been more explicitly damning, as later examples will show.

(d) The same technique was used by the KKE against members of the BMM, in two notable cases. The first concerned a letter alleged to have been written by myself in April, 1943, urging Zervas to attack ELAS; the second concerned a report alleged to have been written by Brigadier Myers in August, 1943, recommending to the British authorities methods of suppressing EAM/ELAS. The former was never produced, and after a few weeks the allegation was tacitly dropped. The latter, however, was published in the Communist newspaper *Rizospastis* in November, 1945; and after reading it I found my mind at ease about the former. The report attributed to Brigadier Myers reflected discredit upon the branch of the KKE concerned in forging it. Not only was it full of demonstrable anachronisms, but it was written in the style of a demagogue inciting a mob to violence; this is not generally employed by regular officers submitting appreciations to their superiors.

(e) The above examples show the danger of crying "Wolf!" too often. When photostat copies were produced by Zervas of letters alleged to have been written by Psaros, the inclination to doubt was almost too strong for the inherent plausibility. The letters were not deeply incriminating, which was a point in favour of authenticity. They simply showed Psaros congratulating himself upon having won, by his masterly diplomacy, the allegiance of every political faith from the Metaxists to the Communists. They also referred to BLOs as "the drunkards." If they were forged, the forger was cleverer than usual, because he made use of the fact that Psaros affected two different styles of writing and signature. On the whole, they were probably genuine; but it does not greatly matter.

(f) The same may be said about most of the documents adduced to discredit EAM/ELAS; but certain exceptions must be made. The most likely to be authentic, apart from the case quoted at the beginning, is a collection of letters alleged to have been captured by Zervas from an ELAS courier during the civil war of 1943. One of these laid down instructions regarding the formation by ELAS units of secret dumps of weapons "for the future purposes of our struggle"; another stressed the importance of "penetrating" the armed forces of the Middle East; another prescribed various tricks for extracting sovereigns from the AMM. These are among the few originals that I have examined. The signatures on them looked genuine, but the fact that they came into my hands from an interested party will render them suspect to the historian.

(g) More serious are the documents brought forward by the enemies of EAM/ELAS after the end of the German occupation. The most important are two papers produced in 1945 implying collusion between EAM/ELAS and the Bulgars; and one produced in 1947 to the UN Commission investigating the northern frontiers of Greece. The first two concern an agreement which the Greek Communists are alleged to have made with the Bulgarian occupation authorities, by the terms of which the administration of Macedonia would be left in the hands of EAM and SNOF when the Bulgars and Germans withdrew, in return for which the KKE agreed to facilitate the autonomy of Macedonia within the Slav federation. The last concerns an agreement which junior commanders of ELAS in Macedonia are supposed to have made to allow the Germans to withdraw unhindered from Macedonia, in return for which the Germans would leave weapons and ammunition in their hands. The first impression which these documents make is that they are, from the point of view of the enemies of EAM/ELAS, literally too good to be true. It is barely credible that the leaders of the KKE should have allowed any document to go into writing, of which not only the general purport, but every word, line and clause, was completely damning. Two things must be borne in mind about these cases. The first is that Communists are habitually averse to committing anything to writing which somebody other than themselves may later have the opportunity of publishing: after all, it was the Russian Communists who first taught the world the danger of such a practice when they opened up the Tsarist archives in Moscow. The second is that the purport of these alleged agreements was to bring about things which were more or less bound to happen in any case, whether such agreement existed or not. The Bulgars knew that the best way of embarrassing the western Allies was to hand over power to EAM when they left, just as EAM knew that Soviet policy in the Balkans was to create an autonomous Macedonia. The Germans knew that any weapons they left behind within reach of ELAS would be used against the British, just as ELAS knew that the Germans were going anyway, and would only take longer about it if they were harassed. In both cases, each knew what was in the other's mind without any written agreements; the course of policy pursued by each would have been the same whether such agreements had been signed or not. What matters in principle about KKE policy is not what it agreed to do, but what it did; when documents relating to the former coincide with the latter after the event, they are just as likely *prima facie* to be forged as to be genuine. But there are corroborative circumstances about one of the alleged agreements with the Bulgars. It purports to have been signed by a Greek Communist and a Bulgarian regular officer at a village in Mount Kaimaxillar (on the Greco-Yugoslav border) in January, 1944. It happens that an American officer of the AMM made a visit to that area at that time in the company of a Greek Communist (Andhreas Tzimas), and in his report on the visit remarked with surprise that an officer in "some foreign" uniform had met them at a village in Mount Kaimaxillar in January, 1944. This report was known to few people apart from myself; almost certainly to no one who could have been interested in fabricating a forgery. The coincidence is at least remarkable; but the authenticity of the other documents considered in this paragraph is improbable.

Since most of the Greek authorities on this period freely use such sources as these on either side, I have preferred not to refer to them at all (except distantly in the quotation from Carlyle at the head of Chapter II). The appendices which follow, however, although many of them are translated from Greek originals, are not open to such criticism.

FIRST DRAFT OF THE "NATIONAL BANDS"
AGREEMENT

Having been prepared by the BMM in March 1943, this version was refined into the form presented here by SOE Cairo. It was eventually superseded by the amended version of EAM/ELAS, which is given in the following appendix.

1. All guerilla bands will be known as National Bands of Greece, which is the only title which will be used by GHQ, Middle East.

2. Greece will be divided into military areas. In areas where bands of only one organisation exist all military decisions will be taken by the military commander of that area.

In areas where more than one organisation exists bands will co-operate under a competent senior military commander recognised by the senior BLO and guerilla bands concerned. Failing agreement they will co-operate through the senior BLO of the area.

3. The bands of one area will not enter into another except by mutual agreement of the military commanders or BLOs concerned.

4. All guerillas of one organisation will recognise those of another. Every guerilla is free to voice his opinion in public provided he does not denounce or say anything against other bands, their principles or ideals, or against any member of another guerilla organisation.

5. Any organisation or persons are free to raise guerilla bands in any area. All guerillas in the same area will have equal rights and, failing the appointment of a senior competent military leader by agreement, all disputes will be settled through the nearest BLO.

6. Bands in one area will give the maximum assistance to those in another on the request of the Area Military Commander through their BLO.

7. All guerilla bands in the plains will respect the rights of bands in the mountains for collecting and obtaining food from the plains.

8. There must be no barbarism against anyone by any member of any band. No one must be kept under permanent arrest or executed without fair trial or without the nearest BLO being made fully aware of the facts.

9. Any Greek guerilla who, up to the date of the signing of this agreement by his previously recognised leaders, has transferred to any other organisation, will be given complete amnesty.

10. All Greeks who enlist in the future are free to join whatever organisation they like.

11. If in the opinion of BLOs there is any failure to carry out the above agreement, GHQ will immediately order the cessation of supplies of war material until this is rectified.

12. These terms to be given publication in the Press, to be read to all guerillas, and recognised by GHQ, Middle East.

THE "NATIONAL BANDS" AGREEMENT

The following is the English text of the final form in which this agreement was signed by the representatives of EAM/ELAS, EDES, EKKA and the BMM at various dates in July 1943. This text was also signed later by the representatives of PAO, and the earlier draft was signed by Athos Roumeliotis, but neither of these signatures was finally recognised by all the other signatories.

1. All guerilla bands will be known for military purposes as the National Guerilla Bands of Greece, which title will be the only one used by Middle East. It is, of course, understood that each organisation may use its own names within Greece and its own system of command.

2. Greece shall be divided into military areas appointed as independent territorial districts. In an area where there are bands of only one organisation, all military decisions will be taken by its HQ in accordance with the orders of the Joint GHQ. In an area where there is more than one organisation, the different bands will co-operate fully in all military actions, either under a joint HQ of the area appointed by the co-operating bands, or under a commander appointed by the Joint GHQ after consultation with the respective commanders and the British Liaison Officer of the area concerned. In special circumstances the Joint GHQ may itself appoint a commander to execute an operation ordered by the Middle East.

3. The bands of one area will not enter another area except in cases of emergency, or as a result of mutual agreement of the respective directing authorities, or as a result of an order issued by Joint GHQ in accordance with the military requirements of Middle East. This clause aims at the insurance of the proper distribution of forces with regard to the local military requirements.

4. All guerillas of one organisation recognise the guerillas of another organisation. Every guerilla is free to voice his opinion on any matter in public, provided he does not denounce or say anything against other guerilla bands, their principles or ideals, or against any member of another guerilla organisation.

5. Any organisations or persons are free to raise guerilla bands in any area so long as they accept the conditions of the agreement and come under the orders of the Joint GHQ. All guerillas within the same area have equal rights. Any disputes will be settled by common agreement of HQs of the respective bands or, if necessary, by the Joint GHQ.

6. All guerilla bands in the plains will help guerilla bands and the civil population in the mountains in the supply of food. The Joint GHQ reserves the right to arrange by mutual agreement between the different organisations the distribution of food supplies in cases of shortages.

7. The bands of different areas will give maximum assistance to each other in cases of military action against the enemy, either when asked by the commander concerned, or of their own accord when the situation demands it. In cases of general action, orders from Joint GHQ should state the extent of help to be given.

8. There must be no barbarism against anyone by any member of any guerilla band. No one must be kept under permanent arrest or be executed without fair trial and complete proof of the facts.

9. Any Greek guerilla who in the past or up to the date of the signing of this agreement has transferred his allegiance to another organisation will be given complete amnesty. All Greeks enlisting as guerillas have been and will be free to join any organisation they wish.

10. All military stores now being sent to Greece should be accepted as a gesture of the United Nations' appreciation of the great and gallant effort being made by their Greek allies to resist and overthrow the Axis. The distribution of stores will be undertaken by Joint GHQ. Any area contravening these conditions will have supplies stopped.

11. For the better direction of the struggle, and for the co-ordination of all military actions, a Joint GHQ will be formed, composed of representatives of all guerilla bands recognised throughout Greece or occupying large areas, as well as a representative of Middle East. Similar Joint HQs may be formed for areas and smaller districts, according to the strength of the different bands. All smaller independent bands may be represented on the Joint GHQ by liaison officers.

12. The role of the British officers attached to Joint HQ's shall be that of liaison officers to Middle East. In cases of disputes between co-operating bands affecting the requirements of Middle East, the nearest British Liaison Officer will be immediately informed.

NOTE.—These terms are to be published in the Press, read to all guerillas, and will be broadcast on the Cairo and London radio stations.

THE ITALIAN ARMISTICE

The following terms were signed by General Infante, GOC Pinerolo Division occupying Thessaly, and the JGHQ, representing the Greek guerillas and the AMM, on 11th September, 1943:

"On this day, the 11th of September, 1943, after the armistice signed between the United Nations and the Italian Government and after the order issued by the C-in-C Mideast, General Sir Henry Maitland WILSON, concerning co-operation with the Italian Forces desiring to undertake the struggle with us against Germany, the JGHQ of the Greek Forces and the General commanding the PINEROLO Division, decide the following:

"1. All Italian forces of the above-mentioned division will withdraw from their stations and will concentrate in places indicated to them by the Greek forces of the THESSALY area, under the cover of Greek forces.

"2. The Italian units, as soon as they concentrate, will undertake, in small units of companies with their HQs, the task of securing the area, incorporated in Greek formations. Italian HQs superior to companies will keep their commanding authority, co-operating with their equivalent in the Greek forces. All officers and men desirous to undertake the struggle against the Germans will keep their arms.

"3. All equipment which is not carried by the Italians must be transported immediately out of the garrisons to a place of security: the surplus to be used by the Greek units.

"4. Those of the Italians not desirous of undertaking the struggle will surrender their arms and all equipment (saddles, etc.) excluding their clothing and boots which they will keep for their own use. The above-mentioned equipment will be used by the Greek forces.

"5. The British Military Mission undertakes to finance the feeding of the Italians on the same basis as that of the Greek rebels. The services concerned will fix details.

"6. The JGHQ undertakes the obligation to send to Italy those of the officers and men so desiring when the military situation allows it.

"7. When the military situation permits and the Italian units adapt themselves to the special type of warfare carried out in Greece, a separate sector of action can be entrusted to units of the Italian forces."

Signed: P. RAVTOPOULOS
COL. CHRIS[1]
S. SARAPHIS
A. INFANTE

Joint GHQ,
Greek Forces.
12th September, 1943.

[1] My usual pseudonym.

DENUNCIATION OF THE SECURITY BATTALIONS

The following terms were signed at Merophyllo, in Thessaly, by the accredited representatives of EAM/ELAS, EDES, EKKA, the AMM, and the Greek High Command of the Middle East, on 19th February, 1944.

"The undersigned organisations, EAM/ELAS, EDES and EKKA, the Greek High Command of Egypt and the AMM in Greece, through their authorised representatives, declare and announce:

"1. That they regard the Government of Rallis and all its appendages as instruments serving the purposes of the Occupation of Greece, supporting it in every kind of tyranny and destruction against the Greek people, and in the suppression of the national struggle for liberation as well as the struggle of the Allied Nations. As such they regard it as the enemy of Greece.

"2. That they regard all who have enlisted in the units organised by the Government of Rallis and armed and directed by the Occupation, namely the corps of Special Security, the Battalions of the Evzones, the Gendarmes and any similar creation of the Occupation or Rallis, as enemies of the nation, war criminals, responsible to the nation for acts of Treason.

"3. That they call upon those who belong to the above-named bodies to desert them *immediately*. No justification of any kind will exist for them after this proclamation."

S. SARAPHIS	K. PYROMAGLOU	D. PSAROS
NIKOLAS	P. NIKOLOPOULOS	G. KARTALIS
(=Petros Roussos)		
for ELAS	for EDES	for EKKA

CHRIS (for Greek High Command and AMM)

G. K. WINES (for AMM, United States component)

THE PLAKA ARMISTICE

This agreement was signed at the Plaka Bridge in Epirus, on February 29th, 1944, by the guerillas and the AMM, to end the state of civil war prevailing between ELAS and EDES.

"In the interests of the total and undivided conduct of the national struggle against the occupation and its instruments, and of the success of the Allied struggle, the liberation of Greece and the consolidation of democratic freedom, and finally of the creation of conditions conducive to the unification of the guerilla army of Greece, the undersigned representatives, authorised to undertake negotiations for the unity of Greece, have resolved:

"1. They accept the proposal of EAM/ELAS for the final cessation of hostilities between ELAS and EDES.

"2. The units of EAM/ELAS and EDES will maintain the positions which they occupy to-day.

"3. The organisations of EAM/ELAS and EDES undertake the obligation of fighting the Occupation and its collaborators with all their forces, either independently in their respective areas or in common by prearranged agreement.

"4. To ensure better opposition against the Occupation, the high commands of both organisations (EAM and EDES) in Epirus will co-operate in drafting a common offensive and defensive plan, specifying the conduct of any necessary manœuvres by either organisation under enemy pressure within the territory of the other, provided that military necessity requires it.

"5. If units of either organisation withdraw from their positions under pressure from the Germans or their collaborators, they will return to them as soon as the enemy withdraw.

"6. A Joint Military Committee, composed of representatives of ELAS, EDES and EKKA, will supervise the observation of these terms and resolve any disputes which may occur. This committee may function with only two members until the arrival of a representative of EKKA.

"7. The AMM is asked to secure from GHQ Middle East the maximum possible supplies for the forces of all organisations in Greece, on the basis of their operations against the Germans and in proportion to the real requirements of the war.

"8. The wish of all Greece is hereby expressed that those who have suffered either from German attacks or from the conflict of the organisations may receive the undivided assistance of all the organisations. The Allied Headquarters is especially asked to come to their immediate assistance.

"9. From the signature of this agreement all those held by either side as prisoners or hostages for political reasons will be released and assisted to go wherever they wish, with the exception of those charged with acts of treason or serious criminal offences, whose names will be notified to the organisation concerned, for trial by the established courts-martial, of which a representative of the organisation concerned will be a member.

It is hoped that these cases will be completed as soon as possible. The release of hostages will take place at the latest within a fortnight.

"10. This agreement takes effect forthwith."

S. SARAPHIS	G. KARTALIS	K. PYROMAGLOU
NIKOLAS		P. NIKOLOPOULOS
(=Petros Roussos)		
for EAM/ELAS	for EKKA	for EDES

CHRIS (for Greek High Command and AMM)
G. K. WINES (for AMM, United States component)

SECRET CLAUSE

The organisations EAM/ELAS, EDES and EKKA will co-operate closely in the plans for "Noah's Ark,"[1] and will facilitate the plans of GHQ, Middle East Forces, including the infiltration of special British and American units designed to take part in the operations.

(Signatures)

---

[1] The code-name for the operation leading up to the liberation of Greece.

THE LEBANON CHARTER

The following is a summary of the Eight Points in Papandhreou's final speech at the Lebanon Conference on 20th May, 1944, the subscription to which of all the other delegates constituted the Lebanon Charter. These points were substantially identical with those already proclaimed by Papandhreou when he first took office on 27th April.

1. The reorganisation and re-establishment of discipline in the Greek armed forces in the Middle East under the Greek national flag must be carried out exclusively on a national and military basis, not on a political basis. The army will carry out the orders of the Government, and cannot possess political opinions.

2. All guerilla bands in free Greece must be unified and disciplined under the orders of a single Government. The guerilla principle of military organisation cannot be a permanent one; but no change should be made at the moment which will lead to a reduction of resistance. Consequently the present situation must be regarded as a transitional one, and the initiative in settling it can only be taken by the Government in consultation with GHQ, MEF.

3. The reign of terror in the Greek countryside must cease and the personal security and political liberty of the people must be firmly established when and where the invader has been driven out. Outbreaks of terrorism must also cease in the towns, Ministers of the Government will be in office in Greece to administer the armed forces and the liberated Greek population. As soon as the presence of the Government in Greece is possible, it must not lose a minute in proceeding there.

4. Adequate supplies of food and medicines must be sent to enslaved and mountain Greece.

5. Greece, when liberated, must be secured the state of order and liberty necessary to enable the people to decide, freely and without pressure, both on their constitution and their régime and Government:
   (a) The special task of the Government of National Unity will be to secure order and liberty.
   (b) The people must be enabled to make its decision as soon as possible.
   (c) On the question of the sovereign power, the political leaders who have joined the Government of National Unity are understood to retain such views as they have already expressed.

6. Severe punishment will be imposed on traitors and those who have exploited the misfortunes of the people. Since this problem concerns the post-liberation period, it is necessary to make clear that the Government of National Unity will continue beyond the date of liberation for such period as the conscience of the nation and its own political judgment may decide.

7. Arrangements will be made in advance, in concert with the Allies, for the satisfaction of Greece's material needs in the way of reconstruction, including such necessities as the provision of outlets for Greek products and freedom of emigration.

8. Full satisfaction of Greece's national claims is called for by the past services and sacrifices of the Greek people. This must include the security of our new frontiers.

U

THE CASERTA AGREEMENT

The following terms were signed at AFHQ, Caserta, Italy, on 26th September, 1944.

1. At a conference presided over by the Supreme Allied Commander, Mediterranean Theatre, at AFHQ, at which the Greek President of the Council with other members of the Greek Government and the Greek guerilla leaders, Generals Saraphis and Zervas, were present, the following decisions were recorded as having been accepted unanimously:

(*a*) All guerilla forces operating in Greece place themselves under the orders of the Greek Government of National Unity.

(*b*) The Greek Government places these forces under the orders of General Scobie who has been nominated by the Supreme Allied Commander as GOC Forces in Greece.

(*c*) In accordance with the proclamation issued by the Greek Government, the Greek guerilla leaders declare that they will forbid any attempt by any units under their command to take the law into their own hands. Such action will be treated as a crime and will be punished accordingly.

(*d*) As regards Athens no action is to be taken save under the direct orders of General Scobie, GOC Forces in Greece.

(*e*) The Security Battalions are considered as instruments of the enemy. Unless they surrender according to orders issued by the GOC they will be treated as enemy formations.

(*f*) All Greek guerilla forces, in order to put an end to past rivalries, declare that they will form a national union in order to co-ordinate their activities in the best interests of the common struggle.

2. In implementation of these decisions, General Scobie has issued the following orders, with which the Greek representatives agree:

(*a*) General Zervas will continue to operate within the territorial limits of the Plaka Agreement and to co-operate with General Saraphis in harassing the German withdrawal within territory between the northern Plaka boundary and Albania.

(*b*) General Saraphis will continue to operate in the remainder of Greece with the following exceptions:

    (i) ATTICA PROVINCE. All troops in this province will be commanded by General Spiliotopoulos, acting in close co-operation with representatives of the Greek Government and assisted by a liaison officer nominated by General Sarafis. To be under Command Force 140.[1]

    (ii) PELOPONNESE. Troops in this area to be commanded by an officer recommended by General Saraphis in agreement with the Greek Government, assisted by a British Liaison Mission. To be under Command Force 140.[1]

    (iii) At a later stage Thrace (including Salonika) to be under command of an officer nominated by the Greek Government.

[1]The official designation of Gen. Scobie's forces. British troops already in Greece were Force 133.

(c) The task of both commanders will be to harass the German withdrawal and to eliminate German garrisons.

(d) As territory is evacuated both commanders are personally responsible to Commander, Force 140, for:

> (i) Maintenance of law and order in the territories where their forces are operating.
>
> (ii) Prevention of civil war and killing of Greeks by Greeks.
>
> (iii) Prevention of infliction of any penalty whatsoever and of unjustifiable arrest.
>
> (iv) Assistance in the establishment of the legal civil authority and the distribution of relief.

A map showing the operational boundaries has been issued to both commanders.

Signed: H. MAITLAND WILSON   G. PAPANDHREOU
General,   Prime Minister of Greece
Supreme Allied Commander,
Mediterranean Theatre   S. SARAPHIS

H. G. MACMILLAN   N. ZERVAS
British Resident Minister ,
AFHQ

Articles of the Varkiza Agreement signed between the Greek Government and EAM delegates on 12th February, 1945.

ARTICLE I. *LIBERTIES*

The Government will secure in accordance with the Constitution and the democratic principles everywhere recognised, the free expression of the political and social opinions of the citizens, repealing any existing illiberal law. It will also secure the unhindered functioning of individual liberties such as those of assembly, association and expression of views in the Press. More especially, the Government will fully restore trade union liberties.

ARTICLE II. *RAISING OF MARTIAL LAW*

Martial law will be raised immediately after the signature of the present agreement. Simultaneously with this action there will be brought into force a Constitutional Act similar in all respects to Constitutional Act No. 24, whereby the suspension of those articles of the Constitution to which reference is made in Act 24 shall be permitted.

Articles 5, 10, 12, 20 and 95 of the Constitution shall be suspended forthwith throughout the country. This suspension shall continue until the completion of disarmament, and the establishment of administrative, judicial and military authorities throughout the country. As regards Article 5 in particular, this suspension shall not take effect in the cities of Athens and Piraeus and their suburbs. Especially, however, as regards persons arrested up to the present day it is agreed that Article 5 of the Constitution is not in force, and that they will be liberated within the shortest possible period of time, the necessary orders to this effect being given to the competent authorities.

Followers of EAM who may be held in captivity by other organisations shall be set free as soon as possible.

ARTICLE III. *AMNESTY*

There shall be an amnesty for political crimes committed between the 3rd December, 1944, and the publication of the law establishing the amnesty. From this amnesty shall be excluded common-law crimes against life and property which were not absolutely necessary to the achievement of the political crime concerned. The necessary law will be published immediately after the signature of the present agreement. From this amnesty will be excluded any person who, being under obligation to surrender their arms as being members of the organisations of ELAS, the National Civil Guard or ELAN, shall not have handed them over by the 15th March, 1945. This last provision concerning exclusion from the amnesty shall be annulled after verification of the fact that the disarmament of ELAS has been effected, since there will then be no further cause and justification for it. Guarantees and details of the amnesty to be provided are contained in the draft law attached to the present agreement.[1]

ARTICLE IV. *HOSTAGES*

All civilians who have been arrested by ELAS, or by the National Civil Guard (EP), irrespective of the date on which they were arrested, shall be set at liberty immediately. Any who may be held on the charge of collaboration with the enemy or of commission of any crime shall be handed over to the justice of the State for trial by the competent courts according to law.

[1]Not included here.

ARTICLE V. *NATIONAL ARMY*

The National Army, apart from the professional officers and NCOs, shall consist of the soldiers of the classes which shall from time to time be called up. Reserve officers, NCOs and other ranks, who have been specially trained in modern weapons, shall remain in service so long as there is a formation requiring them. The Sacred Squadron shall remain as at present, since it is under the immediate orders of the Allied High Command, and shall thereafter be merged in the united National Army in accordance with the above principle. The effort will be made to extend regular conscription to the whole of Greece in accordance with the technical facilities existing and the necessities which may arise. After the demobilisation of ELAS, those men who belong to classes which are to be called up shall report for enrolment in the units already existing. All men who have been enrolled in the units now existing without belonging to the classes being called up, shall be discharged. All members of the permanent cadres of the National Army shall be considered by the Councils for which provision is made in Constitutional Act No. VII. The political and social views of citizens serving in the army shall be respected.

ARTICLE VI. *DEMOBILISATION*

Immediately on the publication of the present agreement the armed forces of resistance shall be demobilised and in particular ELAS, both regular and reserve, ELAN and the National Civil Guard. The demobilisation and surrender of arms shall take place according to the detailed provisions of the protocol drawn up by the Committee of Experts.

The State will settle all questions arising out of requisitioning carried out by ELAS. The goods requisitioned by ELAS, including beasts, motor vehicles, etc., which will be handed over to the State according to the detailed provisions of the protocol which has been drawn up, will be regarded thereafter as having been requisitioned by the Greek State.

ARTICLE VII. *PURGE OF CIVIL SERVICE*

The Government will proceed, by means of committees or councils, to be established by a special law, to the purging of the personnel of the public services, officials of public companies, local Government officials, and those of other services dependent on the State or paid by it. The criteria of which the purge will take account will be either professional competence, or character and personality, or collaboration with the enemy or the utilisation of the official as an instrument of the dictatorship. Officials of the above services who, during the occupation, joined the forces of resistance will return to their positions and will be considered in the same manner as other officials. The above-mentioned councils will also consider the cases of officials who have taken part or collaborated in the manifestations which have taken place between the 3rd December 1944, and the date of signature of the present agreement. Those of them who are found to have been concerned may be placed at the disposal of the State as provided by law. The final disposal of such officials will be decided by the Government which shall result from the elections to the Constituent Assembly. Officials who have already been placed *en disponibilité* by decisions of the ministers, will be submitted to the decision of the council above mentioned. No official will be dismissed solely on account of his political opinion.

ARTICLE VIII. *PURGE OF SECURITY SERVICES*

The purge of the Security Services, the Gendarmerie and the City Police will be carried out as soon as possible by the special purge committee on the same basis as the purge of the civil service. All officers and other ranks of the above corps who fall under the provisions of the Amnesty Law, who during the period of the occupation joined the ranks of ELAS, ELAN, or the National Civil Guard, will return to their positions and will be considered by the purge councils in the same manner as the rest of their colleagues. All the officers and other ranks of the above corps who left their positions between the 3rd December, 1944, and the date of signature of the present document shall be placed *en disponibilité*, their final disposal being left for the decision of the councils to be constituted by the Government arising from the elections.

ARTICLE IX. *PLEBISCITE AND ELECTIONS*

At the earliest possible date, and in any case within the current year, there shall be conducted in complete freedom, and with every care for its genuineness, a plebiscite which shall finally decide on the Constitutional question, all points being submitted to the decision of the people. Thereafter shall follow as quickly as possible elections to a Constituent Assembly for the drafting of the new Constitution of the country. The representatives of both sides agree that for the verification of the genuineness of the expression of the popular will the great Allied Powers shall be requested to send observers.

Of this present agreement two identical copies have been made, whereof the one has been received by the Government Delegation and the other by the Delegation of EAM.

In Athens, at the Ministry of Foreign Affairs, 12th February, 1945.

Signed: I. SOPHIANOPOULOS   G. SIANTOS
         P. RALLIS   D. PARTSALIDHIS
         I. MAKROPOULOS   E. TSIRIMOKOS
         for the Hellenic Government   for the Central Committee of EAM

STATEMENT ON THE
GREEK ELECTIONS AND PLEBISCITE

This document was agreed upon by the Foreign Secretaries of Great Britain and France and the American Secretary of State, and published on 20th September, 1945. Its historical interest lies in the fact that it was the first such inter-Allied statement on Greece in public, and that its effect was to reverse the last clause of the Varkiza Agreement (Appendix I).

"During his visit to London the Regent of Greece had consultations on all the subjects which concern Greece with the representatives of the United Kingdom, United States and French Governments, the three governments which have agreed to send observers to Greece for the elections which are to be held there.

"The three Governments hold the firm opinion that elections for a revisionary assembly should be held as soon as possible. They hope it will be possible to arrange elections before the end of the year.

"Thus a government would be formed which would be based on the wishes of the people and Parliament. The formation of such a government would facilitate the restoration of conditions of stable tranquillity in Greece. Only when these conditions are in due course firmly established will it become possible to hold a free and genuine plebiscite to decide on the future régime in Greece.

The three Governments in full agreement hope and recommend that all parties in Greece with the interests of their country before them will collaborate sincerely and willingly in the execution of this programme which, in their judgment, represents the best hope of orderly and democratic development."

END

INDEX